PROTESTANT AND CATHOLIC

Kenneth Wilson Underwood, associate professor of social ethics and public affairs at Wesleyan University, is director of the Institute of Ethics and Politics. He has an M.A. degree in journalism from the University of Wisconsin, as well as B.D. and Ph.D. degrees from Yale University. He was assistant professor of the sociology of religion at Yale Divinity School from 1949 to 1954, and co-director in 1956 of a Danforth seminar at the Harvard Graduate School of Business Administration on "Religion and Policy Decisions of American Business." The author of *Christianity Where You Live,* he was editor of the Congregational Christian magazine *Social Action* from 1949 to 1952.

PROTESTANT AND CATHOLIC

RELIGIOUS AND SOCIAL INTERACTION IN AN INDUSTRIAL COMMUNITY

by

Kenneth Wilson Underwood

THE BEACON PRESS Beacon Hill, Boston

Library of Congress catalog card number: 57-6529
Printed in United States of America

For

My Mother and Father

Contents

Tables

Maps appear on pages 405-407.

Acknowledgments

Though this study bears but one authorship, it is the product of the thought and experience of hundreds of men and women who live in a place I have chosen to call Paper City. Many were no doubt as concerned as the writer with the nature and meaning of Roman Catholic-Protestant relations in an American community.

During most of the time this book was written, I was a student and then a teacher at Yale University Divinity School. The research and counsel of Dr. Liston Pope, Dean of Yale Divinity School, and of Professors H. Richard Niebuhr, Maurice Davie and Leo W. Simmons, all of Yale University, have been particularly valued sources of encouragement and guidance. I was aided in clarification of my interpretation of this material by discussion of it with students at Yale Divinity School. I am particularly indebted to James M. Gustafson and William Lee Miller, who, I am sure, have taught me more than I ever imparted to them. The searching questions of many students often led me to new research, delaying the completion of the study, and, I confess, contributing to my continued dissatisfaction with the attempt to deal fairly and adequately with the people involved.

Yale University rendered valuable financial aid through a Sterling Research Fellowship, and the National Council on Religion in Higher Education through a Kent Fellowship.

My wife, through her informal conversations with innumerable residents of Paper City and her penchant for reading every line of type in a newspaper—any newspaper—was an extremely valuable research associate.

Miss Helen Fisher helped in the compilation of census data, Mrs. Barbara Nodine and Mrs. Leonta Longman in the typing of the book. Miss Jeannette Hopkins and Miss Janet Finnie gave the manuscript a sensitive and sympathetic editing.

James R. Brown was particularly helpful in his constructive criticism of the manuscript from a Catholic point of view.

Finally I wish to express my gratitude to the Holyoke *Transcript* for permission to quote many times from material which was of considerable significance in Paper City.

Preface

This book is a report on the interactions of Protestants and Catholics in one American industrial community. It is also an inquiry "in depth" into American culture through a study of what is for many of our people the most significant aspect of their daily experience—their religion. By this I mean their convictions as to the most sovereign and reliable reality in their lives, and the institutions in which they express these convictions.

The word to stress here is *interaction.* Churches and people of both religious groups are seen in the ordinary give-and-take of the common life of the community—people reacting to other people as they make contact with each other in business, in neighborhood relations, in the schools, and in the fraternal, recreational, labor, governmental, and political activities of an industrial city. The book provides a study in comparisons—of Protestantism with Catholicism, and of the churches with society. Out of such comparisons, it is hoped, may come a people's self-recognition. "To know thyself, compare thyself to others."

While the facts are presented as objectively as the author can show them, he does not hesitate to attempt to interpret their implications for America and the Western democracies in today's great world struggles. The book offers no blueprints, no panaceas, no easy generalizations, yet it seeks to give meaning to data which originated out of some fundamental questions stemming from the researcher's own views and aspirations. (For a discussion of the point of view of the author, see the Appendix.)

The tone of the book is neither that of sensational exposé nor that of sentimental good will. It seeks to deal with the full richness of the American Christian inheritance. This is a richness which can be seen only if differences as well as likenesses in our major faith groups are appreciated and understood, and not lost in fuzzy talk of common spiritual values and ideals. There is nothing the religious groups need hide, nor the American people need fear, in a frank facing of the nature of the relations between Roman Catholics and Protestants. There are, of course, tensions, anxieties, frustrations and triumphs to be noted in detail. We are dealing with faiths in history, not in some utopia, and we are reporting the *inner* meaning of Roman Catholic and Protestant growth and interaction, as expressed by members of both religious movements.

The author is deeply impressed by the complex and varied forces entangled in the religious relations of the city. The subject demands a look at the whole of society and the use of many resources of social science and theology. The responsibility of men for policy decisions is taken seriously; the book deals mainly with the actions of leaders in the community.

K. W. U.

Introduction

For a brief period in the fall of 1940, Holyoke, Massachusetts, an industrial city of some 54,000 people, held the rapt attention of many religious leaders in the United States. The members of Roman Catholic and Protestant faiths were set in conflict by the attempt of Roman Catholic clergy to keep Margaret Sanger, America's foremost birth-control advocate, from speaking in the First Congregational Church of the city.

The conflict occurred in a community which some Roman Catholic leaders called "the most Catholic city in America," and in a region which some Protestant ministers termed the "birth land" of American Protestantism. An investigation by the major interdenominational agency of the Protestant churches—the Federal Council of the Churches of Christ in America—concluded that the incident, at least for a moment, exposed to clear view the deep involvement of religious loyalties in the entire political and economic life of the community. The local Protestant clergy, pleading for a more extensive investigation of the forces set in operation by the effort of a Protestant church to permit a public dissent to the dominant ethos of the community, argued that the interaction of social and religious movements in Holyoke posed basic issues of freedom and order which people faced in all of Western society. They asked that an intensive investigation of the over-all social and religious impact of Roman Catholicism be made in at least one city in America where the faith was the dominant religious force in the culture.

The inquiry undertaken in the following pages may not be the kind that some of the Protestant leaders wanted. It is primarily a study of the *relations* of Roman Catholic and Protestant churches and peoples. It seeks to describe and to understand not simply Roman Catholicism, but also Protestantism, and to concentrate upon the patterns of behavior of the two faith groups as each is influenced, at least partially, by the activities of the other.

The book seeks to outline these relationships in Part I through "the Sanger incident," the occasion that first called the attention of many people to Holyoke as a city with profound interfaith involvements. The event has a minor significance in the total story of the religious life of the city, but it serves as a prologue to the personalities, institutions and factors that play the major parts in the community and are isolated later for intensive description and analysis.[1]

Part II describes the institutions and organizations developed by the two religious movements—the size of membership and comparative growth of the Roman Catholic and Protestant churches, doctrine and worship, relations of leaders and members, finances and property, association with other churches.

Part III examines the relations of the Roman Catholic and Protestant churches to the class and ethnic lines of the community, the recreational, business, labor and political associations of the city.

Perhaps the religious relations of the community do, as the Protestant pastors claim, become under analysis something of a paradigm of the interaction of Roman Catholic and Protestant groups with one another and with society in America. No claim need be made that the exact state of religious and social relations of the city studied is duplicated in other communities—even those with somewhat the same ratio of Roman Catholics and Protestants, to use but one possible criterion of comparison. The claim can be made, however, that the decisions men face in this city about the relations of their own religious group to other faiths, to social stratifications and to economic and political associations contain the same basic issues with which other men wrestle in our nation and our civilization as they seek to develop significant and creative relationships between the various organizations and interests of their common life.

The community[2] studied was founded approximately a century ago, planned and promoted by Yankee Protestants. They fashioned a city of somewhat diversified industry, but predominantly paper and textile mills, harnessing the water power they saw in the rush of a mighty river through a farm community.[3]

The community came to be characterized regionally as "Paper City," because as a local newspaper noted, "for several generations we have led America in the manufacture of the highest quality writing, ledger, bond and specialty papers." Holyoke is large enough to provide an opportunity to deal with religious relations in a complex urban setting with large and small business and industry; special-interest group activity, such as labor unions and trade associations, political parties and factions; social welfare problems; and popular communications as well as extensive public and parochial school systems. Yet the city is compact and stable enough in its geographical and demographic setting for the people to have some of the personal knowledge of neighbors and leaders possible in a smaller community.

Holyoke has in its short history shifted from a dominantly Protestant community, in terms of religious affiliation, to a dominantly Roman Catholic one. The study of it affords, therefore, some insight into what happens to an American community "when it becomes Catholic." The investigation of religious relations in terms of the "minority-majority" status of the Roman Catholic faith is important in that Protestants often justify their opposition to the extension of Catholic influence in terms of fear of the limitations upon the freedom of non-Catholics which they expect to occur when the Catholic church becomes the "majority faith." The Holyoke situation also affords an opportunity to study any changes which take place in Protestant institutions in response to the increase of Roman Catholic influence.

Although the actual name of the community studied is Holyoke, it will be called in the text of the book "Paper City." This and the use of fictional names for persons referred to in the community will be the only changes made in statements quoted from interviews or published works. In the notes and bibliography the exact titles of sources are given.

The substitution of the name "Paper City" for Holyoke is done for two reasons. It may aid as a reminder that the study hopes to serve as a source of insight into the social and religious processes of many other communities than the specific locale from which the empirical data is drawn. The device may serve also to remind the reader that, although the city described has an objective history which is recorded here, this is not all that is here; the Holyoke described is in one sense inevitably a paper city—the result of one man's response to the events that took place there and his effort to give in writing some form and clarity to the dialogue of the Christian faith groups in the community. A very serious effort has been made to develop an objective and scientific description of the decisions men made in the community and to devise checks upon personal bias in reporting the actions of people and institutions; but the study is still, and rightly, the product in part of the participation of the author in the lives of the people of Holyoke and of his efforts, as well as of theirs, to find meaning in the religious and social encounters of the city.

Roman Catholic-Protestant relations are apparently a subject of considerable interest and concern to the public and to the churches, but little objective research has been done in the field in America. Most of the writing has been of an apologetic or evangelistic nature rather than systematic or scientific in temper.

Several community studies by sociologists deal at some point with the extent of social and religious cleavage and with behavior resulting from it. In some of the studies information has been presented on the impact of religious cleavage upon economic and social life.[4] However, these studies have not developed the relations of church beliefs and practices to cleavage lines, nor made an intensive analysis of the impact of Roman Catholic and Protestant churches upon the total social life of a community.[5]

The Protestant and Roman Catholic churches have established a number of commissions on church, state and education, and various policy statements have been published on particular aspects of religious relations. The National Council of Churches of Christ in the United States of America has established a new Department of Religious Liberty. The most widely organized and most heavily financed organization among Protestants now dealing with religious relations was established in 1948 as Protestants and Other Americans United for Separation of Church and State, a nondenominational, unofficial body.

A flood of books has appeared in recent years on "the Catholic problem," church and state, religion and the public schools, and other subjects related to Roman Catholic-Protestant relations. (See the Bibliography.) The books range in mood and approach from Blanshard's best-selling volume *American Freedom and Catholic Power,* which claims to attack only the Roman Catholic system of power and not the faith, to Stokes's erudite three-volume work on church and state, with its effort to indicate the interrelation of theology and politics. The number of magazine articles on Roman Catholic and Protestant relations has increased greatly in the past decade. (Articles in the *Christian Century* critical of Roman Catholicism increased from fifteen during the first six months of 1939 to a total of forty-two during the first six months of 1949; *America* contained eight articles critical of Protestantism in the first half of 1934, and fourteen in the same period in 1949.[6])

Political controversy over the influence of religious groups in the public school systems has extended from drives for local legislation to prevent Catholic sisters from teaching in public schools in their habits to presentation of test cases before the Supreme Court of the United States. With the important role of America in world affairs, the comparative status and influence of organized religious groups in the nation takes on great importance in the eyes of lay and clerical leaders alike.

Despite all this concern and controversy over religious relations in our society, no descriptive, intensive study has been made of the relations of the two religious institutions in a contemporary American community, and no effort has been made to see these relations as a manifestation of basic assumptions of the churches as to the nature of society. The institutions most directly involved, the Christian churches, have proceeded in their apologetics and strategies largely without benefit of sociological research on the interaction of Roman Catholic and Protestant institutions in American society. Several unpublished, somewhat secretive community surveys have been made by Protestant groups over the past few years. The studies arranged by the churches have been almost entirely unilateral in sponsorship and in source of data and have focused upon what the other faith was doing. Investigators conducting three community studies for one prominent Protestant organization formulating policy on religious relations were instructed to make no contacts with Roman Catholics that would reveal the nature of the studies; for this reason the investigators had little opportunity to secure Roman

Catholic information on the meaning of their own institutional activity, or on their reaction to Protestant behavior.

This study has attempted to avoid the limitations of a one-sided approach by organizing a study involving Catholic sources of information to the same extent as Protestant sources. The researcher was aided in this by the fact that the major part of study was conducted under the direction of a university as part of a doctoral dissertation. The investigator first appeared in the community as a graduate student of Yale University, a Protestant in faith but under obligation to professors disciplined in the methods of social investigation and to an educational institution whose research has been the instrument of no one religious group. Considerable co-operation was obtained from both religious groups on a clerical and lay level, Catholic aid being given cautiously at first and then more freely as the investigator was able to indicate his serious desire to obtain as complete a picture as possible of religious relations. For example, one of the parochial schools' educators, who at first refused to cooperate in the study and then later aided it greatly, explained his attitude as follows:

> The hesitation of Catholic priests to answer your questions is not because we want to conceal facts, but because of a natural first reaction. The church is our home and it is as if you are asking questions about our home and its private life. Yet the questions are important ones and I think that if you will persist and with the approach and attitude you have shown me that you will secure your data. Good luck.

The chancery of the diocese and local priests supplied much data available only through them.[7] The official position of the Roman Catholic bishop of the Springfield diocese, in which Paper City is located, was to put the investigator largely on his own, with a letter of explanation from the chancery that the bishop wanted "the priests to be absolutely free to answer the questions or not as they see fit." [8]

Since the factor of the investigator's friendliness or unfriendliness toward one or more of the religious groups seemed crucial, he and his wife lived at various times during the study in both Protestant and Roman Catholic homes. Nevertheless, the fact that the researcher was a member of one religious group rather than the other was probably not forgotten by most of those who supplied information.

A community study of interreligious relations requires a variety of research techniques or devices. Four months were spent in the establishment of areas of investigation, location of a suitable community, preparation of interview schedules and the development of fruitful hypotheses from published and unpublished monographs concerned with religious relations. During seven months of 1947, the researcher and his wife lived in Paper City and completed much of the field work for the study.

For several years after the basic field research was completed, investigations were made into the movements—religious and social—which originated outside the city but influenced Paper City churches and people. Papal encyclicals, pronouncements and popular material of national Roman Catholic agencies were studied after field surveys had indicated that they formed a part of the educational life of the Paper City parishes. Materials of denominational and interdenominational agencies of Protestantism collected in Paper City were analyzed. Social science and theological studies of political, economic and religious trends in contemporary American life were read, for insight into the phenomena observed in Paper City.

Since 1947, several extended visits have been made to the community to check details and to carry out new lines of inquiry which developed in further study of religious relations. Although the major study was of a contemporary religious situation, historical research was undertaken in Paper City so that processes operative in religious relations could be seen in their vertical as well as horizontal dimensions. The Paper City historical situation is not entirely "unrepresentative" of the social-psychological context of American Catholicism. As Roman Catholic historians have observed, the mood of the Catholic hierarchy in America has shifted from that of a minority religion fighting desperately to meet the needs of impoverished immigrants to that of a church increasingly hopeful of making the great Republic of the West Catholic in practice, aims and ideals.[9]

Unless the text specifically refers to later years, the present tense is used for the years 1947 and 1948. There has been no effort to revise the details of the book up to the time of publication; some of the clergy, politicians, business men and others in these pages have moved away, or died. A more liberal bishop now directs the diocese. Some new data, such as voting behavior in 1948, 1952, and 1956, and the 1950 census statistics, are added. But what has most concerned us throughout are general patterns of action.

In the course of the study, more than a thousand formal interviews were conducted. These included interviews with the following: all the Protestant ministers and Roman Catholic pastors in the community (some were interviewed several times); over a third of the curates; the key executives of eleven industries and eleven retail establishments; three-fourths of the social workers in the city; the leading politicians; principal officers of business clubs and associations, ethnic organizations, major service and social clubs, and labor unions. Enough interviews were also conducted to sample the viewpoints of such special groups as religious converts, Protestant and Roman Catholic school teachers and Jewish leaders. In these interviews a person was asked a variety of types of prepared questions. Some questions requested tabulative information and categorical answers. Most of them inquired into the nature of the person's decisions in areas involving religious relations, sought statements of his policies and positions on issues, and asked for his interpretation of particular problems or situations which had occurred in the community or churches. Most of the written questionnaires were used to secure detailed, specific information requiring research by the person responding. Casual talks and interviews not based on formal questions often yielded important information in areas where people knew themselves to be involved in complex and often inchoate relationships.

The researcher has attempted to assess data from interviews in terms of several levels of observation. What a person *says* he does, or will do, or ought to do is often quite different from what he actually *does*. And what he *thinks* he does, or will do, or ought to do may also be very different from what he does or says. As Robin Williams has observed, "interracial and intercultural behavior is peculiarly subject to discrepancies of avowal and practice. Prejudice is, by definition, something which people are disposed to conceal or obscure under some circumstances." Therefore, verbal statements made in interviews were interpreted in the context of specific action taken by institutional leaders in actual social situations.

For this purpose, interviews with a variety of people influencing and affected by the policy of institutions were necessary, as well as extensive study of literature prepared for the consumption of specific groups: religious periodicals and tracts, papers of clubs, school publications, community newspapers, novels, histories and the like. Personal and organizational scrapbooks, church files, social case records, studies made by various institutional leaders in the community, letters and diaries—all furnished private thought to be compared with public statement and action. The direct observation of such affairs as committee meetings, worship services, church-sponsored suppers, circuses, beano parties, and conferences of social workers, politicians, business and labor leaders supplied important information.

The writer sought to conduct the most intensive and thorough investigation of the relations of Roman Catholic and Protestant groups in an American community as yet done by a sociologist. This study represents one man's serious and honest attempt to understand the decisions of other men, to give them the time and opportunity to speak in intimacy and trust about their deepest aspirations and hopes, their involvements and responsibilities. But neither these intentions, nor the devices of sociological research already described, can guarantee that he has succeeded. When the particular area of human experience under investigation involves the whole life of a community, no methodological device alone can find the central meaning that clarifies. The subject is too complex. As a factory manager said, "What a problem you picked. You'll have to know this whole community, inside out, if you're going to study Roman Catholic-Protestant relations. They are woven into the whole warp and woof of our life."

PART I

THE SANGER INCIDENT

Chapter 1

The Incident

The granting of permission to the Mothers' Health Council to use the First Congregational Church for a meeting at which Margaret Sanger would speak in October, 1940, precipitated a series of events in Paper City which are now referred to by its citizens as "the Sanger incident."

To understand the importance to the Roman Catholic church of the meeting sponsoring Margaret Sanger, it is important to bear in mind that Paper City is located in one of the two states in America which has legally forbidden doctors to provide birth-control information to married persons, even if considered by the doctor necessary for health reasons.[1] In the fall of 1940, the New England Mothers' Health Council, affiliated with the Birth Control Federation of America, was engaged in a vigorous attempt to secure twenty thousand or more certified signatures of the state's voters on an initiative petition to force the legislature to vote in its next session on a bill which would "allow physicians to provide medical contraceptive care to married persons for the protection of life or health," or to refer the issue to the people of the state for a vote in the 1942 elections.

First Congregational Church Action

Part of the campaign for the initiative petition planned by the Mothers' Health Council included a state-wide speaking tour by Mrs. Sanger. Her theme was that the principal issue at stake in the petition was not birth control, but medical and religious freedom.[2] On September 26, 1940, the executive director of the Mothers' Health Council telephoned the pastor of the Grace Congregational Church in Paper City and asked him if he would permit a meeting, sponsored by the Council and featuring Mrs. Sanger, to be held in his church some time in October.[3]

The pastor felt it unwise to give hospitality to such a lecture. He recommended the First Congregational Church, located in the Highlands. This was the area with the fewest Roman Catholic people.[4]

Two days after the conversation with the Grace Church pastor, the executive director of the council called and then wrote to the Rev. Ralph Blanton, pastor of the First Congregational Church, asking him for use of his church for a talk by Mrs. Sanger on behalf of "fundamental civil liberties in the matter of birth control." The letter furnished some information on Roman Catholic attitudes toward outlawing of birth-control information which would be of particular interest to a minister and laymen concerned about Catholic response to the meeting the Council asked for:

> National and state surveys of public opinion have shown that somewhat more than half of the Catholics and a very large majority of the non-Catholics are opposed to legal interference with the rights of parents to avail themselves of the best knowledge that science has to offer in the planning of their families. One of the ten original signers of the initiative petition is a prominent Catholic physician.

The letter enclosed an initiative petition blank containing the proposed change in the state law and giving the names of the ten original signers of the petition.[5] The request for the use of the First Congregational Church concluded with a reminder to the pastor that "most of the non-Catholic church groups [had] declared it to be consistent with the highest morals for parents to use the best knowledge that science can offer in planning for the birth of children."[6]

Mr. Blanton read this letter to the Standing Committee of his church, which had authority to grant the use of church facilities. The minister presented the request without a recommendation for or against the request.[7] He warned the church board that such a meeting might provoke protest and that a favorable response to the letter should be made only if the members were willing to stand by their decision. The board members discussed the possible reaction of Paper City to the meeting in somewhat desultory fashion and reached agreement that they were not worried about Catholic opposition to the meeting. The vote was taken and recorded as unanimously in favor of giving permission to use the church. Only one member of the Standing Committee was absent from the meeting.

The following day, Mr. Blanton notified the state office of the Mothers' Health Council of the committee's decision. On October 10, a field director of the council went to Paper City to arrange a list of sponsors and to make other organizational plans for the meeting.[8]

For nearly two weeks nothing happened on the surface of Paper City about the announced meeting. Many Protestants later explained the silence as a strategic move by the Roman Catholic hierarchy to put the Protestants off guard, and to move so swiftly a few days before the meeting that the Protestants with their decentralized organization would not be able to counter the pressure of quick coordinated action by the Roman Catholic church. Roman Catholic clergy, who participated in tactical discussions about ways to oppose the drive for birth-control legislation, later explained the delay as the result of new plans which had to be made by the hierarchy, since Mrs. Sanger had been expected to appear first in Springfield, where the chancery of the diocese is located. Roman Catholic clergy in that city were prepared to oppose her appearance.

The two weeks of quiet after the announcement of the meeting were interpreted by most Protestant leaders as an indication that the talk by Mrs. Sanger would take place uneventfully. The pastor of the First Congregational Church first "sensed that something very drastic was in the wind" when one of the original sponsors called him Saturday, October 12, to say he wished no further connection with the Mothers' Health Council's sponsorship of Mrs. Sanger's appearance in the city.[9]

The state officers of the council surmised also that the meeting was going to meet strong opposition when they received a wire from the sponsor saying, "I cannot permit the use of my name for committee or to be quoted in connection with lecture in Paper City next week." The council also received a note from the same sponsor saying that he had "advised against having the proposed lecture at this time." [10]

Roman Catholic Action and Protestant Response

On Sunday, October 13, the Catholic pastor of the largest parish in Springfield, the city in which the Roman Catholic chancery is located, issued a statement asserting that birth control is "unnatural" and "detrimental to the interest of our country." He also quoted the Catholic bishop of the diocese as saying that "the birth control of the individual becomes the suicide of the race." [11] Simultaneously, Rt. Rev. Msgr. Edward McGuire, senior priest of the Roman Catholic clergy in Paper City and pastor of the "mother parish," St. Jerome's, read at all Masses an official declaration which had first been prepared in the chancery for use should Mrs. Sanger appear in Springfield.[12] The statement made clear that it embodied the stand of the entire Roman Catholic clergy of the community, and Msgr. McGuire indicated to the press that the clergy had met Saturday evening at St. Jerome's parish house to discuss the birth-control movement and to agree upon a stand.[13]

At the meeting, the specific objective arrived at was to keep Margaret Sanger from speaking in Paper City, and a general strategy was agreed upon, although this was not stated to the press.

The official Roman Catholic declaration began:

> We have been informed on good authority that a campaign is about to be launched in Massachusetts in the interest of the detestable practice of birth control. It is understood that a nationally known defender of this vice, Margaret Sanger by name, is to be featured as a speaker in its defense. The plan, ultimately, is to arouse enough people in its promotion to pass a state law enabling physicians to pass out this type of advice freely, and even to establish clinics for the general distribution of information now prohibited by law.

The statement by Msgr. McGuire continued with an exposition of the stand of the Roman Catholic church on birth control, asserting that for Catholics the teaching of the church is clear enough and that every Pope "has cried out against this sin so contrary to the very end for which the sacrament of matrimony was instituted." [14]

The official pronouncement then concluded with a call to Catholic action:

> Those who are sponsoring this lecture are engaged in a work that is unpatriotic and a disgrace to a Christian community, and for that we condemn them without hesitation. Catholics, of course, will be guided by the mind of Christ and His Church, and will actively oppose any attempt to label this locality as a center of such immoral doctrine.[15]

In interviews with the press Msgr. McGuire made clear that the statement was an official declaration of the sentiment of the Catholic clergy in the city.[16]

The local newspaper, in reporting the declaration the following day, did not quote Msgr. McGuire's final sentence verbatim. The paper reported: "The declaration calls upon all Catholics to actively but legitimately oppose the immoral doctrine as they will be guided by the mind of Christ and His Church." [17] At the end of the local paper's account of the Catholic declaration was a statement by Mr. Blanton, the pastor of the First Congregational Church, that "Miss Sanger's appearance here is not being sponsored by any church group and is not a church function." He said the church had been loaned for Mrs. Sanger's appearance.

The pastor of the First Congregational Church noted the paper's handling of the statement. "Obviously the newspaper saw and appreciated the same element of incitement in McGuire's statement that impressed and disturbed us," he observed in a letter to the director of the Mothers' Health Council. "We shall hope that our meeting Thursday night will be held without untoward incident of any kind." [18]

On Monday all the regional and local newspapers which circulated in Paper City carried the statement by Msgr. McGuire and for the first time the description of the meeting to take place in First Church. The city "was seething," observed a reporter on the local daily newspaper; "Paper City reporters considered the situation too hot for someone going to live here the rest of his life to touch." [19] A reporter from outside the community handled the story.

On Tuesday, October 15, the Rotarians, a service and social club of both Roman Catholic and Protestant business and professional men, met at the leading hotel for its regular monthly luncheon. At this meeting two of the key laymen of the First Congregational Church—a co-owner of the city's largest department store who was also the president of a bank, and an owner of a retail electrical appliance store—found themselves seated between Roman Catholic laymen with whom they did not often eat.[20]

The Catholic businessmen began at once in a friendly, conversational manner to ask what the First Church meant by antagonizing the Roman Catholic church in the community. They asked the Protestants if they did not think it unwise from a business and public relations point of view for them to challenge the Roman Catholic church in a dominantly Catholic city. The Catholic laymen suggested that the Protestant laymen bring pressure on their minister and church board to countermand the permission granted for the use of the church.[21]

The banker was not a member of the Standing Committee and knew nothing of the First Church action except for what he had read in the daily paper on Monday. He confessed to the Catholics that he was at a loss to explain how the First Church became involved in the controversy. He called Mr. Blanton immediately after the luncheon and told him of the conversation with the Catholic businessmen. After the pastor reasoned with the banker that to refuse use of the church now would be "to suffer a humiliating moral defeat," the layman agreed that the church must stand firm. The merchant, on the other hand, seemed to the pastor to be "quite terrified by the specter of economic boycott by Catholics." [22] But the merchant, after conversation with his pastor, agreed that he was "willing to pay the price, if need be, for a strong defense of the democratic right of free assembly." [23]

The pastor spent most of Tuesday conversing with First Church business and professional men who had been approached by Catholics about the action of their church or who were simply fearful that economic pressure would soon be applied against their businesses. None of the men cited any specific economic pressure as being used against them. They were simply afraid that it would soon occur. Many of the men were in retail businesses they believed highly vulnerable to religious boycott. The next morning, the pastor wrote the executive director of the Mothers' Health Council:

> I just want you to know that the people of the First Church in Paper City are standing firm in spite of the terrific pressure which has been applied in almost every conceivable form to compel them to betray their own principles of freedom. It is incredible to what lengths certain people in this city are prepared to go in opposition to Mrs. Sanger's appearance here tomorrow night.[24]

By this time it was clear to Msgr. McGuire and another senior pastor of the city, the two priests who had taken the leadership in opposing the meeting, that no withdrawal of the use of the First Church would take place unless some of the influential laymen of the church were personally approached by the Roman Catholic clergy.[25] The approach of the Roman Catholic clergy was then directed at the First Church trustees, "because," as one of the senior pastors has since explained, "the Protestant church is run by the trustees; they fire the minister and the like."

On the morning of Wednesday, October 16, the banker-merchant who had first been approached by Catholic laymen at the Rotary Club luncheon received a telephone call from Msgr. McGuire asking for permission to call on him in his home. The layman suggested that he himself stop at the rectory on the way to his office, and this he did.[26] Present at the interview were the banker-merchant, Msgr. McGuire and the other senior pastor. According to the latter, the only man now living who was present at the interview,[27] the banker was told in substance the following:

> Mothers' Health Council is not for Mothers' Health; it is for birth control. It is the same outfit that met in a New York hotel and exhibited all the devices of birth control, indeed did everything but commit the sex act in public. The Catholic Church is established by Christ to defend divine laws. God told Eve and Adam to go forth, multiply and replenish the earth. The Fifth Commandment also tells us not to kill, and birth control violates this commandment.
>
> Therefore, the Church would not be true to its calling if it did not fight birth control with all the means at its disposal. Those means will include, if necessary, the use of economic boycott against those who foster the birth control movement and violate divine law.[28]

The Protestant layman, according to the senior pastor, agreed with the priests' statement and said he would do all that he could to prevent Mrs. Sanger from using his church.

The banker after the interview went at once to see his pastor. He would not tell his pastor anything that the priests had said to him in the interview. The pastor quizzed him as to whether the priests threatened economic boycott, but the layman refused to answer. The banker then asked the minister to do something to remove the First Church from further involvement in the birth-control movement. The pastor says he replied, "Let's be honest to ourselves about this situation and admit that we are scared and that whatever we do now we do because we're scared."

The banker's close friends, Mr. Blanton, and the senior priest of Paper City have all speculated subsequently as to why he was so frightened by his interview with the Catholic clergymen. The senior priest says that his own parish had funds of over $30,000 in the bank of which the layman was president; the banker was told that this and other Roman Catholic funds belonging to laymen and churches might be withdrawn in the conflict.[29] One of the banker's closest friends reports that the bank president confided to him that, even before the interview with the priests, accounts had been closed by Roman Catholic laymen who gave as their reason the anti-Catholicism of the president of the bank. The board of directors of the bank was half Roman Catholic and half Protestant, with a long-standing reputation of being highly conservative in business practices. The bank president felt that most members of the board would oppose his involvement in a community issue which appeared to antagonize Roman Catholic clergy and laymen.[30]

The First Congregational Church layman felt that he needed the good will of his board and of his ordinary customers. Although his bank was the largest and oldest savings bank in the community, the local banks had remained more a convenience than a necessity to the major industrialists and the wealthier residents, who had great financial resources outside the city.

The insecurity and fear evidenced by the layman is further explained by his associates as a lack of reliable knowledge as to how great Roman Catholic pressure was capable of becoming. There had never been within the lifetime of the banker and his associates a real test of the ability or desire of Roman Catholic laymen to maintain a boycott over a religious or apparently religious issue. The layman particularly feared a boycott of his store—his chief source of income. Most of the store's customers and 75 per cent of its staff were Roman Catholic. The banker felt that he was much more vulnerable economically than fellow Protestants in First Church who were owners or operators of paper and textile mills.[31]

The layman, attempting to reconcile so many conflicting interests and pressures, readily agreed with his pastor that he was frightened.

He suggested to Mr. Blanton that the First Church should announce, with as little publicity as possible, that it would not be able to hold the meeting because of the illness of Mrs. Sanger.

"You don't mean you want your minister to lie about the meeting—to back down in that way?" Blanton recalls asking.

The layman hesitated and then said that he did not want his minister to do that.

The banker then asked that the Standing Committee of First Church be called into session; he volunteered to bring the committee together. The minister reluctantly agreed.

When the Standing Committee assembled at 1:00 P.M. Wednesday, only seven of the twenty members were present; they alone had been notified of the meeting.[32] Although this group did not constitute a quorum, five of the members asserted early in the meeting that they felt they must assume power to act in the emergency. They expressed the hope that action taken would be approved by the Standing Committee as a whole.[33] The discussion centered on the question: Did the church committee have the right to continue in an action which might weigh economically on other members who could not participate in the official vote of the committee?

First, what evidence was there that the action taken by the committee might weigh economically upon members of the congregation? The banker-merchant who had been approached by the priests, and who was not a member of the committee, was present. He was called upon to tell his story. He informed the Committee that he had been called into conference by two priests about the action of First Church. He did not say that any economic pressure had been exerted or threatened by the priests; he said that he felt, however, that economic pressure might be exerted upon him and that in light of the conference he wanted the committee to rescind its vote permitting the use of the church for the meeting.[34]

Other First Church businessmen who had told the pastor they were directly approached by the opposition declined to report to the meeting what had been said to them about possible economic pressure. These men had called some of the committee members asking withdrawal of the use of the church by the birth-control group on the basis that they feared boycott of their businesses. One of the committee members wrote as follows:

> The question of economic pressure which had been reported to have been brought to bear upon the members of the church was intimated at the meeting. Although members of the committee stated that no such pressure had been brought to bear directly upon themselves, the problems of other members of the congregation whose business or employment was placed in jeopardy by the opposition to this meeting, placed upon the Committee a difficult choice.
>
> Although possibilities of this kind were discussed by the Committee simply in a general way, it was nonetheless in an atmosphere of concern for the economic well-being of the church congregation that the Committee finally took its action.

The men meeting Wednesday afternoon in the First Church were not clear that economic injury had occurred, but they were convinced it could occur if Roman Catholics were antagonized further.

The second part of the general question considered at the meeting was as follows: if economic injury clearly might occur to some member of the congregation, did the church committee have a right to continue in an action affecting some who had no opportunity to participate in the official vote of the committee? The men met to discuss this central question in church polity under circumstances which conditioned their answer to it. First Church is organized under the usual structure of Congregational Christian polity. The Standing Committee has power delegated to it to rent or otherwise grant permission for the use of church property. This polity is based not on a pure "town-meeting" type of democracy but on a representative one with delegated authority.

However, five of the seven men meeting at this special session, the attendance of which had been hand-picked by a man not a member of the committee, claimed the right to commit the church to a new public stand. They did so on the ground that the Standing Committee, composed of a minority of twenty of the church members, did not have the right in a democratic religious body to commit the church to action which might injure members who had no part in the decision. The position of the banker was that neither he, nor any church member, should be exposed to personal suffering from an action on which he did not have a vote.

Other members present at the special session agreed that the first decision of the Standing Committee was not binding on the church members since not all the members of the committee were present (one was absent), and some who were present did not fully understand the situation or had inward doubts about the action taken, even though the action was unanimous.

Two members present at the special session asked that the action of the Standing Committee not be rescinded, for the whole situation represented to them an unwarranted interference in the affairs of the Congregational Christian Church. Other values were at stake besides economic interests of some members—values which the two members felt were perhaps more important to the community. For them, the freedom of a church or group to make decisions without dictation from an outside agency or institution was being threatened. To deny to the central policy-making body of a church the right to take action which might require some sacrifice from church members was to take from that body the power to commit the church to any important action in behalf of the community.

The intent of the members who had been gathered by the banker was soon evident. By a vote of five to two, the permission previously granted for use of the church was withdrawn and the following statement issued to the press, explaining the action:

> The First Congregational Church yesterday withdrew permission for the Mothers' Health Council to use the church building for its scheduled meeting tonight. This action was taken because of the vigorous opposition to the program as reported in the newspapers and elsewhere. The action taken was purely for the sake of community harmony, as the program was not sponsored by the First Congregational Church nor was it a problem involving the teachings of this church.[35]

It was now mid-afternoon of the day before the scheduled Sanger meeting. Blanton notified the Mothers' Health Council of the decision of the First Church laymen and called some of the Protestant pastors in the community to tell them what had happened. None of the ministers offered any concrete aid in the crisis. Most of them thought about or talked over with other ministers or their members the possibility of holding the meeting in their own church.[36]

It seemed to Blanton that the Episcopal minister was most able to aid him and the council in finding a meeting place, for Episcopal polity grants to the rector control of the use of the parish house.

The rector consulted a few members of his church and decided not to offer the rectory as a meeting place.

The pastor of Grace Congregational Church had been openly critical among the Protestant ministers of the action of the First Church. He expressed belief that if the church was going to offer its building to Mrs. Sanger in the first place, it should have known that it had a fight on its hands and been prepared for it—even to the point of having a tent in reserve for the Mothers' Council to use if necessary. "Never raise the devil if you can't bring him down," was his motto, the pastor said.

One minister thought of offering his home for the meeting, but he decided not to after a fellow clergyman pointed out that the home was not really his property, but the church's, and that the property could be placed in danger of damage if the meeting were held there.[37]

After the incident the executive secretary of the Young Women's Christian Association was interviewed by an investigator from the Federal Council of Churches of Christ in America as to why the organization had not offered its building for the meeting, particularly since the national Y.W.C.A. had taken a position favoring freedom for doctors to disseminate birth-control information. The official replied that most of the members of the Paper City YWCA were Roman Catholic, although the majority of the local policy-making board was not. The secretary did not wish to risk antagonizing the membership.

By Wednesday evening, Blanton and the executive director of the Mothers' Health Council concluded that no meeting place would be found among the Protestant churches, and they began to look elsewhere. The council director in Boston called the steward of the Turnverein Hall in Paper City. This hall had been built as a recreation and meeting place for a German mutual benefit and social society. The society had been established in 1864 by German Lutherans, although its membership now included about 15 per cent Roman Catholics. The steward of the Turnverein Hall says that the Mothers' Health Council director told him that he wished to rent the hall the following day for a "social evening with a talk on birth control." The steward gave the council director permission to use the hall. The director then sent word to his Paper City contacts and they spread the information by telephone where the meeting would be held. At noon on Thursday, according to the council director, ten dollars was paid to the steward for the use of the hall and the steward signed a receipt for the fee.

Mrs. Sanger, reached in a nearby city, was informed that the First Church had withdrawn use of their property and that a German Turnverein Hall had been secured. She then issued the following statement to the newspapers:

> I hear that the trustees of the First Congregational Church in Paper City have under severe outside pressure voted to rescind the permission they had granted for the use of the church for a meeting at which I was to speak tomorrow night in support of freedom for the doctors in the state to give birth-control information to sick married women.
>
> I know few of the facts behind the action, but am told that the circumstances constitute so unbelievable a violation of civil and religious freedom as to demand investigation and protest by every person and organization concerned with civil liberties, religious freedom and tolerance.
>
> I understand steps are now being taken to bring to the attention of the public not only in Paper City but throughout the state and the United States the full unvarnished story of minority religious arrogance, bigotry and dictatorial terrorism, which now has so boldly overstepped all reasonable and decent restraint in Paper City.
>
> Of course, I am glad the attempt to suppress my appearance in Paper City has failed. The meeting will now be held in a workers' hall where the working class of people of Paper City, who toil and suffer all their lives, and search for a helping hand, will be able to learn how sinister an influence in the state deprives them of medical knowledge in the planning of their families, which enjoys the moral support of four out of five parents and citizens in these still free United States.[39]

The Turnverein Hall steward thought no more about his rental until he began to receive anonymous telephone calls from people telling him, he says, "what an awful thing I had done, damning me to hell for my hatred of Catholics, and warning me I would lose my job." Friends stopped the steward on the street and asked him how he "could be so stupid as to get involved in such a thing." Some advised him that the meeting would hurt the hall's liquor business done at the bar—an important source of revenue for the other affairs of the society.

The steward thought the matter over carefully. He was not clear in his own mind what he wanted to do. He recalls:

> I felt that this was America and a democracy, and I told some of my friends that I thought a lot of educated people in the country used birth control and it didn't seem to hurt them. I wanted to let Mrs. Sanger speak and yet I didn't want to. I was getting told by my friends how mad the Catholics were going to be, though none came up to me face-to-face and told me how mad they were going to be.
>
> I'm a man that doesn't like trouble. I even quit the Lutheran Church because my wife went to Grace [Congregational Christian Church] and I didn't want to be narrow about it. I always say, your enemies come natural. Your friends you have to make, and I hate to lose them. I was afraid that some narrow-minded Catholics would get me in an alley some night and give me a beating up. That's happened in this town. Then, too, the Irish priests stick close together in this city and they were really mad about Sanger. I was afraid some day they'd tell an Irish cop that I was an anti-Catholic and he'd give me a ticket for drunken driving or the like. I never drank a drop, but they might pull something like that. So I asked the President and board of directors to make the decision whether the meeting should be held at the hall, because I didn't want to make the decision alone.

The senior pastor, who had been so active in the Catholic attack on Mrs. Sanger, recalls asking the steward on the Thursday morning before the meeting why he was renting the hall to the birth-control group. The priest says that the steward told him that the Grace Congregational minister rented the hall without telling the caretaker the intended use of the hall, other than that a minister friend wanted it. The steward informed the priest that the directors of Turnverein Hall were to make the decision as to whether Mrs. Sanger could appear in the hall. The pastor then learned "the identity of the most important trustee of the hall" from a Roman Catholic alderman who knew well the ward in which the hall is located. The senior pastor, Msgr. McGuire, and the alderman then called the trustee. The trustee said that he did not know the nature of the meeting scheduled for that evening in the hall. When the priest informed him, he assured the priest that the Sanger meeting would not be held there.

The steward called the state office of the Mothers' Health Council late Thursday afternoon to inform the director that the hall was not available under any circumstances. The director had already been informed by a newspaper reporter.

Within two hours after conversations of the priest with the Turnverin Hall director, the local newspaper was on the street with a story quoting the president of Turnverein, a Protestant, that the officials "would not have allowed it [the meeting] in the first place, had we known the purpose."

The local newspaper also carried on page one a long account of Mrs. Sanger's reaction to the events.

> Margaret Sanger is coming to Paper City tonight—no one knows where, not even Margaret Sanger.
>
> It may have to be on some street corner.
>
> The birth-control advocate faced late yesterday with the situation of having her permission to use the First Congregational Church here at eight tonight withdrawn was faced at 2:30 this afternoon by similar action on the part of the Turn Hall officials who left Mrs. Sanger "high and dry" as far as any enclosed meeting place for tonight is concerned.
>
> A little disappointed but not too dismayed, Mrs. Sanger, who was coming here under the sponsorship of the Mothers' Health Council in behalf of an initiative petition to amend the state law regarding dissemination of birth-control information, was reached this afternoon at a Longmeadow home where she was being entertained at tea.
>
> Quite taken back by the recent turn of events, Mrs. Sanger in a pleasant but naturally surprised voice said, "This certainly does not seem like the United States. It's more like Russia or perhaps Germany. I really can't understand it."
>
> Asked as to her next move, the 57 year old, twice married birth control promoter, was puzzled, replying, "It may have to be from a street corner. I really don't know. I will perhaps make arrangements before night."
>
> Mrs. Sanger (Mrs. J. Noah S. Slee) travelling in a convertible coupé in her swing through the western part of the state arrived at the home of Mrs. E. C. Lincoln in Longmeadow shortly before this afternoon for tea.
>
> What her program will be for tonight she will decide after consultation with Paper City persons connected with the Mothers' Health Council. There are several in Paper City, the exact number of which Mrs. Sanger could not state.[41]

The senior pastor recalls, "When we read that the birth-control meeting was going to have to be an open-air affair, we knew that it would amount to nothing. It would just be attended by a rabble group." From this point, members of the Roman Catholic clergy appear to have ceased active fighting of the meeting, feeling that it had already been discredited in the community.

The Mothers' Health Council staff and local supporters continued throughout Thursday afternoon without success to find a place. An attempt was made to reach the mayor of Paper City, the only Protestant in an important office in the municipal government, in order to ask for a room in the city hall. The mayor was reported to be out of town.[42] The mayor had previously been called by an officer in the Knights of Columbus, asking him not to aid the birth-control movement by making available city buildings.[43]

The city clerk who had power to grant use of the city hall or municipal auditorium in the absence of the mayor felt that he should not make a decision without the mayor's approval. The marshal of police, requested by a local attorney and the executive director of the Mothers' Health Council to grant permission for a street meeting, was reluctant to do so without consulting the mayor.[44]

Before a decision was reached by the police marshal, a meeting place was found for Mrs. Sanger's talk. The offer came at 6:00 P.M. from what the *Protestant Digest* later labeled a "strange source"—the office of the local Textile Workers' Union, CIO.[45] None of the unions in the city had been approached throughout the search for a meeting place—an oversight "offering interesting insight into the class orientation and thinking of the Protestant churches and supporters of the birth control movement," one union official noted. The officers of the United Electrical Workers (CIO) had on Wednesday discussed the possibility of making available their hall to the Sanger group and reached a tentative conclusion that they would offer it. On Thursday morning a fire inspector came to inspect the hall and told the union officials that no more than twenty-five persons could meet in the hall unless another door was added. The union abandoned its plans.

The decision to volunteer the office rooms of the Textile Workers' Union was made by the secretary of the union, a Catholic laywoman. The power to grant the use of the hall was entirely in her hands, no authorization being necessary from any local union body, since she was a paid representative of the national office of the union.

The secretary did, however, discuss her plan to make the hall available with some other local union leaders. There were several considerations which the secretary has said led her to volunteer the union hall:

> I was burned up that in a town of this sort where I thought we had progressed to the point where freedom of speech was accepted, a group had to fight for a place to meet. Our union had an important stake in the free speech issue, since we were and are now having a difficult time in many communities getting places to meet.

Another major consideration of the union leader was her interest in the personal problems of the working women with whom she came intimately in contact in the union. Over 80 per cent of the 300 women in her union in 1940 were Catholic. She believed that most of her union members wanted medical guidance on contraception more readily available. Most of the girls in the union were young and wanted to keep their jobs; they realized they could not do so if they had children early in their marriages.

The secretary was convinced that her union members already received birth-control information, but from sources not accredited by official medical groups. In 1939, one department of her union contained 120 married women and not one childbirth had occurred among them in the entire year. Because the girls could not receive birth-control information from their family doctor, they "snitched the information," often buying equipment from quacks who charged exorbitant prices for their services. One girl had admitted to the union secretary that she paid $100 as a down payment for birth-control equipment. Another woman with several children had on the occasion of a new pregnancy attempted a crude, self-induced abortion which was nearly fatal. Such things would not be so likely to occur, the secretary believed, if birth-control information was more readily available through regular medical channels. These were the reasons she gave for volunteering the union headquarters.

The most common explanation later suggested by Roman Catholic clergymen who have an opinion on the reasons for the Textile Union's action is that the First Church pastor got in touch with a "pink" professor of a nearby college, who then called his Communist friends in the CIO in Paper City. According to the priests, these people, because they are communists or fellow travelers and hate the church, permitted Mrs. Sanger to come into their union offices.

At eight o'clock seventy to one hundred people who had been notified by "a system of grapevine telephone calls" crowded into two small rooms of the Textile Workers' headquarters and overflowed into the corridor. The setting of the meeting startled many of the Protestant laywomen who entered a union office for the first time. To reach the meeting they passed by three policemen and no spectators, climbed a narrow flight of stairs in a dilapidated red-brick store and office building, walked past a door bearing the legend "Socialist Meeting Hall" to the Textile Workers' office, there to be confronted at once by a mammoth "F.D.R." campaign poster.

The Sanger Meeting

The meeting was opened by a short statement from the director of the Mothers' Health Council thanking the Textile Workers' Union for use of its rooms.[46] He said that the invitation and the audience were proof that among intelligent people everywhere there is a bond of interest greater than race or creed. The minister of First Congregational Church then gave a short talk stating that he was present at the meeting because he believed strongly in the right of free speech and the right of petition. He said that his church had merely given permission at first for the Sanger meeting in defense of these principles and that the movement to which the meeting was dedicated was no problem of the church nor sponsored by the church.

The third speaker was a political science professor in a private college near Paper City. For him the meeting showed a "spirit of determination on the part of some people not to sit calmly under this cycle of tyranny which appears to be sweeping over the world." He hoped that the meeting "would be an object lesson to those who learn too slowly." He explained his support of the meeting also as a defense of "the principle of free speech and malice for none and charity for all."

Mrs. Sanger then spoke, standing in the doorway connecting the two small labor union rooms. The meeting was being held in significant rooms, she noted, for at the bedside of a dying mother in a New York tenement the movement began. Mrs. Sanger pleaded for the people of Paper City "to aid in making it possible for doctors to give contraceptive advice to married people, for the people in this state are being denied the right to receive information which they want."

During the past generation the facts of birth control have been denied the working class, she said, noting that those who can afford to pay doctors for such information can get it, while the workingman's wife who wants to bring up her children as well as she can does not have access to the information. If birth-control information were available to working people, one-fourth of all deaths of infants and mothers might be eliminated, Mrs. Sanger said.

The child labor problem can never be solved by legislation, Mrs. Sanger declared; it must go hand in hand with control of the size of the family, so that there may be four children instead of ten in a family which can afford only four. Many other social problems which confront the world today, she said, have their source in the endless chain of children coming too fast for the health of the mother and the earning capacity of the father.

Mrs. Sanger stated that the people who are opposing her movement should remember that they had to fight for their rights. The people of the United States are not going to stand being deprived of civil liberties much longer. All religions, she said, have the right to express themselves, but when religion steps out of the sanctuary of the spiritual atmosphere, and descends to the market place, then people have the right to criticize it just as they would any other group.

Reports of the meeting by the three newspapers covering the event represented different emphases and interpretations. Two of the papers, both published outside Paper City, attempted to bring the reader straight factual news stories, giving information as to what was said. The Paper City *Transcript* story featured the controversial rather than the informational aspects of the situation, and did not report in any way the arguments given by Mrs. Sanger for birth control or the speeches of the local ministers in behalf of civil liberties. "Hardship cases" cited by Mrs. Sanger as resulting from laws prohibiting doctors from giving birth-control information were not reported; the *Transcript* writer only referred to them as "too emotional to be convincing." [47]

Chapter 2

The Aftermath

"What began as a simple little thing like the announcement of a birth-control lecture," as one Protestant woman said, became within a few days the subject of a city-wide conflict involving deep religious, economic and political forces and the major leaders of the community. Prominent businessmen appeared terrified. Politicians went out of town. A janitor who prided himself on being a friend of everyone began to receive anonymous phone calls threatening his job. A fire inspector arrived to inspect and then to condemn a union hall. The incident cut deep enough and widely enough into normal patterns of community and church life to induce many attempts to interpret its meaning.

The event was interpreted by city leaders in terms of the continuing problems of achieving free and ordered relations between people in the community. The event was related by the religious leaders both to the past internal life of the churches and to their impact upon over-all social problems of the city.

General Response to the Incident

The leadership in Paper City was divided between two groups. In one group were those for whom the major role after the incident was restoration of at least the surface order and harmony which had characterized the relations of the religious groups before the controversy. This role served their interests better than any further probing into the sources of the conflict. The other group, representing the minority, was composed of people who wished to stress the continuing underlying tensions and basic differences between the two faith groups which they believed the incident revealed. They wished to point up the conditions necessary for a more vital religious diversity and for a "more confident and genuine unity" in the community.

The dominant desire of community leaders—editors, politicians, businessmen, Protestant lay church leaders, Roman Catholic clerics—was to end all external signs of conflict between religious groups in the community as soon as possible and to return to the *status quo*. Overt tension such as was present in the Sanger incident was regarded by most Paper City leaders as bringing discredit upon the community. The discussions of most leaders were not evaluations of whether Roman Catholic action had been coercive and destructive of the Protestant faith. Nor did leaders speculate as to whether Protestants showed inadequate religious conviction to meet successfully a powerful and tense test of its faith. Further talk about the incident was to be discouraged; the city was to be helped to forget.

Appeal to local pride was an important theme in published statements pleading for the cessation of open hostilities. The Paper City *Transcript* editor wrote the day after the event a leading editorial entitled "An Issue That Was Badly Handled." The statement was intended to place the controversy in a simple and casual context. The editor first noted that "Margaret Sanger's appearance netted an extraordinary interest because of the circumstances connected with it." The editor stated:

> . . . the lecture would have been passed over in the usual way but the announcement of the lecture involved one of the Protestant churches.[1] Immediately there is the issue of churches divided on this issue. The Roman Catholic Church has a very definite world-wide policy on the matter of birth control.[2]
>
> Here in Paper City no one anywhere wants any division among our churches. We have through the years established a high degree of unity among our churches on all civic community problems. We want to hold on to it, to develop it further.

The editor then noted that "something happened yesterday at a neighboring city which makes a very refreshing contrast" to the Sanger controversy:

> Mrs. Clifton Johnson, the mother of five children whose devotion to her and whose inspiration from her [*sic*] are a great satisfaction to her as the years roll along, spoke at the fall Association meeting of Congregational churches. She took up the declining birth rate

> throughout the country. Her plea was that the church body to which she was speaking make an effort to realize that having a family is the most worthwhile thing they can do. . . . "Find your happiness in simple things," said Mrs. Johnson, "not always in feverish delight."

The *Transcript* editor then closed the editorial with an appeal that "all of us do some quiet thinking about this issue which has so stirred us for a day or two."

The *Transcript*—Paper City's only daily newspaper—published on Friday, October 18, three letters to the editor about the Sanger incident. But thereafter the paper printed nothing more on the conflict, except for a two-and-a-half inch story stating that an investigator from the Federal Council of Churches of Christ in America was in the community studying the events leading up to the Sanger meeting. The results of the Federal Council investigations were not reported in the paper.

Mr. Blanton, who was now the leader of Protestants holding that present religious and social relations in Paper City did not insure "the rights of a free church in a free society," found that his activities were given much less space in what is probably the most important communications medium in the community—the local daily newspaper. During the seven years of his ministry in Paper City before the Mothers' Health Council asked him for the use of his church, the *Transcript* gave his personal views and his church's activities 661¼ inches of news-column space; in the seven years after the event, news reports on the pastor and the church totaled 57¾ inches of copy, most of which came in the final year of the last seven.[3]

The mayor, a Protestant in a dominantly Roman Catholic community and therefore one of Paper City's most convenient symbols of municipal tolerance and good will, also aided the restoration of community harmony by emphasizing in frequent speeches immediately after the incident the small importance that should be attributed to the "slight flare-up" and suggesting that "everyone forget about it as soon as possible." In an interview with the Federal Council of Churches investigator in November, 1940, the mayor had apparent difficulty in recalling any details of the Sanger incident. He asserted that anyone had always had a right in Paper City to hold a meeting. If any group scheduled a meeting and then called it off, that was their own affair. He viewed the loose talk in the community that hoodlums might have been permitted to interfere with the meeting as an entirely unwarranted insinuation that Paper City lacked adequate forces to maintain law and order.[4]

The professional organizations for lawyers, doctors, social workers and teachers in the city did not discuss the incident in their meetings, while it was occurring or afterward. None of the officials of the associations made any public statements about the incident.

The labor secretary, a Catholic, who had offered the Textile Union headquarters to Mrs. Sanger received no personal condemnation of her action by priests. In a mimeographed newsletter she explained her action to union members as a "defense of freedom of speech in Paper City." No criticism came to her from members. A few letters from Catholics outside the union condemned her action, but more letters were received commending the union "for saving the community from the disgrace of offering no meeting place to a group wishing to assemble peacefully."

Msgr. McGuire, who two Sundays before had voiced from his pulpit the official Catholic opposition to the Sanger appearance in Paper City, made no other statement on the incident than to announce that pamphlets on the birth-control issue were available on a stand in the rectory for all laymen interested. Mrs. Sanger continued her tour and spoke in eleven other cities in the state without public opposition by the Catholic clergy.[5]

The diocesan press maintained its editorial fight against the political drive of the birth-control advocates in the first issue of the *Catholic Mirror* following the Sanger incident in Paper City. The journal took up again one of its major themes, the identification of the birth-control advocates with the "interests and foibles" of the wealthy class.[6] Mrs. Sanger was quoted as saying, "What we are trying to do briefly is to level the unequal birth rate in this country, so that people with intelligence, means and health will have more children, and the poor, sickly mother will be allowed to space her pregnancies."[7] The editor of the *Catholic Mirror* commented on this statement as follows:

> That these "people with intelligence, means and health" are not reproducing their kind in sufficient numbers to guarantee their future existence is obvious to all. If you doubt it, read over the lists of

> players on the college football teams. Better still, read over the lists of young men to be conscripted for national defense.
>
> Yet these Olympian Puritans (the names of the Sanger committee read like a roster of the Puritan descendants) have the rank gall to number the mothers of our fighting youth among "the poor, sickly," to imply that they are lacking in intelligence. Vigilant pastors in cities and towns of this diocese where Mrs. Sanger Slee was advertised have awakened the populace to the true object of her mission.

The birth-control issue, before the incident to some extent but now even more so, was understood by clergy of both churches as a composite symbol, freighted with a multitude of class, political and ethnic, as well as religious, loyalties.[8]

The leaders of the minority faith sought to keep the people of the community sensitive for a while to the need for greater clarification of the fundamental differences and agreements between Roman Catholics and Protestants as to the conditions of a free society. They found themselves cast in the difficult role of disturbers of order and fraternity in the community; yet they did not want the incident dismissed as of little significance. It was, for many of the Protestant clergy at least, a momentary revelation of the weakness of their movement and of the precarious existence it had as a vital and unique element in the community. The pastors of most Protestant churches on the Sunday after the incident noted before their congregations the "general growth of intolerance within the United States in the past few years," to quote one sermon, but they did not, except for Mr. Blanton, make specific references to the events surrounding Mrs. Sanger's appearance in the community.

There was in the community obviously considerable unorganized, but intense individual support of efforts by Protestant leaders to make the incident an occasion for re-examination of religious relations. A Protestant, writing to the *Transcript* the day after the Sanger meeting, observed: "Democracy is more than majority rule. Democracy involves recognition of minority rights. But this also means that the minority must ask for those rights. We imagine they have community harmony of a sort in Munich or Madrid. They can have it." [9]

For a few articulate Protestants, the incident was an exposure to something they had known but not wanted to face—"a minority afraid to make a scene." One Protestant wrote:

> If we didn't believe it before, now we know, that here is a community where the majority rules inviolate and where the minority is too timid or indifferent to ask for free speech, free assembly, or any other right. . . . Mrs. Sanger was surprised at what she met in Paper City. Nobody in Paper City was surprised. This is our way of life. . . . The whole country ought to know by now that there is still a city where intolerance and fear are the ultimate government.[10]

The desire of the Protestant pastors to keep the incident alive until some adequate interpretation could be presented to the community, and their great concern to show after their defeat "that the Protestant churches are organized," prompted the Ministerial Association to appeal to the Federal Council of Churches of Christ in America "to make the Sanger affair a case study and give it adequate publicity." In November, the Federal Council received a statement signed by ten ministers in Paper City asserting that "the interests of community, state and national harmony demand a disclosure of all the facts which are possible to learn and a consideration of steps to be taken to insure the continuation of a free society." [11] The ministers suggested that "a public meeting" be conducted in Paper City "at the earliest possible moment to investigate all the circumstances and facts surrounding the recent events in the city." The pastor of the First Congregational Church also wrote to the Council for Social Action of the Congregational Christian Churches asking for aid "in using our defeat in the service of the ideals of freedom."

In a conference of Federal Council secretaries and the Council for Social Action's director, it was decided to send an investigator to Paper City to make a quiet study and then to publish the results in *Information Service,* a weekly research publication of the Federal Council. After the investigation, a 4500-word report was published by the Federal Council. The report was not mentioned in the local newspapers, but a summary was made by a newspaper of a nearby city with some circulation in Paper City. The report cautioned the community that "to ignore it [the event] would be like ignoring a fever as a temporary incident, because beneath it was some cause of social ill health." [12]

The incident still serves as a point of reference for people in the city interested in maintaining a sensitivity "to the differences between the Roman Catholic and Protestant faiths." When religious relations are discussed at length among Protestants, the conversation usually turns to the Sanger incident as the occasion when the problems of Roman Catholics and Protestants living together in a community were presented in their most disturbing and perplexing aspects.

The response of the Mothers' Health Council and supporters of the initiative petition on dissemination of contraceptive information was to make no attempt to hold further speeches in Paper City. The next decade of work by "planned parenthood" groups was largely done "underground." Strategy was planned at secret meetings. Local membership was carefully concealed. What leaders termed a "Know Nothing" attitude was adopted toward inquiring reporters. Careful investigation was made of Roman Catholics before allowing them to co-operate with the movement for fear they might be aiding the opposition. Organization leaders claimed that their furtive methods and the attention given the birth-control cause by opposition to the Sanger meeting made signatures more easily obtainable for the legislative petition than before the controversy.

Implications of the Incident for Internal Life of the Protestant Churches

After the incident, the Protestant congregation chiefly involved set about restoring "good will" among members. The importance of diverse points of view within the church was reasserted as well as the necessity for members to respect the "good faith" in individual actions taken during the events. Some church members held strong convictions about the implications of the incident for Protestantism; but no corporate discussions of the meaning of the incident for the church took place, except for a meeting of the Standing Committee in which the chief concern was to see that agitation ceased over action which had divided the members.

The few letters written to Mr. Blanton by members of his church supported a firmer stand for freedom of speech and for facing directly the issues raised by Protestant weakness under pressure. Excerpts from these letters follow:

> I have always taken pride in the liberal and broadminded attitude which old First Church has always taken where civil and social matters were concerned. Now I feel a personal shame because of notoriety recently given our church. Insofar as I know, this is the

first time in our history that we did not have the courage to back up our convictions, but let outside factors bring pressure to bear in determining our actions. . . . As a loyal supporter of old First Church, I demand that the action of the people involved in denying the use of our hall to Margaret Sanger be publicly repudiated.

At our last group meeting the question about Mrs. Sanger came up and a fine lady of an earlier generation than mine said, "Why did we have to have a thing like that at our church?" And I said, "Because we have a right to have it if we so choose, and I certainly am going Thursday night to hear Mrs. Sanger."

The night you came home from your vacation you said at supper, "The idea that America has to ask Hitler to allow us to bring the children from England safely here," and I say, "The idea that we have to ask the Catholic priests (the Irish priests) whom we can listen to and where."

I herewith tender my resignation as deacon of the First Congregational Church. Considering recent events, I am convinced that I do not possess the proper qualifications to hold any church office at this time. It is impossible for me to perform the functions of a deacon, or any other church function with the idea always in my mind that whatever I do or say must be pleasing to the Catholic bishop of this diocese, and in accordance with the teachings of the Roman Catholic church.

For the last twenty years, the First Church has meant much to me, because of my opinion that it stood for something. Today I am puzzled to know whether it does or not. There is always the possibility that in the future, as in the immediate past, Protestant church officers may be instructed by the Catholic bishop to reverse their stated opinions, and to rescind their votes, to suit his pleasure. This I have not done, and never will do.

Therefore I feel very much out of place, and I am convinced that my resignation is necessary for my own peace of mind, and for the good of the First Congregational Church.

Will you please see that this matter is given immediate consideration and acceptance?

Although the minister made clear his opposition to the church's withdrawal of permission for Mrs. Sanger to lecture, he sought after the incident to end the tensions in his congregation. Yet he did not want the event to close without awareness by members of the difficult problems raised by the affair. His approach is indicated in the statement he read to his church at the Sunday morning service following Mrs. Sanger's appearance in Paper City:

I am sure you all must know that the events of the past week have been a trying ordeal for both your minister and the official members of our congregation. For days the spotlight of local, state and national attention has been focused upon us and the story of what we did or failed to do has been carried over the press to every part of the country.

Those of us who have shared the responsibility for the decisions made have had to make them in the very midst of all the noise and turmoil of a great struggle, when judgment is difficult and wisdom is hard to command. It is a time when we need most to understand each other and to realize in fellowship that crisis can be opportunity as well as disaster.

That a mistake was made somewhere along the path we have travelled together on this issue—*We Are All Agreed;* at just what point that mistake was made—*We Are Not All Agreed.* This is what we should expect wherever the right of disagreement prevails, and we want to preserve that right within a fellowship which has stood historically for the defense of the ancient liberties of free men, both within and outside the Church. Let us also remember that only those who never do anything are those who never made mistakes. We, at least, did something, although we may not, even yet, see clearly just what it was.

Crisis is the growing edge of personality for the individual; it is also the growing edge of the life and spirit of a community of faith. Out of frustration comes new achievement; out of defeat comes a greater triumph; out of death—the resurrection of new and nobler life. May this be, by the grace of God, the ultimate meaning for us all, of the valley of humiliation through which we have so recently walked together.

The Standing Committee as a whole was dissatisfied with the rescinding action taken by a minority of its members. In a meeting on the Sunday following the Sanger meeting it accepted "under protest" the action of those "who had cancelled the meeting in First Church," but further resolved: "to affirm its complete confidence in the integrity of those who so acted under the strain of extraordinary outside pressure; its faith in their purity of motive, and of its sincere appreciation of their deep concern for the best interests of the church and the welfare of the individual members of the congregation."

The Standing Committee also issued a statement clarifying the position of their minister during "the Sanger matter" and affirming the "continued and increased regard of our congregation for our minister and that under stress he has proven himself a worthy member of the ministry of the Congregational Churches through whose instrumentality the seeds of individual, political and religious liberty were implanted in New England."

The Protestant church defeat was bitter enough to turn ministers other than Blanton to examination of the institutional life of their churches. A month after the incident, the investigator for the Federal Council of Churches found ministers and laymen disturbed by the lack of co-operation among Protestant leaders and in favor of the formation of a Protestant Council of Churches in the community. The Protestant church had at the time of the controversy one interdenominational organization—the Ministerial Association. It did not meet to take action in the crisis.

Some ministers, sensing the weakness of local Protestant comity, believed that the Federal Council should have done more than publish a study. They wanted a national Protestant agency to be represented in the community with extensive resources to "expose the situation on a national level" and "to produce resolutions denouncing the incident in the public press." But most ministers felt the Federal Council had done all it could do for Paper City.

The Federal Council report indicated the questions being asked by the pastors about their institutions and mentioned the great importance economic interests had had among leading Protestant laymen. The report sought to lessen the Protestant leaders' sense of failure to resist Roman Catholic pressure. It focused its criticism upon Roman Catholic views of society and religious relations as the source of the conflict. "Theoretically, it is the duty of the minority to persist in advocating its cause whatever the opposition," the report noted, "but this is perhaps too much to expect when the other side gives the impression of having the weapon of economic boycott up its sleeve and being ready to use it." [13]

The Sanger incident revealed the crucial importance of the attitudes of business and professional laymen toward community religious relations. The Federal Council investigator observed that "the chief reason why the union stood ground on Sanger speaking in Paper City and the Protestant church did not is to be found in the differences in the interests and social background of the people who influence most the policy of the two institutions." [14] Older business and professional men, the report observed, hold the major positions of leadership in the Protestant churches in Paper City; young women run the union. The decision to withdraw permission for Mrs. Sanger to speak in First Church had been taken largely by older businessmen. The occupational and class composition of the policy-making boards of this church and other old-line Protestant churches in Paper City is dominantly business and professional, upper-middle class and upper class. Therefore, the pattern of opinion among these occupational groups on the course of action the First Church should have pursued or did pursue in the controversy is highly significant.

A systematic sampling of the membership of key Protestant church boards and of Protestant business and professional people indicated a decided majority agreement (82 per cent) with the First Church's action to withdraw Mrs. Sanger's permission to lecture after the Roman Catholic church evidenced such strong opposition. The great majority of Protestant business and professional men believed that "the First Church would have been wise not to have become involved in the issue in the first place."

"What else could the First Church have expected?" a hardware merchant asked. "The Catholic church won't change and it's obligated to crucify whomever tries to get birth control into town even if all the Catholics practice it." The majority were also certain that the Protestant banker involved had information that a boycott would be attempted against his business; they "would have done much the same thing he did to make sure the business was not boycotted."

A minority of the businessmen believed that "when Protestants get in a position such as the First Church did, they have to show some courage." Most of these men were active in manufacturing, an economic area believed to be less vulnerable than retail business to pressure by local consumers. None of these men claimed to know with any assurance what his own action might be if a "show of courage" cost the disruption of his business affairs. "I know one thing," said a paper manufacturer; "as soon as I saw that a religious stand of mine was creating trouble in the plant and was hurting the morale of the labor force, I'd pull out of the religious issue double quick. I'm in business, and business comes first with me. I might as well be honest about it." A manager of a paper-processing plant doubted "if any economic boycott would have worked on [the banker's] store or bank," and believed "the First Church scared too easily." A cotton-mill owner said, "if they had told me they were going to boycott me, I'd have told them to go to hell." Then he reflected a moment and added, "Of course, you never can be sure; you never can be sure what they'll do because of religion."

Implications of the Incident for Church Relations to the Community

Throughout the controversy the supporters of Margaret Sanger's appearance in the city pleaded their case almost exclusively in terms of civil rights and the sociological and medical evidence of personal hardships encountered by inadequate knowledge of birth control techniques. The Protestant leaders and the Mothers' Health Council supporters dealt very little with the religious doctrines and theological concepts of their own church tradition involved in the controversy. Blanton, major spokesman of the Protestant ministers at the Sanger meeting, as already observed, interpreted his support of the meeting as a desire to defend the right of free speech and assembly. Neither he, nor any other Protestant spokesman, deepened the meaning of the issue to indicate to the public the differences between Protestant and Roman Catholic concepts of how knowledge of truth is attained and other fundamental theological issues involved. As the investigator for the Federal Council of Churches of Christ in America concluded: the Protestant leaders were sincerely concerned to achieve a free church and a free society, but they expressed to the community little of the theological or religious reasons for wanting such freedom.

None of the Protestant ministers described for the community the precise or concrete action by the Roman Catholic church in the Sanger controversy which, in their view, violated minority liberties. They were in agreement that the Roman Catholic church had tried "to manage" the First Congregational Church and thus "had interfered with Protestant freedom." But during the controversy, the Protestant leaders could provide no public information as to the specific means the Roman Catholic church and its members had used or planned to use in opposing the Sanger meeting. The pastor of the First Congregational Church had reached the most carefully thought-out position among Protestant leaders on the civil and religious liberties involved in the Sanger incident. He stated his position as follows in an interview:

> The Roman Catholic leaders are unwilling for us to act on our faith. They will not uphold in this city the right of the minority to express itself, for the minority to them has no possible truth in it. It is the pressure of latent power, which is always present and which can be used overtly if necessary, that has the decisive influence in silencing the minority in a community such as ours. The Catholic priest has a right to talk to a Protestant layman, of course, but if the power of suppression is there, and the people know it, then it does not have to be used, not even hinted at, to get suppression of liberty. Religious and civil liberty is not a technical crossing of a line; it has to do with power realities in a town and how they are used.
>
> If the Catholic power is here, there is no use in our trying to get rid of it simply by persuasion. If Catholics use power, then we use what power we have, or acquiesce to decreasing influence. This is a necessary level of religious relations. It may not be the highest level in this situation, but a necessary level. The Protestant must adopt a *quid pro quo* relationship on some matters in our situation. For example, the Protestant is a fool to let a priest drag him into his rectory and talk to him when a Catholic layman is given no recognized right to talk to a Protestant minister about religious and moral matters.

The conclusions of the investigator of the Federal Council of Churches were similar to those of the Congregational pastor. The official declarations and action of the Roman Catholic clergy in the Sanger controversy encouraged Catholic laymen "to take the position that minority opinion, must, if possible, be denied free expression in open meeting." [15]

The Roman Catholic clergy, in contrast to the Sanger supporters, dealt with the affair in public statements as involving *purely* a religious issue and having nothing to do with civil liberties.[16] The incident, they contended, was occasioned "simply by the violation of divine and natural law by the proponents of birth control"—a law interpreted correctly in its specific implications solely by the Roman Catholic Church. The priests involved in the controversy felt that any disagreement with their judgment on this issue was an attack upon the church. For a minority group to reject publicly the Roman church's position was to break the harmony of a community based on general acceptance of divine institutional authority on a crucial moral matter.

This official Roman Catholic approach to the Sanger incident is revealed in the statements made by Msgr. McGuire in an interview with the investigator of the Federal Council of Churches soon after the controversy. Msgr. McGuire began the discussion with a declaration that birth control is morally wrong and that the law proposed by the Mothers' Health Council was morally wrong. The Congregational church, he contended, had proposed to hold a meeting and feature a nationally known speaker in advocacy of this law; therefore it was the duty of the church to teach against it.

The investigator then said to Msgr. McGuire, "It is perfectly understandable that a leader in the Catholic church should teach against such a meeting, or should denounce it if he wishes, but I have heard that members of the business community were seriously alarmed by talk about an economic boycott."

Msgr. McGuire replied, "That was far from our minds, although we do know that when people become aroused such things might happen. Religion has been the occasion of more wars and hatreds than anything else." [17]

The position taken by the other senior priest most directly concerned in the controversy, is also based on the judgment that birth control is a violation of divine law. For the priest it is not possible that the Roman Catholic church could err in the interpretation of the literal or specific implications of God's commandment not to kill.[18] Sexual intercourse must not be separated from the risk of begetting a child. This ethical judgment is reinforced for the pastor by historical and sociological data which he has spent years in collecting:

> Mrs. Sanger and her crowd have already lost America her next army. If we fight Russia as we may have to do then we are already licked by the birth-control people. I was in France and I saw what happened there. The Germans had superior numbers and just took over, that's all. The French had better equipment than the Germans, but numbers defeated them. The same thing is happening here. Statistics tell us that by 1960 we will just be holding our own or beginning to lose numbers.

The pastor in his defense of divine law feels justified in using economic boycott and says matter-of-factly that he and Msgr. McGuire did use it in the Sanger controversy. He considers a Christian a poor one "who holds economic or political interest before the maintenance of religious laws," and he asks, "Do Protestants have no religious laws they value so highly they will sacrifice economic or political rights to defend them?" The opposition may hold that civil or economic freedoms have been violated or infringed and this may be so, but for the priest such a violation is not as important as the maintenance and defense of the divine law violated by birth control.[19]

All the Roman Catholic pastors in Paper City were in agreement that when a minority in the eyes of the Catholic church definitely violates God's laws, the church must at times seek to deny free expression in open meetings of the minority's views. The disagreement among the priests was only on what they termed "a stategic or tactical level." A minority of four pastors did not approve the tactics used in the Roman Catholic church's fight against the Mother's Health Council in Paper City. They believed that other ways of opposing the movement could have been used which would have been more successful in decreasing its influence in the community. This disagreement as to tactics was never voiced publicly and the Roman Catholic pastors maintained a solid front of agreement during the controversy. Most of the direct action taken by priests during the incident is traceable to the two senior Irish Catholic pastors discussed above. Both of these men had reputations among the Catholic people of Paper City for a greater strictness in interpretation and enforcement of the moral and religious duties of laymen than most of the priests.

Roman Catholic laymen with positions of leadership in Catholic organizations such as the Knights of Columbus, the Catholic Girls Association, Catholic Library Association, sodalities and benevolent societies generally agreed with the action of the priests in the incident and their interpretation of it.[20] Representative comments of the Roman Catholic lay church leaders follow:

> The use of economic boycott in the Sanger fight is in accord with canon law. I studied for a while to be a priest and I ought to know. Canon law forbids birth control universally. So the church must run [*sic*] whatever economic and political methods are available to fight an action against religion. (An officer of a French Canadian benefit society)

> No individual has any right whatsoever to interfere with divine

law. And birth control is an interference with divine law. The priest doesn't have to place on me any moral obligation to fight against birth control; the obligation is already on me in divine law. We chased out Margaret Sanger, you might as well say, on a pure and simple religious issue. Wouldn't you stand up for your religion and fight damn hard if anyone openly attacked it the way the Sanger crowd did? (An officer of the local chapter of the Knights of Columbus, one of the influential Catholic laymen in Paper City)[21]

The largest proportion of people who disagreed was found among well-educated Catholics in upper class business or professional positions in the community[22] who interpreted the boycott action as the result of ways of thinking developed by an older generation of priests and by laymen who were not yet aware that Catholicism was no longer an "immigrant faith."

Summary

The Sanger incident appears as a comparatively simple prologue to the complex drama of religious relations in one American community. But it does highlight many aspects of Paper City life that must be probed more deeply. It is a significant fact that in Paper City the birth control issue was the one on which Roman Catholic leaders made their major attempt in this century to achieve community conformity to their religious ethic. That only a minority of the Catholic clergy should seek to use the religious, social and political power of the church on this issue, while the others stood by, is symbolic of the limited scope of Catholic efforts to achieve community agreement on moral standards. The event is a symbol also of the fundamental difficulties many Catholics have had in Paper City in appreciating the public processes in which minority views are respected and common interests discovered in a highly pluralistic society.

The incident is also a miniature of Protestant problems in approaching contemporary culture. In this incident Protestantism was able, albeit haltingly, to affirm the right to act of a particular minority; but it showed little ability to affirm in the midst of a specific community event the larger religious and moral requirements of a free society.

The testing of Protestant conviction by Catholic action came to the oldest of the Protestant churches in the city—the First Congregational Church. This church stands ecologically at the pinnacle of social success and power, on the crest of the commanding Highlands overlooking the city. When the test came to this church, the pastor and the laymen found that they had no experience in discovery of religious convictions held in common among themselves and in the community at large, and no ability to act on conviction in a disciplined manner. The church fellowship was torn apart by social and economic forces which dictated the final decision. Wealthy Yankee businessmen did not will or have enough access to the political power in the city to obtain a public meeting hall. Refuge for the meeting which their wives attended came from a social source no Protestant had thought to ask—a labor union. During the incident, the First Congregational Church pastor stood before the city as perhaps the most honored and personally respected of the Protestant clergy, but unsustained by a community of believers.

PART II

THE CHURCHES IN THEMSELVES

Chapter 3

A Protestant City Becomes Catholic

"And yet this is New England. This is the land of the Puritans, to whom Frenchmen and Papists were an abomination. If I am to believe the evidence of all the writings about me, the tables have been turned." Thus a French Catholic novelist of Paper City wrote recently.[1] Paper City, according to several priests, has within the lifetime of some of its citizens changed from a dominantly Protestant community to "probably the most Catholic city in America."

Documentation of the extent to which Catholicism has actually dominated the religious membership of the city is our main concern in this chapter, but there are important corollary developments in the population of the community that need to be understood. Six basic facts about the people of Paper City emerge from a study of the census statistics.

Stable Over-all Population Trends

The first of these facts has particular significance for the Sanger incident. This fact is that Paper City is not located in a boom area of America, demographically speaking. We are dealing here with a city in New England, an area hard pressed to hold its people over the decades of rapid economic growth in the nation (Table I). The religious movements are interacting in a community with comparatively static over-all population trends. Yet in recent years Paper City has not been the least expansive in the state; only three of the nine major cities in the state held their population size as well in the decade from 1940 to 1950.[2]

Paper City had its first census in 1850, one year after the community's Yankee promoters had succeeded, with the hard labor of Irish workers, in damming the river which was to provide the power for industrial development. The population was 3,713—enough to support a few provision and clothing stores, a weekly newspaper, four Protestant churches and several saloons.[3] But the city was slow to grow industrially until after 1870. The next two decades were Paper City's years of greatest industrial expansion, and its population kept pace, increasing from less than 11,000 to more than 35,000 —the most rapid rate of growth in its history. The city reached its population peak in the post-World War boom (over 63,000 people in the year 1923), then it declined steadily until in 1950 the city had less than 55,000 people.

The contraction and expansion of population affects to some extent clerical concern over religious relations. The pastor emeritus of the Second Congregational Church noted in 1900, in an address commemorating the fiftieth anniversary of his church, "Unless a town be increasing in population, you cannot have a thriving and expanding Christian community. The former presupposes the latter." This pastor had come to Paper City when it was growing rapidly in population and wealth. During his ministry of fifteen years, the city nearly quadrupled its population, and his church's membership rose from 163 at the time of his ordination to 405 at the close of the year he resigned. The pastor had a benevolent attitude toward the Roman Catholic church's increase of membership: as the population of the city increased, he said, all the churches could expect to increase in members and strength.

By contrast the Paper City clergy live today in a community which no longer foresees an era of rapid expansion of population and religious membership. They make decisions in a city almost stable in its population growth. Churches cannot hope to increase their membership and their institutional strength simply by waiting for the city to grow bigger. The pastors believe that new church membership is recruited largely among children born into the church-going families and occasionally among people with church backgrounds who move into the community, rather than by conversion of non-church people to membership.

In such a situation there is great interest in the maintenance of at least existing membership numbers and ratios. Comparative losses or gains of membership among particular churches are more conspicuous and serious than in a city with an expanding population. The birth rate of present membership takes on more importance than if new membership were constantly available from an influx of people into the community. The churches in Paper City find demographic trends conditioned by formidable social and economic forces beyond their control—class, work patterns, housing, etc.[4] Therefore, factors which the churches feel they may be able to influence to some extent—such as morals in regard to use of birth control methods and the size of the family—may possibly take on greater importance to religious leaders than in areas where population is expanding rapidly.

Perhaps this "tight" population situation is related to the fact that the most overt attempt of the Catholic clergy to mold Protestant church action and the morality of the community in the past two decades—the Sanger incident—centered in their enforcement of the church's strictures against birth control. The Catholic church has placed high priority on the importance of this ethic in communities all over the world, but the concern may have been intensified among the Paper City clergy. Many Protestant ministers whose churches are now surrounded by Roman Catholic people think, to quote one pastor, in terms of "the alarming growth of the Catholic population in America," and of the Catholic policy in Paper City "as a larger strategy to increase the power of the church by outbreeding the Protestants."[5]

A Catholic City From Its Early Years

The second important fact about Paper City's population is that the community has been predominantly Roman Catholic in its religious affiliation throughout most of its history. The long association of Protestants and Catholics in the building of Paper City distinguishes it from most American communities, even from many other New England communities. As a local Roman Catholic church historian has indicated:

> Catholics were so late in their settlement in this New England Puritan stronghold that when they arrived, it was to find cities and towns firmly established and operating under a long history of orderly government. An exception to this general condition is the case of Paper City . . . incorporated in 1850, but two years after the arrival of the first band of pioneer Catholics in that town. . . . In 1857, only nine years after the appearance of the first Catholics, a new parish . . . St. Jerome's was established.[6]

From 1870 (only fifteen years after the town's official formation) until the present, Roman Catholics have outnumbered Protestants in the community. Paper City became the first community in the western part of the state and in the Roman Catholic diocese in which the Catholic population was the larger religious group.[7]

In 1906, Paper City, with a population of approximately 50,000, reached the high point of Catholic representation in the community—35,000 Roman Catholics, representing 70 per cent of the total population.[8]

Paper City has had one of the longest periods of Catholic dominance in American culture. For only the first two decades of its history were there more Protestants than Catholics. It is true that much of the surrounding area remained more Protestant in religious composition, and that the Protestant Yankees occupied such prominent positions in the economy that their influence far outweighed their numbers. But nonetheless, no city could be better chosen to show what life is now like in an American city long under pervasive Catholic influence.

The Catholic priests do not consider that the majority or minority status of the Roman Church is as important a factor in conditioning the programs and policies of the church as the Protestant clergy do. The priests stress the fact that the Catholic church holds to certain basic religious beliefs which are not founded upon social or historical conditions and which are the basic determinants of the church's attitudes toward other religions. There are, however, at least minor aspects of adaptation of the methods of the church in realizing its religious goals which do change somewhat with the census.

The Protestant pastors believe, on the other hand, that the Catholic as well as the Protestant churches adapt their programs in important respects to population trends. For example, a Congregational minister said, in presenting a long, scholarly paper to a study group of Protestant laymen on "Catholicism, Past and Present":

> Most of us are much too conscious of the effect the distribution of the religious population has upon the pattern of life here in Paper City and over the nation for one to elaborate. The Roman Church in North Carolina, with its six to seven thousand Catholics (we have

that many in one parish) manifests qualities never even suspected in a city like ours. In a community where I lived for five years, the local Benedictine priest, serving a parish which extended over an area with a radius of twenty-five miles, was one of my most intimate friends, a frequent guest in my home and I in his. He was a member of the local ministerial association and a willing and eager participant in union Thanksgiving services and other community enterprises. . . . Here in Paper City, I am unable to establish a friendship with any priest, no priest of the Roman Catholic Church belongs even to a service club, no religious baccalaureate service is held for graduating classes of our public schools since priests are not permitted to share public worship services with Protestant ministers. . . . The pattern of life changes with the census.

In spite of the importance that the Protestant clergy attach to religious membership data, they have instituted no population studies, and have made little use of available information.[9] Three Protestant ministers in Paper City had accurate knowledge of a study made by the Massachusetts Council of Churches summarizing data from church yearbooks and the 1936 federal religious census. This study estimated Roman Catholic religious membership in Paper City as 65 per cent of the total population and Protestant religious membership as 16 per cent. Uninformed opinions of almost all Protestant and Roman Catholic clergy, education leaders, YMCA and YWCA secretaries, social workers, journalists, politicians, labor leaders and businessmen put the percentage of Roman Catholic religious membership much higher. The estimates are usually that Catholics compose 75 to 85 per cent of the population and Protestants only 10 to 15 per cent. The median estimate was 80 per cent for the Roman Catholic religious population—considerably above the most accurate estimates obtainable.

Most Roman Catholic religious leaders claim the city as "one of the most Catholic in the United States" and estimate the Roman Catholic percentage to be approximately 75 to 80 per cent of the city's population. One priest, the most active participant in community activities of all the Roman Catholic clergy, has said on several public occasions that the city is 88 per cent Roman Catholic.

There are no entirely reliable and exactly comparable statistics for recent decades on the numerical strength of Protestants and Roman Catholics in the city and the membership of individual churches and denominations. However, enough information is available to permit satisfactory generalizations about present total church membership of Roman Catholics and Protestants.[10]

In 1946, 65.6 per cent of the total population of Paper City was Roman Catholic. Protestants made up 12.7 per cent of the population; Jews made up another 3 per cent of the community (Table II). This religious membership represented 81 per cent of the people of the city. The peak of Protestant numerical strength in proportion to the total population during these decades came in 1936, when Protestants composed 16 per cent of the population, although their absolute numerical strength was less than in 1926. The peak of Roman Catholic strength came in 1916.

In the past three decades, there has been no great shift in the proportions of Roman Catholics and Protestants in the total population. There is some evidence that Protestants lost ground slightly from 1936 to 1946 in relation to the total population and to the church-affiliated population, after a steady, though minor, increase in proportionate strength from 1916 to 1936. The possible significance of this fact in terms of varied responsiveness of religious groups to economic growth will be noted later. It is hard to account for the shifts in terms simply of factors within the churches themselves and their relations with one another.

At present Paper City has eleven Roman Catholic churches, eighteen Protestant churches, one Christian Science church, one Greek Orthodox church and two Jewish synagogues (Tables III-VII). The six major Protestant denominations (twelve churches) have within their membership 95.8 per cent of the affiliated Protestants in the community, and have held approximately the same percentage since 1916. These twelve major Protestant religious centers minister to 12.2 per cent of the community's people. The Roman Catholics have ten religious centers which minister to 65.5 per cent of the population. The Roman Catholics average 3,887 people to each church; the Protestants average 388 people. These figures will be significant in observing the differences in the professional activities of the religious leaders, particularly the tendency of the Catholic priests to confine themselves even more narrowly than the Protestant pastors to traditional worship and educational activities of the churches.

Paper City, in comparison with the thirty cities in the state with a population of 25,000 or more, was in 1940 one of the most Catholic communities in the commonwealth.[12] Only one other city had as large a percentage of Roman Catholics in the total population. Only three other cities in the state, by a slight margin of 1 or 2 per cent, have as great a proportion of Roman Catholics among those people who identify themselves with a religious faith. Paper City has a substantially greater percentage of Roman Catholics in the religious population than does the state. (Table VIII).

When Paper City is compared with the nation, the Roman Catholic nature of the religious population is accentuated. In the decades from 1916 to 1946, the Roman Catholic population in the nation was never greater than 18 per cent (Table IX) or less than 15.8 per cent. But in Paper City the Roman Catholic population ranged between 65.6 and 56.8 per cent of the total population. The rate of Roman Catholic growth in the nation has been less rapid than in Paper City. Further, in the nation, the Protestant growth has been steady and substantial, but in Paper City, where Protestants are in a decided minority, they have not quite held their own demographically.

A Comparatively Low Birth Rate

The third population fact about the community is this: a Catholic city is not necessarily a highly fertile city. Social and economic factors in Paper City operate to reduce the power of religious pressure against the use of artificial means of birth control. This fact no doubt contributed to the concern of some Catholic leaders with population trends in the community expressed in the Sanger incident.

Intensive analysis of the pre-war census data of 1940 indicates that the birth rate in Paper City was lower than that of the state and nation (Table X and XI). As might be expected, a declining proportion of young people and an increasing proportion of elderly people accompany the decreasing birth rate (Table XII).[13] The policy of the mills of employing more women than men because of the skill of women in textiles and paper work and their willingness to work for lower wage rates is an important factor in the excess of women over men in the city. The presence of more women than men has been true since 1860 (Table XIII). The industrial situation is a factor also in the low percentage of married women and married men in the city in comparison with other communities in the state (Tables XIV and XV), and in the low birth rate of the married women. The percentage of the female population gainfully employed in Paper City has always considerably exceeded that of the average percentage in the state (Table XVI). The employment policy of the mills is facilitated by other factors, such as weak labor organization and the closely knit family structure of the working population.

The End of the Immigration Influx

The fourth demographic fact of some consequence in religious relations is that the comparative growth of Roman Catholic and Protestant groups has ceased in the last four decades to be appreciably influenced by immigration from other lands. The number of foreign-born in Paper City has decreased since 1910 (Table XVII),[14] and with this trend the ratio of Catholics to Protestants has stabilized. Up until this the Catholics received their chief increase in membership from foreign immigration.

The end of the immigration influx has contributed to the great interest of the clergy now in the comparative ability of the churches to win converts. Data on conversions indicate, however, that the numbers claimed by either movement is too slight to affect the membership ratios appreciably. In 1946, the Roman Catholic church in Paper City secured 36 converts[15] (Table XVIII), a successful year in comparison with 1936 when 18 converts were won to the faith. In the same year converts from Roman Catholicism to Protestantism were 29 (Table XIX). Protestants, with approximately one-fifth the membership of the Roman Catholics, have secured in the years from 1942 to 1946 almost the same number of converts each year as the Catholics.[16]

Paper City Catholicism rates considerably below the conversion achievements of the faith in the diocese as a whole, and in the nation. In 1946, the Springfield diocese, in which Paper City is located (with a Roman Catholic population of 505,000), reported 617 conversions.[17] If the Roman Catholic population of the diocese had achieved the same proportion of converts as in Paper City, the diocese would have secured only 486 converts in 1946. In the nation, the Roman Catholic population achieved in 1946 one convert per 260 members;[18] in Paper City one convert was gained per 1,029 members.

The most spectacular gains in membership for each faith group appear to have been made by winning the participation of non-affiliated people, particularly from 1916 to 1926 (Table II). Senior priests in Paper City believe that the great increase in the proportion of Roman Catholics in the religious population from 1916 to 1926 must be attributed to more adequate records kept by the church and to a big expansion of the physical facilities of Catholicism in the city.

The Suburban Expansion

The fifth fact about population trends to be noted in Paper City is the movement toward the suburbs, a phenomenon common to urban areas all over America. During the decade from 1940 to 1950, while there was almost no increase in the population of Paper City, the metropolitan district (which includes Paper City and the neighboring rural areas, towns and cities) grew about 12 per cent. Small suburban towns located near Paper City, such as South Hadley and Longmeadow, expanded greatly.[19] As early as January 4, 1920, the mayor of Paper City wrote: "The practice of our people leaving Paper City for a near-by outside suburban district should be checked and discouraged. It tends to leave Paper City lean while these respective places bask in a steady growth and prosperity." This movement has accompanied the breakdown of ethnic areas in the city and the close alignment of ethnic-oriented recreational and social activities with the Catholic churches. The tensions created within the religious movements by these changes will concern us in detail in later chapters (particularly Chapters 13 and 14).

Labor Mobility and Religion

The final fact to be noted about Paper City demography is more speculative than the others, for it involves the relationship of many religious, social and economic factors. There appears to be some basis for speculation that the Protestants are more mobile in the search for better economic opportunities than the Roman Catholics. The relevant observations are these: Substantial and sustained downturns in the number of wage earners are always accompanied in Paper City, as in other cities, by a decline in population, but the decline in population always lags behind the decline in employment (Table XX). So too, long-term increases of employment opportunities augment the population size, but not in direct proportion, because of the great flexibility in the labor-force potential of the population. Paper City's flexibility in this respect is very great indeed. Although Paper City's wage earners increased from about 9,000 to 13,000 between 1940 and 1950, the increase in the total population was a slight 2 per cent at best.

For three decades (1910-1940), comparatively poor work opportunities pressed the people to leave the city and seek employment elsewhere. But when World War II opened up new work and the labor force expanded over 25 per cent, there were still enough people ready to work in the community so that only a very slight influx of new people was needed to fill the jobs.

The people of the city, for many economic or social reasons, would appear to have a very high potential ability for labor mobility. The city has a comparatively large percentage of unmarried men and women. They might be assumed not to have heavy family responsibilities and could "travel light" in search of new opportunities in an expanding national economy. Because home ownership is also comparatively limited in Paper City, the problem of selling property is often not involved.

But obviously there are tremendous ties that bind the people to the city and pull against the economic pressures to move to other communities with better job opportunities. What are they? It may be that a significant characteristic of this city, with its large Catholic population, is the power of tight-knit familial, ethnic and religious associations to limit labor mobility. Comparison of the impacts of religions upon these associations become highly pertinent in the study of the forces that influence the rate of economic expansion in a society. As we have seen, the Protestant churches in Paper City proportionately lost membership during the period of great post-war national economic expansion (in which the city participated less than many other industrial centers in the region and the nation), while the Roman Catholics "held their own." Perhaps Protestants tend to be more mobile socially and more responsive to economic developments than Roman Catholics because they have less strong individual ties to or dependence upon particular ethnic, familial and religious associations and institutions. Is there, for example, a Protestant family ideal which places less stress upon maintaining large cohesive groups than the Catholic ideal? And is the Protestant family ideal and relatively greater economic mobility related to the individualistic and pluralistic religious and church experience of Protestantism, while the Catholic family ideal and comparatively less economic mobility are related to a more structured, authoritative, mediated religious experience?

The significance of the impact of religious differences upon labor mobility, if it can be ascertained, depends both upon one's value judgments as to the importance of economic growth and material productivity in the society and upon one's factual knowledge as to the importance of labor mobility and entrepreneurial aggressiveness.

The clergy of Paper City reflect little upon such matters. They view the population data almost entirely in terms of the relative strength of the churches, with no understanding of the data as a possible clue to the varied responsiveness of church members to social and economic change and as an expression of their own religious institution's assumptions about the good society. The minority sensitivity of the Protestants and the majority confidence of the Catholics lead Paper City citizens to assume that the Roman Catholic population is greater than it is and that the Protestant population is less than it actually is.

Chapter 4

The Role of the Churches in Man's Salvation

"Protestants agree with Roman Catholics on the spiritual side of man's redemption. It's the mechanical side coming to focus in their doctrine of the church's role in salvation with which we disagree." This remark from the pastor of the First Congregational church is representative of the appraisals by the clergy of the central issue in disputes over doctrine and worship between Protestants and Roman Catholics. They focus upon the role of the visible religious organization in relating man to God.

The degree of isolation which the religious institutions attempt to enforce in the relations of members with nonmembers, the religious structure which they seek to maintain in the community, and their general theories of society are deeply involved in their interpretations of the role of church organization in man's salvation.[1]

Not all the differences in doctrine and worship between the Roman Catholic and Protestant religions in Paper City can be summarized in the next three chapters. (See the Appendix for a chart of the major theological characteristics of the Catholic church, the Protestant churches and the sects.) Doctrine and worship are dealt with in their relation to the development of two distinct religious movements in the community, and with the general areas of agreement and tension which have developed between the leaders over the role of their respective institutions in the salvation of men.

For both Protestant and Roman Catholic leaders, the "life, death and resurrection of Christ" is interpreted as of supreme importance in man's reconciliation with God. Their mutual involvement in the world as Christians is founded in this single event in which, for them, the nature of the creating, governing and redeeming God is best revealed. They return to this fact even in their dependence upon varied interpretations of it for the basis of their separate existence as religious communities. Without Christ neither Roman Catholic or Protestant churches would exist.

But the question is at once posed, how do men receive, hold to and express this fact of faith in God revealed in Christ? Are the religious associations or institutions which men form necessary instruments or media by which men are "brought to God"? If so, in what ways?

Justification by Faith—The Protestant Interpretation

The most fundamental doctrinal issue about which disputes over the role of the church in man's salvation appear to revolve, in one terminology or another, is the one which several Protestant leaders believe to have been at the center of the Protestant Reformation which broke the unity of Christendom in the Western world. This issue was posed in the Protestant principle of "justification by faith alone."

This debate[2] goes on almost constantly within the Protestant churches and sects, and between them and the Roman Catholic leaders.[3] The sects in Protestantism in Paper City are chiefly confined to the "storefront" religious groups, such as Jehovah's Witnesses, Polish Evangelistic Assembly and Gospel Hall. The Protestant churches are the congregations of the "old-line" denominations —mainly Episcopalian, Congregational, Presbyterian, Methodist and Baptist. The debate between the religious groups is not usually in the terms of the Reformation and its slogans, "the sufficiency of Christ," "justification without works through faith alone," and the like, although the sect leaders and the Roman Catholic press and clergy particularly continue to use the traditional slogans.

Protestant leaders chiefly represent the justification by faith principle as a protest against the identification of the "sources of salvation" or the "reality of God's grace" with any action or instrument of any individual or institution.[4] "No group or institution can claim that its works, its sacraments, or its doctrines are divine or that they save man. This claim belongs only to the God revealed in Jesus Christ," a speaker at Gospel Hall observes. He adds:

> If salvation is a gift then you can't work for it. It's either a gift or works. For Protestants it's a gift from God. In the Catholic church salvation is mostly works; "do this, the church tells you and do that"

> the priest keeps saying. But Christ came to seek and to save the sinner. When he went, he said, "It is finished." Sinners are saved by the sovereign grace of God, not by fulfillment of laws and works of individuals or of churches. Paul said, "By deeds of law shall no flesh be justified." That was what he learned on the Damascus road—that he was on the wrong track.

The justification by faith principle is most unitedly and consistently employed by the Protestant leaders against the "deification by Catholics of their church institution," with the sects being the more persistent and continuous in their application of the principle to Catholics within their worship and teaching activities.[5] As one sect leader noted, "When the priest says that men can always find God in the Mass, or that certain religious acts recommended by the church earn eternal reward, or reduce a person's time in purgatory, the priest is giving an importance to particular institutional devices which belongs only to God."

Differences clearly arise between Protestant leaders in their interpretation of the implications of the justification by faith principle for their own organizational life. They are united in their rejection of the institutional form of the Catholic church, but there are great tensions among them as to the form by which their protest is to be expressed. Deep within the sects, such as the Polish Evangelistic Assembly and Gospel Hall, and also to some extent within the leadership of the Baptist, Methodist and Congregational churches, there is an anti-institutionalism, a sense of Christ being in protest against the institutional expression of religion.

This anti-institutionalism is not simply the assertion that when the gospel is apprehended by men, it is necessarily no longer wholly transcendent or wholly spiritual, embodied as it is within "earthen vessels," in a particular time and place. It is the assertion that the more complex the development of doctrine, worship and organization, the greater is the compromise and corruption of the gospel, and the less vital is the Protestant protest against Catholicism. It is the denial of religious significance and importance to the patterns of meaning and the forms of association developed within the church community. This is one of the most puzzling and profound aspects of Paper City Protestantism, in which apparently fundamental problems with which the movement has always wrestled in its history are made grotesque and urgent by the pressures of a dominant and ever-present Catholicism. The social aspects of the Protestant churches remain great—the professional prestige of the clergy is bound up with "keeping the show going" and with providing "more and more organizations to give people a chance to get together,"—even while the anti-institutional versions of the justification by faith doctrines are most stridently maintained. Thus no serious attempt is made to provide a theological understanding of church organization or periodically to re-examine it critically in relation to a changing society.

The sect position is representative of what H. Richard Niebuhr has termed the "Christ against culture" point of view.[6] This frame of reference seeks to affirm the sole authority of Christ over the Christian and to reject the world's claim to loyalty. Within the Protestant sect, the world becomes the society outside the religious group. Society is evil and, therefore, to be abandoned, withdrawn from, rather than transformed. There is no need for elaboration of doctrine to clarify the sect's relation to the complexities of society around it. There is no need for development of worship forms to express the relation of sacred and secular symbols in the culture. There is no need for development of organization to carry the content of the gospel to the various specialized centers of modern society.

But some institutional expression is inevitable, and the Protestant sects of Paper City have tended to form small perfectionist groups, with enough doctrinal and cultic development to establish group consensus as to the meaning of the Scriptures, to express one's sanctification through charitable acts for fellow members, and to provide opportunity for informal witness and for a corporate prayer life. The sect groups look upon their simple form as the correct expression of the justification by faith principle. Christ is in protest against all the religious and secular forms outside the sect.

The institutional form of most Protestant churches in Paper City is a much more loose aggregate of individuals than the sect groups, meeting occasionally for social fellowship and for participation in a service of worship or cultus which has as its major act the expression by a professional leader of his personal convictions. The supporting doctrinal position for this institutional form represents much more complex phenomena than that of the sects. The dominant theology is an interpretation of the justification by faith doctrine in much the same individualistic terms as the sect. God's redemptive work is accomplished apparently through a direct, separate, vertical relationship to man. The usual Protestant clergyman shares the sect leader's suspicion that the more elaborate he makes the religious institutional forms and the more self-conscious he is about organizational problems the more he compromises the gospel. At least this is the prevailing public ideology he perpetuates.

The Protestant church leaders, on the other hand, combine with the justification by faith doctrine—or more accurately, add to it—a doctrine of sanctification expressed as high optimism about the power of "the Word," when persuasively preached, to make men desirous and capable of loving their fellowmen. For most of the Protestant clergymen, the traditional Protestant church form is a satisfactory expression both of their understanding of the Protestant belief in justification by faith alone and an optimistic belief in God's power (operating through good preaching) to help men follow the law of love.

The most widely accepted role of the Protestant pastor is well expressed by the minister of the Second Baptist church as "preaching that if men will but be obedient to the principles and ideals which Christ exemplified, then there can be a peaceful and prosperous world for all." For the pastor to carry out this role, the Protestant church does not need disciplined and complex development of doctrine and organization. The Protestant church's form itself is in many ways an expression of the best social ideals of its most prominent laymen—an association of independent individuals, zealous in maintenance of their freedom and autonomy. To use Richard Niebuhr's types again, this is a "Christ of culture" position.

This inattention by the Protestant clergy to the development of institutional and community life is part of a broad theological, professional, and cultural pattern—a strong reaction against Catholic emphasis upon the religious significance of organization; a particular view, growing out of this reaction, of a central Protestant doctrine, justification by faith alone; a great emphasis upon the preaching function of the ministry, a specialization no doubt encouraged in seminary training and by the limited contact of the church with laymen; and finally the reduction of the Christian gospel to an idealistic ethic of love.

Yet these pastors live in a community where the Catholic church is dominant and its members in the majority. The pressures created by this situation have brought a challenge to many Protestant pastors and they experiment spasmodically with forms which will "resist Catholic expansion more adequately" than their present programs. But this "experimentation" reveals the great difficulty Protestant leaders have in relating theology and sociology and in making their faith "work" in the community.

There is a minority of Protestant leaders (represented chiefly by the pastors of the First and Second Congregational Churches) who tend to interpret the justification by faith principle within a "Christ transforming culture" theology. They seek to discover an affirmative, ordered and continuous response to the activity of God within all religious and secular organization. They view society not as wholly evil, to be rejected or replaced, nor as fulfilling the demands of Christ, to be accepted. They view it as corrupted and needing constant transformation and conversion.

These pastors work within Protestant churches which have long been established and are stoutly defended by most Yankee laymen. Their concern about existing Protestantism reflects, like that of the other pastors, their deep involvement in the survival and power needs of their own religious institution before the pressures and questions of Catholicism. But their concern also reflects an awareness, greater than that of the other pastors, of the distinct and determining influences of the "secular" institutions upon their laymen.

They see about them a community with an influential popular press—a daily newspaper, a radio and TV station—with simple "catechisms," elaborate "doctrinal" pretensions, and capsules of meaning and motivation prepared by efficient staffs. They see the impact of the "high priests" of mass advertising in the magazines, movies and radio networks which come into Paper City. They see the disciplining of men within the economic and political interest groups of the community. And they wonder if there is within the

Protestant interpretation of justification by faith the basis for an institution which is neither an anarchic Protestant fellowship giving little religious significance to the church, nor a hierarchial, authoritative institution identifying salvation with itself—a position which they associate with Catholicism.

Expression of the justification by faith principle is to be found in that institutional life in which leaders do not claim for doctrine, worship and polity God-like attributes of absoluteness and correctness always to be defended against new forms of doctrine, cultus, and polity. "The grace of God is expressed through forms but is not to be identified with them," said the pastor of the First Congregational Church. "Neither sect form nor church form saves." The sect's adherence to simple expression of belief, its limited use of symbols in worship, its equalitarian organization can be made as absolute and rigid a form as any elaborate ritual of the churches.

There is present in Protestantism a greater fluidity, dynamism, tension in its institutional forms—doctrine, cultus and organization—than in Catholicism. Protestantism has a greater openness to new developments than Catholicism and correspondingly less power to order and discipline. Yet within a great deal of Protestantism—sect as well as church—there is also a static and dogmatic adherence to certain institutional forms as the correct or best protest against Catholicism.

For basic theological reasons all Protestant churches and sects, including the Episcopalian, stop short at some point of the doctrinal, worship and organizational development of Roman Catholicism. Protestantism introduces more "open-ended" expression of doctrine and rite, greater lay participation in the formation of belief, greater reluctance to locate within particular offices powers to formulate "right" doctrine and acts of worship binding on others.

Three types of fairly stable institutional responses—the Protestant sect, the Protestant churches and the Roman Catholic church—can be delineated in Paper City faith groups. But the differences between Protestant sect and Protestant church are less significant for Paper City than the general distinction to be made between Roman Catholic and Protestant developments in doctrine and worship. The movement from sect to church, as described by such scholars as Liston Pope and H. Richard Niebuhr, must not be conceived as an inevitable expression of institutional development, through a smooth, unbroken continuum from the Protestant sect to the Catholic *ecclesia.* It is true that the tensions evident within Protestantism over the "inadequacy" of its doctrine and polity are often posed by the participants in terms of becoming more or less "like the Catholics."[7] And there have been Protestant sects which have developed into churches, and groups have then split off to establish associations of more enthusiastic and informal camaraderie.[8] But the movement from sect to church in Paper City has never been on a continuum from Protestant sect clear over to Roman Catholic church; there have obviously been strong theological and social factors operating to prevent this.[9]

Justification by Faith—the Catholic Interpretation

The Catholic pastors assert that they do not see any point to the Protestant criticism of Catholicism on the basis of Protestant belief in "salvation by faith" and "the sufficiency of Christ." The pastor of St. Jerome's parish, the "mother church" in Paper City, says:

> We can do nothing by ourselves toward our salvation. In this the Protestants are right. But once we are given grace or supernatural power by God, we can co-operate with it. We can increase and develop grace through our personal efforts. Once we are given grace by God, we can through our own actions merit eternal rewards. This is important. Christ bore the penalty for man's original sin, but not for sins committed by man after baptism when he is freed from his original sin. Christ won for us by his merit the power of meriting eternal reward.

The pastor of Immaculate Conception parish comments:

> For Catholics, as for Protestants, man's salvation is beyond his own power to achieve. No man comes to Christ unless God draws him. It is by the act of faith that man first sets himself on the path to salvation, and that act is God's gift. Protestants do not realize that Catholicism is a religion of faith. In the act of faith, the individual sees that the things God has revealed are true.

Where then is the point of Protestant dispute with Catholics about justification by faith? It enters again at the point where the church assumes its place in the act of faith. The pastor of Immaculate Conception continues:

> For the Catholic, the act of faith is an act of trust in the church. For the church is the instrument, the institution through which Christ saves. The church would not be possible without the life and death of Christ in history and his continued activity in the world now. The church's infallible teaching authority, its power to save sinners is evidence of Chirst's power, of his sufficiency. Christ understood that men would need a divine institution on earth to direct them to Him.

From the same theological position the pastor of St. Jerome's parish explains in a sermon to his people their access to Christ through the church:

> Christ asks that you come to Him by taking His blood. But many of you would not come to Mass if you did not know it is a sin not to. The church knows this. It saw communion attendance was falling off among early Christians. So in 1215 A.D. the church made it obligatory, a law of the church, to take communion once a year on pain of excommunication.

For Catholics the necessary contribution of Christ to man's salvation was the establishment of His church. The commission given by the Lord to Peter, "Thou art Peter and upon this rock will I build my church" is interpreted by the Catholic clergy as the singling out of an individual to establish an unbroken continuity of spiritual power in the world—the apostolic succession. It is a commission to institutionalize God's dealing with His children.[10]

When Christ founded His church 1900 years ago, the Catholics argue, He gave it two wonderful powers which distinguish it from the Protestant churches, which make it "surpass all other institutions and organizations" and establish it as "the Kingdom of God on earth" for which "every gain is a gain for truth." A manual of instruction, widely used for instruction of laymen, describes these powers as:

> (1) Teaching and legal powers in which the Church partakes of God's divine authority and cannot be deceived. By these powers man is brought to God.
> (2) Sacramental powers by which the Church brings God's grace to man.[11]

In the Roman Catholic church, then, Christ has, for the Catholic believer, bridged the boundaries between God and man by the establishment of a particular institution. Each form of this institution takes on great importance. From the church's doctrines the Catholic receives God's answers to questions of faith and morals; from its sacraments he receives the power to do works which win for him eternal rewards.

While Protestant interpretations of the relation of faith and institution will not permit a precise definition of the role of the church in the salvation of man, the Catholic clergy locate absolute saving power within a *particular* church and in a *particular* place. The priest's education of young people, where doctrine tends to be reduced to the basic core of conviction desired, leaves no uncertainty as to the identity of "God's church." For example, a catechism reads:

> Q. Which is God's church?
> A. The Catholic Church is God's Church.
> Q. Why is this His Church?
> A. The Catholic Church is God's Church because Jesus, the Son of God, started it when He lived here on earth.
> Q. How long is it since Jesus lived on earth?
> A. Jesus lived on earth over 1900 years ago.
> Q. How old is the Catholic Church?
> A. The Catholic Church is over 1900 years old.[12]

This institution stands, for the Catholic, above culture, above the finite, earthen, limiting factors of society. It has a form independent of all other institutions—a form not to be judged by the standards used for other institutions. Catholic identification of the Lordship of Christ with a particular institution is a fact of overwhelming importance.

Definition of Catholic Church Members

When the Catholic pastors in Paper City speak of the church and its members in the widest sense, they include, as one priest said, "all those in heaven, purgatory or on earth who belong to the Communion of Saints." There is some difference among the priests as to whether those on earth (the church militant) who are to be saved are to be identified with membership in the visible organization of the Roman Catholic church, or whether the church must be thought of as embracing all those in the visible membership and those in other religious organizations who are to be saved. The latter theoretical position is the dominant one among the clergy; the former is dominant among the layman's understanding of the priests' position. In either case, the phrase, "outside the Church there is no salvation" is held to be correct.

The Papal position has been taken that it is "necessary to salvation that every human creature be subject to the Roman Pontiff" (Pope Boniface VIII in the Bull *Unam Sanctum,* November 18, 1302). The Roman Catholic church is defined by the priests and by discussion guides (such as Father Betowski's *The True Church*) used widely in the parishes, as the society composed of all the faithful, who profess the faith of Christ, partake of the same sacraments, and pursue salvation under one common head, the Holy Father, the Pope who is the visible representative of Jesus Christ.

These are representative expressions by the priests:

> We don't tell our people that the Protestants are going to hell. We tell our people that more Protestants will probably go to heaven than Catholics who think they'll go and won't. If a man is sincere in his religious beliefs and lives by them the best he can, then he has as good a chance to go to heaven as Catholics.

> What is meant by the doctrine outside the Church is that all those who seek to live by the highest they know, and who have no doubts are really Catholics. If they doubt the Protestant church and stay in it, they can't be saved.

However, in application of these principles by the priests to specific Protestant groups in Paper City, the possibilities of Protestant inclusion in the church become more narrow. For example, one of the priests quoted above, when asked whether the people in the Polish Evangelistic Assembly were in the church, observed, "All the people in the Assembly are divorcees, people who can't be married in the church. They know they are doing wrong. They will not be saved." And an Irish priest, asked about the Protestant group nearest his own parish, replied, "They don't have any religion. All their minister knows to do is fight the Catholics. He is the most wicked minister in the city. How can people who let a man like that lead them have any religion?"

The Catholic Position on Correct Doctrine

The certitude of access to God and to knowledge of His will through the Catholic church in the teaching of Paper City's priests is epitomized in the statement of the pastor of Holy Rosary parish to children on the occasion of their first communion:

> You are going to be nearer to God through the acts of goodness you are going to perform. You are going to come to love even more the precious church that God has given the people. You will know now where God can always be found. You will know right from wrong. You are the hope of your parish, your city and your country for your faith is sure.

For the Catholic leaders, religion without an established body of truth is about as sensible as civil government without a constitution.[13] The primary and ultimate test of religious truth is the growing, infallible teaching of the church, an institution which existed before the Bible and has preserved the true meaning of the Bible.[14] It is the content of this tradition which the faithful must know above all else. This can be seen in examination of devotional and educational material distributed to families and in the diocesan press itself. For example, a booklet recommended by priests for "Family Life in Christ" gives in detail the duties of parents in "preparing the child for his first Mass," in "following the liturgical cycles in the home" but does not mention the reading of the Bible.[15] To a critic who asks, "Why are Catholics not allowed to read the Bible?" [16] a columnist of the diocesan magazine answers:

> The Church permits and encourages the faithful to read the Bible but only in versions approved and annotated by her. Some versions of the Bible pervert the meaning of the Sacred Text. . . . The ordinary laymen . . . may unwittingly imbibe heretical ideas and thus imperil his faith. Hence the Church forbids her children for their good to read versions of the Bible which she has not authorized or approved. She is the divinely appointed teacher of revealed truth and the authentic interpreter of the whole Scripture. She must preserve the stream of Divine Revelation from pollution.[17]

The product of this type of authoritative definition of truth is a systematic and detailed codification and rating of beliefs and correct conduct. The priests display great unanimity as to which of the doctrines are most essential to the maintenance of the church and of lay faith, and therefore to be stressed in limited contacts with members. These doctrines are rarely argued out or reasoned out with laymen. They are affirmed over and over: Jesus Christ is God. Christ died for us on the cross and rose from the dead. Christ lives in His Mystical Body, the Catholic Church. Jesus Christ, True God, and True Man, is really present in the Blessed Sacrament. The Sacrifice is that of the Cross. The priest in the confessional has the power to forgive sins. The Blessed Mary is the Mother of God. Almighty God has given the church revealed truth. These are the fundamental Catholic dogmas on which the institution of the church is built. And they are the ones which are presented most frequently to laymen in the Catholic diocesan press and in sermons.[18]

The description by Protestant leaders of the Catholic doctrinal system as one which claimed exactness and precision in its interpretation of the will of God, of right and wrong, is accepted as correct by Catholic clergy. This is the distinctiveness and greatness of Catholicism, a *Catholic Mirror* editorial observes.[19] A writer in a Catholic pamphlet widely distributed to laymen in Paper City affirms that:

> Today the Christian Church (except those persons who have quit to follow their own mind on things) has a neat and most systematic body of principles covering every human act. No Christian need worry or fret over whether he is doing wrong. After more than nineteen centuries of helping people, the Catholic Church knows very well the difference between right and wrong.[20]

How is the Catholic Church able to develop this detailed and inclusive body of principles? The answer the priests give, in the words of one pastor, is that "a law of God governs men, antecedent to the Mosaic Law and the Sermon on the Mount and of far wider obligation and application, to which all men are subject. This is natural law, the result of man's discernment of God's eternal laws by his reason and without the revelation of Christ." The church is able to correct any false discernment of this law in the individual or in a temporal organization of society. Moreover, there is no conflict between what God reveals his will to be in the natural laws rightly discerned and in the Gospel. The revelation of the Gospel is simply added on to the demands given men in reason.

The results of this combination of belief that the church has been given power to define right and wrong and the absorption of a natural law ethic into this authoritative system are to be seen in detail throughout the various social areas of this study with which the church makes contact. The priests believe that the church knows what the *general* structure and characteristics of a Christian economic, social and political order are. There are, of course, autonomous areas in temporal affairs where no moral issues are at stake. And there are moral areas, the priests are aware, in which Catholic ethicists are not agreed. But in the crucial issues of faith and morals, a Catholic position is believed by the priests to be defined. Debates over Catholic morality in relation to issues, such as ownership of property and the role of the state in economic affairs, going on within the scholarly journals of the church are almost never reflected in the diocesan press or in the educational programs as developed by the clergy for the parishes. Positions on detailed issues are often taken in the diocesan press with no indication that they may not necessarily express God's will or may be simply "common opinions" which the priest expects only the pious to keep. In the official diocesan journal, "the Catholic viewpoint" has been expressed that "it is most un-Christian in its suppositions to imprint [Christmas] cards, for example, Elsie and Robert Jones, when Elsie and Bob are really Mr. and Mrs. Bob Jones. In a Christian family the father (or husband) comes before the mother (or wife)." [21] The "Catholic viewpoint" is also expressed on the way in which a girl's appearance "in shorts in the presence of others will lead her into sin: 'she who ignores the little things will soon fall' says the Holy Ghost in the Bible." [22]

The Protestant Reaction

The religious leaders of Paper City think they live in a society in which men are increasingly confused as to what they believe about God and about their responsibilities in the world. In an address in 1947 before an overflowing crowd in a Catholic high school auditorium in Paper City, Bishop Fulton J. Sheen described modern man: his daily work is composed of specialized tasks that give little opportunity to see the whole product toward which he contributes. He views economic and political events which determine his life as beyond his understanding or control. He feels surrounded by people with moods as fluctuating and uncertain as his own. In such a situation, said Bishop Sheen, "Man seeks an absolute, a church, infallibility. Seeking a dogma, he finds economic determinism, Communism, and it fills the void created by loss of faith. Into the void of modern man must come the Catholic faith with its true doctrine."[23]

The fundamental error of Catholicism, said two Protestant pastors who heard Bishop Sheen's speech, is that it has always sought to appeal to man's hunger for certainty by assuming a too easy and precise overcoming of the differences which exist between God and man. Parochial Catholicism has affirmed that the church has the resources for a detailed knowledge of the will of God. The general Protestant position on the "degree of certitude given to Christians" is presented in a sermon by the pastor of Paper City's largest Protestant congregation:

> We have an accumulation of evidence to back up our faith, but it is still and must forever be a venture of faith. Any spiritual reality is by its very nature beset by doubt. Paul in First Corinthians (2:14), as I understand him, is saying "Everything about life is mysterious. God is too great for a little human mind to comprehend. Our earthly measuring rods are too short."

The sermon notes a tremendous hunger among men for some absolute or certain answers to their predicaments. But the alternative before the Christian is neither to flee to the authority of a religious institution nor to affirm a complete scepticism, as if nothing can be relied upon. The alternative is to make one's relative discernments of the truth and the good with courage and with faith in the God who judges and sustains all persons and institutions.

No one individual or group, including the Pope when he speaks on matters of faith, can claim to have final, infallible knowledge of truth, the same pastor said in another sermon. The only final authority that men must obey is God in Christ, for He alone is without sin. All men and institutions are under judgment and all men have a right of conscience over against all forms of authoritarianism. The Protestant heritage, then, is "one of an open Bible." There is nothing binding on man except what he receives in his own study of the Scriptures and meditation upon the insight and experiences of fellow believers. No institutionally located authority exists which interprets the Scriptures in an infallible way. "We cherish [this situation] even though groups spring up with wrong or peculiar notions of Biblical interpretation. That is the only way of real freedom and true progress."

This is the core of conviction which composes the theological thought of most of the Protestant pastors on the church's role in the development of doctrine. But, again, it is to be noted that Protestant doctrinal expression receives its most explicit and forthright formulation as a protest against the institutional development of the Catholic church. Very little is directly said about the role of the Protestant church in the development of beliefs of laymen.

For example, the pastor of the Second Baptist Church, in an outline of Protestant belief for new members, observes that Christians should join the church "to be partners with Christ in the building of his Kingdom." He warns that the church "is in the front-line trench in the battle for righteousness and against evil." But the nature of the church's activity in clarifying the issues for which men fight, the symbols under which they gather and the organization for utilizing the resources of the individual members are not indicated. The Protestant church leaders assume that a religious community will emerge from the common response of believers to the Word of God in Christ and not from any concern for a systematic design and a precise program.

For the minister to imply that one's religion requires a specific act in society is to violate the justification by faith principle and to make religion into a legalistic code. A common theme in Protestant sermons is that "the Protestant religion is a religion of love. The Scriptures indicate that love is above the law. When we try to say what love is we had best look to Christ and say, he expressed what God means by love. Christ is always overcoming and breaking through codes and laws and revealing new possibilities to Christians."

The proper role of the minister is widely conceived to be that of clarifying the general moral and religious goals for men, and leaving to each individual the working out of the specific relation of the goals to his life and the means of achieving these objectives. This approach is indicated in two fairly typical sermons by a Protestant pastor, one on "The Word of Power for an Age of Power" and the other, "Jesus, Joy of Man's Desiring." Here is the central message of each:

> This is the day, my friends, of either-or. Either we study God's word and inculcate his spirit or we will blow ourselves forever off the stage of this universe. It is either the Bible or bombs and oblivion for this generation. It is either Christ or curtains for us. There is no other alternative. Does someone say, "Pastor, do you really believe the Bible could change all of this?" Indeed I do. If a wave of Bible reading which was an intelligent seeking for truth, should flow across this land and the world, we'd take it for Christ.

> It is becoming increasingly apparent that unless he [Christ] does come more fully into our lives, civilization is lost. Where we have dodged him and avoided his program we have run into difficulty and struggle and hardship and bloodshed. Where we have uncompromisingly accepted him, he has worked out our problems amazingly. He is a long way from being the Desire of nations yet, but I believe that is coming and is the only hope. If nations right now invited him to the peace table, what miracles he would work across this earth!

A minority of pastors say they are concerned to develop among their members some sense of what are the essential principles of faith, while avoiding standardized codes of legalistic religion. They wish to broaden the areas in which faith is articulated, and to avoid a retreat to general principles away from concrete decisions that must be made in society. They wish to see clergy and laymen seeking together to define what are for them true convictions, with awareness of the relativity of their expression and without the security of church authority. They wish to see these convictions worked out in relation to the precise and present decisions to be made in Paper City. For example, two of these men have supported the work of the Council for Social Action of the Congregational Christian Churches against some lay opposition as "an important aid to the clarification of the implications of the Gospel for our present situation." And they have organized intermittently small study groups composed of laymen from a variety of vocational backgrounds on Christianity and social issues.

In regard to the sects (and also the Lutheran church, which has a conservative orientation toward Biblical theology), religious certitude is present on the basis, to use the words of the lay leader of Gospel Hall, of a belief in "the Bible as the verbally inspired word of God, inerrant and authoritative from cover to cover." The problem of development of doctrine is looked upon primarily as that of study of the Scriptures as "the only and all-sufficient rule of faith and practice." Any tenet of belief, the pastor of the Polish Evangelistic Assembly said, "which cannot be proven to be based on the Scriptures cannot be an object of faith." The sect criticism of both Catholic and Protestant churches is that a vast body of beliefs about church forms and about the world have been elaborated without use of the Bible as the fundamental point of reference. From the Scriptures, the sects derive a new law, a code of conduct which is limited in its concentration upon the virtues of religious zeal, temperance, industry and purity of speech.

The Protestant and Roman Catholic churches and sects participate in a search for answers to the ultimate questions of man's existence in society. At times the leaders of these institutions appear to each other as men who know they must honestly face deeply felt and profoundly different convictions, and yet who also know that they can understand and appreciate one another because they are sustained by a common faith in a reality transcending their historic manifestations. On other occasions, the confrontations seem to be taking place between antagonists who can represent the positions of others only in stereotypes as if there were no faithful basis of understanding or empathy.

Chapter 5

Worship in the Churches

Nothing within the lives of the people of Paper City expresses more directly and symbolically the nature of Protestantism and Catholicism than the corporate and personal acts intended to express the experience of the holy. No attempt will be made here to describe the varied private or personal acts of reverence and their significance in religious relations. What concerns us in the main are the ritualistic, sacramental, corporate acts of worship carried out within the physical settings provided for that purpose in the religious institutions, though discussion of these will sometimes carry us into interpretations of personal worship experience.

The principal issue between the religious movements over the nature of worship is posed in an opening story for a series of sermons delivered in 1947 by the pastor of the only Presbyterian church in the city. This series was widely discussed in the church for it represented the first attempt of the pastor, as he described it, "to put on the line" the basic distinctions between Protestantism and Catholicism. The series was titled "Some Positive Reasons Why the Protestant Church Is the Greatest Religious Movement in America." The story was about a member of his church, who was a nurse and worked in the Roman Catholic hospital in the city. She became engaged in a discussion with the chaplain of the hospital over the question of "where the Christian finds God." In the course of the discussion the priest took the nurse into the sanctuary of the Catholic church near the hospital, and pointed to the altar and the tabernacle. "There is where God is," he told her, but the nurse replied, "No, this is where God is," and pointed to her heart.

The issue the story poses is this: in what way is God present in the corporate acts of reverence carried out within particular religious institutions? More specifically, the Catholic church by making the Mass the central cultus poses the issue as *the meaning of the sacraments.*

The story also suggests the main directions taken by the religious leaders. The Catholic church asserts the assured presence of God within each local Catholic church particularly through the transformation of natural objects into the body of Christ. The Protestant churches assert that God cannot be identified with any act or object of worship, that no object takes on sacramental significance apart from the faith in the individual. Most of the Protestant churches tend in their institutional form to localize the manifestations of the holy in the individual, in his act of personal decision.

The affirmations, tensions and ambiguities already described within the Protestant churches over the relation of faith in Christ to institutional forms are expressed in Protestant worship and the leaders' interpretation of it. Most of the Protestant pastors have sought to say that "sacraments" and rites of the Christian church can merely "symbolize Christ's presence." Catholic sacramentalism, according to the ministers, seeks to make God's grace a tangible, though special, object which can be grasped and handled like other objects. The Protestants maintain that no man can touch or localize God in a particular object or thing. The object which serves as a holy symbol remains what it in itself is; it is a holy symbol only as it is an "outward, visible sign of spiritual Grace experienced within man." Thus, one pastor told his congregation the story of Moses and the burning bush and contrasted its meaning with the Catholic view of sacred objects. "Moses was told he was on holy ground," the pastor noted, "but all it was was a bush and soil. Therefore, the holy ground must be something in the self."

No symbol, no communion table, no bread and wine has religious meaning apart from the faith within the man who sees the object. A Congregational pastor takes the young people in his confirmation class up to "the altar" of his church and tells them that there is no sacrifice, no physical change going on during communion. "It is a communion table pure and simple. I don't want to claim that special materials or rites have a holiness in themselves. God is for Protestants best found in the individual act of faith in Jesus Christ as Saviour. This faith changes man's attitude toward the symbolic acts which Christ instituted for remembrance of Him. A new relationship between God and man is established through man's awakened conscience," the minister explains.

This Protestant view of sacraments is, of course, accompanied by a general belief that God can be present in the church building in a manner no different from that of any other place. The walls of the church are extended to include the whole of man's life, and in the analogy of a Congregational booklet of instructions for new members, the church building is like the home of a large family. Every member, just as at home, should see that the building is orderly, clean and comfortable, and that all while in it are cordial and friendly. A pastor reported that he "should have known better than to try recently to make the church into more of a sanctuary. I gave up when the janitor kept right on coming up front at the beginning of each service to fuss with the hymn numbers."

None of the ministers, with the exception of the Episcopalian pastor, has sought to present to laymen the metaphysical and theological issues involved in the differences of Protestant and Catholic views of the sacraments and of nature, other than the symbolic or metaphoric one described above. They reject the Catholic sacramental concept chiefly as "impersonal," as a failure to see that no act of cultus is holy apart from the faith of the "new being in Christ." They do not seek to deal with philosophical problems such as the relation of body and soul within personality. They reject the idea that God in Christ can be placed "in a little box on the altar," to quote a local Catholic catechism. But they have developed no concept for Protestantism of the way in which God makes nature a bearer of His grace that deals with the philosophical and theological concepts on which the Catholic priest has developed his sacramental claims.

The pastorates of several of the clergy have been characterized by a great deal of experimentation with and manipulation of external worship forms in response to various pressures of laymen for "more meaningful worship." This experimentation goes in the direction both of sect informality, zeal and antisymbolism, and of churchlike concern for greater order, solemnity and pageantry. It often involves the same pastor in sermons against the idolatry and externalities of the Catholic cultus and the introduction of worship forms suggested by Catholic usage. The major direction of the experimentation is toward a calculated, rationalistic appropriation by the pastor, or a worship committee, of various symbols and rituals available in traditional Protestant and Catholic worship and in popular rituals of the culture outside the church. The new forms seldom emerge out of the experience by the congregation or groups within it of the meaning of the Christian faith in their common life. The experimentation evidences some lay dissatisfaction with and indifference toward present Protestant worship.

The Protestant pastor's chief response to lay indifference to worship is to spend more time upon his sermons in an effort to make them more interesting, exciting and expressive of his own faith. For the center of the Protestant cultus is the sermon, as the Mass is the center of the Catholic. The sermon is the major act of the preacher, the rite through which he most fervently hopes God will express His presence, as the transubstantiation of the elements is the major cultic act of the priest. The personal persuasion and intensity of conviction of the pastor expressed in the preaching of the Word is the major answer of the Protestant minister to lay indifference.

Case Study of an Eclectic Protestant

The ambiguities and tensions in the Protestant clergys' approach are most conspicuously expressed in the actions of the pastor of Grace Congregational Church, a laboring-class congregation composed in large part of former Catholics. The minister in talking about Protestant worship said that "the church is just like any other place where people take their troubles in prayer to God." Yet in the vestibule of his church he has placed a large plaque bearing a quotation given him by an Anglican pastor:

> . . . When you reach this church never stay outside; go in at once. Time spent within is exceeding precious. In church bow down at once, very humbly to pray. In prayer remember the Presence into which you have come. Never look about you to see who is coming in, or for any cause whatever. It matters nothing to you what others may be doing; attend to yourself; fasten your thoughts firmly on the holy service; miss not a word. . . .
>
> Do not cover your head until you are outside—the church is God's House, even when prayer is over.

During a recent Sunday service the pastor made an announcement reminding members "of the little chapel open to you every evening, with candles burning to invite you to prayer," and in his sermon cautioned his audience against "Catholic talk that the early church had robes, candles, incense, big ceremonies and rituals and that therefore we should have such things now. Don't you believe it. Not a word of it is true. Not a word."

The order of worship for his Sunday morning "preaching service" is an eclectic mixture of church and sect cultus. It includes more formal creedal statements by the congregation and minister than any other Protestant church, including "Exhortation by Minister," "General Confession," "Declaration of Absolution by the Minister," and an "Affirmation of Our Faith and of Our Covenant." But the service is also characterized by several informal announcements: "When I look at the empty seats this morning I am glad that it doesn't rain every Sunday. Which reminds me to tell you not to forget our mid-week service. Mrs. Chitabar will speak and I hope we have a fine attendance." The pastoral, invocational and benedictory prayers are offhand, personal instructions to God and to the congregation by the pastor. A typical pastoral prayer begins:

> We'd like to take a little time in our prayers this morning, Lord, to ask that we be like the hundred and twenty in the early church that had such enthusiasm they soon had themselves thousands of members just as we can here if we have the enthusiasm.
>
> We are thankful, Our Father, for that wonderful evening last Tuesday when a great crowd turned out to hear the Mt. Holyoke College girls sing. Such evenings bring the girls closer to the church and give them unity, too. . . .

A typical benediction ends: "And now may we think on these things spoken this morning. May we understand what we mean by the Chritsian faith and the like. Amen."

The introduction of new symbols within the cultus of Grace Church has been chiefly by commission of the pastor, reflecting his own deepest interests and loyalties, not those of the congregation. The prayer chapel is dominated by enormous paintings of campus scenes, faculty portraits, and emblems in stained-glass windows from the nearby college alma mater of the pastor. The most expensively furnished room of the church is a "study," furnished by a wealthy textile manufacturer. It is a place of thirty-eight stiff, antique "noble chairs" (as they are described by the pastor in his public "log" of church activities) and of books from a gentleman's library, featuring uncut eighteenth- and nineteenth-century English literary works. The room stands open but unused by members of the church, except for meetings called by the pastor to care chiefly for the financial and property concerns of the church.

In this church as in others in the city, some laymen press their pastor for symbols as "impressive as the Catholics," and for "as big a public observance of Holy Days as the Catholics." Others revolt against "aping the Catholics" and oppose "making the worship hall look like a Catholic church." Here also groups of laymen have maneuvered and counter-maneuvered over "having the choir loft removed from its exalted position and the communion table with a cross on it placed in front of the baptismal font"—all without benefit of open discussion by the laymen and pastor of the nature and meaning of worship.

Worship in the Protestant Sects

In the sects, where the pristine experience of the members' break with the Catholic church is often expressed, the most radical rejection of the sacramental objects of the Catholic and Protestant church tradition occurs. ("If Christ came to most Catholic and Protestant churches, he wouldn't get any further than the door. He'd see people bowing before images and passing the collection plate and he'd leave.") The worship services of the sects are characterized by a rejection of formal orders of worship, of passive listening and restraint, and of extensive use of symbols. Almost none of the calculated experimentation with "more meaningful" worship forms is present.

Each sect meets in a rented room invariably furnished with a plain speaker's rostrum, an upright piano, folding chairs, and a table piled with tracts at the door. The walls are usually plain, without the symbol of the cross. The room of the Jehovah's Witnesses offers one variation—a huge chart on one wall recording the hours of various types of evangelism done by each member.

The members usually participate in services which are conducted by laymen, except for the Polish Evangelistic Assembly, whose members when there were no more than eight sought out a part-time pastor, so greatly did they feel the need for a leader. Each sect has a general pattern of worship which is not formally recognized and allows great spontaneity and wide participation by laymen. The Gospel Hall sect believes that "the Holy Ghost if allowed to work can still control the church" and members wait in silence until one of them is moved to contribute the selection of a hymn, the reading of scripture, the offering of a prayer, the preaching of a sermon, or administration of holy communion.

The only act which has sacramental significance for two sects—the Gospel Hall and Polish Study Group—is the reading and group commentary upon the Scriptures. For the Jehovah's Witnesses the central act is the reading of and exegesis by members upon the most recent issue of the *Watchtower*, the major study publication of the sect's national office. Each issue is read aloud, paragraph by paragraph, by a member. After each reading, the leader asks for "comments" or "further evidence" or "more points" until almost all members have made a short speech interpreting the *Watchtower* or have read aloud another section of the magazine. Many members come to meetings with every line of type underlined in pencil, so intensive has been their study of the *Watchtower*.

The main worship service of the Polish Evangelistic Assembly, which is composed almost entirely of converts from Catholicism, represents a mixed form derived from both Catholic and Protestant worship experience. The group is composed almost entirely of adult Polish people who speak English with difficulty. The service usually begins with the singing of two hymns and a forty-five to sixty minute sermon in Polish by the minister, followed by spontaneous prayers and "personal praise of God." Members kneel on the floor, facing toward the walls of the room for privacy of meditation. The prayers and witnessing mount in fervency amid weeping and cries of anguish and relief. Members are believed sometimes to be given the gift of tongues. The pastor reported that visiting missionaries had identified "Indian and Chinese languages spoken fluently." Almost simultaneously over the room there comes a lull in the prayers. The minister begins to say over and over in a soft, slow, quieting voice, "Thank you, Jesus, Halleluiah. We love you, Jesus, Halleluiah. Yes, yes, Halleluiah," until the crying has ceased and the room is silent. The service is over and the members walk out of the room with almost no conversation.

Catholics who once knelt before an altar now kneel in a barren furnished room; who once heard a ten-minute sermon peripheral to the major act of worship now listen for almost an hour; who once prayed prayers of the church now pray long personal, spontaneous petitions to God; who once brought their rosaries to worship now bring Bibles; who once confessed their guilt to a priest now cry out their anguish in the midst of fellow-believers and hear the prayers for quiet and peace from a part-time minister. Such is the old and new in this sect's worship.

Catholic Worship

"Is Jesus in every Catholic Church? Jesus is in every Catholic Church. Where is Jesus in the Church? Jesus is in the tabernacle on the altar. Who places Jesus in His little house on the altar? The priest places Jesus in His little house on the altar."

This is part of "First Communion Catechism" prepared by a Paper City priest, and in wide use in the instruction of young people of the Roman Catholic church in the diocese. This claim to objectification of Christ and of God's grace usually gives both the leadership of the church (who make possible the presence of infinite being in an exact, finite place) and the organization of the church (which assures the perpetuation of such sacramental power in the leadership) a sacred or divine character in the eyes of believers. Catholic rituals and sacraments narrow and particularize the area in which men look for God's sure manifestation more than do Protestant cultic acts, and therefore develop a different attitude toward the visible church. This is of great significance to the relations of Roman Catholic and Protestants in the life of Paper City.

Here are some of the interpretations given by priests of the worship life of the church:

> How does the priest bring Jesus from Heaven to the altar? The priest brings Jesus to the altar by changing bread and wine into the Body and Blood of Jesus.
>
> When does he do this? During Mass—at the Consecration.
>
> Does Jesus ever come out from His little home? Yes; He comes out at Communion time during Mass. Why does Jesus come out from

His little home? Jesus wishes to go into the souls of the boys and girls and of the men and women who wish to receive Him.[1]

Realizing that Jesus, my God, my inspiring and powerful Helper, is waiting for me in every Catholic church, I now resolve (do not make the resolution unless you mean it) to visit Jesus in His tabernacle home in some Catholic Church every day, if possible, even if only for a few minutes.[2]

Life for a Catholic without a priest is so tragic . . . We know that they alone have the power to bring God from Heaven to earth within our reach, and that we sinners can become saints by partaking of His Body and Blood.[3]

Catholic church attendance is not simply a "duty and privilege such as responsibility to one's family," to use a representative phrase from a Protestant sermon on "loyalty to the church."[4] It is, as the pastor of Holy Rosary parish said in a sermon, the "only assurance that a man will keep his faith." For the priests, "the beginning of the end of faith is when the Catholic quits going to Mass." It is also the "beginning of the end of man's hope for eternal life."

The zeal and devotion of the Catholic church member heightens the chance of the sacrament "working." This subjective, personal aspect of faith is referred to in sermon and article.[5] But the crucial difference stressed by the priest between Catholic and Protestant rites is in the Catholic belief that the grace of God has an objective expression independent of the personal relations between the transmitter (the priest) and the recipient (the layman) and independent of the religious convictions of either. Thus in the Mass, the office of the priest assures the performance of the act of transubstantiation. The natural elements are then transmitted to the participants. The element itself now has power to transform man's spiritual life. Man's nature is changed by God's transmission of a new divine nature within the church and by means of the grace-filled material of the sacrament.

This interpretation of the relation of nature and sacrament, of nature and grace, is the basis for the concept of miracles which permeates the life of the church, from the short stories in the diocesan journal to the establishment of statues in the church yards of Paper City. The usual plot of a story in the *Catholic Mirror* is something like this: Catholics are in personal trouble. A father and mother with their child have been evicted from an apartment and have searched in vain for another. In their difficulty they are aided by a Catholic "stranger"—a priest, a nun, who is the instrument of a miracle. The family is directed to an apartment which they can afford by a priest who appears on the street. Then the Catholics aided are given a sign that a miracle has been done. In this case, the mother turns to thank the priest but finds only a religious medal where she last saw him.[6] Or again, the pastor of Holy Rosary parish designed a statue at the beginning of World War II duplicating the Infant of Prague statue, with a sailor, soldier and airman kneeling before it.[7] The pastor had the statue placed in the church yard. "During the war most of the men on going into the services or their families left candles burning for one dollar a week in the name of the Infant of Prague," the priest said. He claimed that this action "was followed by a miracle. The parish lost only three men in the war. A neighboring parish had three times as many in the service as our parish," the pastor observed, "but it lost forty-eight men, so you see the statue worked." [8]

Instructions by the local priests for the laymen give detailed directions for preparation for worship, gestures and thoughts during it, and sometimes calculate the exact amount of temporal punishment remitted by indulgences:

> Your preparation for Holy Hour should start as you enter the church.
>
> Upon entering, take holy water on your fingers and make the Sign of the Cross fervently and correctly: with the fingers of your right hand *touch* your forehead, breast left and right shoulders, while saying, "In the name of the Father, and of the Son, and of the Holy Ghost." Then join your hands when saying, "Amen." (100 days Indulgence.)
>
> When inside, look at once for the sanctuary lamp. This light will remind you that you have entered the home of Jesus. Turn your eyes from the light to the tabernacle, the little house on the altar where Jesus actually lives.
>
> As you walk toward a pew, keep looking at the tabernacle and think of Jesus Who dwells there. Show your desire to be close to Jesus by selecting a place as near to the altar as possible. At the pew, genuflect, that is, touch the right knee to the floor and whisper, "My Lord and My God."

> When you enter the pew, go in as far as possible and thus show your welcome to others who may come to visit Jesus with you. Kneel, make the Sign of the Cross (50 days Indulgence) and put your mind in a spirit of prayer. Your prayer is a Holy Hour to be spent in loving union with Jesus, the Son of God.
>
> Bow your head each time the name "Jesus" is mentioned. (50 days Indulgence.)

The sermon is of minor importance in the Catholic Sunday morning service or Mass. It is usually no more than eight to ten minutes in length. It is prefaced by the priest's reading of a selection from the Scriptures. Usually the reading is rapid and sometimes intoned almost as if it were liturgy. The Scriptural reading is seldom used as a basis for development of the sermon. The sermons are usually straight, rational expositions of doctrine with much less general use than the Protestant pastors employ of devices to interest and persuade (such as illustrations, narrative, dramatic figures of speech, personal witness). The role of the priest in the service is primarily that of performance of the ritual, not of instruction. At the Sunday morning services, in most churches, collections are taken for sittings during the sermon; these are fifteen cents each and involve a good deal of noisy change-making by the ushers. At the close of the service, most of the members leave the sanctuary without comment to one another. "Should we talk to our friends in church?" asks a catechism written by a local priest. "No, in church we should talk only to God, the Blessed Virgin and the Saints" is the answer.

Some sense of the differences in the Catholic church and the Protestant churches can be gained from the observation of comparable points in the services of worship. The service of the 8:30 A.M. Mass in several of the Catholic parishes begins promptly as the tabernacle light goes on over the altar with the march of children, separated by sexes and age, up the center aisle of the sanctuary, the scouts in uniform and preceded by American and Christian flags, the groups of children genuflecting in unison at signals from the nuns accompanying them. In the Protestant church services the children usually arrive with parents, or in straggling groups from Sunday School classes to be seated noisily and talkatively in the front seats for a children's sermon by the pastor. In one church after this sermon a lone Brownie scout in uniform (at the suggestion of the pastor) carries an American flag to lead a group of children out of the worship hall.

Or to make another comparison, the major city-wide meeting of Catholic laymen in 1947 ended with a Mass and candlelight service in which men stood in the darkness of a church and repeated their Catholic vows. The major city-wide meeting of Protestant laymen in 1947 was for a speech by an out-of-town lecturer on the relief program abroad. The supreme act of Catholic worship—the Mass—is interpreted by the *Catholic Mirror* as "community action" in which Catholics receive a supernatural element, changed from a natural form by the God-given power of the leader of the church.[10] In the Protestant church, the major act is the hearing of the interpretation of the word of God by a pastor or in the sect the discussion of the Scriptures.

Chapter 6

The Faith of Laymen

Thus far this study has concentrated upon the religious beliefs of the leaders of the churches. We turn now to the beliefs of ordinary laymen without prominent roles in the churches. To present as economically and coherently as possible a great deal of data, composite profiles are presented of the religious beliefs of four families representing significant types present in the city. These profiles indicate the extent to which the thought patterns of the clergy are a part of the habitual approaches of laymen to religion.

Roman Catholics and Protestants are divided significantly in terms of class and ethnic group—a generalization to be documented in detail in later chapters. Important differences do not exist doctrinally between all these groups, yet within both religions, meaningful distinctions can be made between beliefs of the better educated, well-to-do people of the upper and upper-middle class and those with grade and high school education and lower and lower-middle class status. Within these two general configurations of belief, responses to specific issues are made—such as the means the churches use to witness to their beliefs, and the role of the pastor in the layman's discovery of truth.

The religious frames of reference of four families are presented: upper-class Roman Catholic and Protestant families and lower-middle class Roman Catholic and Protestant families. Both of the Protestant families belong to churches. The sect laymen are excluded from discussion here, since rank and file views are very close to those of the lay leaders described.

In none of the following composite profiles is an actual family described. Rather the ideas and experiences of several individuals are compressed, but without loss, it is believed, of their representative nature.

Protestant Upper-Class Family

Mr. and Mrs. Alvin Stuart live in a twelve-room house in Highland Park, an area which real-estate dealers call "an exclusive, $45,000 and up suburb." About two-thirds of Highland Park residents are Protestant, the remainder Catholic. Mr. Stuart is general manager of a local mill, in which he owns a considerable block of stock. Mrs. Stuart, mother of Susan, age ten, is active in the Junior League and a Vassar College graduate. The family church is First Congregational. Mr. and Mrs. Stuart attend services about twice a month. The Stuart family has traditionally gone to First Church, a tradition begun early in Paper City history by Alvin's grandparents. Mr. Stuart appreciates his Protestant background, "but less in a church way than my forebears." However, he is on the Standing Committee of the church and "a pillar," according to Mrs. Stuart.

Mr. Stuart "cannot see much difference between Protestantism and Catholicism on religious ideas such as the way of salvation. I know lots of Catholics," he observed recently, "and they've got the same religion I do." After some reflection he added slowly, momentously, "I think we are all Christians under one God." Mr. Stuart took a religious attitude test prepared by a lay member of his church and given to a men's discussion group which asked, "When we pray, do we pray to Jesus as God?" He answered "Yes" along with twenty out of twenty-five in the group. What Christ did for men was to provide "them with an example to live by," Mr. Stuart believes. He thinks the minister of the First Church "is a wonderful fellow," but Mr. Stuart does not go along with a lot of his theology, "particularly when he gets to talking about original sin."

Mrs. Stuart says that she was "never bothered about such words as sin, hell and the devil until Susan began to hear the little Catholic girls talk about them" and then questioned her mother as to what they meant. Mrs. Stuart told her closest friend, "I try to be a tolerant person, but I don't know what I should do about Susan. I hate to keep her from playing with Catholics. Yet she doesn't get enough religion in Sunday School of a kind that gives her satisfactory answers to such things as Catholics ask her. I'm too confused to know what Protestants should believe about all that Catholic business of purgatory, mortal sin and damnation. And I'm better off than most mothers, I guess; I attend a study club in the church where we have papers on religion." Mrs. Stuart is of the opinion that it is "bad to have children have sin in their souls since modern psychology is against guilt feelings in people."

Recently Susan wanted to know why she could not join the Catholic church with two friends who were taking lessons prior to confirmation. Mrs. Stuart explained that "the Catholic religion is a *hard* religion, much harder than Protestants'. You have to go to Mass every week and all sorts of hard things." Mrs. Stuart did not tell her child, but she feels the Catholic religion is "built on fear, and that Catholics go to church out of fear." She worries because her Polish Catholic maid, Josephine Witrobski, transmits her religious fears to Susan. "One night she told Susan the devil was going to get her, and Susan hid under the covers, she was so scared."

Sometimes Mrs. Stuart has not controlled her displeasure with her maid's religion. Recently, when the maid complained about the weather hurting her legs, Mrs. Stuart in a bantering way said, "Oh, Josephine, go light a candle in the church and the pain will stop," and Josephine replied in broken English with her stock answer to all Protestant comment on her religion, "Priest, he good man."

The aspect of Protestantism most prized by Mr. and Mrs. Stuart, as they have often said, "is the independence of judgment in contrast to the dogmatism of Catholicism." The heart of Protestantism for them is not particular theological doctrine so much as the attitude of tolerance and respect for the individual's search for truth. Mrs. Stuart after her experiences with Susan is less strong on this point than her husband. She would like to find "some people or books that commend themselves as authoritative because of their superior knowledge of Protestant religion." When Mr. Stuart discovered that one-third of his discussion group at the church agreed in an attitude test that "the Bible contains all the necessary information for Christian guidance and living," he was astounded. The Bible is not an all-sufficient guide for him. "Practical judgment from experience is a valuable contribution to Christian living," he believes.

Mr. and Mrs. Stuart have some of the restiveness of their minister about the worship patterns of their church. Mr. Stuart was recently asked to give a "layman's address" and in it he quoted with approval the statement that "the danger of Puritanical solemnity is still upon us. In our services, we might well consider many things which were swept away by our forebears in their zeal to get away from frills." Mrs. Stuart is also convinced that Protestants neglect the "beauty of religion." She says, "Frankly, I don't want to hear a sermon every Sunday. I would like a minister with enough imagination to draw occasionally from the rich store of religious literature and read to us. Particularly, I'd like him to do this when he knows he has prepared a sermon that just hasn't come off. I want to know what men in moments of great crisis and of religious fervor have said about God. And I don't want cheap music. I want the treasures of great religious music of the ages."

As to the ethical implications of his religion, Mr. Stuart made clear in his layman's address that, "I feel I have a right to expect that the church shall be a beacon, showing the way with a minimum of turns and grades, to a Christian life. The Protestant preacher of today has a select group to whom he delivers his message. They are the leaders in the community who demand and need the bright light of inspiration that the minister must supply. In my opinion," observed Mr. Stuart in his address, "the church should not take up the gauntlet for every cause that rears its head. In the larger issues of the day, it seems bold presumption for the church to dictate policies in economics, politics and social questions, when experts in those fields cannot agree on a course of action."

Mr. Stuart observed to an associate at the mill recently that, "One thing you can say for the Catholic priests is that they have seen the menace of Communism and aren't getting mixed up with Reds in this country." Mr. Stuart insists to his minister that he does not wish to divorce religion from life. He was pleased to see that only two men out of twenty-five in his discussion group agreed with the test statement that "the primary concern of a Christian life is to reach heaven in the hereafter." But he was very perturbed that only a majority of fourteen agreed that a "person who lives up to his highest ideals is a Christian." For Mr. Stuart, the sum of Christian ethics is that each man respect his own conscience.

No religious or moral witness of fellow Protestants has produced in Mr. Stuart the feeling that class or economic interests may have distorted the dictates of his own conscience. Mr. Stuart's ideal church is a projection in great part of his ideal business—industrious, frugal, efficient, inspiring in its optimism and satisfying in its culture and good works. Mr. Stuart heartily approves a pamphlet appealing for funds for the liquidation of the debt of his church, particularly the final page of copy which after enumeration of the good works of the church reads:

> One would assume that the cost of maintenance and operation of such an organization would be enormous. However, such is the official management of the Church that the entire administration and operating costs are held within an annual budget of only $25,000, this amount being subscribed by free-will offerings, and most of which is disbursed within Paper City.

Mrs. Stuart feels that she has no "world-shattering ideas" on the similarities or differences between Protestant and Catholic religions. For her the differences between the moral views of the clergy are important. The Catholic priests, she observes, "are more broad-minded and not so petty as the Protestant clergy on such things as drinking." She saw a group of soldiers in a bar in Boston flocking around a priest who had come in for a beer. "They laughed and joked and had a good time. There is something earthy about most Catholic pastors that we don't get in our ministry very often," she said.

Upper-Class Catholics

Mr. and Mrs. Edward Connelly live in the Highlands near Holy Cross which is their parish church. Mr. Connelly is a manager and stockholder of a large mill in the city. He is a thin, energetic, conscientious man who has worked hard to achieve his present business position. He is one of the few Catholics among the top management of his company. Mr. Connelly "does not talk religion in business or in social life," and he does not hold a position of leadership in lay organizations of his church. He goes each week to Mass and to communion monthly. He believes that he can choose the Catholic doctrine which he wishes to believe without accepting the entire Catholic theological system.

Mr. Connelly—a methodical man—divides Catholicism into three parts, "philosophy, ceremony and politics." As for the first, he says, "I agree with love of God and neighbor and the like of that. All religion goes along pretty much the same on that." The chief difference Mr. Connelly can see between Protestantism and Catholicism is that "Catholicism is a little more strict in its interpretation of what men must do." As for ceremony, Mr. Connelly observes that "Some like a show of religion. They want the lace curtains of religion. Some like their religion with the minister in business clothes. I like mine with a show, so I go along with the Catholics on that."

Now as for politics in religion, that, for Mr. Connelly, "is where the trouble comes. I don't go along with rank and file Catholics who don't know enough history to appreciate the Protestant fears of the political ambitions of the priests," he explained to a Protestant acquaintance. Mr. Connelly wishes to see the Protestants maintain an active educational program of their own. "Protestant churches have a hold on some truths; the Catholic church does not necessarily have all religious truth." Mr. and Mrs. Connelly look with tolerance but with a certain aloofness at the submissive way Catholics of the lower classes follow instructions of the priests. They were "more than a little embarrassed" at the agitation of Catholics over the appearance of Mrs. Sanger in Paper City.

Mrs. Connelly has tended over the years to participate less and less in sodality and parish functions and is now active in a woman's club with a mixed religious membership. The club does not discuss religious issues, but on one occasion Mrs. Connelly asked to talk privately to a Protestant member to explain to her what Catholics meant by the doctrine of the Immaculate Conception, when the woman had jokingly referred to the unexpected pregnancy of a friend as probably an "Immaculate Conception."

Mrs. Connelly has made less effort than her husband to evaluate or to distinguish the aspects of her religion. She likes the "sense of antiquity of the church." She feels that she has all the freedom of thought she wants within her faith. To her, "most of the rules of the church are good." She finds the diocesan magazine, the *Catholic Mirror,* distasteful in its emphasis upon Irish history and issues. She feels that there is great social pressure from Catholics in her circle of friends to go to church, and believes that if "they thought

I didn't go to church, they would not talk to me. The most important religious duty for maintaining a standing in the community is to go to church."

Mr. Connelly doubts that there is any difference between Roman Catholic and Protestant social ethics. Both churches want people to live better lives, to have higher standards of living. Mr. Connelly has read none of the social encyclicals of the Popes and knows of no instance when Catholic moral teachings have influenced or been considered in decisions made by him in business or politics. He feels that one "carry-over value from Catholic moral teachings has been to make the demands of Catholic labor leaders reasonable."

During a social evening in Mr. Connelly's home attended by four of his Catholic friends and a Protestant, the conversation settled on the Sanger incident. Mr. Connelly expressed the belief that, "If action to defend a moral position taken by a priest [such as opposition to Mrs. Sanger's appearance in Paper City] seems like a sin to me, then I am not bound to take action." A visitor disagreed on the grounds that "If a priest places a moral obligation on a Catholic to take certain action, it is a sin to disobey. If the layman thinks the priest is wrong he can take the obligation to a higher authority in the church. In the Sanger incident the bishop had stated the obligation upon Catholics to oppose her, and such a position was not likely to be changed. A layman could leave the church if his conscience did not agree with this position," the friend explained. "A Catholic is bound to these alternatives—obey the priest, appeal the priest's interpretation of moral law, or cease to be a Catholic." Mr. Connelly, acting the genial host, said that was what he really meant.

Protestant Lower-Middle Class Family

Mr. and Mrs. John Baker own and operate one of the fifty-odd "living room" stores in Paper City. Mr. Baker's is a delicatessen, located in a frame house in which the front room has been altered to become a shop, with the usual equipment—a cat, a partly paid for frozen food display cabinet and a house telephone with a large sign announcing a ten-cent charge for local calls. Baker and his wife are Baptists. Mrs. Baker was a Presbyterian, but both she and her husband like the preacher at the Second Baptist Church, a "very friendly, kind man," and the people better than those at the Presbyterian Church.

The Bakers are parents of Ned, a little boy who is at present the prize pupil of the Baptist Sunday School. The superintendent, on an inspection of the classes, asked a children's class, "What is God?" No answer was ventured after a long silence, except by Ned, Mrs. Baker relates. He then said, "God is spirit," and when asked by the delighted superintendent, "Where do we see God?" Ned replied, "In people." The incident was recounted in the church and the parents have been congratulated by several customers for having a boy who "really knows his religion." The boy, Mrs. Baker explains, had been taught from a Presbyterian catechism she received when in Sunday School.

Many of the fundamental Protestant evangelical doctrines concerning the nature of man, of sin, of the sovereignty of God, of salvation by faith, are not a clear or expressible part of their religious ideas, although their attitudes are informed by many assumptions related to these doctrines.

Mr. and Mrs. Baker reject certain symbols of faith in Catholicism. Thus, Mr. Baker sees the major trouble with Catholics is that "they believe everything the priest tells them." By contrast, Mr. Baker makes his moral decision by "thinking over what the minister says in church, praying, and what I receive is final for me."

Mr. Baker used to work on a truck with a Catholic who tipped his hat and made the sign of the cross whenever he passed a Catholic church. One day when the Catholic did this, Mr. Baker asked him why he didn't tip his hat when they went past the Second Congregational Church. "There's just one God, you know," Baker recalls saying, "and He's in there as much as He is in your church." But Mr. Baker finds it difficult to explain the religious beliefs which prompted him to say this, other than that "Catholics always think they alone have God and that we don't."

To ask the Bakers the meaning for them of the doctrine of "justification by faith alone" produces only an embarrassed admission of ignorance. But they note that "Protestants do not think they *have* to go to church, cross themselves, say beads and do all those things to be saved."

Mr. Baker is careful in his business not to say anything that would indicate his religion because he is "in competition with many Catholics." Although Mr. and Mrs. Baker do not talk religious differences outside church, they have an abundance of disconnected stereotypes about the Catholic religion in comparison with Protestantism. Mr. Baker believes that "the Catholics have changed the way men are to become Christians from the way Christ had in mind. No one went to confession before the Last Supper, like the Catholics do." Mrs. Baker sees the major differences between Catholic and Protestant ideas of salvation as this: "Catholics have priests, saints, Mary and I don't know who else between Christ and people, while Protestants have no one between Christ and themselves. Catholics must find it hard to get close to Jesus."

Mrs. Baker says that the Catholic girl who keeps store sometimes when she or Mr. Baker cannot be there (they both take part-time jobs in the mills) told her, "We are not supposed to read the Bible. The priest tells us what we are to do." Mrs. Baker believes that it says on the Catholic Bible "not to read it too much." The Catholic Bible, she is certain, "has an awful lot in it about the Virgin Mary."

The most positively impressive thing about Catholicism to the Bakers is "the respect shown for the church by Catholics." But they do not want Protestants to have "the Catholic attitude of fear of the priest and of not going to church." They think Protestants could have more of the Catholic attitude about worship. Mr. Baker recalls going once with a Catholic to a service. "I don't believe the friend said anything about it, but he showed by the way he acted that he had a lot of respect for being in church." Mr. Baker wishes "Protestants showed more respect for the church, like the Catholics do." He objects to the way "bedlam breaks loose as soon as the sermon is over" in his church.

The chief difference in Protestant and Roman Catholic ethics for Mr. Baker is that "Catholics have a comfortable, easy religion. All the Catholics have to do is to follow the forms, go to confession, go to Mass, pay the priest, and all their sins are erased and they can start over. They can drink, gamble, run after women, cuss all they like. But if I do something wrong, it bothers me for weeks." The main thing in the Protestant religion for the Bakers is learning to be good. "We run an honest store. We never shortchange or short-weigh anybody," says Mrs. Baker. "That's being a good Christian, as I see it."

Lower-Middle Class Catholic Family

John Kane has been a policeman for the Paper City police department for almost twenty years. He, his wife and their only child, a boy now in high school, live in a frame house in Ward 3. Mr. Kane is reluctant to make any observations on the differences of Roman Catholic and Protestant religions beyond what all his friends note—that Catholics have more loyalty for their church than Protestants. He doesn't know why, but they do. Mr. Kane does not try to learn anything about other people's religion or much about his own. "All I do is try to follow the rules the priest gives," he explains. I know if I get to thinking about all the problems in religion, it will just worry me and I won't be able to work out any answers anyway."

Ultimate authority on religious matters is the priest. When the Kanes became involved in arguments about religion, they refer to what the priest said when they or a friend asked him for an answer to the question raised. "You may say I accept blindly what is told me, and perhaps I do," Mr. Kane explained recently to a Protestant. "But in parochial school we had an explanatory hour of instruction by the pastor. I learned there to ask questions of those who know more about religion than I do. I could always see there was logic behind the answers to questions I asked. So I reached the conclusion that the reasoning and the answers are there. Whenever I am bothered by my religion or by something done by the priests, when I have doubts, I have decided it is my fault; and now I seldom have doubts."

In a recent discussion over whether Protestants will go to heaven, Mr. Kane maintained that when he was in parochial school the nuns told him that to be a Protestant meant to be in danger of loss of salvation; that is, unless the Protestant never doubted his faith. Since a lot of the Protestants Mr. Kane knows have doubts about their faith, he is not sure now whether all these Protestants are in danger or whether there were more details to the doctrine which he has forgotten. However, he is certain "that the church has worked it out right."

Doctrinal issues between Protestants and Catholics summarized in such terms as "Salvation by faith alone" have never been presented to the Kanes in any reading or conversations. Their interpretation of the Protestant Reformation reflects the stereotypes of the diocesan journal. So far as they can figure it out, the Reformation was the result of the personal whims of a few leaders—particularly Henry VIII and Luther, more being known about the former than the latter. "Damned if I don't wonder sometimes why Protestants don't question how their religion came into existence," Mr. Kane remarked. As he understands it, and he cautions that he "may be 100 per cent wrong, the main idea behind the Protestants when they left the church was to get freedom for every individual to think whatever he wants to think." For Mr. Kane this idea has no appeal. "I go to church to learn to think something correct," he observed.

Mr. and Mrs. Kane never doubt the rightness of any religious or moral teaching of the Catholic church. They are not aware of any degrees of moral obligation upon laymen or of varied degrees of authority for the various laws of the church. On certain issues they sometimes keep their own counsel or exempt one moral act from the priest's province, "to be settled with God alone," reflecting the variety of pressures and influences in Paper City culture upon them. For example, Mrs. Kane has the ambition of sending her son to a private school rather than to a parochial or public school, and works part time in order to do this. She feels this will mean "greater social opportunities" for her son. She has not talked with the priest about her son's schooling for she "knows what he would say."

The only time that Mrs. Kane felt some conflict between what "Christ asked of her and what the priest demanded" was over her use of artificial means of birth control. This is how she worked out the problem in her mind after much thought and prayer. She accepts

> everything else the priest says as a demand from the church and therefore on my conscience, but I feel the priest should not have a say in this part of my marriage. I feel I am a good Catholic, and still I cannot obey the law on birth control. I couldn't go through bearing a child again. I came near to dying with Joseph. It is sometimes hard for me to go to confession, and I do not go as often as I used to. It is hard to confess the same sin over and over. I feel the sin of birth control is up to my Lord. I answer to him for what I have done.

I tell the priest what I am doing. I do not feel that I am in conflict with the church greatly on this. The church is right that it is a sin. I do not doubt that. I am now pretty much at peace with my God. This is not so with my sister who worries constantly about what she is doing.

The Kanes like the feeling of stability and certainty in moral requirements of their faith. They do not expect the church to change its position on birth control or any other moral law. "The Ten Commandments don't alter and the church's interpretation of them doesn't." They feel that all in all they do a "fairly decent job of living up to the moral laws and religious duties of the church" and they feel assured that they will find their way to heaven and eternal life. An "eleventh commandment" which John Kane has added to his code is "Don't be careless of your job." "The one unforgivable vice in Paper City," Mr. Kane heard his father say once, "is not getting drunk and beating your wife, but being lazy on the job."

Mr. and Mrs. Kane go to Mass regularly each week out of a variety of feelings. As Mr. Kane said, "I have a feeling that I must go or suffer damnation and I also want to go because I like the ritual and the effect of it." The Kane's knowledge of Protestant worship is fragmentary and confusing to them. Mrs. Kane several years ago had a Protestant girl stay over Saturday night at her home. She has never forgotten how this girl "on the spur of the moment decided she was going to church Sunday morning. At the church she took communion without fasting or confessing or any preparation." Mrs. Kane did "not see how she could think of her sins that quickly."

The Kanes do not know the reasons for all the feast days, nor the meanings of many of the rites, but the Mass and the worship services have a solemnity and dignity which do not escape them. Their daily life is marked by a series of personal ritualistic acts associated with their religion—from the prayers Mrs. Kane says for her husband whenever she hears a police siren, to Mr. Kane's careful observance of religious or folk rules that "we should pray for everybody we dream about."

The Kanes say they are "live and let live" people, and they are not "out looking for fights for the faith." They do not think that the priests will have many occasions when they will need Catholics to take action to defend the faith. "But if the priest puts a moral obligation on you to take certain action against people who threaten the church, then it is a sin to disobey." Mr. Kane believes his priest in the message read about Mrs. Sanger coming to Paper City put a moral obligation on him to oppose her coming. On such occasions, he would use economic boycott or similar measures of joint, organized action.

Summary

The central import of the past three chapters on belief and worship is this: the Catholic layman's religion, if it reflects that of the priest, will bind him to an institution for salvation and give him a trust in and loyalty to his church which most Protestant laymen cannot have. The institutional attachment of the Catholic produces an assurance about the precise content of his religion which the Protestant cannot or does not gain from his church.

The ordinary Catholic priest and layman does not have enough knowledge of his faith to answer charges against it by the secularist or the heretic, but his institution, he is convinced, does have. And that is all that he considers necessary. The Catholic's role then is to live by the rules—chiefly the religious precepts stressed by the priests and the hierarchy—to love and care for the institution, to defend it when it must be defended and to advance its religious influence when the opportunity is available.

There is obviously no monolithic, Catholic "lay mind," but rather a variety of levels and types of relations to the "institution of salvation." The upper income, well-educated Catholic laymen are much less receptive to clerical guidance as to the practical social implications of moral and religious laws of the church than are the lower income, more poorly educated Catholics. The former tend also to be much more appreciative of the role of the Protestant churches in supplementing or correcting Catholic action. As Catholics become more highly educated and more expansive in their associational experience (usually a corollary of an increase in income), they appear to be less rigid in their doctrinal content and less dependent upon Catholic moral teaching for their judgments of "correct" action. On basic religious matters—which they tend to confine to worship and sacramental observance, and to doctrinal matters on the after life, the role of the church as a channel of grace etc.—they respect the church deeply and support its demands with enthusiasm. The Catholic clergy face a tremendous challenge to relate fundamental theological beliefs to lay patterns of meaning in the social order.

The institutional expression of the theological positions of the Protestant pastors and laymen is principally a witness to freedom from authoritarianism. Protestant laymen by doctrine and worship are chiefly oriented toward the autonomy of their own consciences in matters of religion and toward suspicion of individuals and institutions which claim absolute knowledge of the will of God, or assured power to save. Many of the Protestant clergy are now beginning to feel that probably their most pressing doctrinal problem in a community such as Paper City is to develop a Protestant concept of the nature and role of the church in man's salvation. Over and over laymen assert (and also the Protestant clergy, sometimes in wonderment) that the most obvious and persistent differences between the two religions is that one commands intense loyalty to and identification with a particular institution while the other does not. Most laymen cannot explain this, but they know that it is so. And they believe that this is the major contribution of doctrine and worship to Catholic and Protestant cleavage.

The theology of the "professional" leaders is reflected in the thought of the laymen, the germinal ideas often stripped of qualification and major emphasis alone remaining. The religious community is clearly an important source of personal identification to Protestants and Catholics, but men derive different things from their belonging to it. The Catholic religion tends to unify believers as members of a visible institution with superior and assured power to save. Protestantism tends to bring believers into a tenuous association, more generally social than sacramental, and to remind them of the importance of the "pure" conscience and the responsibility for individual decision.

No one community of belief has a determinative hold on the fundamental orientations of laymen to life.[1] There is a creative freedom and a mysterious unpredictability to men's actions and thoughts. The self comes into being through a complex involvement in many associations. The power of family, class and ethnic groups are still great in Paper City culture and for some men may be more determinative of the character of their decisions than association in the church. There are situations where income, educational and residential similarities between Catholic and Protestant are deeply related to common habits of thought about events in the world. But it is also clear that persons do internalize the meanings of the Christian faith and in part at least respond to social situations in their light. Personal identity is formed out of participation in many groups and the continuing pattern of meaning which emerges becomes the core of the self. The church as an institution reshapes its habits of thought and patterns of meaning, as does the self, out of the continuing interaction and communication of men—lay and cleric. Yet there is some continuity in the church institutions and in the selves that come into being through these social processes and we can anticipate to some extent the way groups and persons will act and react to various situations. Moreover, there can be discerned a common center in these religious communities: the God known in Jesus Christ, and in the Scriptures.

Chapter 7

The Spiritual Authority of the Religious Leader

The clergy are the professional and most active leaders of the religious institutions in the community. What is the nature of their authority in their relations with the laity? By "authority" we mean not merely the power to command the action and service of others, for a man may be able to control another and yet lack authority. Nor do we mean merely status or position by itself, for a man without prior status can have more authority than a man with superior rank in an organization. By authority we mean the established right to act as a leader of men—to make judgments about their past and to anticipate their future, to form policies, to deal with controversies. The emphasis in authority is upon right and responsibility, not power or status. What gives the bishop, priest or minister the mandate to speak and act as he does; what are the theological and social grounds of his legitimacy?

Do the grounds of authority differ significantly for Catholicism and Protestantism? Do the relations of a Protestant clergyman with the "standing committee" of his church differ from the relations of a priest with a group of laymen in his parish during a discussion of religion? Yes, they are different, provided one looks at their whole doctrinal and institutional context and the interconnections of all the factors. Paul Blanshard claims that a distinction may be made between Roman Catholicism as a system of power and as a religious faith.[1] This is a distinction Catholic leaders often seek to make also. It has its uses in analysis, but it may, if pursued too rigorously, ignore the profound involvement of Catholic polity with Catholic theology and philosophy. By the same token, the failure to see the difficulties for Protestants in giving institutional and organization expression and form to their religious conviction is to ignore an important clue to the theological nature of Protestantism and its peculiar contributions to the understanding of authority.

There are two types of authority exercised by the clergy of Paper City, the first having two important sub-types. Once these are understood, some significant distinctions can be made within and between the Roman Catholic and Protestant movements.

The first type of authority might be called "charismatic" (a term Max Weber uses in his study of authority in religious institutions).[2] This is authority which evidences *charisma* or a gift of grace. It is authority grounded in the special divine quality or spiritual endowment which is thought to have been conferred by a supernatural being. This gift fits the recipient for the life, work or office to which he has been called. It makes possible miraculous or supernatural powers of healing, speaking, prophesying and inspiring.

Two sub-types of charismatic authority designate different claims to the locus of the special endowment—in (a) the office and (b) the person. Official charismatic authority is derived from the institution, the church, which has received the spiritual gift. More exactly the authority is derived from the office one holds within the institution. Power, status, and property to manipulate or channel the instruments of grace and to define or teach the truth are in the office; therefore distinctions between those who hold the office and those who do not, between clergy and laity, are basic distinctions, related to God's conferring of spiritual gifts.

The second sub-type, personal charismatic authority, is grounded not in the rights of an office, but in the person, in his conviction that he has himself experienced divine grace and in the qualities which give evidence of this experience in him. The experience is not dependent upon status or position within an institution, but upon a supernatural being whose gifts of grace are accessible to all men, with or without office. The claim to authority rests upon the person's belief that he has been called by a Being greater than himself to carry out a particular mission. It is a mission with an intensity and distinctiveness that are truly the person's own. But the actual authority also depends upon the conviction of others that the qualities and experience of the person are those which the Being they know in faith would confer.

The second type of authority is "rational" authority. The right to leadership is grounded upon the nature and necessities of organization, which can be understood by all intelligent and sensible men. If men are to act in a coordinated fashion, someone must assume responsibility to develop rules and norms of conduct and apply or enforce them in an impersonal and impartial manner. Some division of labor must take place, so that special skills may develop and a variety of functions be performed effectively. Positions or offices must be organized on some general principle of hierarchy, so that responsibility is focused and lines of communication established. Various patterns for appeal of decisions from lower to higher levels, for selection and recall of officers, may be developed. The general legitimacy of this type of action is founded not upon supernatural gifts but upon the natural and reasonable requirements of organization.

The Roman Catholic church has sought to utilize both charismatic and rational types of authority in its conception of the clergy and the hierarchy. It has sought to maintain a distinction between them, making clear that the major ground for the action of the clergy is its charismatic or supernatural authority, with primary emphasis upon official charisma, that is, the association of God's grace with various offices of the church. The authority as exercised has its universal claims upon men. The church has insisted that the particular forms of rational authority developed by it are not held by the church to be mandatory for other types of organization but are forms which serve the distinctive spiritual functions of a religious institution. Thus the types of authority are to be distinguished even though related in the life of the church.

The Protestant churches have, by contrast, made no such systematic effort as the Catholic church to develop an institution which combines all types and sub-types of authority, even though all the types and sub-types can be discerned, in some degree at least, in various aspects of Protestantism. The major Protestant image of itself is that of a movement grounded in the personal charismatic type of authority, dedicated to the transformation of the whole function of leadership and the nature of authority. Most Protestant leaders feel that these various types of authority cannot be added one to the other (as they believe the Catholic church claims to do), since they represent developments which are often antagonistic or in tension. Rational authority, conceived as the demands of nature and reason and expressed in every organization, has serious moral and religious issues at stake within it. The Protestant leaders note that official charismatic and rational types of authority are to be found in the heavily institutionalized and settled religions; these tend toward a conservative acceptance of the existing social system from which status is derived, and toward development of routine areas in which the official charismatic authority is asserted. The personal charismatic leader, Protestant leaders believe, is always in some sense a radical or a revolutionary, setting himself in conscious opposition to established aspects of the institutions in which he lives and works. Yet a serious problem emerges in this thinking about the ministry—a problem already observed in its theological expression in Chapter 4. If the personal charismatic protest is to break old forms and to give more adequate expression to religious faith in a given situation, it must of necessity take on some visible, concrete sociological form. When this occurs, an authority secondary to the transcendent reality claimed as source of the charismatic protest is always created—the ministry, the church. Where, then, does Protestantism stop short of Catholicism in its claims to authority?

In this chapter the problems which center in Roman Catholic and Protestant approaches to charismatic or supernatural authority will be examined. In the next chapter the problems of rational authority and church bureaucracy will be the focus of attention.

Official Charismatic Authority in Catholicism

The major ground for authority in Roman Catholicism, as already noted, is official charisma. The structure of the hierarchy is held to be a divinely appointed instrument whereby the faith is preserved, truth discovered and the efficacy of the sacraments conveyed. "If anyone says there is no hierarchy in the Catholic Church by divine institution, consisting of bishops, priests and deacons, let him be anathema."[9] Catholic polity is not to be separated from Catholic salvation because both are related, the one essential to the other.

God's gift of grace is expressed in two types of official power—the power of the orders (administration of the sacraments) and the power of jurisdiction (teaching of Catholic doctrine).[4] All priests have by their ordination received the power to transmit God's grace through the sacraments of the church. The power of the priesthood is transmitted in a physical manner in the ceremony of ordination by the bishop who stands in the unbroken succession from Christ to the apostles to the Roman Catholic bishops to the priests. The Catholic diocesan press refers to the priest as "another Christ," who can do "what no angel can do," who can "command the Son of God to come down from heaven to the altar" in the rites of the church.[5]

The power of jurisdiction resides in full only in the Pope whose authority is over the whole Roman Catholic church; the bishops have this power over the priests and the lay people of the diocese, although not in full.[6] The priest has the right to interpret the moral law to the layman, not to promulgate it. In principle the priest is to indicate to the layman the various levels of obligation upon him in obeying or conforming to the teachings of the church. The Catholic layman rarely has these distinctions clearly in mind for the various requirements of the church and they are not often made explicit in the press or in sermons. A "creeping infallibility" over all the areas the priest feels strongly about is the result. If a layman wishes, he can appeal the priest's interpretation to the bishop, but the priests of Paper City know of no case when one of their number was overruled.

A Catholic pastor interprets his jurisdictional authority thus:

> If I find a Catholic doing things that are immoral and tending to lose his soul, then I have a right, first, to advise him, then if he persists, to forbid him such an act, and if he still persists, to draw the line and cut him off from the sacraments and eventually from the church if he continues. Or suppose a man is associating socially in a club with a certain group. Suppose that this group gets to talking ideas which threaten his religion or morals. Then I must forbid him to participate in the group. A group in which Protestants insisted on talking about religion to him might be such a group. The man is obviously caring more for social matters than for religion, so his soul is in danger.

In summary, then, as the *First Communion Catechism* quoted earlier observes, "The priest of the Catholic Church is the living representative of God upon earth." Therefore, boys should "tip their hats or salute him and girls should greet him with respect."

In only two of the Protestant churches—Episcopal and Lutheran—do the pastors claim a charismatic authority in matters of faith by nature of their clerical office. Most of the ministers of Paper City recognize that they have been assigned "different functions than the laymen, such as administering the sacraments and preaching of the Gospel," but these functions are not in themselves held to make the ministers more spiritual or a more certain channel of grace than members of the laity. The interpretation by most Protestant ministers of the meaning of their ordination and official charisma is similar to that voiced by a Methodist pastor:

> I have no authority because hands have been laid on me in my ordination. There was no alchemy of the spirit which gave me new powers. Whatever religious leadership I give is independent of what external things may happen to me. The authority I have is what any layman can have; it depends on what I believe and witness to in my own character.

The sect leaders also claim no official authority; they are self-designated and self-called. They believe that people recognize the gift of God when it occurs and do not believe in ordination. "The acts of man can give no spiritual gifts."

In the Protestant churches, appeals are occasionally made for respect of the ministerial office and guidance in faith without concrete designation of the authority involved, but with observations upon the Roman Catholic polity. For example, in a celebration of fifty years of service by the Reformed church pastor, the president of the synod said:

> I wish to take my texts from two verses in the last chapter of Hebrews: "Remember them which have the rule over you, who have spoken unto you the word of God." (Hebrews 13:7) And "obey them that have the rule over you, and submit yourselves: for they watch for your souls, as they that must give account, that they may do it with joy, and not with grief." (Hebrews 13:17) These are words a generation like ours needs—obey, submit, rules, discipline, order. These are words we do not hear much of these days.
>
> I took a walk this morning and passed the statue of our Lord in front of Sacred Heart church. A communicant rushing by tipped his

> hat. I suppose our Calvinist forefathers would have called this act idolatry. But I noticed with respect the obedience and reverence of Catholics for their clergy. If we had some of their discipline and submission to religious leaders, it would help us Protestants.

Personal Charismatic Authority

The Roman Catholic church bases religious authority chiefly upon official, not personal, charisma. However, the importance of the personal influence of the priests is not overlooked. Few priests or Catholic laymen believe that the personality and character of the pastor—short of disavowal of the faith and public scandal—*substantially* affect the religious life of the parish. The religious message of the priest is more the product of his institution than his own reflection; hence the common and accepted practice among priests of using the prepared sermons of scholars of the church. The curates are not pressed by the pastors to associate closely with laymen in order to provide a moral and religious example. They are expected to maintain lives that are largely separate from laymen; it is assumed that this will aid in maintaining a lay picture of the priest as morally different or superior. The priests do not express either the extreme sense of pressure upon them for maintaining a strict and specific personal moral code or distinctive and personal interpretation of the Gospel that Protestant ministers do. For example, the pastor of the Precious Blood Church explained the policy of his parish as follows:

> We are all human and if the laity saw that some of the priests drank or neglected their work for recreation or did other things they did not approve of, it would be hard on their faith and respect for the priest. They think priests are different and this is well. Our job is to keep the faith.

The relation of laymen and pastor is based chiefly upon the assumption that the individual layman directs his attention to learning the religious frame of reference defined for him by the clergy, rather than upon the assumption that the layman is to accept or reject the interpretation of the pastor in light of his own convictions, to add to or to share in the formulation of the doctrinal position of the church.

In the eyes of the priests, Catholic lay leadership is to implement the position defined by the hierarchy of the church. As an officer in the Knights of Columbus said:

> The good Catholic layman expects to be held in line by the priests. We expect the priest to lay down the moral law. We don't go to priests asking them to rethink their ideas on a moral issue, because it does not suit our interests or our version of the situation. But Protestant laymen do. Take the birth-control issue. The Protestant ministerial association was quick to jump on the bandwagon, because they discovered that birth control was popular with their people.

When the director of the parochial schools of Paper City was asked:

> Do you in your teaching and counselling place the greater emphasis upon the discipline of the pupil in the fundamental truths, learning self-restraint in order to master truths which he may not yet fully understand, or upon allowing the pupil liberty to express his individual interests and insights, to question truths until he accepts them fully?

he replied:

> We place the greatest emphasis upon learning self-restraint in order to master truths which may not as yet be fully understood. We listen at times to the expression of individual interests, but are always on the alert to strive to seek a reasonable balance between discipline and freedom, always careful not to jeopardize the truths of our religion.

And the pastor of Holy Rosary parish said:

> The Catholic will recognize the teaching power of the church by accepting wholeheartedly the doctrines it holds. The man who will not condemn all the church condemns and who accepts only some of her truths but rejects other, simply cuts himself off from the church. It's a yes or no proposition—Do you or don't you believe the divine teaching authority of the church? Will you submit to her laws and teachings or won't you? If yes, then the church makes available her sacraments to you and guides you to heaven.[7]

Catholic pastors were told that many Protestants found a tension existing between what they believe God's will to be as revealed in Christ and what the pastors in their church interpreted that will to be. Could this tension exist for Catholic laymen? The priests were unanimous that no such tension or conflict was possible for a Catholic—or he would not be a Catholic. He would have lost his faith.

The Catholic clergy are quick to note that Protestant leaders protest against a Catholic system of defining truth which has careful institutional checks and resources while affirming that not the Pope but every single Protestant is infallible. This, the Catholic diocesan journal observes, quoting Theodore Maynard, is "straining at the Catholic gnat and swallowing the Protestant camel." [8]

The pastor of Holy Cross parish speaks for the Catholic clergy when he says:

> The Protestants say the Bible speaking to the individual conscience is the rule of faith. We say that, too, but we say each individual must not rely on his own interpretation of it. If there is no higher court to which the individual can appeal, chaos is the result as in the Protestant churches. For that reason the Catholics have one faith and the Protestants have a hundred and fifty faiths.
>
> The government of the United States recognizes it must have a Supreme Court to interpret the law, and the Church recognizes that there must be a final court to interpret the Bible and to settle the disputes. The final and infallible authority for Catholics is the Pope when he speaks of faith and morals. From the Pope, the bishops and the priests receive their authority to teach the truth.

The Catholic clergy believe Protestants view the doctrine of papal infallibility as implying that the Pope can make no mistakes. The doctrine to Catholics means that the Pope may make mistakes, even on questions of faith and morals, as a private teacher, but that when he as head of the church defines an article of faith or morals intended to bind all members, God protects him against error.

Protestant Institutions and Personal Charismatic Authority

The reliance upon the personal charisma of the clergy as a basis of church polity is much greater in the Protestant churches than in the Roman Catholic. Most Protestant pastors in Paper City view their own moral and religious qualities and convictions as the chief, if not sole, basis of their authority; for some it is also the major source of the church's effective witness in the community.

In a situation characterized by "normlessness," or an inability to achieve any meaningful synthesis of theology and sociology, this authority emerges as of overwhelming importance to the pastor and as a "solution" which is "Protestant" in its emphasis upon individual conviction and avoidance of the machinery of an institution.

The Protestant pastors have elevated this personal authority over that of the office as part of a fundamental belief that no one can truly be said to be a member or a leader of a religious movement until he has internalized at least part of its value system and has come to believe that its norms and doctrines are in a very intimate way his own, that he understands them and has experienced their meaning. The goal is for each laymen to be a "pastor," to express his own personal authority.

What most of the Protestant pastors mean by the concept of the "priesthood of all believers"—to which they often refer—is the right and duty of each member to assume responsibility for having his own religious convictions and for judging for himself the rightness of the beliefs of the minister. As one Congregational pastor observed, "The pastor's position on a religious issue can have influence only to the extent that laymen regard the position as their own. The minister is a minister to a layman only to the extent that he speaks to the layman's understanding of his religious needs and is regarded by the layman as a person of integrity and wisdom."

The chief institutional expression given the principle of the priesthood of all believers has been the protection of the freedom of each member to hold his own religious beliefs, to stand alone against conformity asked by others. In most of the churches, particularly those of the "free church" and congregational tradition, each member or a minority of members has had the right of absolute veto of any action taken by the committees of the church which they deemed harmful to their interests or against their interpretation of "the right." This is the basic principle involved in the Sanger incident, the major test of the Protestant conception of the church and its authority by the Catholic clergy during the past two decades.

The elaborate Catholic development of "infallible doctrine" is countered usually among Protestant clergy by assertion that the Protestant church stands for the autonomy and authority of the conscience of each member. Recently the Presbyterian pastor outlined his next sermon to a fellow minister as follows: "The sermon will get at the core of the whole conflict between Catholicism and Protestantism. It's on Catholic institutional authority versus Protestant individual authority. I'm going to tell my people that we Protestants think it is more fundamental to do what our consciences tell us to do than to have an institution tell us what to do."

The Protestant church leaders also contrast their stress upon "individual responsibility" with Catholic insistence upon "individual submissiveness" to the doctrinal teaching of the church. "How can laymen develop any sense of personal responsibility," one minister asks, "if they are given no opportunity to work out what is right and wrong?" Another pastor characterizes the Catholic system of moral teaching as "one in which responsibility for moral decisions is developed only at the top where rules are made and enforced. The role of the layman degenerates into one of snitching—trying to do something without being caught by the priest."

The "way one becomes a Christian" for the Catholic is characterized by most Protestant pastors usually as "submitting to the church." The way one becomes a Christian for most Protestant pastors is by an "individual act of decision to accept Christ." In a prepared outline for members, a Baptist pastor enumerates the ways in which salvation occurs:

1. Levi became a Christian by forsaking a lower life and by following Jesus. Luke 5:27-32
2. A sinful woman was forgiven because she dedicated herself to Jesus in a spirit of self-sacrificing love. Luke 7:36-50
3. Zacchaeus became a Christian by making up for the wrong he had done, and by giving generously to the poor. Luke 19:1-10
4. The Philippian jailor became a Christian by "believing in the Lord Jesus." After being baptized, he ministered to Paul and Silas with brotherly love. Acts 16:25-34
5. Becoming a Christian is a PROCESS as well as an EVENT.
   a. It means growing in grace and in the knowledge of our Lord and Saviour Jesus Christ. II Peter 3:18
   b. It means casting off our sins and giving ourselves in a steadfast loyalty to Jesus, running with perseverance the race that is set before us, looking to Jesus the pioneer and perfecter of our faith. Hebrews 12:1-2
   c. It means attaining spiritual maturity, according to the measure of the stature of the fulness of Christ. Ephesians 4:11-16

The mark of the Protestant-type personal charismatic leader by his own interpretation of his role is confidence in the message and mission "given" him by God, combined with a realization that it is also his own at every point and therefore fallible and needing correction by others. Actually Protestant clergy usually veer toward emphasis upon one or the other of these attributes—awareness of one's own "given" mission, or the need of correction by others.

The first type is represented in the pastor who exalts the role of "prophetic leader" above all other roles. He seeks to challenge the congregation with an "uncompromised presentation of the highest Christian ideals" in relation to "controversial issues." The order of church life where this type of personal authority exists is that of a small circle of devoted disciples, loyal to the pastor, within a larger congregation priding itself on its support of a free pulpit while rejecting most of the positions voiced there. This is the basis, for example, "on which the Grace Congregational Church has," in the words of a layman, "been held together over many lean years—respect for the pastor. Many of us would have left the ship long ago if it had not been for loyalty to our minister." (The personal nature of membership in the church is symbolized in the "Membership Certificate"—a four-page leaflet with a picture of the church building on page 1, a picture of the Last Supper on page 2, and a picture of the pastor on page 4.)

Significantly educational or worship experiments in the life of the churches have rested for the most part upon the personal charismatic authority of the pastor. ("My people love pageantry, but I just don't have time to think up something for them each Sunday.")

The second pattern of clergy-lay relationship is based not so much on the importance of the mission of the pastor as upon his sensitivity to the wide and varied sources of charisma in the congregation. This position sees the prophetic pastor as a poor representative of the truly Protestant leader, because his message does not represent the consensus of the church members and their correction and supplementation of the pastor's views. Representatives of this position hold that in the first type of church, when the position of the pastor is tested by pressures in the community, no support among laymen is found to exist. This is precisely the charge made by some ministers against Ralph Blanton in the Sanger incident; but it is also the situation he sought to avoid by having the Standing Committee decide for itself whether it desired the speech in the church.

In a few of the churches, this second type of clergy-lay relation becomes anti-authoritative. The pastor becomes so sensitive to the wishes of various groups of laymen that no direction or guidance comes from the pastor, and "democratic Protestant leadership" is interpreted as "the willingness not to press for any position of one's own."

Most Catholic pastors characterize the entire Protestant cleric-lay relationship in the city as representing this second type of authority, or anti-authority. They state that the motive for this type of relationship is the Protestant ministers' great reliance upon the financial support and good will of affluent laymen for their security and advancement. One Catholic pastor observed:

> The Protestant clergy get their pay from laymen and are hired and fired by them, so they have to do what the laymen want them to do. But no laymen run the priest in the Catholic church. He is more independent. He does not have to worry about what hundreds of people will think. He has the discipline of one—the bishop who speaks for the church. His job is to interpret the laws of God to the people. If the people do not follow them he simply says, "You are beyond the pale," and attributes it to human frailty.

In their extreme forms both of these Protestant developments represent "leadership" without genuine authority. The "prophetic preacher" becomes the lone voice with no influence upon his parish; the "group-sentiment" pastor supplies no direction to the opinions of his congregation.

There is a nonmanipulative aspect to personal charismatic leadership; its authority roots in a gift of God. Yet the whole Protestant church system rests heavily upon some approximation to this type of leadership.[9] When the real authority is not forthcoming, when a sense of personal purpose is lost, the pastor in a Protestant church is under much greater institutional pressure than the pastor of a Catholic church to affect personal religious conviction and piety, to provide in some way a pseudo-personal charismatic leadership. The charismatic urge to communicate a message and to arouse people to action in light of it is replaced by preoccupation with mastery of techniques of speaking effectively for immediate response, with becoming a "great personality," with development of a distinguishing public "flair," with "prophetic utterance" which has the appearances of being daring and the harmless irrelevance of sweeping generalities or of single-cause fanaticism. The minister no longer feels laid hold of by a message "not his own," but by professional pressure to direct reading habits, conference attendance and personal associations toward the supply of illustrations, gimmicks, angles, catch phrases which will give a momentary "kick" to his sermons.

The pseudo-prophetic pastor is often a man who passionately wants the church to "say something" or to "do something" in love of God and man but who has given up the possibility of developing among his laymen any sustained, corporate efforts to examine their common life within the Christian faith.

A few Protestant pastors in Paper City know that their own relations with laymen at many points resemble these patterns; yet they are also keenly aware that the authentic "prophetic voice" emerges from a religious community, the result of the interaction of the pastor's own disciplined prayer and study and that of various groups within the church as they seek to discern the activity of God in the world from the "mind of Christ."

In many of the Protestant churches it is difficult for the pastor to find a consensus of belief that is the product of a religious community; there does not seem to be any priesthood of believers. The main categories of analysis and occasions of disciplined study have been supplied by the special political and economic associations of the city. No groups of laymen bring before the congregations their vigorous examination of the significance of their Christian faith for specific areas of culture—business, labor, press, politics. There are only the Sunday sermons, the social gatherings of the church with attendance chosen by ages and sex, the "big program meeting" with guest speakers answering perfunctory questions on a "one-night stand"; and from these no conviction with a common point of reference or loyalty emerges to withstand the cohesive force of the secular disciplines of the community. In this context arises the pseudo-prophet, determined by his own study and force of expression to fill the void of authority created by the lack of religious community.

Yet in a few Protestant churches the order of the church emerges out of the continuing attempt of the church to witness its faith in particular social situations. Church members seek within a community of believers for institutional structures which will reflect faith in the God of Christ, which will allow room for genuine diversity and common action, both arrived at without fear and within a context of mutual love and respect.

Chapter 8

The Organization of the Religious Community

At the most carefully prepared and widely attended meeting ever held by the Protestant Council of Churches in Paper City, the main speaker described the "rising tide of Catholic power in America," and concluded that "individual denominations can alone do nothing against it. A *united* stand against Catholics' claim that theirs is the only true church must be made." The unity sought, he explained, "is a *spiritual* unity, a unity of fellowship. There is no hope in the world except in fellowship." Protestant unity in Paper City against Catholicism should be "a fellowship of *independence* in which no Protestant group is asked to give up anything at all."

This is a fairly representative Protestant statement of the problems of organization and rational authority. Protestants know they are living beside a religious movement much more unified and cohesive than their own. Sometimes they identify that cohesiveness with power and influence, with an organization more formal, coercive and hierarchical than their own. Basically they are suspicious of a unity that is not born of a greater voluntarism, greater independence and diversity of judgment than in Catholicism. But they do not probe much deeper into the problems of corporate action; Protestant unity is to be "spiritual" and it is to involve no sacrifice "of anything at all." Can there be "fellowship" which brings unity out of diverse positions, without some reorientation of the positions of the participants through serious and prolonged wrestling with common problems? The Catholic church by its very presence keeps pressing the Protestants to clarify what kind of community its "fellowship" represents. The Catholics know that development of rational organization always involves the establishment and recognition of some norms of action. What are the sources of moral principle and their function in Protestant conduct? The Catholics know that rational organization always involves clear division of labor and co-ordination of resources. What does the Protestant pastor conceive his role to be? The Catholics know that rational organization means some hierarchy of power and responsibility for the exercise of social control. Is there to be any ordering of Protestants in the "fellowship" to achieve common objectives and, if so, on what terms is influence exercised? If there is to be "no giving up of anything" in Protestantism, can there be any meaningful unity amid her diversity?

The Catholic Church and Organization

The local Catholic pastor has much more sense of a clear division of responsibility and of territorial limitations for his work than the Protestant minister does. The Catholic pastor sees his role as the administrator of the sacraments within a certain number of blocks of the city, enforcing religious precepts and moral principles not developed by him but by authorities above him. The Protestant pastor often says that "the city is his parish"—meaning that his members usually live in all parts of it. Even though he has his "sermon aids" (such as the *Reader's Digest* sermon outlines and Halford Luccock's collections of sermons), he still is expected each Sunday to preach a sermon that bears the mark of his own personal confession of faith. The Catholic pastor spends less time than the Protestant pastor in the "running of committees." His responsibility for parish organizations is more formal in its relation to laymen, and he delegates more responsibility to subordinates—curates, nuns, and so on. The Protestant pastor becomes more involved than the Catholic pastor in the personal problems of recruiting and training lay leadership; this activity takes more of the minister's time, but it appears to keep him better informed of lay attitudes toward the church. The much greater size of the membership in the Catholic parish than in the Protestant congregation often contributes to a more functional and formal relationship of the Catholic pastor to the person seeking counsel than found in the smaller Protestant churches.

One of the fundamental differences in orientation between Catholic and Protestant clergy is that the Catholic pastor thinks of the authority for formulating basic policy for the parish, for defining the content of the faith, and for settlement of controversies as centering in a few places of power and as originating and being exercised from the top down. The Protestant pastor, on the other hand, is conscious of himself as the initiator of all basic tactics and strategy for the congregation, even though his proposals are extensively debated by the members. He has responsibility for thinking through a Protestant approach to the whole city, just as do the other ministers. He must be informed, if he can, about the religious thought of a number of initiating centers of equal status in the institution (such as the various boards of a denomination) and must resolve their differences for himself. The stress upon local congregational autonomy is greatest in the Congregational, Baptist and Methodist churches, which have the largest Protestant congregations in the city.

These differences between the roles of the Catholic and the Protestant pastors should not overshadow the involvement of both in the difficult search for the implications of their faith in the changing, concrete problems continually confronting them in the stream of persons who come to them for counsel and aid. Both Protestant and Catholic pastors are deeply involved in the running of organizations, in the bureaucratic problems of religion. This does not bother the Catholic pastor so much as the Protestant, for the latter has a much more personally charismatic conception of the ministry.

Furthermore the emphasis upon the greater hierarchical development in Catholicism should not obscure the way in which responses to local problems and needs by Paper City Catholics does have important influence upon the policy decisions made in the centers of greatest power. Communication runs both up and down in the system. But within the Catholic church the real responsibility for initiating long-range, general action and for evaluating local developments rests in the higher levels.

The definitive power for policy-making is located in the office of the bishop. The bishop is responsible to Rome; for him the criteria of his success are those established by the Holy Father, the Roman Congregation and Papal Advisors, and recognition within the church depends upon his direction of his diocese by these standards. The bishop has some autonomy in the development of strategical emphases or goals for the diocese.[1]

The bishop has done little to encourage group discussion among the pastors of Paper City of the policies established by the hierarchy for the diocese and community. During an entire year, no meetings may be held for the purpose of local Catholic pastors discussing common concerns, the local clergy taking no initiative to meet together for fear of censure, even though many feel strongly the necessity for such occasions. No discussion of relations with Protestants has taken place during the past five years, so far as the clergy can recall. When Protestants seek to discuss the policy of the church in religious relations, priests often stop conversation with some remark such as: "I understand your point of view, but I have a bishop over my head." Responsibility for policy-making cannot be located at the local level; so discussion is made to seem futile.

Centralization of policy is used as an excuse for inactivity or indecision at each level of the organization. Developments in Paper City's parochial high-school system illustrate the tendency. The system is formulated on a parish basis and represents a highly inefficient use of building and teaching facilities. It reflects the tendency of some of the older pastors to think only in terms of their own parishes, rather than in terms of the entire city. Some of the priests and the public superintendent of schools estimate that three thousand more students could be served in the four existing parochial high schools if a joint program were developed on all levels. Yet it took four years for one pastor, working carefully and judicially, to secure a joint athletic coaching staff for the four high schools. This was the first integration of teaching staffs in the system.

In a polity where genuine exchange of ideas rarely takes place between bishop and pastors, pastors and laymen, the response of the church to social change, to overtures from groups wishing to establish closer relations, is exceedingly slow. If the top hierarchy is weak, local leaders may wait years for the possibility of a basic change in policy with the elevation of a new bishop to power.

The polity does give considerable autonomy to the local parish in carrying out traditional activities of the church, allows for lay "politicing" with the priests about such things as the social activities of the parish, the building plans of the parochial school, and permits particular emphasis on whims of the pastor (for instance, Sacred Heart parish pastor's dislike of gambling as a source of revenue for the church). Elderly pastors who are in accord with a conservative policy, centering in the usual educational and sacramental interests of the church, have a strong sense of freedom and contentment within Paper City's Catholicism. Pastors and curates who desire leadership in new policies, particularly in social-moral areas, have felt circumscribed by a bishop who, as one priest observed, is "sick and does only what is necessary to get by" and who, therefore, "avoids getting into public fights." [2] On rare occasions, a curate has attempted to develop through his own initiative a program which he considered important, such as support of certain union organizational and educational activities in Paper City, only to be transferred to parishes where such opportunities are not available. In the most recent instance, a young curate of Holy Rosary parish, who taught labor education courses in the Textile Workers' Union, was transferred to a rural parish.

The Catholic church has, during its hundred years in Paper City, witnessed an organizational revolution in the economic and political institutions of the community. An agrarian community of small farms and retail stores became in two decades a mill city dominated by absentee textile "lords"; the business leadership was rocked by the efforts of workers to organize unions and by the break-up of inefficient trusts under competition into more manageable units; and the expansion of welfare services made the municipal government the city's "biggest business" and a subject of increasing political activity. The Catholic church has been able to maintain an independent existence amid the rise of big, specialized, secular organization, its own polity less subject to challenge from within by new, diverse sources of authority than that of the other major organizations in the community.

Roman Catholic pastors insist that different problems of authority are involved in the discussion of secular organization and church polity. Safeguards against abuse of power—such as those introduced in business through collective bargaining or in government through democratic political reform—are not necessary to achieve responsible action within the church, the priests claim, principally because the church is responsible to God. Such a system of authority could be cause for alarm in other institutions, the priests observe, but not in an institution which has a divine mission and whose leaders know they are judged by God. Democratic and Protestant arguments have no relevance for polity of a church which is a divine institution; in turn, the church polity is not intended as the church's example of how society should be organized, for society is a temporal order and not a supernatural order.

The principles used in organizing the clerical offices of the Catholic church are extended into the ranks of laymen. Although most of the officers and members of parish committees are laymen, the pastor of the parish, in consultation with the bishop, makes the important decisions about the purposes and activities of the parish societies. The bishop consults with a prominent Catholic layman, trained in law and business, about many of his financial investments affecting Paper City churches. The power of dispersal of funds and accumulation of parish debts does not reside in lay hands in Catholic polity. Pastors vary in the extent to which they consult laymen on financial plans; the higher the income level of the parish, the more the Catholic pastor tends to consult lay leaders. In many parishes, the only financial accounting by the priest is an oral annual report of receipts and expenditures.

The priests have a strong sensitivity to the political aspects of their leadership, that is, their power to influence action on an issue, so they are careful to discover what kinds of action laymen or groups are predisposed to take to defend the laws of the church. One pastor stated his conception of rational authority as follows:

> I must always remember that a pastor has to be on the winning side a good bit of the time. He can't lose too often and keep the respect of his people. He is the leader and he has to show he is. It always seemed to me that Protestant pastors either never demanded action from their laymen on religious issues or were running so far out in front of their laymen that nobody was following.

Organization of lay ranks has been facilitated by the fact that the hierarchy is working in Paper City with laymen who, more recently than most Protestants, have had minority experience in combining to use contention tactics.[3] The Catholic laymen have a strong sense of the necessity and rightness of powerful clerical and lay organization to protect the interests of the church. (Protestant leaders have exercised great power in Paper City culture, but for the past two or three generations it has been chiefly through action of individuals wielding power within the established economic institutions. The mobilization of many people to engage in overt protest has not been a recent or extensive experience of most Protestant lay leaders.)

Most Catholic laymen believe that they experience in Paper City's economic life no greater share in actual policy-making processes than within their church.[4] Although the basic policies of the parish societies are clerical decisions, most of the Catholic lay leaders express a strong sense of freedom "to maneuver," "to politic," to discuss with the pastors and curates the social and educational activities of the parish.[5] They look upon their church polity as a part of the "American scene" as much as other institutions in Paper City.

Protestant Churches and Organization

The commonly expressed belief of Protestant pastors and laymen that "what really matters in a church is personal religious conviction" serves poorly to illuminate power relations and structure in religious organization. Yet the pastors are inevitably deeply involved in the problems of organization and of operating a physical plant. Most of their time actually is taken up with calls upon members, securing leaders for Sunday schools, for men's clubs and women's circles, in seeing that the church property is cared for. The status and advancement of the pastors within their denominational ranks seems—if the questions asked of the pastors by the national and regional church offices are an important clue—to be based chiefly upon the fulfilling of the external, rational criteria of organization, such as increase in numbers of members and participants in various activities, sale and use of various materials, size of financial contributions to nationally promoted programs. Some of the pastors express a sense of burden from too many meetings to attend, and talk of "taking a small church where a man can concentrate on religious work," where he would no longer be involved in the minutiae and routine of extended and sometimes purposeless organization. Others have settled into professional roles in which considerable pride is taken in "making the wheels go round," and in which absorption with the mechanics of group activity has been accompanied by a narrowing of what the pastors conceive to be their "religious concerns."

One of the most remarkable aspects of Protestant organizational activity by the pastors is that most of its elaboration has not been accompanied by explicit and serious theological debate as to its meaning. Most of the developments of Protestant church organization and of the pastor's routine in support of it have not been subject to critical discussion of the norms guiding them in relation to the traditional and fundamental doctrines of the church. One of the corollaries of this seems to be that the organization which is established within the churches consists in great part of aimless and amorphous committees spending a great deal of time in handling church property, selecting officers to call meetings to select officers, discussing for hours trivia in planning social gatherings of the church, and the like.

The organization, in formal terms, developed within the Protestant churches is lay-administered. In most churches, officers of the major boards are held responsible to the congregation as a whole and are elected under a representative form of church order. In some churches, the boards are self-perpetuating, and future membership is selected by present members in close consultation with the pastor; yet these boards, too, are in principle subject to review of the entire congregation. However, in many churches great numbers of the members of the congregation have so thoroughly identified religion with a particular institution, and responsibility for looking after its interests becomes so routinized under a paid professional leadership, that the pastor and his interpretation of his role becomes the most crucial single factor in the organizational life of the church.[6]

The chief activity of the church is to keep before individuals in the congregation, through the affirmations of the pastor, the ideals and message of the Christian faith. Such a function does not require strong organization of ministers or laymen within the church itself. The life of the community is to be changed through the persuasion of laymen influential in economic and social organizations outside the church. The process of persuasion does not involve the Protestant churches in formation of disciplined groups of men to influence particular vocations in the community, to penetrate the popular press and special interest groups, or to engage in protest action on a series of interrelated public issues. This kind of witness presumes a rational analysis of the community and the formulation of norms from the faith which is not a part of the authority of Protestant leadership.

The Paper City churches whose leadership expresses in sermons and interviews the widest social-moral concerns are the most indifferent to the development of rational organization. No other major institution in Paper City professing interest in achieving freedom and justice in the community has given as little attention to the means of achieving these goals.

Protestant Interdenominational Organization

The clergy's and laymen's experience of polity within Protestantism is characterized by localism, decentralization, autonomy of members in their various congregational groupings. Almost no effective organization has been developed across denominational lines for discussing common concerns of the faith, for pooling financial, property and leadership resources in relating the churches to various aspects of community life. Laymen are informed by most pastors in classes and sermons that the congregation belongs to and contributes funds to a local council of churches, the Federal Council of Churches of Christ in America (now the National Council) and the World Council of Churches. But the pastor usually explains that "these relations are voluntarily made for purposes of fellowship and service, and there is no authority which can hand down orders to any local church" (to quote one statement to a pastor's class). The principle dealt with most, according to the pastors, in description of the relations of denominations is "the independence of the local church."

The ecumenical movement in Protestantism must be regarded for Paper City largely as a top-level affair. The usual church member experiences no organizational life beyond the local church. He is aware of no over-all Protestant programs for influencing or interpreting American culture in which his church or denomination is to take part. He reads none of the literature produced by the top-level interdenominational agencies expressing an emerging "open-ended" consensus among Protestant leaders on the relation of theology to various areas of society or vocational groupings.[7] And this literature is only occasionally processed and meagerly summarized for lay reading in the denominational literature most widely circulated in the churches, and through which the ecumenical agencies have their chief access to local congregations.[8]

The Ministerial Association, begun in 1918, has as its constitutional Objects of Association "the promotion of Acquaintance, Fellowship and Mutual Helpfulness among the ministers." [9] At the first meeting of the association a motion was made that the objectives of "discussion and such action as may be considered advisable for the benefit of the community" be added to the constitution's statement of purpose of the organization. The motion was defeated and no changes in the objectives of the association have been made since. The present minutes generally describe the association as a "fellowship which makes no theological commitments."

The association has never engaged in a systematic discussion of the over-all program of the churches in relation to Catholicism in the city. Ministerial co-operation has centered in planning occasional interdenominational worship services, vacation schools, annual city-wide youth rallies and farewell meetings for ministers going to new churches.

The Protestant ministers see their ministry as calling for "all round" concern about people and the community, and believe that when a minister becomes a specialist, he necessarily "abstracts" a "part" of life from the whole. This means actually that each minister pursues highly individual interests of his own—such as fighting for dissemination of birth-control information, studying the number of Catholics in city government and public school instruction—or devotes his time entirely to the operation of the traditional services of his church.

The highest level of co-ordinated action achieved by the association has been to develop a policy that individual ministers will not make controversial public statements on social or religious issues separately, but will make them together. Such statements have been made only on a few social issues—gambling and transportation of parochial students in public buses. The co-ordination ended when effective opposition developed to statements.

The major financial and leadership resources of the Protestant churches in the association are focused in the Second Congregational church, and a virtual monopoly is held by the three strongest churches—Second Congregational, First Congregational and Episcopalian. The other churches expend their energies in simply maintaining traditional services. Support for any program costing money, such as a religious census or a religious education program, must come largely from the strong churches.

The second interdenominational agency formed by Protestants in Paper City was the Council of Churches, organized in 1942, twenty-eight years after the first committee of the Ministerial Association had been appointed "to investigate the matter of a Federation of Churches." A quota of ½ to 1 per cent of the operating expenses of each member church makes possible an annual budget of approximately $500. With this the council is charged by its constitution

> to express through fellowship, cooperation and service the essential unity of the Christian church; to provide an interdenominational agency for cooperation of the churches in Christian education, comity, social relations, united worship, evangelism, World Christian Fellowship and such other service as may achieve more effectively the objectives of the Christian religion; to study the religious needs of the community and devise plans through which those needs can be met.

The major activity of the council is a meeting once a year when Protestant unity is discussed and reports are given by the committees of their activities. Suggested activities involving any careful organization or extensive financial support have been turned down after consideration of the difficulties. On this basis a city-wide religious census has been rejected, a newsletter and publicity program, and a week-day religious education proposal made after extensive work by a small group of concerned laymen. The Protestant churches, while talking more of the necessity for interdenominational unity, have not appreciably altered the extreme congregational autonomy of their rational organization.

In summary, the Roman Catholic church has not had the difficulty of the Protestant churches in giving organizational form to their religion. The Roman church represents a precise and comprehensive system combining charismatic (personal and official) and rational authority—the major ground being official charisma.

The Protestant churches display an uneasiness and indecision over the problems of authority not present in Catholicism. For Protestant clergy, their reaction to the Roman Catholic system has deepened both their general predispositions to be anti-authoritarian, at least in ideology, and their tendency to make the personal charismatic authority of the Protestant minister carry most of the burden of the institutional development of the church. Since real charismatic leadership is both uncommon and important, pseudo-charismatic qualities are developed—sociability, facility in providing momentarily arresting interpretation of the gospel and similar qualities. And since organization is necessary for the performance of the many social and religious functions which laymen desire, the Protestant ministers have found themselves deeply involved in the running of committees and property and other works which their seminary-inspired pictures of the ministry have not prepared them to see as meaningful and important. Paper City Protestantism is most dramatically exhibited in the ineffectual efforts to co-ordinate church activities and the slight attention given by Protestants to any ecumenical consensus on the relation of Christianity and society.

The people of Paper City are confronted by two major religious institutions representing both deep variances and similarities on the crucial level of polity where the impact of movements in society is often decided. Both institutions embody in mixture all types of authority. But the dominant tendency in Roman Catholicism is toward bureaucratic organization without the liberating influence of truly charismatic leadership originating from a variety of sources and forceful enough to bring about new directions in church policy. On the other hand, Protestant polity is represented by individual subjectivism, an unrecognized institutionalization of personal charismatic leadership among the clergy, inability to achieve expression of religious conviction disciplined enough to influence effectively a highly organized society. Protestant leadership fights the pull either toward vague consensus without clear purpose or "prophetic" leadership without community; while in Paper City Catholicism the drive is toward precise authoritative positions cut off from lay understanding and decision.

Chapter 9

Bingo and Building Funds: The Financial Problem

The financial apparatus of an institution—even a bingo game—is part of a whole complex of factors which disclose influence and power in a community. The religious leaders are acutely aware of this, and at times no issues in religious relations seem to be more important to them than those growing out of disputes over the financial practices of the two major institutions. Opposition to the gambling activities of the Roman Catholic church brought the Protestant pastors to their greatest activity in Paper City politics since the Sanger incident in 1940.

Finances and the Social Structure of the Churches

The Catholic church throughout most of its existence in Paper City has sought financial support largely from laboring people, while the Protestant churches have received their major income from middle and upper classes. This fact has influenced the development of somewhat different fund-raising devices in the two religious movements. Religious leaders have tended, however, to interpret practices different from their own almost entirely in moral terms.

The official diocesan history remarks on the financial sources of Roman Catholicism in the period from 1850 to 1870:

> They could not give much, these humble hewers of wood and drawers of water, but, from their small wage of sixty cents a day, they gave what they could and began the golden chain of Eucharistic temples which runs, like the finger of God, through our western counties.[1]

By 1947, the mean annual income of each consumer unit of the labor force in Paper City was $1500.[2] This is the class which composed 62.8 per cent of the church's membership in that year.[3] The

Catholic leaders believe it has been necessary, because of the low income of members, to rely upon oblique methods of fund raising, that is, income not from direct gifts to the church but from the expenditure for other activities—mainly amusements and gambling (a form of chance investment in items not obtainable with a low income).[4] Carnivals, penny socials, circuses, beano and various lotteries have been used to a much greater extent by Catholics than by Protestants. These methods have also aided laboring-class churches to reach financial sources outside the parish membership. The use of such indirect methods is not to be explained purely on class terms, but this is one factor.

The Catholic Church and Gambling

The differences between Catholic and Protestant fund-raising methods are seen most graphically in the comparison of laboring-class Catholic churches with upper-middle class Protestant churches. The upper-middle class churches of both groups have a great deal of similarity in their financial systems. Funds from envelope giving and from fees are adequate to support the regular activities of Holy Cross, the upper-income Catholic parish in the city. No circuses or bingo games have been used to raise funds in this parish, although occasional lotteries have been conducted to finance special programs of societies in the parish. The first $100,000 for the building of Holy Cross Church was raised when most laymen in the parish subscribed 5 per cent of their income for one year.[5]

The use of gambling as a source of income for the Catholic church decreases as the class ladder of Paper City is ascended, and opposition among Catholic laymen to gambling as a financial device of the church increases.[6] Members of Holy Cross parish often express embarrassment at the "financial antics" of the lower-class Catholic churches and sometimes make apologies to Protestant friends for financial tactics of the Holy Rosary pastor whose parishioners live in working-class Ward 1. They point out with pride that, in their parish, "Father never has to ask for money. He just thanks us for giving so generously."

The decision as to which churches will be permitted to organize lotteries, circuses and beano is made by the bishop, so that funds can be channelled to the parishes most in financial need. Also, competition between Catholics for city-wide participation in church gambling activities is avoided and financial programs can be adapted more adequately to the interests of members. The two churches in the city's poorest ward (Ward 1) have exclusive rights to city-wide gambling programs—Immaculate Conception to beano; Holy Rosary to monthly lotteries and an annual circus. All other Catholic churches can operate socials and bazaars and most do.[7] At the height of the efforts of Immaculate Conception parish to pay for a new church building, a car a night was given away and special buses were run from neighboring towns to bring the people who participated in beano.

The most spectacular of the Catholic gambling programs is carried on by Holy Rosary parish. The lottery is called a "monthly offering." With this phrase, as the pastor has pointed out, a federal admissions tax does not have to be paid on lottery tickets which permit people to attend a social affair and drawing for prizes.[8] The pastor had printed on the tickets, "I have given a donation of one dollar to Holy Rosary Parish." The practice instituted by Holy Rosary is now generally used by the Knights of Columbus, Order of Hibernians, Immaculate Conception parish, as well as many Catholic parishes outside Paper City.

The Holy Rosary lottery is run in co-operation with eight parishes in communities near Paper City. The parishes sell dollar tickets for the "monthly offering," and keep half of all money collected. The other half is sent to the pastor of Holy Rosary who, in his words, "provides the set-up."[9] In the parishes participating, books of twelve one-dollar tickets are distributed to adults and children of the parish. The seller returns ten dollars to the parish and has two tickets to sell for his own income. This is considered a large financial inducement to most people in the parishes, and the streets of Paper City are often busy with children selling the tickets.[10]

"The annual Holy Rosary Lawn Fete is," according to the pastor of the parish, "the crowning achievement of a life of fund-raising for the love of God, which began with the best little beano game you ever saw on the lawn back of my first parish house." The fete (Protestants call it a "circus") has become in the five years of its existence "New England's biggest and best fete," in the judgment of the pastor. A giant banner across the main street of Paper City acclaims each year the "Holy Rosary Lawn Fete. You've seen the rest. Now see the best." The three-day fete in each of the past three years has grossed receipts of $70,000 to $80,000 and made net profits for the parish of $40,000 to $50,000.[11]

The fete is run with consummate professional showmanship by the pastor. The appearance of the circus or fete in the city is timed with the co-operation of the mayor, who grants permissions for use of city lots, so that it is the first carnival production each year in the community. Thus, the fete does not suffer from earlier competition. For weeks before the fete five- to seven-column advertisements are placed in the local newspaper promoting the event.

The ads, often written by the pastor, announce the event as a "sensational jet-propelled production which ROARS into stratospheric speed at the opening." The fete has, according to the advertisements, "gigantic value awards—six cars including a Packard, one aeroplane, one truck, $4,000 in cash to be given away." The fete features a $15,000 stage spectacle with "fourteen spectacular attractions," including the "highest paid single act in the world" and another act of "Canine Cleverness and Comely Young Ladies." With the fete are Baby Beauty Contests, Mr. and Mrs. Paper City Contests, and a Start a Chicken Farm Contest.

The fete extends over a four-acre lot on the edge of Ward 1's working-class tenements. The local newspaper estimates 22,000 people attend its three days of activity. The carnival rides for children, the circus acts, the gaming booths are supplied by the Lagasse Amusement Company, an organization which specializes in Catholic carnivals.

The approach to the grounds is indicated by a powerful searchlight cutting back and forth across the sky. Popular music from records played over a public-address system fills the air, broken occasionally by the voice of the pastor of Holy Rosary parish: "Admission to the grounds, thirty-five cents for adults, twelve cents for children. Folks, if you are going to the mammoth show buy the ninety cent ticket and save a nickel. . . . Don't forget Saturday all children are our guests. To them admission to the circus grounds is absolutely free. We want all of them to see our wonderful show. . . . This big spotlight has a million, a million, candlepower, so they say. I never counted them. . . ."

The building nearest the entrance to the fete grounds is a tenement. The lights are on in an apartment on the ground floor. On the living room sofa sit two plump, bead-eyed teddy bears, and on the mantel are two dolls and two papier-mâché religious statues, all prizes from the circus gaming booths.

The ticket windows for admission to the grounds are manned by curates from Holy Rosary parish. The first sight on entrance to the grounds is a large canopied tent with the sign "DIRECTOR." Seated beneath it on a Morris chair is the pastor of Holy Rosary parish. He holds a microphone in one hand and operates the control box of a public-address system with the other. The pastor is an impressive man—large, white-haired, red-faced. He sits with great dignity and poise facing the people as they enter the grounds through the gates. He flicks a switch. The music stops and the pastor says, "Now wouldn't you like to win an automobile or an airplane? We're giving away twenty. Isn't that something?" The switch is flicked off as people come to greet him on arrival. He is seldom alone under the canopy during the evening.

In the center of a circular, sawdust midway is a first-aid tent operated by a uniformed nurse. Around the edges of the midway are the gaming booths: Bingo, Quizzo, Dice Wheel, Hit the Bottle, Dart a Prize, Ring a Prize, Pick a Duck, Try Your Luck, Chuck a Luck, Win a Whip, Try a Trick, Pick a Tip, Honest Kelly the Kandy Man—twenty-five in all. The counters of the games are arranged so that the wheels and operators are in full sight. The grounds are heavily policed; many priests walk about the midway. The people play the games in quiet, earnest decorum, in sharp contrast to the blare of the music. No groups of people play together; the participants almost always are alone or with one other person. The booths are run almost entirely by teen-age boys and girls of Holy Rosary parish, instructed by a few professional men with the circus. Two booths have religious objects such as crucifixes for prizes, but most have carnival items—baby dolls, candy, paper animals. One booth has kitchen utensils for prizes; three have money prizes.

At one end of the midway, canvas screens block off from view the showgrounds where grandstands have been erected around a wooden stage. Here "High Wire Wonders," a "famous Dog and

Pony Circus," Watkins Chimpanzees, a bear called "Big Boy," cyclists, teeterboard stars, and Will Hill's elephants can be seen from bleachers for sixty cents, completing the evening's entertainment.

The fete is given greater status in the community by several policies pursued deliberately by the pastor of Holy Rosary parish. The priests of the parish are conspicuously present during the proceedings. The finances of the fete—gross and net income—are reported to the local newspaper by the pastor of Holy Rosary parish at the end of each season with a statement of gratitude for community support, for the aid of the mayor, for the Board of Public Works, for the Police Department and for "all others who contributed to the success of the fete." [12] The pastor of Holy Rosary parish is regarded throughout Paper City as the most co-operative of the priests in various social welfare programs and is the only priest who gives money regularly in his and his parish's name to the city-wide social service programs of Red Cross, Community Chest, cancer drive, and others. Sums of $500 to $2,000 are given with a statement that the parish is grateful for the community-wide support of Holy Rosary's fund-raising program.

The pastor is convinced of the importance of his particular fund-raising talents to the church. "My predecessor was a very saintly man, but the church needs more than that," he observes. "My predecessor did the praying; I do the paying." The pastor stated in an interview in 1947 that his parish had paid off an indebtedness of $500,000 since he became pastor, mainly through the gambling activities of the parish. He estimated that the parish had spent $250,000 in redecoration of the interior of the church and the parish buildings, and that it carried over a million dollars' worth of insurance on property.

The pastor believes that he has the support of all the people in Paper City except the Protestant ministers. "They know how much I get and they know the money goes to support eight other parishes. That's why they hit at me so hard."

The personal candidness of the pastor about his methods of fund-raising and devotion to financial campaigns on a lottery basis are generally regarded as an asset in the church's public relations. A prominent Catholic once remarked to the pastor that if he had gone into show business instead of the church, he would have been a millionnaire. The pastor's reply—"No, I wouldn't have; I'd have been in jail"—has become a part of the folklore of Paper City.

The interest of the Roman Catholic church in gambling as a source of income is indicated by the pastor's estimate that in the last five years Holy Rosary parish has received and spent over $1,-250,000, almost entirely from gambling enterprises.[13] The pastor claimed that his parish in 1947 would "make a half million dollars." The pastor believes that the parish "does the biggest business of its kind of any church in the United States. We are unique. When I tell the curates how big an affair we run here, they can't believe it. They have to come here to Holy Rosary and see it to believe it."

Holy Rosary is "the smallest parish in the diocese [sixteen blocks] and has the biggest income in the city and perhaps in the diocese," according to the pastor. The staff of Holy Rosary parish numbered forty-five persons including sixteen nuns, five housekeepers and two curates. The income from the gambling is shared with eight other parishes, two of which are in Paper City—Immaculate Conception (French) and St. Michael's (Greek). Funds also go to a Catholic orphanage and day nursery in the city. None of the churches in the system receives, according to the pastor, less than $500 a month, a few, $1,500.[14]

The use of gambling devices by the Roman Catholic church has increased during the century of its existence in Paper City, although the real income of its members has increased.[15] This situation perhaps reflects an increasingly marginal conception of church support in family budgets—coming after food, clothing, shelter, amusements and transportation have been paid for. The Catholic church has sought to identify or relate support of religion with these central concerns. Prizes at most socials and lotteries are groceries, cooking equipment, cars, as well as frivolous items such as plastic and paper dolls. The major support for the churches' gambling devices for fund-raising purposes—if the votes cast in one referendum vote on legalizing beano are an adequate indication—has come from the lower income wards.[16]

Protestant Reaction to Catholic Gambling

Most Protestant ministers in their sermons regularly attack "gambling in every form" as a "source of corruption to the morals and social well-being of the community." They often refer to the dangerous sanction given to gambling by the financial practices of the Catholic church. As early as 1912, the community's chief Protestant spokesman against the Catholic church's use of gambling observed:

> It is wrong for churches to run games of chance in connection with entertainment, and equally so for societies to conduct similar plans. We lack a high keen moral sense if such things do not shock us. One way and a most successful way to stop church and society gambling is not to buy a chance. Gambling is the spirit of selfishness and the essence of meanness in the last degree. The fascination of the game is great, hence the danger of permitting any laxity in this direction.[17]

In 1947, the Protestant ministers of the six largest congregations in the Council of Churches made a statement, widely publicized, against "gambling in every form" and urging "the responsible officers in our city administration" to make "an earnest and sustained effort to restrain and ultimately to abolish the gambling trade which appears to be flourishing in our midst." [18]

The political pressure against the ministers by the mayor and other officials and the action of the Catholic church (reported in detail in Chapter 20) was immediate and intense. When the Protestant leaders attack gambling in Paper City they are striking at the major financial sources of the Catholic church in lower-class areas. Their attempt to arouse public opinion for political activity against gambling in the city could have been expected to bring the power of the Catholic church immediately into play.

The great preoccupation of the Protestant pastors with the "evils" of gambling in comparison with other social problems can be explained in part by the Protestant ministers' awareness that the gambling issue is close to Catholic and Protestant institutional interests. The ministers have at no time in the past decade dealt publicly and at length with their religious and ethical reasoning for absolute condemnation of every form of gambling. And they have made no public statement as to the relation of the widespread practice of gambling to the recreational and economic problems of the community.

The Catholic pastors in Paper City maintain a common front on the ethical harmlessness and legitimacy of gambling as practiced by the church.[19] Statements by the diocesan press on the ethics of gambling are much more reserved than those of the local priests. The official position on gambling as summarized in the diocesan paper, the *Catholic Mirror,* is that gambling is not to be extolled as a virtue or condemned as an intrinsic evil. "The evil is not in the use of this recreation or transaction, but rather in its abuse." [20] Gambling to be licit or morally acceptable must be "well conducted," meeting these conditions: the gambler owns and is at liberty to use what he wagers; the gambler acts of his own free will; there is some sort of equality between the parties participating—that is, the games are run honestly.

The more closely the priest is involved in gambling activities for his parish the fewer reservations he has on the moral abuses possible from gambling, particularly if conducted for good causes, such as support of the church. The pastor of St. Jerome's parish observed, "There is nothing morally wrong with gambling. How can there be? The Protestant minister will say nothing—not a peep—about adultery being practiced in this city. But he'll shout about gambling." The pastor of Mater Dolorosa parish does not believe that church beano or lotteries are gambling. "The church is against gambling. I'm against gambling. But a man buying a ticket from his church and putting beans on a card for an evening is not gambling." A French Catholic editor of a weekly newspaper, president of the Franco-American Club which collaborated with the Immaculate Conception parish in raising funds through beano, summarized the position of lay supporters of church-operated gambling in a public letter:

> To characterize beano simply as "gambling" does not resolve anything. Gambling! It is gambling if you use the word to mean that it implies an element of chance. Then you will have to condemn every game which has an element of chance without exception, from baseball, football, boxing, up or down. . . . Well-conducted beano is an innocent pastime which may become a profitable pastime for some good cause when people choose that easy means of raising money, as has been the case of Immaculate Conception in Paper City. Here, the utmost honesty has always presided at every gathering. . . . Nobody ever got poor from the money he spent in Immaculate Conception hall and many were greatly helped by the prizes they recovered.[21]

Almost all the Catholic priests associated with the gambling enterprises of the church also defend local nonchurch gambling activities, such as betting and book-making on horse races. The priests argue that people will engage in such activities—whether legal or illegal—and that "it is better for local people to benefit from the operation of the gambling than for outsiders." The bishop of the diocese and the priests opposed the establishment of a state lottery.[22] The involvement of priests in gambling activities is accompanied by the practice of drawing no distinctions between church and non-church operated enterprises and of not stressing to laymen the morally dangerous aspects of gambling. The priests more frequently argue the innocence and inconsequential moral nature of all gambling in the city.

Protestant Finances and the Social Structure: The Role of Paternalism

The Protestant ministers are most critical of the ethical effects of Catholic church-sponsored gambling; the Catholic priests are most critical of the moral implications of Protestant paternalism—the easy reliance of churches upon a small number of well-to-do laymen for their major financial support. The priests' conception of Protestant church finances is chiefly that "a few wealthy people give the money—thousands of dollars at a time." They believe that "all Protestant churches have big endowments so they don't have to worry about support from the nickels and dimes in the collection plate as we do." [23]

There is some basis for the Catholic interpretation of the upper-class nature of Protestant financial sources as paternalism. A careful study made in 1943 by the Second Congregational Church of the giving by its laymen over the previous five years indicated that this upper-middle class church was relying upon 31 members (4 per cent of the 738 membership) to give 40 per cent of the annual income. The annual budget was approximately $20,300 at that time. Fifteen per cent of the membership contributed 63 per cent of the annual income.

The church made the study in order to set goals for gifts toward liquidation of the church's $50,000 debt. A booklet was published for the membership indicating the past pattern of church support and strengthening it by recommending that an even smaller group be asked to give an even larger proportion of funds toward the debt liquidation than in the past. Thus, 25 members were asked to give 50 per cent of the fund to be raised, 10 members another 10 per cent, and 100 more members 20 per cent of the fund. The remainder of the 603 members were expected to give but 20 per cent of the fund. This plan was developed by a laymen's board composed almost entirely of upper-class laymen. It is fairly representative of the financial structure of all the middle-upper class Protestant churches and to some extent of the churches attended chiefly by laborers. A few families are looked upon as the major contributors and leaders of the church by both ministers and rank and file laymen. In the Second Congregational Church in the 1930's, when three large contributors died, the congregation cut the budget $4,000, the sum which the men had usually given.[24]

The pattern of Protestant church support and leadership chiefly by small groups of relatively well-to-do people in Paper City is visible also in the laboring-class church, Grace Congregational. For over three decades, the pastor of this church has been the city's most vehement speaker against the Catholic church's use of gambling for fund raising. While the major Catholic solution for deficits in laboring-class churches has been gambling, Grace Church has found its solution in upper-class paternalism. The Protestant churches of Paper City have found no way to finance religious institutions in the lowest-income areas so that educational programs, adequate professional leadership and meeting places can be obtained without reliance upon solicitation of personal gifts from upper-income people—solicitation which on occasion has involved the pastor in carrying out actions which advanced the private interests of donors. (For instance, one pastor called on influential men who were his personal friends in order to advance the political ambitions of a donor.)

Grace Church represents the chief conscious effort of middle- and upper-class Protestants to reach laboring people in Paper City. It was begun in 1879 on a high level of idealism as a Sunday School and Mission by a few well-to-do mill owners who contributed their money and time to the founding of a Sunday school and finally a "laboring man's church" in Ward 2. Their inspiration for the project came from a sermon preached by the pastor of the Second Congregational Church on "Doing Something Definite for the Master."

The church throughout its history has had a paternalistic financial structure. After seventy years of existence, laymen and minister still rely upon financial gifts from Protestant mill owners; one-fourth of the budget comes from outside the membership. Grace Church has not developed into a financially free Protestant laborers' religious institution. The minister who has served the church for forty-five years conceived of the institution largely as a mission supported by the affluent and saw nothing detrimental to the morals or morale of the church in "begging," as he termed it, "for gifts from Paper City's best people."

In 1906, twenty-seven years after Grace Church's founding, a new building was erected. The program for the dedication services notes that thirty-five Protestants outside the church gave $12,470 for the building; the members gave $632.50. The building committee, the program notes, consisted of three prominent mill owners "constantly seconded and aided by the church committee of Grace Church." Grace Church received a regular "missions" stipend toward the pastor's salary from Second Congregational Church until 1937. Until then the church had been so reliant upon the mother church for support and direction that almost no laymen's organization had been developed—a standing committee, property trustees, church council were nonexistent.[25]

The paternalistic structure of the church has been expressed in part of the worship material of this church. A cross composed of fourteen large bricks was recently erected in a parlor of the church to commemorate the fourteen Second Congregational Church men who founded Grace.[26] On important occasions of the church, the "Grace Church song" is sung. The words of this song, composed by the minister's wife, read:

O, years ago on Race Street men who now are known to fame
Organized a Sunday School
For the boys and girls of Paper City, and eagerly they came,
And were taught there the Golden Rule,
And were taught there the Golden Rule.
There were teachers from the Mother Church and Superintendents too;

Their names we ever shall revere.
But the school became a Chapel and that building would not do;
So they bought this site so dear.

CHORUS:

Oh, Grace Church, oh, Grace Church, you have grown 'til you're known this country o'er,
May you live on and work on, 'til your task on earth shall be no more.

For several years two of the most influential Protestants in Paper City—one a textile manufacturer and community philanthropist, the other a paper manufacturer—contributed $2,700 apiece to the pastor for Grace Church, a sum composing over half the church's income. But the older men interested in Grace Church as a "family charity" are passing from the scene and the church will have to rely on the resources within its membership.

The minister of Grace Church believes that he has tried "every acceptable method of securing support from rank-and-file membership." He has deliberately patterned financial appeals to the membership after several Catholic devices used in laboring-class churches, such as the "annual coal offering." The pastor has sought to cultivate special gift offerings for various Protestant days, as the Catholics do for feast days. Grace Church promotes Reformation Day, anniversaries of the pastorate, anniversaries of the founding of Grace Church as well as Easter and Christmas, as special gift days.

Grace Church, although taking over many of the financial devices of the laboring-class Catholic churches, does not run gambling programs. Grace's standing committee has at various times debated the "advisability of adopting gambling as a means of church support" but the opposition, chiefly from the minister, has been sufficient to discourage it. The church has held bazaars without gambling booths.

The Protestant sects of Paper City, which also serve laboring people, have secured financial support from the voluntary and spontaneous gifts of members. Most of the sects take no collections at their meetings, the gifts being made at various times to a member designated to receive them. However, the sects support little property, their funds going chiefly into missionary work. The Lutheran church is supported almost entirely by voluntary gifts from its members, but it differs from Grace Church in its stronger ethnic alignment, a greater representation of skilled workers and its more systematic designation of the role of the church in the salvation of men.

Protestant Financial Contributions to Catholic Churches

Despite Roman Catholic criticism of Protestant upper-class paternalism, the financial structure of the Catholic church has throughout Paper City's history also been related to Protestant businessmen's philanthropy, although not to the same extent as the Protestant churches. The Catholic hierarchy during the earlier years acknowledged often and publicly the financial contributions of Protestant leaders to the development of its institutions.[27] But a shift in policy has occurred in recent years.

No priest in Paper City would now acknowledge in an interview that Protestant contributions had been made to his parish for any purpose—even for church buildings in the past. The pastor of Holy Cross parish, whose laymen systematically canvassed leading Protestant businessmen when the new million dollar church was being built,[28] reported that the parish "has received no gifts from wealthy Protestants. If they did give anything, they would expect more favors." The pastor of a Catholic church to which a Protestant family claims to have given a window is "sure that a Protestant in Paper City wouldn't permit a window to be given in his name to a Catholic church."

The Protestant ministers and a good many of the Protestant laymen believe that a shift in policy is taking place within the Catholic church, that the pastors no longer expect large funds from Protestants for church buildings and no longer seek to cultivate them as before. When, however, Catholic building drives are conducted for community projects, such as a new Catholic hospital, systematic solicitation of Protestant business and professional men is made.

In the nineteenth century the collaboration of Protestant mill owners with the financial programs of the priests was much closer than now. In the first three decades of Catholic church establishment in Paper City it was common practice for the mills to deduct from the wages of the Catholic workers the amounts they proposed to pay for church purposes and on pay day to deliver the sum to the pastor.[29] The Catholic priests had access to the pay roll records of the mills so that they could know the exact income of their parishioners. Over the years, and particularly during the Catholic expansion in Paper City, the Protestant-controlled Water Power Company contributed more free land to the Catholic church than to the Protestant churches.[30] These grants are recorded in Catholic parish histories. A local Catholic novelist-historian notes that every Catholic church in the city received some gift from a Protestant textile mill owner.[31]

Doctrine and Financial Apparatus of the Churches

A major doctrinal issue—that of justification by faith or works—is thought by some of the Protestant clergy to be involved in the methods of fund-raising used by the diocesan office of Catholic charities and social work. This office engages in a great deal of mail promotion, and some Protestants in the city receive the appeals. In this literature the Protestant clergy claim to see abuses which they believe occur inevitably once the merit concept of religion is given a place in the scheme of salvation. For them the worst assumption—which they think is back of financial appeals such as those used by the diocesan charities—is the belief that man can by his own acts manipulate God, influence His punishment of man in this world and the next and assure God's reward of man for good deeds on man's own terms. Good works, such as charitable offerings, they charge, become associated with earthly and heavenly rewards in a direct cause-and-effect relationship. Religion becomes, according to one of the Protestant ministers, a matter of "I've burned my candles, done the stations and left the coppers in the box; it won't be long before I'll be getting results."

Such a morality, these Protestant clergy claim, injures the cause of deep religion which attributes salvation entirely to God and which lifts man to a higher relationship than *quid pro quo* with God. These Protestants hold that when man has done all he can, he should still feel a deep sense of humility and inadequacy before the demands of God. One Protestant pastor said:

> When a man seeks to do good works, to act charitably, to strive for justice, he must not think, as do the Catholics, that they contribute to his salvation. The Catholic believes he is saved in graduated scales,

that he goes through various stages of merit. A Protestant must never think that he can merit salvation. Christ did all that was necessary. Man can never earn or merit salvation. He should do good acts in gratitude for what God has given him. His faith in God would not be of much stature if it did not express itself in good works.

The theological statements of most of the Catholic pastors on the relation of faith and works of merit represent in composite a view something like this:

> Christ tells us of the great reckoning which will take place in the last days. Some souls will be damned because they have led bad lives and some will be admitted to glory because they will deserve it for the good lives they have led. Doing meritorious work does not make God our debtor as the Protestants claim. God simply promised an eternal reward for those who are good. This reward is a gift, as the Protestants say, but it is a gift because God set it as the end of man's action and because he sent Christ who won for us the power of meriting rewards.

Some Catholic pastors, who use the fund-raising literature under criticism by the Protestants, nevertheless have serious reservations about it. They feel that such appeals would do well to make clear the fundamental concept of the church—that no acts of charity alter the fact that satisfactions must be made for one's immoral acts and that justice must run its course. These Catholic pastors have not criticized the literature in their contacts with the laity, though it does not represent so balanced a theological position as their own.

While not promising forgiveness of sins or direct remission of punishment by the clergy in return for a gift of money, the literature does relate good works directly to specific rewards. For example, the Holy Family League of Charity in its appeal for funds for orphans usually distributes letters to members like this:

> DEAR LEAGUE MEMBER:
>
> In return for your generosity to the orphans, you are favored with rich blessings; you are remembered—every day—in the powerful prayers of more than five hundred orphan children; you are remembered also in weekly Masses, as well as special weekly devotions in the orphanage chapel; you can gain special indulgences.
>
> You have problems and difficulties, disappointments and sorrows; and yet, like other league members, you must often realize the unexpected courage and comfort that comes to you as a result of these orphan prayers.[32]

A leaflet of the Holy Family League announcing a Double Novena with "eighteen weeks of prayers by orphans and nuns" is entitled "Are You Satisfied with Your Life?" It asks, "Are you happy? If not do you want to be? Are you sickly? Then you want health. Are you a failure? Surely you want to be successful. . . . Have you a pet ambition? . . . Is God good to you?" The leaflet contains a petition sheet listing needs to be checked—"happiness," "suitable apartment," "happy death," and the like—which will be placed on the altar of the orphanage chapel for the Double Novena. The leaflet then says:

> God answers the prayers of orphans. Here is proof from what others have written to us: "Walked for the first time in two months . . . successful operation . . . cure of deafness . . . comfort and peace . . . my soldier son safe . . . doctors astonished at recovery . . . a lovely baby brightens our home . . . no longer worried or confused . . . my sweetheart promoted." [33]

The Holy Family League of Charity also sends to its members a card for the wallet which lists the benefits "As an Orphanland Helper." It notes that "*Orphans* and other League members pray for you every day . . . helpers with dues paid at time of death continue for five years as departed members. . . . Indulgences, plenary and partial, can be gained during life and at the hour of death." [34]

The Catholic pastors make no charges against the Protestant churches for manifesting a merit morality in their financial program. This does not concern them in the enunciation of Protestant heresies. Although financial appeals of the Protestant churches are sometimes related directly to a merit morality, the development has not been so greatly systematized and so intimately related to worship practices and to support of specific church projects as in the Catholic church. Some of the Protestant pastors preach that support of the church will "make us happier," "less frustrated," and "will lead to a more peaceful and just world in which to live." A debt-liquidation campaign pamphlet of the Second Congregational Church began its explanation of why people should support the drive with the words: "No other organization, religious or otherwise, offers so much for so little as does the Second Congregational Church." Yet within this church and in the majority of the other

Protestant churches the doctrine of "salvation by faith, not works," is fairly consistently expressed in the teaching of the ministers.

Polity and the Financial Practices of the Churches

The fund-raising methods of the Roman Catholic church are more highly rationalized and inexorable than those of the Protestant churches. The class factors may be of some importance in this development, but apparently of more direct force are the types of authority instituted by the churches themselves as expression of their religious beliefs.

The Catholic church has adopted in most parishes the envelope system by which members make voluntary contributions to the church. The system is used in all Protestant churches, but not in the sects. The Catholic envelope system is much more specific than the Protestant in its designation of the various church activities and organizations to be supported by gifts. Beyond the regular support of the Catholic parish, its priests and nuns, one or more causes or organizations outside the parish appeals each month for funds by means of special envelope offerings. A letter by the bishop is sent appealing for funds, or a representative of these organizations comes into the parish to make the various collections. For example, an envelope is designated each year for a subscription to the diocesan magazine. The Protestant churches have no such identification of the religious press with regular support of the church.

The Catholic priests administer a financial system in which specific stipends fixed by the Provincial Council, or by a conference of bishops with approval by the Pope, are received for the various sacraments. In the churches where the envelope system is used, a pew charge for Mass is designated, and in the laboring-class churches the charge is collected by laymen at the doors or in the pews. The Protestant churches do not designate specific fees for their functions.

The social pressure of public reports upon individual giving through notices on church bulletin boards of delinquent members and through the publication of the envelope contributions of each member and circulation of the report to all the church constituency is also much more widely used in the Catholic churches than in Protestant churches.[35] The Catholic appeals for funds are much more constant and comprehensive than in the Protestant churches.[36]

The official charismatic authority of the priests is so great and the organization of the financial apparatus so extensive, that socially compulsion is used despite lay protest. The greater sensitivity of the Protestant pastor to lay response and the highly personal basis of his authority militate against so extensive use of such methods in the Protestant church as in the Catholic church.

Comparative Financial Support by Members of the Churches

Religious relations are influenced not simply by the fund-raising methods of the respective churches, but also by the degree of their effectiveness, since the ability to develop property, to educate membership, to employ professional leadership are all dependent upon the financial resources of the institution.

Charges and countercharges are made by Protestants and Catholics as to the extent of financial support given by members of each group to support its church financially. The difficulty of securing data which is comparable on the financial contributions of Catholics and Protestants to their churches is so great that only slight attention should be given to the statistics available.[37]

It would appear that Protestants support their local churches financially more strongly than the Roman Catholics. The Catholic reliance upon gambling as a financial device may not be influenced simply by the class source of the church's membership, but also by the low level of response to traditional fund-raising devices in all class groups.

Property

Some indication of financial support by members of the religious movements can be obtained from data as to the property accumulated by the churches. Here again, the class basis of membership as well as differences in doctrines of the church are involved. Protestants have property now evaluated by the city assessor at $1,624,-670. The total value of the Roman Catholic property is similarly estimated at $3,591,700. The Protestants have accumulated property which in 1946 was the equivalent of $226.70 for each member. The Catholics had property in 1946 worth $93.70 per member.[38]

Many Protestants have taken pride in the fact that their church leaders are less preoccupied with securing funds for buildings. There is strong evidence in parish records and church histories that the Catholic leaders have been more vocal and have devoted considerably more energy than the Protestants to raising funds for church property. Yet the Protestant churches have developed in terms of their size of membership a more impressive quantity of property than the Catholics. The contrast in Protestant and Catholic property per member is impressive also because of the fact that much of Protestant funds went into community property—such as the Paper City hospital—which is not under Protestant church control, although the chief financial sources are Protestant. The explanation lies partly in the fact that most of the money for the Protestant property has been contributed by a relatively few wealthy people. This is best indicated by the fact that approximately one-fourth of the Protestant property wealth—a memorial chapel—was the gift of one man.

The achievement of a large building program chiefly through many small gifts rather than through a few large ones necessitate, in the minds of the priests, a tremendous and constant absorption in the task of accumulating property.[39] The Roman Catholic property is widely dispersed with little correlation of cost with the income level of the parish members. The most costly French church is in the poorest French parish; the second most valuable English-speaking parish church building is located in the parish with the fewest middle- and upper-class Catholic people.

The erection of the costly Catholic churches in Paper City has been accompanied by a proportionate growth of *esprit de corps* among Catholic rank and file and a respect for the power and authority of the church.[40] In the midst of the building drive, sharp criticism was expressed by many Protestants of the financial strain imposed on the poor, of the failure of Catholics to contribute to the social work and relief needs of the city because of their concentration upon building up church property, of the great contrast between the wealth being developed in the Catholic church and the poverty of the members.[41] But on the other hand the architectural dominance of the Catholic churches in the city became symbolic of a new social status of Catholics in the city;[42] there is an outspoken admiration, particularly among Protestant businessmen, for the wealth, the financial acumen, thrift, and persistence of the Catholic church. Respect for the power of property and wealth is great in all areas of Paper City culture. The financial practices of the churches are of very great importance in the total impact of the churches upon the culture of the community.

Chapter 10

Tolerance and Religious Liberty

Profound religious diversity exists in Paper City—a fact of enormous importance in the life of any community. But even more important is how men live with this fact. Do they refuse to admit it? Are they unhappy with it, seeking a unity of religious belief? What do they say about religions other than their own? What means do they use to propagate their own faith? Do they seek association and co-operation with members of other faiths? If so, on what terms? These are the questions which now concern us, with particular attention being directed toward the thoughts and actions of the leaders of the Roman Catholic and Protestant churches.

Catholic Approach to Religious Structure of the City

The ultimate goal of the Roman Catholic church, as the priests of Paper City understand it, is to overcome the religious diversity of the community and to develop a common culture unified about the Roman Catholic faith. The Catholic church, whether in a minority or majority status in Paper City, has maintained the fervid desire to become an all-embracing institution capable of directing the whole of the religious and moral life of the community. The ideal or preferred religious community of the priests is not that in which men receive religious knowledge from a variety of sources, but one in which there is a unity of religious loyalty and belief in the true church.

This ideal does not exclude the prudential "acceptance" of the existence of the Protestant churches in Paper City and in the nation, and of other associations claiming to be "secular" or "religious," which seek to influence the culture. The priests expect that the Protestant heresy will continue to exist in their lifetime of work and beyond. They assert that the operative ideal for them is not elimination of the Protestant faith and achievement of a united Christendom in Paper City; it is the achievement of a Catholic ethos or frame of mind throughout the society. This does not necessitate the elimination of the Protestant churches. It does mean in the lifetime of the priests the extension of recognition of the spiritual superiority of the Catholic church and the reduction in influence of the Protestant churches over the life of the city.

"The core of the matter in the relations of the churches," a rabbi in the city observed, "is the Catholic proposition of 'You serve God in your way and we in His.'" On religious principle, no other religious or secular group can be regarded or treated by the true Roman Catholic as on a parity with the Roman church in the eyes of God, or more importantly, as a source of religious truth not obtainable in the true church.

Some of the curates expressed an appreciation of Protestantism in Paper City as a challenge which keeps the Catholic church alert and active without critically threatening its liberty. But this appreciation is not an expression of respect for or recognition of the Protestant religion on the basis that in controversies between the two faiths some error as well as some truth might conceivably exist on both sides. The non-Catholic position is at best to be regarded as discerning some truth already known by the church, but this truth is always inexorably compounded with error.

The statements of the Catholic clergy have sought to reconcile two fundamental principles and their related tenets. The first is that Catholicism is the only true religion, that although the church does not claim exclusive knowledge of truth, it claims to be the only institution with whole and exact knowledge of religious and moral laws.[1] Ideas or activities which do not correspond to the truth or the laws of morality have no right to exist, to be propagated and expanded in influence.

The second fundamental principle is that of the law of love, or fraternal charity. Persons reared outside the visible Catholic church are to be treated kindly by Catholics because of the law of fraternal charity, that regardless of creed or race every man has a claim to the supernatural love of his fellowman, because he is made in the image of God and is at least potentially the recipient of the church's sanctifying grace. Those outside the visible Catholic church will be treated mercifully by God because of their invincible ignorance, by their belonging to the Catholic church even without knowing it (for there are several ways of belonging to the church) and by their discernment of part of the church's truth apart from her teaching.

How can the devout Catholic priest or layman serve both of these principles? Some have developed what appear to them to be neat and balanced statements reconciling the principles for their major area of responsibility.[2] Other leaders are in considerable tension and confusion as to the ways in which these principles can best be served in concrete situations.[3] Is evil to be tolerated or is it to be repressed by private coercive measures and the power of the state? Or is repression of evil not to be regarded by the church as an absolute, God permitting evil to exist in order to serve higher or more general goods, such as love between men?

The general picture which emerges from the action of the Catholic clergy toward other faith groups is that the principle of fraternal charity often tends to be subordinated or submerged, and understanding of its requirements transformed by the church's promotion of its creedal superiority. The fostering of a society with diverse religions seeking an opportunity voluntarily to associate and share religious truth cannot be accepted on religious principle as necessary for the maintenance of fraternal charity. So persons making the principle of spiritual authority the center of their religion always threaten the structural bases of charity and community.

Yet the Catholic church's accommodation to religious diversity has become a part of the city's life. Many people now think of the variety of faiths as a clear and ultimate objective of the church rather than in part, at least, the necessary accommodation of Catholicism to the city's history and culture.

The Catholic approach to religious diversity reflects a variety of complicated factors. The Catholic clergy are now the leaders of the majority religion in the city, but they are also leaders of a people many of whom have had long experience as ethnic, economic and religious minorities. They are accustomed to the social isolation occasioned by the efforts of "native" groups to limit their activity. They are accustomed to the minorities' cohesive and defensive drives for power. The clergy are also leaders of many Catholics who have achieved high social status and influence, some wanting to use their new position aggressively, others feeling a tremendous stake in the community harmony and the status quo. Ethnic and class background of membership and leadership are deeply involved in the actions of the Catholic church toward other groups (as will be noted in detail in Chapters 12 and 13), but the church's claim to religious superiority and universalism is undoubtedly a determining factor.

Catholic Education About Other Religions

What one religion has to say about another influences the attitudes of its members toward the liberties extended to the other religion and toward association and co-operation with its representatives. The Catholic church believes this to be so. It devotes considerable attention in its church press, in parochial-school classes and parish societies for young people and adults to Catholic apologetics and indoctrination which will anticipate religious questions that may be raised in contacts with Protestants.

The children before teen age are taught only Catholic doctrine on the theory that any mention of the claims of other faiths or their beliefs about the Catholic faith will simply confuse them. But the children are informed with some regularity, as the pastor of St. Jerome's parish phrased it, that "unfortunately non-Catholics are not taught these truths and that Catholics should feel sorry for them."

In adult education, no systematic presentation of any aspect of the doctrine of the Protestant religion is given; refutation is chiefly made of Protestant charges about the nature of the Catholic faith, or brief caricatures of Protestant beliefs are presented before their refutation. For example, an article in the diocesan journal about "Faith and Works" will describe Protestantism as a religion holding "that only faith is necessary, not works," and will then give the Catholic doctrine of the relation of faith and works.[4]

There are two major themes in diocesan literature about the nature of Protestantism. The first is the highlighting of the differences between Catholics and Protestants to the virtual exclusion of common characteristics and values in order to exalt the superiority and truth of the Catholic faith over all other religions and "sources of error." The second is an emphasis upon the threats to the religious security of the Catholic minority by the bigotry and aggressiveness in some Protestantism and by certain forces, chiefly communist, using Protestantism, and the necessity for a strong and cohesive defense of the rights of the true faith.[5]

The first pattern of belief is indicated clearly in the church's treatment of the sources of the Protestant movement, the Reformation, or "revolt" as it is termed by many Catholics. The second is highly evident in the approach to Protestant critics. The general picture given of the Protestant Reformation is unvarying wherever it appears in the Catholic educational system; it appears most starkly in the diocesan press. The following is a paraphrase, with direct quotations, of the version given to students in the American history textbook used in the parochial schools in Paper City.[6]

> The so-called Protestant Reformation was a religious revolt, not a reform, which "cut up northern Europe into scores of petty sects, all separated except in their common hatred of the older Catholicism." The history of the revolt is to be considered "as this hatred was carried over to America and persists even today in many localities of our country."
>
> The immediate causes of the "Protestant Revolt" were partly economic, partly political, partly religious, partly the personal ambition of leaders. In terms of economic sources, Europe was growing rich and hard, and among the prosperous individuals "there was a growing envy of the riches of the Church and irritation with her taxes, her assessments, and, what is more important, with her restraints on individual cupidity."
>
> The political sources of "the revolt" were chiefly, according to the textbook, "the spirit of nationalism," which "sought to keep within its own frontiers the source of all religious power. It did not look with favor upon membership in an international organization, even though the Church was international because its Divine Founder had so willed it." (The diocesan journal, the *Catholic Mirror*, summarized the rise of the Lutheran faith in an article on the Protestant Reformation as follows: "The new religion based on justification by faith alone was able to make inroads under the stimulus of power-politics and armed might."[7])

The "religious reason for revolt" was the resentment of the authority of the church in civil matters. Two important complaints mentioned in the textbook (but not dealt with in the accounts of the diocesan press) "were the avarice of churchmen and the failure of many of them to make their lives agree with the principles they preached." These complaints were against "individual members of the Church and not against the Church."

The "sorry business" of the revolt was begun by a German monk, Martin Luther. "His break with the Church was occasioned by envy because the Pope had entrusted the preaching of an indulgence to the Dominicans, and Luther was himself an Augustinian." [8] Other Protestant leaders were Zwingli, "an apostate priest" in Switzerland, "best remembered for his smashing of works of art," and Calvin, a "morose and gloomy man," who placed the "shadow of eternal damnation on everything he touched" and "burned Servetus, a Spanish refugee, because he dared to differ in religious belief."

The text does not describe the results of the Protestant revolt or reformation; but the booklets used in parish instruction, the diocesan journal, the lectures of parish priests, the local Knights of Columbus paper report on disastrous consequences. Luther was so disturbed by events following his revolt that he regretted his break with the Catholic church and "even advised his mother to die in the Catholic faith," [9] a Sunday-school leaflet notes. When this "renegade monk, Luther, started the Reformation, he struck no blow for peace; he threw open the doors for numerous troubles that plague humanity. Centuries ago when the world was Catholic there was a tribunal which was accepted by all. The world is no longer united in religion and men seek in vain to establish a court because they have forgotten God." Thus a Catholic priest and Lenten lecturer informed the Knights of Columbus.[10]

The responsibility which the Protestant Reformation should assume for modern war is made even more pointed by an editorial in the *Catholic Mirror:* "World War I and II, with the burden of all our modern woes, were the logical outcome of Luther's teaching. . . . The line from Luther to Hitler runs straight. Hitler brought the doctrines of Martin Luther to inevitable conclusion." [11]

As to the effects of the Protestant revolt upon religious beliefs in general, the official diocesan magazine makes this editorial observation:

> Is it not true—and the question is here asked only in sorrow—that outside the Catholic church the great religious truths have been one by one done to death and buried by the preachers? Count only some of the casualties: the inspiration of the Bible—the divinity of Christ—even the existence of a Personal God—the facts of hell—the next world, eternity with God, as a man's supreme concern.[12]

Catholic pastors sometimes observe to Catholic laymen, often in as blunt fashion as the pastor of Holy Rosary parish, that "the Protestants have no religion. All they do is negative. They were called Protestants originally and that's what they are. They just exist to protest against the Catholic church."

The Catholic pastors' picture of Protestant doctrinal diversity in comparison with Catholic unity of belief is epitomized in the words of Father Hall, the hero in *Let's See the Other Side*, a pamphlet widely recommended to Catholic laymen. Father Hall asks people who want to be acquainted with "the other side":

> Which other side? Shall I study . . . High Church or Low Church Episcopalianism? Shall I run with the fundamental Methodists? Or with the Unitarians who have scrapped the divinity and the miracles of Christ? Shall I be a Seventh Day Adventist or a Holy Roller? Or should I perhaps follow the new revelations of Judge Rutherford, Jehovah's Witness?[13]
>
> But here we are, we Catholics, united in all the essentials, unswerving in our devotion to an historic truth . . . and there are our adversaries, who agree on nothing, are united on nothing . . . and get together in name only, a name that is the most ridiculous of negativeness—Non-Catholics.[14]

The second major theme in Catholic education places Protestantism in the context of "increasing and widespread opposition to the Catholic Church." "Forces of bigotry working overtime" within Protestantism, but not representing all Protestants, are an important part of this increasing anti-Catholicism. Protestant opposition to the church is but part of the "world-wide ideological war within the shooting war" with communism as the major enemy.

If the Catholic layman in Paper City has absorbed his church's education, he thinks of himself not as being on the side of a majority (which is the situation both in the diocese and in Paper City itself [15]) or even of a disciplined minority with power to deny the freedom of others, but as the victim of persecution. The diocesan magazine, parochial school texts, official histories of the diocese re-create frequently the Catholic massacres by Protestants in Ireland, the martyrdom of Catholics at the hands of New England Puritans, the Bible Belt KKK's (Ku Klux Klan), and the APA's (American Protective Association).[16] Much of the doctrine in the Catholic press is presented as an answer to "false charges" of other religions; the criticism of another religion takes place always in the context of a Catholic answer to attacks by that religion, but the substance of the charge is not repeated.[17] The church press has kept alive the Catholic sense of outside threats and has heightened the internal cohesion, the tendency toward isolation and centralization of control within the Catholic group.[18]

The theme of constant attack on Catholics by Protestants is usually accompanied in the church's literature by optimistic assurances that the Catholic faith is growing in influence as the major minority in a nation composed of a multitude of groups and of "seventy million Americans who profess no religion at all," and as the faith increasingly acknowledged by authoritative leaders as the source of democracy, freedom and strength in the nation.[19]

The official journal of the diocese and important Catholic leaders in Paper City have often associated Protestant criticism of Catholicism with communism. They do this by claims both that the criticism "gives encouragement to the communists to attack the church" and that it is inspired by men sympathetic to communism or ignorant of the way in which they are being used by communists.[20] A *Catholic Mirror* reprint from *Our Sunday Visitor* observes, for example:

> . . . in many respects they [Protestant attacks] have been inspired by communists, even though churchmen have hardly been conscious of it. The blasts against the Vatican and the Catholic Hierarchy of various countries from Moscow are always featured and amplified by communist organs in the United States; they are carried in the secular press as news, and because they are not answered they feed the prejudices of people ill-disposed towards the Church.

> But any attack on the Catholic Church by communists, atheists, and other anti-Christian organizations injures the cause of Protestanism and helps the cause of communism, whose chief non-party support comes from bigotry, hatred, religious disunity.[21]

Many of the forces of bigotry working within Protestantism or using its symbols are said to be "financed and aided by Red agencies." [22] The readers of the *Catholic Mirror* during the 1945-47 period might have assumed that the *Protestant,* extreme left-wing magazine without official status in any denomination, was one of the major Protestant publications, since it was referred to more often in that period than any other Protestant publication.

A statement issued to the Associated Press by the editor of the *Catholic Mirror* after a lecture by Bishop G. Bromley Oxnam said: "Bishop Oxnam is a fellow-traveler of the communists and uses the word 'democracy' as a good Soviet does. His approval of lax divorce laws and of contraception would make his Protestant ancestors turn over in their graves." [23]

It would appear that in much diocesan literature which deals with the relations of Catholics and Protestants, the tendency is toward posing the two religions as representing truth against error, white against black, religion against secularism (or Protestantism, for they are largely synonymous in diocesan literature), the true faith against the enemy. Thus "It is Catholicism—and only Catholicism—which offers untemporizing and effective resistance to the vicious violence of Caesar against the Church." [24] "It is Catholicism—and Catholicism alone—which still logically believes in those words of the Declaration of Independence about 'inalienable rights.' " [25]

Under the influence of this material, a rather pervasive attitude becomes evident among Catholic laymen who rise to leadership of the parish societies. It is epitomized in the words of the president of a city-wide Catholic Action society: "When it comes to religion, we are 100 per cent right. Period. And if you're 100 per cent right, then you should never yield on a point." [26] The giving-up of certain tenets of the faith while holding to others becomes an act of treason and of succumbing to communist devices.[27] And fraternal charity for a person of another belief sometimes becomes only pity and sufferance.

Catholic Interpretation of Majority Rule

In situations where the Catholic church is under direct attack (as by Oxnam), the clergy and professional leadership usually interpret the Bill of Rights and American freedom as that of protection of "minorities against the caprices of an unjust majority." [28] In Paper City, however, where Catholics have been in the majority for several decades, the principle of majority rule over community morals is more frequently and generally advanced, by church leaders in positions of public influence, as a basis for restraint of minorities and of special favors for the church.

The principle as developed by the Catholic leaders gives little attention to the corresponding principle of majority responsibility for the maintenance of the liberties and opportunities of non-Catholic groups. The use of the principle is indicated by the priests' response to questions about the basis of the Catholic church's use of economic force to oppose Margaret Sanger's appearance in Paper City in 1940 and its use of the power of the state in Italy to give special privileges to the Catholic church over Protestants.[29] A representative statement of the Catholic clergy follows:

> In a Catholic community such as Paper City, where a Catholic moral code is accepted by the majority of the community, such people as Margaret Sanger should not be brought in to disturb the public. The Catholic church should do all it can to keep such people from appearing. It isn't a matter of religious liberty, but the preservation of the moral and religious laws that are a part of the life of a community. We are against the communists for the same reason. They have no right to speak wherever and whenever they please, because they seek to destroy the government and the public institutions of the majority of the people.

The Catholic clergy believe that the Vatican opposed equal religious liberty for Protestants in Italy on the same basis of "majority rule." One pastor expressed a characteristic opinion:

> In Italy, Catholic religion and morals are the basis of the country and of the people's way of life, for the church is in the majority. In a country where this is so, the church should be favored in the laws and opportunities of the state. The Protestants in Italy have gone out of their way to be nasty. They say there is nothing to the Catholic religion. They put a Methodist school up right across the

hill from the Vatican just as if flaunting us. This kind of action by a minority naturally makes the Vatican doubt that they should have as much liberty as the Catholics in the country.

Catholic Concepts of Religious Liberty

The common denominator of all anti-Catholicism, as the Paper City clergy and the diocesan press see it, is the "liberalism which will not limit man's choice of what he may profess." [30] The church, the *Catholic Mirror* affirms, is "for liberty which is the right of men to seek truth, to seek God and to acknowledge the divine authority to which obedience is due." [31] Since the church alone understands the whole and true nature of religious truth, it can be said that "the Catholic Church alone has defended religious freedom." [32]

The *Catholic Mirror* notes that the Committee for Constitutional Government prints and distributes an essay by a sixteen-year-old girl on "What American Democracy Means to Me." The girl writes that as an American she is at liberty to "go to any church I wish to—or none at all." The journal then editorializes:

> Taking that to mean that she considers herself, as an American, free to believe in God or to deny His existence, we must conclude that with that as a premise this school girl will have trouble reaching objective conclusions on the meaning of American democracy.
>
> Our rights are God-given. How then can we be free to ignore God? Are we free to obey or disobey the law? Throw out God and American democracy goes to pot.
>
> The essay we quoted above was copyrighted by the "Committee for Constitutional Government, Inc." The poor simpletons. Using the law of the land to protect beliefs which if put into practice will sabotage the government they are working to defend.[33]

The priests of the city accept the constitutional liberty of conscience for such people as atheists as a part of American Catholicism; but they interpret this liberty to be a private matter, not to be given public or institutional expression. One Catholic pastor voiced the prevailing interpretation thus:

> In this country where all profess the liberty of conscience, no one has a right to prevent a man from professing his views as an individual, if he is honest. But we ought not to let atheists speak on the radio, or be given the opportunity to reach great numbers of people if we claim to be a Christian country. We can't be atheist and Chris-

tian at the same time. I guess as long as it's in the Constitution we couldn't hold it's not in the Constitution to permit an atheist to speak. But if this is a Christian country, we ought not to allow an atheist to go out and propagate his beliefs. We should say it's all right to be an atheist if you keep your thoughts in your conscience.

The basic presupposition of the church's approach to religious diversity in Paper City is that religious liberty is a liberty different from other liberties—a liberty belonging to the supernatural order, not to the natural or civil order—and that the church must claim superiority in the supernatural order.[34]

When non-Catholic religious groups use their freedom to advocate publicly a position which seriously challenges the religious beliefs of the Catholic church, as in birth-control controversies in Paper City, then "civil liberties are no longer involved. The issue has become a religious one in which God's law is defied, and the church cannot give in to the defiance of God's law if it has the power to prevent it." [35] "Divine law is always above civil liberties."

So long as men in the civil or political area propagate what the Catholic clergy believe to be civil or political ideas which do not involve matters of "faith and morals," then these men should have equal liberties. But "when religious issues are raised, that's another matter. All groups should not be given the same opportunity to propagate religious ideas. The Vatican policy on the new constitution [established by the civil government in Italy in 1946] was right. It was for equal civil liberties for all men of good will who act according to their conscience and not maliciously or prejudicially, but not for equal religious liberty for all in a dominantly Catholic country." [36]

Means of Advancing the Catholic Faith

There is no question but that every issue involving faith and morals, as the church sees it, is an important area of action for the true Catholic. The problem remains as to what means are considered morally permissible by Catholics in achievement of the church's objectives. The basic issue here is whether the goal of religious unity through acceptance of the church's authority is to be advanced by noncoercive and persuasive methods or through coercive or forceful restraint, such as economic boycott, denial of public meeting places through influence upon the government, and the like.[37]

There is no doubt in the minds of the priests or most lay leaders of parish and city-wide Catholic societies that such private non-governmental coercive action as economic boycott is, from a moral standpoint, permissible to enforce the laws of the church against non-Catholics—"just as it is permissible," one priest noted, "to go to war if the cause is in the eyes of the church right." The question for many of the Catholic leaders is whether the action will be effective in achieving a limitation of error and whether this particular type of action will jeopardize the winning of converts to Catholicism or to a greater truth than that enforced by the coercive action. Two-thirds of the Catholic pastors expressed the belief that witness to the principle of fraternal charity might be more important than economic action against non-Catholics over the birth-control issue, if non-Catholics appeared to be particularly offended or aroused by this type of pressure.

Only a minority of the priests—one-third of the pastors—have regularly used the economic boycott as a tactic to limit or check the action of non-Catholics. These men have used and threatened to use the considerable economic power of the church as a consumer of goods (such as groceries) and services (such as banking facilities) to fight supporters of the birth-control movement and signers of petitions for a referendum on the transportation of parochial students in public buses. Some priests have fostered the boycotting action by laymen by informing them of certain businessmen or employees who were acting against the moral laws of the church and therefore should not be supported by Catholics.

The support of overt, coercive measures, such as economic boycotts, against non-Catholics comes chiefly from Catholics whose main social activity is found within the parish societies of the church, whose occupations do not require harmonious relations between people of various religions for success, and whose education is of high-school or grade-school level. Some Catholics who participate in such pressure report that they were "unaware of their power as Catholics until it was pointed out by the priests." But such devices as economic boycott are part of minority tactics which, although used in Paper City now principally in issues which are given a religious angle, have also been used by municipal employees (mostly Catholic) against retail store owners who as members of the Taxpayers Association, sought to freeze or cut their salaries; by newspaper readers against the political position of the local newspaper; and in other cases.[38]

The boycotting action against Protestants is usually undertaken by laymen who see it as a necessary and wholly laudatory defense of the church against "bigotry." They do not question in any serious way the rightness of the moral position of the clergy. For example, the action against a Protestant grocer who signed the petition written by two Baptist ministers calling for a referendum on the transportation of parochial students in public buses was promoted by a Catholic layman. He observed:

> I always thought of Mr. Edwards [the grocer] as a nice fellow until I saw his name in the paper as a signer of the petition, but now I think of him as a religious bigot. If you are fighting bigots and you know you are right, then where do you draw the line? I don't know exactly, but I'm sure you don't draw it at political pressure or economic boycott.

The priests make their decisions about the use of methods of influencing the activity of non-Catholics with a highly prudential sensitivity to the public reaction, the different attitudes of laymen in their parish, and the relative influence of Protestant groups. The senior priest of Paper City observed when seeking to explain his own willingness to use economic boycott in the community that the "methods of combatting error, the severity of the priests in keeping the laws of the church, depend upon the nature of the country, the community, the people in it."

The priests are quite aware that the restraining influence of such overtly coercive action as economic boycott, although of high concern to the Protestant leaders, is a minor aspect in the total weight or impact of the Catholic church upon the life of the community. Much more important to the actual liberties or opportunities of Protestants to influence the community are the actions of Catholics practicing their faith within the press, business, labor unions, social work, municipal government and the public schools.

This type of "internal" influence is looked upon with most favor by the Catholic laymen in positions of major influence in the community. Overt Catholic action of the boycott variety is referred to by Catholic business and professional people as that of "ignorant masses," "chest wallopers," the "lunatic fringe." The priests who foster such methods are also regarded as belonging to another era of minority Catholicism; these priests significantly are located in the middle-lower parishes, not in the upper-income parishes.

A Protestant bank director asked a Catholic priest whether he would like to talk with a Protestant clerk who had signed a petition written by his pastor for a referendum on the public transportation of parochial school students. (The bank director wished, in his words, "to build a backfire so that an economic boycott by Catholics would not take place against my bank as was at the time taking place against another bank where a Protestant clerk had signed the petition.") The priest could reply that he did not wish to speak to the clerk, because he understood "how people sign petitions without knowing what is in them."[39] The priest made his decision with clear knowledge of the power of the church, which the director had acknowledged, a power indicated sometimes by the action of zealous laymen and priests as well as by more subtle and indirect influences.

On occasion priests have stopped coercive action taken by laymen to enforce what the laymen thought was a religious position when the action did not support church policy. For example, after the Alfred E. Smith-Herbert Hoover presidential campaign, a Protestant clerk of a Protestant-owned shoestore remarked in the hearing of a Catholic customer that the Catholic church had voted the nuns for Smith but that this was still not enough to elect him. The customer engaged the clerk in a fistfight in the store. The story spread in the city and the store was boycotted by Catholics. The owner went to the senior priest to explain the incident and solicit his aid in ending the boycott, reporting to him that his business had fallen at least 70 per cent because of the boycott. The priest had a score of nuns from the diocesan children's home buy shoes at the store at various intervals during the following day—and the boycott ended. The clerk was dismissed, and he moved from the city soon afterward.

The varying Catholic pressures upon two Protestant sects—the Jehovah's Witnesses and the Polish Evangelistic Assembly—reflect to some extent Catholic sensitivity to comparative and shifting factors of power and influence in religious relations.

The Jehovah's Witnesses, with a nationally demonstrated capacity for vociferous defense of their religious liberty, have experienced no pressure from Catholic action in the community. They sell their magazines with headlines announcing "Ireland Divided and Confused by Religion" and "Anti-Clericalism Sweeping Over Italy" on street corners. They have held a regional convention attended by seven hundred in Paper City. They have been assured by the chief of police, a Catholic, that, if they have any coercive action taken against their distribution of literature, they should let him know personally.

By contrast, Polish Catholic converts who formed a sect now called the Polish Evangelistic Assembly had difficulty in obtaining a central room for meetings in the city and in securing public announcement of their meetings, in part because of pressure from Catholic priests.

The group sought a room in a building managed by a nondenominational agency, the Family Welfare League. The league president consulted the mayor, who advised him that the Catholic church would not co-operate with the agency if the Polish group were allowed to use the hall. The league president then conferred with the senior priest of the city, who confirmed the mayor's judgment. The agency then refused the hall to the Polish Assembly.

When the Polish group was able to locate another public room, in a building partially abandoned for structural reasons, the hour and place of the group's meeting was announced in a local newspaper, along with announcements of other religious services. After the first appearance of the announcement it was withdrawn by the newspaper. A member of the newspaper staff after much questioning finally informed the minister of the Assembly that the pastor of the Polish Catholic church had protested against the announcement on the basis that it was not good for the faith of the Polish people and that they resented the announcement. A few other Catholics also protested.

A few weeks later the announcement was restored to the paper. An employee of the paper explained to the Polish Assembly pastor that this was done when a Protestant manufacturer, hearing of the action by the newspaper, threatened to withdraw his company's advertising from the paper if the announcement was not published. The financial pressure on the paper was then explained by a representative of the paper to the Polish priest, and the announcement was restored without further Catholic protests.[40]

Protestant Approach to Religious Structure of City

Most of the Protestant clergy in Paper City believe that a community and a nation with a diverse religious structure are essential for the discovery of truth, maintenance of freedom and development of strong religious commitment. The survival of the Protestant type of religious institution depends upon the preference by all groups for a highly pluralistic society of autonomous units. The dominating theological conviction in the Protestant position is the belief that God is not at the disposal of any one individual or group and that no religious institution can encompass the whole of religious truth. Society must be built upon genuine respect for the religious judgments of others—"the recognition," as one minister said, "that I may be wrong and that the next man has a right to his beliefs because he may be right."

Thus the pastor of Paper City's largest Protestant church observed in a sermon on "The Basic Principle of Protestantism":

> The pattern of authoritarianism contained such elements as these: UNIFORMITY of religious worship. Both state and church (for the two were united) insisted that every citizen had to worship God only in the approved manner. OBEDIENCE was expected of the private individual, CONFORMITY to the COMMAND of the higher authorities who presumably were alone competent to declare what was the right and true faith and worship. These authorities laid down what was ORTHODOX and what, accordingly, was to be humbly received by every Christian. These authorities were the CLERGY, supported by the MONARCHY. If an individual showed any tendency toward independence of thought or belief there were ways of COERCION, for the pattern of authoritarianism was finally that of INTOLERANCE.
>
> The pattern of private judgment was quite a different one, and it contained such elements as these: DIVERSITY of religious worship, for with the individual free to think and to explore for himself there are bound to be diverse opinions. Christians banded themselves together in voluntary associations where they all met as equals. They believed themselves to be competent to determine what was the true Christian

> faith. They were a body of LAY men and women, and their ministers were in essence only lay men set apart for the ministry of the Word. There was among them a spirit of DEMOCRACY and FREEDOM. It was a way that taught and required TOLERANCE. . . . Nor would I have anyone think that I regard one of them wholly bad and the other wholly good. As a matter of historical fact, authoritarianism does not always end up in intolerance, just as the right of private judgment does not always mean tolerance.

However, a minority of Protestant religious leaders look upon the diversity of churches in Paper City as a condition of error, in which the truth—focused in their own religion—has been rejected. These leaders represent the Protestant sects (Jehovah's Witnesses, Polish Evangelistic Assembly, Gospel Hall), the cult (Christian Science) and the Lutheran Church.

Protestant Education About Religious Diversity

Most educational activities and literature originating in Paper City Protestant churches and intended for laymen have dealt comparatively little with the nature of Catholicism and the approach to be made to it. No systematic and sustained attempt is made to immunize members against specific "errors" of the other faiths.

On the other hand, some of the denominational Sunday school literature coming into Paper City in recent years has shown a greater concern or preoccupation with the problems raised by Catholicism than with Protestant relations to any other group in American culture.[41] Denominations which have been making intensive efforts to understand their history and the theological sources of their movements have concentrated in some Sunday school lessons on the issues in the Reformation. Vital differences and conflicts between the Catholic and Protestant faiths have been stressed at least as much as the areas of agreement. For example, in one denomination's literature for senior and intermediate levels, responsibilities for intergroup tension are clearly shared in "recognition of the common tendencies to pride and arrogance in men." But the fact that the Roman Catholic and Protestant denominations do not work together is attributed largely to the "official and rigid position" of the Catholic church.

Within the Sunday schools and regular adult discussion groups of the three major Protestant churches, the education on Catholicism has been confined in the past five years to a forum conducted by a Roman Catholic layman, a Jew and a Protestant. Some literature has been prepared by denominational and interdenominational national offices of the churches about religious relations, but none of the church pastors or religious education workers have used this material in the youth or adult education programs during the past five years.

Various unofficial groups in the Protestant churches are producing material, some of it strongly critical of the Catholic faith and expressing great alarm at the influence of Catholicism upon American life. However, literature produced by the *Christian Century*, Protestants and Other Americans United for Separation of Church and State, Religious Liberty Association and *Converts* Magazine (these vary considerably in mood and competence) is not circulated among laymen by the clergy in Paper City as regular study material for education classes or for general readings.

The only education most Protestants receive in their churches on religious relations is from very occasional references by the minister in sermons to doctrinal areas of agreement and disagreement between their own religion and Catholicism. This is never done as a systematic analysis of the way in which different theological assumptions and social sources influence the relations of the churches in the community. Eighty per cent of the ministers report that no more than two of their sermons a year deal explicitly with doctrinal likenesses and differences in the two major religions. The possibilities of abuse of power and position by all religious groups is a major theme in these sermons, and the history of bigotry within Protestant ranks in early New England is often developed.[42]

Sermon manuscripts evidence an increasing consciousness also of the Protestant minority position and of concern for restraint to be exercised by the majority faith. One pastor was so agitated by Catholic pressure that he observed, "The most dangerous trend in America—and the one that is headed for national disaster if not stopped—is not anti-Jewish, anti-Negro, or anti-Catholic bigotry, but anti-Protestant bigotry."

Most converts to Protestant churches receive no systematic or formal religious instruction when they become members.[43] In the Protestant church drawing most heavily for its membership from

Catholic converts, no instruction comparing Roman Catholic and Protestant doctrine or institutional policies is given to new members. Approximately two-fifths of the church pastors say they make some comparison of Protestant and Roman Catholic theology in classes for new members.

Protestant educational policy reflects to some extent the assumption of a pluralistic religious society in which each group operates its own affairs with a great deal of autonomy. It reflects also in a number of churches the desire to avoid "highly controversial topics," in the educational life of the church or "charges of intolerance." The religious education director of the largest Protestant church said:

> Discussion comparing Roman Catholicism and Protestantism makes for enemies and bad feeling. People in our Sunday schools have friends that are Catholic and they are apt to go out of here and say their teacher said such and such about the Catholics. That would lead to misunderstanding. I personally wouldn't risk talking Catholic-Protestant differences in a town like this.

In contrast to the other Protestant churches, the Lutherans, who make a claim similar to the Roman Catholics' of having the only religious institution without creedal error, conduct a systematic education of laymen in "the errors of the Roman Catholic church." [44]

Protestant Concepts of Religious Liberty

The Protestant pastors are of the general conviction that genuine religious liberty exists in a community when beliefs are propagated "competitively," to use their favorite descriptive word. By this they mean that there is a genuine give and take, a rivalry for truth creative for all, and a peaceful adjustment of differences without pressure, coercion or fear. The increasing intransigence of the Protestant pastors against any act of the Catholic church which increases its influence can only be understood from the fact that the pastors are convinced the Catholic clergy in Paper City are not in competition with them, but in conflict—that they would, were the Protestant churches weaker, seek to reduce Protestant liberty and public witness as an act of Catholic loyalty to "truth" and triumph against "error."

Most of the Protestant pastors—the major exceptions are the Lutheran and sect pastors—stress that they do not know what over the years would be the result of full religious liberty in a city. "The result could even be the loss of one's religious faith as he now knows it," according to a Baptist pastor. "But a vital religion cannot be produced by destroying the freedom to deny faith. If a church believes in religious liberty, it must permit people to do what it claims is evil, stupid or nonreligious." The pastor of the Second Congregational Church believes that "the whole secular drift in American life is a part of Protestantism, not Catholicism, in the sense that if we are to let people think in their own way, then we must also give them the right to deny all religious reality."

Protestant Means of Achieving Religious Liberty

Catholic action poses for Protestant pastors the kind of questions about the relation of power and liberty with which they find it very difficult to deal. All but two of the Protestant church pastors and sect leaders reject "the use of coercion or pressure by laymen or clergy on people who differ with them in religious conviction."

Most pastors claim that there are distinctively religious means of influencing other people, of expressing deep convictions, and that a church can and should confine itself to them. These are worship, teaching, preaching, publishing the gospel—activities listed in their description of religious liberty.[45] The tension most Protestant pastors envision for a "genuine religious community" does not involve the kind which takes place between institutions more rigorously organized than their own.

Such experiences as the Polish Evangelistic Assembly's efforts to achieve freedom of assembly and the First Congregational Church's involvement in the Sanger incident have given Protestant religious leaders some reason to reconsider the relation of religious liberty to economic influence and discipline of belief to freedom of belief. Protestant ministers were asked whether they would consider it morally permissible for them to ask Protestant laymen to use their economic power, as did the businessman who used his influence in behalf of the Polish Evangelistic Assembly, in order to resist what the ministers felt was a severe infringement of religious liberty or of a moral principle. Their answers gave qualified support to the idea:

As a matter of principle, I think I could sanction use of economic pressure if I thought a matter of morals or religious liberty was involved. But in policy, I can't think of an instance in which it would be desirable to use economic pressure. In the instance of the Polish Evangelistic Assembly, I imagine the newspaper could have been handled in some other way. It just never crossed my mind to ask a layman to use such a thing as economic boycott. I'm totally dumb, if I thought I should, as to how I would go about getting it done. [Pastor of the Episcopal Church]

I just don't think I can answer the question [about the use of economic boycott to restrain infringement of religious liberty]. Emil Brunner has pointed out that Protestants don't have any theory of justice and I guess he is right. I'm just not clear in my thinking at this point. I don't think meeting the pressure of a Catholic priest upon a paper with counterpressure of economic boycott was what Jesus taught.

The more I think about it, I suppose that there would be some situations, such as the Catholics' actions against Mrs. Sanger, when counter economic or political pressure might be used. But I'd have to know exactly what kind of pressure was to be used before I would support it. [Pastor of a Congregational church.]

There are situations when it is necessary to deal with religious relations in Paper City on the level of simple justice when no higher level can be achieved, when economic power is used to counter economic power for religious interests. But we must always work for a transformation of the relations into a finer expression of love of neighbor. [Pastor of a Congregational church]

A Ministerial Association's committee on religious and civil liberties existed for five years (1934-39) and then dissolved, reporting there were no issues or infringements to be investigated in the city. The phenomenon looked for was a rare overt incident, not the complex of factors which make for comparative influence of religion in a culture and mold their relations.

A few pastors have at times articulated to laymen the broad and complex ramifications of religious liberty in Paper City, but they have done this largely in private conversation and letters rather than public discussions. The approach of these pastors is indicated in a letter written by the minister of the Second Congregational Church to a paper-mill owner after a conversation with him about religious liberty and religious relations in the community. The minister stated that he was, like the layman, in favor of "better religious relations," but not if they always had to be purchased "at the expense of capitulation to the demands of the Roman Catholic church." Decision and action, the pastor sought to say, on one issue—such as public funds for transportation of parochial-school students—involve the issues of how a majority decision in the community is to be arrived at, the relative influence of the church on the opinion-molding agencies of the city, and the long-term intentions of each religion. The letter then concluded that Protestants who were really aware of "the aggressiveness of the Roman Catholic church in this country at the present time are afraid that if we begin to give a foot, they will soon demand a mile."

Chapter 11

Interfaith Association

The Roman Catholic church has given almost no encouragement to the participation of laymen or clergy in conferences or associations for the purpose of establishing areas of co-operation and greater understanding between religious groups. Such participation has been considered a field for "experts" only and careful rules for procedure have been defined.[1] Interfaith participation in worship has also been interpreted as a source of sin and guilt.

The dominant consideration in this policy is the effort to maintain the superiority and monopoly of the church in religious matters. The more dogmatically religious beliefs are held by a religious institution, the more precise and thorough are its efforts to protect or isolate members from association with representatives of error. Catholic pastors believe that fraternization of their members with Protestants is usually at the cost of the unity and purity of Catholic faith and morals, a decrease in members' intensity of Catholic conviction and even loss of members. The Catholic pastors recognize that in an increasingly mobile and diverse society such as America the associations of Catholics and non-Catholics will expand, but they do not look with favor upon this development from a religious standpoint. As one pastor in a parish of working class people noted, "Interfaith associations are increasing among our people, but the church is not encouraging this. Protestants have different morals than we do. They believe in birth control, divorce, and euthansia. They talk that stuff to our people, undermining their morals and spreading doubts about the Catholic faith."

The policies of the pastors toward association between Catholics and non-Catholics appear also to be a defense against defections from the church's own ranks as well as of her claims of superiority in religion. Association of Catholics and non-Catholics in a social way, some pastors also observe, increases the number of mixed marriages, in which the church—indeed all churches in the view of the pastors—loses more members than are gained.

Most Protestant church leaders have not evidenced as consistent and determined a policy on the association of members as the Catholic clergy. The norms generally professed have been for free and intimate exchange of ideas about religion with people of other faiths. But the relation of these principles to traditional Protestant theology has seldom appeared clear or integral. And vague preference for free association has been challenged by obvious Catholic intent to isolate members and to control all exchange of religious ideas. Only the Lutheran church and the sects have maintained unambiguous objectives—but these have been to isolate and monopolize the social and religious associations of members as has the Catholic church.

Most Protestant ministers find themselves less and less concerned about breaking down barriers to association and discovering ways of communicating with Catholics about religion. They still profess, as a tenet of their faith, the necessity for a society with varied sources of truth; but their long-term lack of direct relations with Catholic leaders appears to contribute to their tendency to dismiss the Catholic church as a possible source of supplementation to some of their own religious and moral assumptions. A pastor summarized the pragmatic and indecisive mood of most Protestant ministers as follows:

> We appear to be trying increasingly to isolate Catholics and Protestants. If we're going to do this, we'd better have the same approach as the Romans and make it appear as an accepted and natural part of our doctrine. Our policy must not appear as anti-Catholic, but as an inherent part of the Protestant church. We had better get some theology and policy quick on relations with the Catholics.

Historically, Protestant clergy have stressed that community is not so much a matter of having common interests—though these are certainly present and important—as it is a matter of mutual love and respect.[2] The emphasis within this view upon the free pursuit of a variety of interests has been used by some Protestant leaders to show the affinity of religious concepts of community with Yankee economic ideology. This ideology stresses the belief that the competition of units independently pursuing their own concerns (and not seeking or not able to destroy one another) will produce a harmony of interests within the society.[3] In the religious sector, unity and harmony are to emerge out of the stimulating, but not destructive, competition of each religious unit in the search for truth. The tenseness of the Protestant clergy over religious relations betrays the effort to retain the central assumptions of this ethos, while increasingly aware that many of them are no longer widely held.

The canon law of the Catholic church designates five types of co-operative discussions, that is, discussions with the purpose of joint or common action on the part of two or more persons to obtain the same ends:

> (1) those which aim at union of religions on the basis of the lowest common denominator;
> (2) those which try to imbue their participants with a respect for the diverse religious beliefs of others;
> (3) those which have the immediate purpose of bringing one or more non-Catholics into the true Church of Christ;
> (4) those in which participation is concerned with moral, social or civic issues and does not include matters of faith;
> (5) those which envisage a formal discussion from which the ends set forth in the first two types of co-operative discussions have been excluded and in which the primary purpose is to foster personal tolerance or a spirit of Christian charity.[4]

The law forbids the first two types of conferences at all times. The other three types are permitted if the circumstances make them morally acceptable. The third type of conference has rarely taken place in Paper City.[5] In the fourth type of conference a spiritual and interconfessional unity on a distinct nonecclesiastical plane is envisioned by the church interpreters, since "the union of all men within . . . the Roman Catholic Church is not practicable at the present time." [6] In the fifth type of conference to foster personal tolerance, the most important prudential circumstances are anticipated attitudes of non-Catholic participants, the safeguards taken against "religious indifference" and against "respect for diverse religions of others." [7]

Interfaith Co-operation on Moral and Social Issues

The Roman Catholic pastors, with two exceptions, do not believe that co-operation on any moral and social issue of deep concern to the church (the fourth type of discussion) is possible with Paper

City Protestant leaders. The location of the two pastors who hold some optimism about and desire for future intercreedal co-operation is significant. One is pastor of the upper-class Holy Cross parish of the Highlands where optimism about religious and social harmony and agreement is greatest among Catholic laymen. The other is the pastor of St. Michael's, a Greek ethnic parish of the Roman Catholic church. This priest, appointed under another diocese, came recently to the city from a community where Catholics are in a minority. He believes more efforts could be made by Catholic leaders to co-operate with Protestants on such issues as housing, health, and communism.

The other Catholic pastors are unable to think of any social reforms in the community on which the churches could unite; hence they do not desire conferences with Protestants on these matters. The Catholic clergy, when questioned about co-operation on such specific local issues as housing, generally regard the obvious religious separation as an argument for their own inactivity in these areas. For example, a pastor of a parish located in one of the poorest wards in terms of housing observed: "I was for going into the housing matter. I offered to help out financially or anyway I could with a project, but then I saw if I did there would be such a fuss from the Protestants, more housing would get built if I stayed out."

The last successful wide-scale co-operation of Roman Catholic and Protestant clergy in Paper City on a moral issue occurred in 1877 with the launching of a temperance movement. Inaugurated by the Baptists, the campaign soon worked closely with the Catholic temperance societies. Sunday evening union temperance meetings in the city hall were held for several weeks with Protestants and Catholics attending.[8]

Today, most Catholic pastors and lay leaders of parish societies talk about the impossibilities of co-operation by the churches on moral-social issues as follows:

> If the Catholic clergy came out for action on a social problem, the Protestants would oppose it. Nothing could be accomplished by attempting a joint statement or action. [Catholic Pastor]
>
> The thing for us to do is just to go on as we have, each going his own way with as little attempt to develop co-operative relations as possible. [Catholic Pastor]

> When a man has been taught from the cradle that his religion is the only true one and he knows his salvation is in that religion, it is natural that he can't understand how anybody can have any other religion, and finds it hard to co-operate with those who have such different morals and beliefs. [Lay woman leader of a parish sodality]
>
> There is nothing that can be done to get better co-operation. We don't agree on anything, except that there's a God. I read this morning about the Episcopalians adopting the Planned Parenthood League. What can you get co-operation about there? We say our position on birth control is God's position. The Episcopalians say it isn't. Should I go and try to talk to them? That would only cause trouble. [Catholic Pastor]

The priests have been reluctant to participate in public rituals and ceremonies affirming solidarity or co-operation of religious groups in the city. Jewish religious leaders made the most recent effort to secure public association in order to prepare a float for the Victory Celebration on V-J Day. The Jewish leaders planned a float bearing large Norman Rockwell pictures of the "Four Freedoms" and the slogan "Let's All Pull Together and Win the Peace, Too." Clerical representatives of the three faiths—Catholic, Protestant and Jewish—were to pull the float. Four Catholic priests were called before a curate of the Holy Rosary parish was found who agreed to pull the float. A few minutes before the parade was to begin, the curate told the Protestant pastor and rabbi that he felt he should go ask the senior priest on the reviewing stand if it was all right for him to participate. The parade was delayed until a decision was made for the curate to pull the float.[9]

The Protestant pastors are as convinced as the Roman Catholic clergy that no community issues can be found which could be a basis for coaction of the churches.[10] The Protestant clergy comment to one another in terms such as these: "If the Catholic clergy would endeavor to get better housing for the low-income people of Paper City I'd walk down the street arm in arm with Father McMichael"—the Holy Rosary pastor. But they have not in this century invited the Catholic clergy to take a stand with them on a public issue in which the economic or political welfare of Catholic people was deeply involved and in which the position of the Catholic clergy was not as yet precisely indicated.

Conferences for Personal Understanding

On the clerical level no friendships exist between the faiths; contacts seldom go beyond formal greetings on the street or at public meetings. Two of the Protestant ministers say that they are on "conversational terms" with Catholic pastors, but "do not talk religious matters." None has a relationship to a priest in which they talk about problems involving the relations of the two faiths. The few conversations most ministers have had with priests have been telephone exchanges between the pastors, such as "to clear the referral of a boy found stealing in a church to the proper agency." No controversial personal issues, such as interfaith marriage, are dealt with. No priests have visited the offices or homes of the present ministers in Paper City. One minister visited several times with a Catholic pastor, now deceased, in the priest's parish office; the priest twice accepted invitations to visit the home of the minister, but canceled both appointments.

Much of the ministers' information about local Catholic practices is based on a miscellaneous and unsympathetically interpreted collection of "crisis" incidents in which they have been called into "funerals which priests will not handle because of the family's attitude toward the Catholic church," alleged snubs by priests at public meetings where the minister was to give the benediction and the priest the call to worship, and similar incidents. The Protestant clergy have undertaken no systematic study of the Catholic church in the community through use of its locally published literature, or of the Protestant churches' role in light of data gathered, in spite of their general feeling that they "live with the Catholic problem day and night." [11]

Most of the Protestant ministers still talk about wanting friendships with the priests and of trying to establish more personal contact with them, but the intensity of this desire may not be great. One of the ministers who expressed in formal interviews a strong desire for a more cordial and friendly association with priests called a Protestant real-estate dealer to ask him not to sell property close to his parsonage to a priest for a residence, because the minister did not wish the priest in the neighborhood. ("The minister sure is sensitive about the Catholics getting too close," the real-estate dealer observed, "but he can't understand my not wanting to deal with Jews.") Clerical relations are put by several pastors on a *quid pro quo* basis. A Congregational minister stated:

> When Father Nolan [senior priest, known popularly as "the Builder"] died in 1910, all the Protestant clergy attended his funeral, except the Lutheran pastor. I arranged our attendance. A little later, Dr. Palmer, the pastor of the Second Baptist Church, died after twenty-seven years of service. Not a single priest came to the funeral. So that was the last time the Protestant clergy ever attended a Catholic priest's funeral in Paper City. We feel the road must run both ways.

The priests make clear that they do not desire any more contacts with the Protestant clergy than now (even less, if possible), and that increased personal contact will have to be on terms of a shift in the attitude of Protestant ministers toward such issues as birth control, gambling, transportation of parochial students in public school buses. For example, one priest ceased speaking on the Catholic religion before a synagogue discussion group and a college class on the basis that the leaders supported the petition for referendum referring to the voters the issue of transportation of parochial students in public buses.

The priests have over the past decade severed what contacts did exist with religious leaders of other faiths.[12] As the *Catholic Mirror* bitterly observed in an editorial, "The unanimity with which Protestant ministers in this valley are putting their names to a petition to deprive children attending Catholic schools of the right to transportation on school buses, makes one wonder if they will have the courage next year to invite the Catholic clergy to join them in the observance of Brotherhood Week."[13] An elderly priest in Paper City is of an opinion unanimously shared by his colleagues:

> It is no use to try to get priests and ministers together in this city. The Protestant ministers have taken stands on so many terrible things that we priests feel we cannot associate with them. Recently, for example, I was invited to give an invocation at the Paper City Hospital commencement service for graduating nurses. I found out that a minister who had preached against the laws of God and had signed the petition on transportation of parochial students was to give the benediction. I suppose he's sincere, but I talked it over with

three other priests here and we decided we couldn't associate ourselves with a man like that. So I refused to go. You see, on religious matters we are so poles apart there is no use in trying to get together.

The nurse planning the convocation sent two letters to the senior pastor, inviting him to participate in the program; but she received no reply. She then telephoned the pastor. She later reported that the pastor asked, "What responsibility do I have to the city hospital?"

The nurse paused, unable to think of a reply.

The pastor then said, "You have chosen for the program a minister who advocates race suicide. I can't be on the same program with a man like that."

The Protestant pastor was the minister of the First Congregational Church which had given Margaret Sanger permission to speak in his church. The senior priest had given the invocation at the previous year's service when the Baptist pastor, a Protestant of less public reputation in the community for advocating the right of doctors to disseminate birth control information, had given the benediction. On this occasion the senior priest refused to hold any conversation with the minister.[14]

In general the priests display an intense lack of respect for all the Protestant pastors, as men with whom they want no further social or religious contact. These are representative comments:

I definitely am not for any "fellowship" meeting with Protestant ministers. They are so intolerant there would be nothing but more tension caused by our getting together. Besides, I don't think the ministers are really sincere. I asked a friend of mine about that, a priest who had been a Protestant minister and was converted. And I was sorry to hear him say, "No, I can honestly say I don't think they are."

I've watched Protestant ministers in this city for forty years. Take [a local minister]. I know he does dishonorable things in his ministry.

I know Protestant ministers better than any other priest in the city. I meet more of them because I get around to more of the community affairs than any other priest. And I'm convinced they are not sincere. They can't be sincere and be for divorce and murder through planned parenthood. They'll practice abortion right along with their people and that's murder, pure and simple. They are hypocrites. They smile and greet me so nice when I meet them and then fight me in their gambling pronouncements as soon as they leave me. They hate me. I don't hate them. I just feel sorry for them. They have no position, no program, so all they do is protest. I tell you, I'm through co-operating with the Protestant ministers. They are a dishonest, insincere lot.

Efforts to develop formal conferences or discussions dedicated to the explicit ends of "personal tolerance," friendliness and understanding between the religions have originated exclusively from non-Catholic groups. Protestant leaders have made attempts at such conferences only in the past fifteen years. In the period of Protestant dominance, apparently, from historical records now available, no initiative was taken by the Protestant churches to develop such conferences. The social isolation of Yankees from Catholics was much greater in the nineteenth century than at present. After the Protestant churches became a distinct minority, and the full impact of the Catholic policies of isolation and religious neutralization of all mixed association developed, the Protestant clergy expressed some interest in sponsoring public occasions when interfaith discussions could occur.

Various attempts have been made by three Protestant ministers and a rabbi, all unsuccessful, to have the local Catholic clergy participate in establishing a local Conference of Christians and Jews. The first meeting to attempt organization was held in 1936 with Dr. Everett R. Clinchy, director of the National Conference of Christians and Jews, and George N. Schuster, Catholic president of Hunter College. Three Protestant ministers were present, but no priests, although invitations had been extended to several. Subsequent meetings did not succeed in enlisting Catholic clerical support or in locating lay Catholics with views of the relations of the churches similar to those of Protestants. During national Brotherhood Week a priest can usually be secured to give a talk on a radio program with a minister and a rabbi. After the most recent program, the priest explained that he had prepared two scripts: one which he read on the program and one to be read in case the other men attacked any aspect of the Catholic faith.[15]

The attitude of Catholic laymen who are leaders in Catholic organizations is typified by a leader in the Catholic Teachers' Association in the city:

> Discussions of religion by Protestants and Catholics at joint meetings are a waste of time. Suppose we were invited to send a representative to such a meeting. We would send an outstanding layman who would be solid and set on the Catholic point of view. The Protestants would be fools not to send the same kind of man. So the meeting would have leaders polite but set in their ways. You can call it prejudice or narrowmindedness or what you like, but if I were there I know nothing would be said that would change my view one bit.

Under the impact of Paper City's religious relations, many of the basic assumptions which the ministers believe to be back of such interfaith movements as the National Conference of Christians and Jews no longer have a compelling significance for them. They do not believe that the conflicts and suspicions that arise between the religious groups stem in the main from ignorance—that if members of the religions only come to know one another better they will realize they all share a common belief in a personal God or the Golden Rule and that conflicts and suspicions will cease, or, more important, cease to be necessary.

Many of the Protestant pastors believe that, the more they and their people have come to know about Catholicism, the more tension and antagonism they have felt toward that faith. They have misgivings about what one minister terms the "brotherhood-smotherhood" approach. They feel that the few meetings initiated by men associated with the National Conference of Christians and Jews in Paper City attached too great importance to securing superficial agreement on a few simple and general theological or charitable concerns, but that this agreement had little to do with the deeper political, economic and religious issues in the relations of the churches, which called for more serious probing than anyone was willing to undertake. Therefore the Protestant ministers have mustered no enthusiasm for the National Conference program and have devised no alternate program.

Association in Worship

The isolation of Catholics from Protestant services of worship is as rigidly governed and defined as discussions for co-operation.[16] The *Catholic Mirror* commented upon participation of Catholics in a New Year's Day prayer service in a non-Catholic church:

> Some of our Catholic people apparently do not realize that we are not allowed to take an active part in non-Catholic religious services. To do this is to be guilty of the grave sin of heresy, and causes irreparable scandal. . . . From the newspaper write-up and editorial comment the impression was definitely given to the citizens of the community that Catholics, Protestants and Jews had "united" in a religious service in a Protestant church under Protestant auspices "to signify their spiritual unity." If the Catholics who participated were not guilty of formal heresy, they certainly gave very grave scandal.[17]

The Protestant churches, with the exception of the Lutheran church and the sects, have made no effort to discourage or stigmatize attendance at Catholic services of worship. All the ministers but one thought "interfaith programs which include worship at churches of all the major religions" would be a valuable part of a Protestant church's education of members.

Patterns of isolation of Catholics and Protestants carry over into funeral and burial arrangements. None of the three Protestant funeral directors in the city does over 2 per cent of his business with Catholics.[18] In several instances, priests have spoken to Catholics who have patronized Protestant directors, inquiring why they did not patronize Catholic directors.

Occasionally converts to Protestantism have been reclaimed by nonconverted relatives to Catholic burial ground, and in some instances the family maneuvering for location of the deceased involves the local clergy. The city's best-known incident concerned Michael Ryan, a former principal of a public school who left the Catholic faith. Ryan never became a member of a Protestant church, but he printed and circulated a letter to his friends saying—that he "expected to die very soon," and that he wished "to be buried in Forestdale Cemetery" (a Protestant burial ground). His letter read in part:

> My monument has already been erected there. I am taking steps thus early to avoid any trouble when I do pass away. I have known of persons to be taken to Catholic cemeteries and masses said, when they were not Catholics at all and had said so. The church thus got the fees for the graves and for the "masses" which were said for them. This can easily be done when some of the family are Catholic, for they favor the priest as a rule. I have the kindest feelings toward Catholics, for they have always used me well, both in school and outside, but I have no confidence in the clergy. They wait until one is

dead, and then come and claim the body on the ground that he was "baptized" a Catholic. They get their strength from children (baptism), and the dead.[19]

After his death, relatives removed his body to a Catholic cemetery. They sought to sell his monument in Forestdale Cemetery, but a Protestant pastor induced officials of a nearby Protestant-founded college, also residuary legatees of Mr. Ryan's estate, to object. This discouraged the sale.

Influence of Laymen Upon Church Relations

The isolationist policies of Catholic religious leaders have evidently been strengthened by social attitudes of many Catholic laymen. At least class and ethnic discrimination by Yankees is often offered by the priests as a defense of the church's isolation of members from other religions. "Do you think it is all the Catholic church's doing that members are isolated?" a French Catholic priest asked in explaining the church's associational policy. "The wealthy Yankee Protestants have made the French know that they are not welcome at their affairs. They have looked down on the French and treated them as inferiors so long that the French have come to distrust everything about the Yankees."

Some variance in attitude of priests located in an upper-class parish such as Holy Cross can be observed in comparison with priests of other parishes. The priests of upper-middle class parishes report slightly more association and co-operation of Catholics with non-Catholics, and they express more interest in its continuance.

Many Catholics have come up from the tenements in the lowlands to achieve upper-middle class status as owners of retail stores, printing shops and similar businesses. They have experienced in their lifetime the restraints placed upon a depressed economic and ethnic minority. They express the superiority of their religion in more militant, "go-it-alone" terms than either submerged economic groups or ones who have had wealth and status for a long time.[20]

The most powerful lay pressures against the policies of the Catholic priests come from the upper and upper-middle class members who have stable positions of great prominence in the economic, social, and political life of the community. Their attitudes are reinforced by the ideology of Protestant laymen of similar social status. These laymen have in recent years been tending toward increasing association across religious lines, particularly in economic affairs, while the clergy have tended toward greater isolation. These laymen believe that they have a great stake in maintenance of harmony and unity among the churches. Church practices which create tension complicate economic and social pursuits involving personal relations with people of a variety of faiths. The symbols of their creed are "co-operation and good fellowship between religions," "equal treatment for all religions," "tolerance of and freedom for all religions."

Nothing is more acceptable to these laymen on public occasions than professions of peace, harmony, friendship and co-operation between the churches as the goal and fact of Roman Catholic-Protestant relations in the city.

"Paper City glories in her various religions; all differences between them have always been overcome successfully and easily," one of the most prominent Catholic businessmen is fond of saying on public occasions. The mayor frequently refers to Paper City as the "friendly city" and the "most tolerant, democratic city in America." Most business and professional men can recall events revealing religious cleavage in the city only with visible difficulty.[21] Their public belief is that ministers and priests are getting along better all the time and that community causes are bringing them closer together in their approach to religious relations. "It is a wonderful sight," a Catholic lawyer recalled, "to see clergy of all faiths sitting and joking together at a Community Chest dinner." A local newspaper editor in speeches still recalls "the exciting symbol of the representatives of the three faiths side by side in the Victory parade."

On the façade of the Veteran's Building, the most costly and modern municipal structure in the city, inscribed along with such sentiments as "Banish War," "Enthrone Peace," "Heroic Women, American Mothers," and "Liberty, Political, Economic," is the slogan "Religious Freedom Glorifies America." The words were sent by the Rt. Rev. William Cardinal O'Connell to a committee seeking what the chairman of the committee called "sentiments which would represent all the people of Paper City."

The church obviously appears to many laymen chiefly in the

role of a stabilizing influence upon the community; the extension of its authority promises even greater harmony. The isolation of Catholics from contacts with specifically interfaith programs also appears to the laymen as a policy which reduces the possibility of friction, a policy which is emulated in the social order by refusal to become involved in religious discussions and issues with non-Catholics.

For the priests, the problem of restraining laymen from direct action does not bother them so much as that of achieving greater lay concern to act. The effect of a pluralistic culture, of groups outside the church competing for the time and loyalty of laymen, impresses them. With such concerns, the priests believe that they are performing the role of a majority religion with great restraint and charity, that they have seldom sought to create religious tension in the community, and have used their influence overtly only under the threats and activity of anti-Catholic forces.

Protestant Laymen and Religious Diversity

The indecision of the Protestant clergy about association with Catholics has enhanced the influence of Protestant laymen who for social and economic reasons know precisely what they want in religious relations, who counsel the Protestant pastors not to raise controversial issues in the community, and encourage them to take their cues from the Catholic church as to the amount of interfaith association and co-operation to pursue. What most Protestant business and professional people mean by religious "harmony" and "unity" is the avoidance in church and economic associations of the introduction of controversial religious issues to create divisions. Some of the counsels offered by Protestant laymen as *modus operandi* for religious unity in Paper City follow:

> Never get involved in politics or religion, never sign petitions on religious issues. Don't do anything to antagonize the Catholic church. [Manager of textile factory]
>
> Talk religion in church but never talk religion with your business associates. That's how I get along. [Supervisor of paper plant]
>
> When you're in business in a town 85 per cent Catholic you can't go out crusading, carrying the torch for Protestantism. Why man, this place gets hot when anyone tries to point out religious differences. People get rocks heaved through their windows. The kids in

school get it taken out on them for what their parents say. I suppose if I came up against the Catholic problem all the time like the ministers do I would get hipped on the subject. But my advice to them is not to draw out differences publicly. What good does it do? It just causes hard feelings. [Owner of large retail store]

All of us have to live together and we do live together without much strife. I'm proud of the fact that Protestants have contributed to community harmony by not fomenting religious issues and not being adamant when they are raised. [President of bank]

In a city 85 per cent Catholic it is too late to make public issues. I'm a strong believer in the Protestant religion. In a town like this its main job has got to be to keep harmony. [Superintendent of paper mill]

The Protestant laymen have arrived at these views under a variety of pressures. They are impressed by the intransigence of the Catholic church on issues that matter to it and by its majority status. They protest against the irrelevancy of many "church" issues, such as gambling and transportation of parochial students, which excite the ministers; these are not issues which appear crucial in their own lives. They believe they have kept freedom in Paper City in the areas which matter most—"the chance to run a business profitably," to "make a good living," to practice medicine or law successfully. "So give the Catholics their transportation and their birth-control laws," one businessman, a wholesaler of construction supplies, observed; "these will not change our control of business in the city."

Some of the laymen are confused and torn by varied church and business claims, even while supporting the harmony pleas of business associates. A manufacturer, scion of an old Yankee family and a layman of the Second Congregational Church, said:

I can argue this Catholic-Protestant business a dozen different ways. I do with my wife regularly. "What will you accomplish," I'll say, "by standing up to the Catholics? You'll not change their view of their church. You'll just make them more loyal under attack." Then she'll say that I'm unwilling to defend the religious convictions that have been the basis of this country when I'm in a powerful position to do it. Then I argue that my plant would be vulnerable to economic action by Catholics. But I get to thinking: What would the church do? Withdraw workers? Even good Catholics won't stay out and starve. But what do I want to make them do a thing like that for? Hell, I don't know where I stand. I'm just interested in maintaining good business relations in the plant, not in promoting righteous causes. My first responsibility is to the plant.

Some of the nominally Protestant laymen advocating a policy of "harmony" acknowledge their skepticism and indifference toward the traditional beliefs of the church.

> I don't give a damn what a man's religion is. I go to whatever church is convenient. I like some things about all of them. [President of jobbing business, prominent in local Masonic lodge]

> Once you cut through all the words, religions are pretty much alike. People are born into a religion and don't select it, anyway. [Clothing retailer]

> I try never to know what a person's religion is. Religion is the last thing I'm interested in. [Wholesaler]

These men are not without strong loyalties—to economic and social status already achieved. These are loyalties capable of moving men from popular appeals to unity and tolerance based upon indifference toward historic faiths, to dogmatic exclusion of groups which threaten social interests. It is significant that the Protestant Junior Girls' Association, an organization chiefly devoted to fashion, beauty and recreational programs, is the only social or religious organization of Protestants which has instituted in the past ten years an economic boycott against a Catholic store owner; this was done because they understood, incorrectly, that her refusal to give a talk to the club on fashions was because the club was Protestant.

A great deal of overt exclusion and prejudice is directed against the Jew. In a community situation where there is enough of a balance of power between Catholics and Protestants to threaten costly reprisal to overt prejudice against either major group, and where the delicate relations of Catholicism and Protestantism often bring suppressed aggression, the Jews offer a convenient and weak scapegoat. Catholic and Protestant real-estate agents, bankers and merchants often evidence considerable reticence in talking to outsiders about Catholic-Protestant relations, while volunteering to discuss the "Jewish problem."

Many Protestant ministers have found, after sermons on relations with Catholics, that lay men and women are suddenly aroused to demands for "quick and effective action" against "the destroyers of American democracy"—demands which then vanish with the realization that action would invite strong reprisals and require sustained interest, given the complexities of Paper City's religious and social structure. For example, the wife of a businessman wrote her pastor:

> What is to be done? . . . What can we, as Christians and militant ones, I hope (too long have we been pieces of cooked macaroni) do here in Paper City, to become a strong, united minority? . . .
>
> I have a real feeling of affection for some Catholic women I know, but a holy rage (I hope it is holy) possesses me when I think of our Constitution, Bill of Rights, and all that America means, being swept aside to make way for a totalitarian state which means lack of progress and a stifling of all liberty and thought. I can *almost* understand the Ku Klux Klan, so much do these things mean to me. Cannot something be done—quickly and effectively?

Characteristically, the husband of the letter-writer chastized his minister for telling her "that stuff about Roman Catholicism and getting her excited," and his wife for forgetting that he had a plant to run and that he "couldn't have her involved in controversy." No further interest was expressed to the pastor by the laywoman.

Laymen who do not profess rejection of traditional Protestant concerns but who pragmatically advise that the churches should not "rock the boat" are probably the most direct and influential pressure upon the Protestant pastors. One businessman wrote in reply to his pastor's request for funds to support the varied denominational work of the church:

> Sure I will give $100.00 to benevolence, but none to social action. Social action of our churches is a personal pain in the neck to me. . . . The Baptist Church of Paper City has recently made fools of its members—has done much harm to the community—has given me sleepless nights—and the cause was foolish and impossible of accomplishment before it started. [Reference is to a public statement by two Baptist pastors and several members asking for a referendum vote on use of public funds to transport parochial students.] The First Congregational Church made fools of themselves and their members in Paper City only two years ago [Sanger incident]. We have to live in Paper City, and direction of these problems should be in the hands of those who know the community if it is to succeed.

The ministers find themselves not in the role of majority leaders with a stake in the order and stability of the community (a role which many have experienced in earlier pastorates) but in the uncomfortable role of minority agitators, accused by their own leading laymen as well as by Catholics of intolerance and of disturbing the harmony and peace of the community. The minority role is strange to most of the ministers and they are not happy in it.

In summary, then, the dominant approaches to the relations of the churches in Paper City are those of the Catholic clergy and influential Protestant and Catholic business and professional people. The accommodation of the interests of these groups represents the actual power structure of Paper City's faiths and ultimate loyalties. The religious leaders pursue their various policies of isolation and the laymen adapt to them by confining religious discussion to church activities. Social harmony in the community is achieved at the cost of religious profundity.

PART III

THE CHURCHES IN THE COMMUNITY

Chapter 12

Class and Parish

"I'd like a home in Holy Cross parish." This is how a shopper for a new house in Paper City often expresses to his real-estate agent a desire for a "higher class" residence and a break away from a section of the city still dominated by strong ethnic loyalties and associations.

"Next thing you know they'll be joining the Second Congregational Church." This is the derisive remark of a Roman Catholic fireman about a family which has left his own lower-middle class parish for a suburban home.

"A man can get ahead—meet a lot of fine people—in our church too. I keep telling our people, there is more money here than they will admit." Thus speaks the minister of Grace Congregational church, located in a working-class area of the city.

"We have everybody in our church from charwomen to bank presidents," proudly says the pastor of a Protestant church which has only three families of wage workers in it.

"The love of French language and culture is dying in our people. What will happen to the faith and to the parish? Already the bishop has his eyes on our parish for an Irish priest," laments the pastor of the oldest French Catholic parish in the city.

"They [the French priests] can't continue this ridiculous effort to hold back change. Catholic faith is not dependent on a language. Observe the Irish," notes the pastor of the oldest English-speaking parish.

These remarks are indicative of the concern the people of Paper City have about the relation of parish lines and church membership to the class and ethnic strata of the community. What we seek to answer in this and the following chapter are questions such as these: How closely can various class, nationality and religious lines or groupings be identified? Are there important tensions or conflicts arising between class and ethnic groups involved in the relations of the churches? To what extent do social and religious loyalties and struggles reinforce one another? To what extent do the churches bring people of diverse social backgrounds into the same congregation or parish? Do the churches vary significantly in the degree they seek deliberately to control the social composition of their membership? (See the Appendix for a discussion of the methods used to obtain answers to these questions.)

Paper City people "place" or "locate" their neighbors in terms of three broad economic classes. First, those who because of high professional or managerial skill or wealth are at the top of the existing social order—the upper class. Second, those who by and large find themselves at the bottom of the same social organization, having only manual and service techniques of simple skill—the laboring class. Third, a middle group composed of persons who for the most part are neither very near to the top nor very near to the bottom of the social structure and know this, as do their neighbors, and who are found primarily in the white-collar occupations requiring clerical, managerial aid and exchange skills.[1]

Fairly general agreement exists in Paper City as to the specific occupations which belong in the three broad classes. In ranking the occupations, people consider factors such as skill and training required, education, income, amount of privileges, control over affairs of the community and leadership opportunities which are concomitants of the vocation.[2] For example, the occupations most commonly or generally associated with the three classes are as follows:

I. Upper Economic Class: Mill owners, mill executives (superintendent or above), bankers, large-scale proprietors, publishers, brokers, large-scale construction company owners. Professions with high income return: physicians and surgeons, lawyers and judges, highly skilled engineers and architects.

II. Middle Economic Class: Professionals with comparative low income, semiprofessionals and small proprietors: clergymen, teachers, musicians, social workers, small retail store owners and managers. Mill officials below superintendent: foremen. Clerks, salesmen, white-collar workers. Craftsmen of traditionally skilled occupations: carpenters, electricians, masons, machinists, molders, plumbers. Textile and paper skilled work: mule spinners, typesetters, tending of most skilled paper machines, loom fixers. Service —protective: policemen, firemen.

III. Lower Economic Class: Manual operatives in mills and repair shops requiring little skill: pulp beaters, paper finishing room operators, ragpickers, weavers, spindle tenders, ring-spinners. Service—non-protective: domestics, janitors. Common laborer in non-industrial areas.

Social, ethnic, economic and religious factors combine to produce a variety of strata within the three general social classes. For example, the "upper class" has at its apex a group of self-consciously elite Yankee families who represent ancestral lines established early in the industrial history of the city. They have their own social and literary clubs with no Catholic or ethnic groups represented. Objective data of occupation, income and place of residence may place some Protestants and Roman Catholics in the same economic class, but subjective data such as "consciousness of kind" and degree of esteem evidenced in visiting and freely associating in activities with one another, dating with intent to marry, reveal cleavages within economic classes based on religion and nationality.

Social Classes and Church Membership

Most of the Catholic pastors adapt the approach of various church programs explicitly to class characteristics of the parish. The Protestant pastors seldom plan educational and financial programs in terms of class differences in membership. The Catholic leaders have a view of society which assumes and accepts a more rigid ordering of the economic positions of men than do the Protestant leaders. The Catholic pastor views the one-class parish as a natural and expected adaptation of the church to the social structure in the city. The church serves men within their various stations in life; it sends clergy to the laboring man, to the wealthy; it does not seek to draw its parish lines or plan its programs to bring men of diverse social classes into association.

The Protestant church pastor, on the other hand, not only feels it is a moral stigma if his congregation does not have "charwomen as well as bankers" but is highly defensive about any general tendencies of his church toward lower-middle and lower-class membership or lack of opportunity for social mobility within the congregation. A minister of a largely middle-class downtown church lowered his voice to a whisper to report to an out-of-town visitor, "I have a labor leader in my church. I'm not sure whether he's CIO or AFL, but he's not too popular with the other men—a little too aggressive." A minister with a predominantly labor constituency complained that some of his members who were "not very sincere or earnest" would "leave to go to an uptown church so they could meet some wealthy people. But we do right by our people," he explained. "We have a lot of people of influence here, too." The Protestant pastors seek to deal with each member as an individual, avoiding public recognition of class distinctions in their program.

Within each of the two religions are three distinct types of congregation: 1) the predominantly labor class church, with more than 70 per cent of the members working people; 2) the church, with more than 70 per cent of its membership in the middle or labor classes; 3) the church with more than 70 per cent of its membership in the upper or middle classes. (The names and number of churches in each of the three categories and the percentage of the total Roman Catholic or Protestant membership which each category contains are indicated in Table XXII.)

The Roman Catholics are most heavily represented in membership among the distinctly labor churches (52 per cent in comparison with 33 per cent of the Protestants) while the Protestants are most concentrated in churches combining middle and upper class groups (42.5 per cent in sharp contrast to the 13 per cent of Roman Catholic membership in such churches).

There are significant variations and similarities in the manner in which the Roman Catholic and Protestant religions have adapted to the class structure of the community. (Tables XXIII and XXIV give the class composition of each Protestant and Roman Catholic church or parish.) Both groups in terms of total membership cut widely into all classes of Paper City. Both groups tend to segregate the classes into separate churches. However, the Roman Catholic churches have developed a system of separation more explicit and thorough than the Protestants, that is, membership in the individual

Roman Catholic church follows class lines more neatly and precisely than in the individual Protestant churches.

Sixty-five per cent of the Protesants of laboring or lower class status are to be found in the labor churches, while 77 per cent of the laboring people in the total Roman Catholic church membership are located in the seven labor churches. Also, the Catholic labor churches are more predominantly one-class than the Protestant labor churches, with little representation of the middle class and no representation of the upper class. Only the small sect groups among Protestants are entirely or overwhelmingly one-class. Further, the upper-middle class Catholic churches have a smaller labor representation than the Protestant upper-middle class churches. The middle-labor class churches are very similar in both religious groups.

In short, the Catholic class pattern for each church is much less varied than the class pattern of the individual Protestant churches. In only 2 Catholic churches are enough representatives of other than the predominant class present to compose 30 per cent of the total membership. In these 2 churches, which have 27 per cent of the Catholic membership in the city, chiefly lower and middle classes are brought together. In 7 Protestant churches, constituting 65 per cent of the Protestant membership, the 2 minority classes comprise over 30 per cent of the membership.[3]

In comparing the over-all class make-up of the two religious groups, the chief difference to be noted is that the Protestants draw a much larger percentage of their total membership from the upper class (14 per cent) than the Catholics (1.2 per cent). Both religions have about the same proportion of members in the middle class, and Catholics have approximately 10 per cent more in the lower class. (See Table XXVI.)

Various Protestant denominations have become identified with particular economic groups, and Paper City's citizens can construct a generally accurate social scale for them, corresponding to that in Table XXVII, ranking denominations from upper to lower class. Usually, the Congregationalists are ranked before the Episcopalians as an upper-class denomination, largely because of the concentration of prominent mill operators and professional people in the First and Second Congregational churches, overshadowing the large labor membership of Grace Congregational Church below Main Street. These two Congregational churches are often referred to as "Marshall's and Jackson's church" and "Palmer's church," so important have been the roles of these mill-owning families in the lives of the churches. Second Congregational is the only church in the city where the ushers at the regular worship service wear morning coats, striped trousers and wing collars. The church constituencies cut across all income levels, but the mill-owning, mill-managing Yankee occupies a position of such great economic power and conspicuousness in Paper City history that the identification of most Protestants with the upper class is a prevalent stereotype.[4]

Social Ecological Areas of the City

Paper City's residential, business and industrial locations are far from formless. There is a pattern and order to the territorial system with areas having different social character and significance for those who live in them. Actually the social areas of Paper City are more readily evident than in most communities, since the industrial, business and residential locations were laid out well in advance of their development. Most citizens in Paper City have an everyday working knowledge of the various areas of the community described here. For them the Flats, South City, Ward 4, Springdale, Elmwood, Oakdale, Highlands, Highland Park have social meaning and rank.

The areas, through property costs, rental levels and other social pressures, operate selectively so that individuals of similar social status tend to live in the same neighborhoods. Paper City's ecology is almost diagrammatic, the mill sites, business district, homes of workers, owners and managers having been planned on paper before the city development was begun.[5] Through many social controls (not the least of which was the Water Power Company's powerful resistance to the building of bridges across the Connecticut River to permit suburban growth away from its own property[6]), community expansion came in fanlike fashion and concentric half circles out from the industrial area.

An observer looking west from the hills above Paper City sees the river make a great turn as it flows south into the Lowlands. Crowded into the land in the bend of the river is the heart of Paper City. (See maps, in the Appendix.) In the middle of the sprawling U formed by the river is Main Street, along which the major business and commercial establishments are located. To live below Main Street is to live "across the tracks" where the canals supply power and water and the mills and tenements utilize space allocated with an engineer's precision. Almost the only plots of grass below Main Street are in the parish house yards of Holy Rosary, Precious Blood and Immaculate Conception. Above the center of the city is a broad, tree-lined boulevard called Hill Street. This crest marks the "best" residential areas, the homes becoming larger and the yards more expansive as the crest becomes higher in its sweep from south to north. The ecological pattern is simple—a social ramp from the working class tenements in the Lowlands up the hill to the well-to-do residences. There is a continuous increase in social status as one moves up to the Highlands, with the exception of a small area near the dam, which has, with the Flats, long been a point of entry into the city for immigrant groups.[7] In the last decade of the nineteenth century, the business center was nearer the Lowlands and the best residential areas were along what is now Main Street.

The major social areas of the community need to be described before church parish lines, membership and property can be located in meaningful ecological terms.

I. *Upper-Class Residential Area*

This area is known to everyone in Paper City as the Highlands or Ward 7 (Map I). It is the place of residence of the mill owners, top business executives, proprietors of successful retail and wholesale establishments —all with large incomes. The neighborhood farthest from the city, labeled "Large Estates," is the central location of the upper-upper class, old Yankee families. Highland Park is a new, but expensive housing area with some Irish Catholic, but largely Protestant families. Using all the criteria of best housing available in census data, Ward 7 ranks above all others.[8]

The lower part of Area I is in a transitional state between upper-class and upper-middle class status. Many of the spacious homes built by the textile and paper mill owners in boom days are now maintained for largely sentimental and social reasons, the owners increasingly building new homes in neighboring small towns. The Highlands is an area of the middle-aged and elderly, not of youth (Table XXVI). The Highlands has the smallest percentages of foreign-born people of any ward. The area is largely native Yankee and second and third generation Irish and French in composition.[9]

II. *Middle-Class Residential Areas*

A. The two major middle and lower middle class residential areas (Elmwood and Oakdale) are composed largely of small inexpensive single dwelling homes and duplexes with small lots and neighborhood developments. The people who live here are white-collar office workers, salesmen, semiprofessional people, artisans, small merchants. As these people make more money they move farther north on Hill Street into the Highland area or into small neighboring towns.

Ward 3 which includes most of this area has the largest proportion of people between 25 and 65 years of age of any ward in the city (Table XXVII). Ward 3 (and Ward 5 which has the same data) has the second largest percentage of native born, indicating the extent to which former immigrants have been able to make the move from the tenements of the Flats.[10]

B. A commuters' area of middle-class homes is located on the periphery of the city and along roads leading into it. Particularly to the north, past the large estates, office and skilled workers share space with gasoline stations and roadside eating establishments along a major national highway.

C. Toward the center of the city and Ward 5 is a third area of middle rank dwellings. It is composed largely of old (pre-1900) but substantially built apartment buildings and tenements, inhabited largely by elderly people with small family units. In the decades from 1880-1900 this district was known as Church Hill and was the first location of the more elaborate homes of the mill owners and operators. These homes have now become funeral parlors, professional office buildings, small stores and apartments.

III. *Business and Commercial Area*

The old business district, noted on Map I, has become a center for French, Jewish and Greek ethnic stores and short-order eating places, wholesaling establishments, small hotels of "ill repute" and itinerant lodging, of second-run movie houses catering largely to working people's diversions. This is clearly an area of deterioration, with former ecological glories but a memory. The central business district is six blocks up the hill from the old one. Within its seven blocks are the major department stores and clothing retailers, the best restaurants, leading hotels and first-run, gilded movie houses.

IV. *Industrial Area*

The boundaries of this area are clearly determined by the location of three levels of the canals which supply water and power for the mills. The mill sites were carefully blocked out by the first promoters and the plan adhered to by the Water Power Company which subsequently assumed control of the industrial real estate and water power in the city.

The major industries are located along the three levels of canals. The water of the river is drawn off by the dam into the first canal, used and then poured into the second canal on a lower level of the slope. The last series of mills is located along the third canal and the water after use by the mills is returned to the river.

V. *Workers' Residential Areas*

In these areas, most of the workers live in five-story tenements, most of them built before 1900 by the mill owners to utilize the space close to the mills as frugally as possible. These tenements have now been sold by most of the companies. In these areas are the worst housing conditions of the city (Table XXVI). See also Wards 1 and 2 in the Lowlands, Ward 4, once known as the Patch, and Ward 3, particularly the lower part on Map III.

In Paper City the wards with poorest housing facilities are the wards with the most children and young people. The greatest concentration of foreign-born people is found in the working-class areas. Distinct ethnic neighborhoods are still maintained in Wards 1, 2 and 4, although they are to some extent overlapping and diffused. The lower section of Ward 4 is the most recent point of entry for immigrant groups; Poles are the dominant ethnic group here.

Such factors as low rentals, easy accessibility to work, coterminous ethnic and church life and social pressure enforcing segregation of "undesired people" have operated to keep the immigrants in the worker tenement areas.

The workers' housing areas have been the ports of entry into the city not only for the immigrant Catholic groups, whose flow has largely ceased, but are also now the first location of Protestant people who come to Paper City seeking work from rural and village areas of the state and region.[11] This development has not been understood by the Protestant churches whose leaders have thought of the areas "below Main Street" as entirely Roman Catholic. The most visible symbol of the old Protestantism in the workers' wards is the German church, and of the new, the Negro store front church.

Workers, middle and upper class people tend to live in isolation from one another, or at least in sections of the city which are clearly recognized by the community as of different status and social composition. The workers and upper classes are the most isolated in residence. In prosperous times, the people who are able to accumulate some money move from the worker wards into the middle class residential areas to the northeast. Between 1922 and 1929 a gain of 36 per cent in population took place in the middle-class areas with a decrease of 21, 23, and 14 per cent in the three industrial wards. In the depression decade from 1930 to 1940, when the total population of the city declined, the only ward which increased its population was Ward 1, a worker area with the poorest housing facilities.

Social Areas and the Churches: The Parish System

The Catholic church's response to ecological changes and development of social areas has been deliberate and systematic, based on a policy understood in its major features by the local religious leaders.[12] The Catholic adaptation has been a matter for high strategy, considered as so important to the institution that major policy decisions rest with the bishop of the diocese, not local priests. The Protestant adaptation has had a pattern also, but it is not the result of a conscious system or policy by the ministers; it is the product of decisions arrived at separately by the most influential laymen of each church who in their decisions sought to keep up with the social mobility and change of residence of their own group.

The Catholic adaptation to the ecology of Paper City has in general been the traditional one for this church—division of the community into parishes, each one with a church governed by one pastor popularly and officially recognized as responsible for all that affects the religious and moral life of the people in his area.[13]

The parochial system is a *human* institution in the eyes of the church, a result of administrative experience and insight, but according to a Catholic interpreter it is "the most likely sociological factor for strengthening the inner structure of the Church and for channeling the influence of Christianity to the larger community and nation."[14] The parish system in Paper City is a complex one. The factors considered by the bishop in location of parish lines are these: the population trends in the city and the number of people necessary to maintain parish life and provide adequate financial sources in a new area of the city, the national loyalties of the clergy and people, the class make-up of the Catholic constituency in the residential areas, and the political boundaries of the community. The major determining factor in the estimation of the Paper City clergy and of the chancery is the first.

The Catholic clergy, particularly the Irish, have demonstrated a remarkable ability to anticipate and to use population trends in the city in order to secure excellent property locations. They have also skillfully used the parish system to develop units that would assume responsibility for their own property and leadership as soon as Catholics became numerous enough in a certain area of the city.

This "high strategy" was manifested first in the bishop's selection of the priests for the mother church in the community. The first two priests, who built St. Jerome's and introduced organized Catholicism to the community in the nineteenth century, were men of great dignity and gentleness of manner, so cultured that they commended themselves to the community at large.[15]

By 1866 Paper City was clearly becoming an industrial community with a large Roman Catholic population. The gentle, cultured priest was replaced by Father Thomas J. Nolan—aggressive, quick-tempered, rough, property-minded, sensitive to population and general ecological trends in the city. He became known in the period from 1866 to 1910, during which he guided the expansion of the English-speaking Catholic church in the community, as "Nolan the Builder." With clear vision of the patterns of growth in the city and with faith in his parishioners' support of the church, he bought hundreds of thousands of dollars worth of real estate for his own parish and for others to be formed.[16] The funds came in part from the bishop, in part from the pastor, but mostly from loans made through banks.

As early as 1890, the bishop had foreseen the need of a parish in the Highlands to serve the well-to-do Catholics moving into the area, and had purchased land there. The Holy Cross parish lines (Map II) were created in 1905 in the face of bleak financial prospects.[17] For over twenty years the parish worshiped in a brick hall constructed so that it could be turned into a school. In 1929, an English perpendicular gothic church was erected in a commanding position on the hill overlooking Paper City,[18] a great ecological triumph of Irish Catholic expansion in the city. The building was worth upwards of half a million dollars and featured what the brochure in celebration of the dedication described as "probably the largest organ in any Catholic church in the United States." The writer of the brochure, impressed by the location of the church, observed:

> Motorists approaching Paper City over the range . . . have their eye arrested by a specific object in the landscape. Heart and mind,

> if as sensitive as the eye, have been arrested too. The object is a massive square tower, bearing aloft a cross and below the tower a cruciform church. Facing the town, then, we face this supreme symbol, the Cross, on its hill top. Below it, on all sides, the city. Behind it, miles of valley, bounded by hill-ranges against the sky.[19]

With the establishment of Blessed Sacrament parish in Ward 6, a network of English-speaking parishes encompassed the city, and church buildings existed in all its major areas.

The Parish System: Class and Political Lines

As already noted the Roman Catholic church separates economic classes within its membership more precisely than the Protestant churches. The chief device used in this isolation is the parish system, the lines of which conform neatly to the major social areas (see maps).

At most points ward and parish lines are very similar—a pattern to be expected with Paper City's planned spatial arrangements. In some instances the parish lines preceded chronologically the establishment of ward lines, and the men who drew the ward lines followed the patterns of the church, but in most instances the hierarchy had the ward lines to aid them in the establishment of parochial lines. The deviations of parish and ward lines are always significant; the parish lines are closer than the political boundaries to the "natural" social lines of the community, that is, they encompass like residential areas into one territorial unit.[20]

The power to establish the final parish lines of the community rests entirely with the bishop. Priests and laymen in Paper City were consulted for information, and special religious censuses and surveys were often made before new parishes were established. Local priests and laymen have opposed the decisions made by the chancery, with varying success.[21] Parish lines, once established, tend to be kept, since periodic change would invite continuous pressure from priests to shift lines in order to increase membership in their parish.

The parish system is a territorial adaptation to the city's social structure. This adaptation is relevant to a number of social relationships. Marriage, recreational associations and education are to a great extent local matters.[22] The politics of the city are to some extent ward politics. Ward 2 is "Father McMichael's ward," and his presence at all political rallies and big social occasions is expected and courted by the precinct and ward politicians.

There are, however, many organizations and social relations that are formed about issues and interests much larger than the parishes. The parish system, while simplifying the constituency and the responsibilities of the pastor, also cuts him off from many dynamic movements in the community. The concerns of the parish priest tend to center in the religious and educational life of the parish. Yet most of the political-moral issues with which the politicians wrestle involve the whole of the community and the actions of agencies outside the parish on state, national and international problems. The social system of Paper City reflects the city-wide maneuvering of special interest groups. The local Catholic pastor leaves the church's program for such groups to the diocesan hierarchy; but this means that leadership, as in the labor unions, is drawn out of the parish for education and then not reintegrated in any way into the religious life of the major social unit of the church, the parish.

The parish system reduces the preoccupation of laymen with social advancement through the choice of the religious group with which he will associate. If a Roman Catholic has achieved the social status of upper class, the process of residential selectivity has already operated and he lives in the Highlands and accordingly belongs to Holy Cross. Protestants probably more often make calculations about the chances for increasing their social status by joining an "uptown" church.

Ecological Areas and the Protestant Churches

In the Protestant churches the major unit of organization is the congregation, a group of people voluntarily united in their desire for a particular type of religious and social leadership and service, rather than a group of people territorially selected for the reception of generally uniform doctrine and cultus. Little precise relationship exists between the residential areas occupied by Protestant church members and the neighborhood in which their church building is located.[23]

Since virtually half of the Protestant members go to churches located outside their social area, the ministers do not attempt in their association to distribute responsibility to one another for reaching the people of any given area of the city.[24] The Protestant churches have steadily withdrawn from the major working-class areas into an eight-block pocket in the center of the city. Members in the major Protestant churches are now almost nonexistent in Wards 1, 2, 4, and even 5; yet there is considerable evidence that these are the areas where most laboring-class Protestants on entering the city from rural and village areas live.[25]

The area in which the Protestant churches now cluster was, in the decades from 1870 to 1890, the major residential area for upper and upper middle classes. In these decades, not only the Methodists and Baptists moved their churches from the flats into the area, but also the Presbyterian and Reform groups built their first churches there, and the Second Congregational Church moved four blocks to be more centrally located in the new residential area. "The churches were probably the most important single conscious factor in the social evolution of the city," an historian observed, so closely did the Protestant churches follow their most affluent members up the hill.[26] None of the major denominations was to have the funds or inclination to move again.

Today the Protestant churches have approximately three-fourths of their financial investment in property located in an area increasingly invaded by commercial interests, with the smallest percentage of young people and the highest percentage of people over sixty-five in the city.

The laymen who assumed major responsibility for raising funds for the buildings and for location of them in Ward 5 were largely the well-to-do members of the congregation.[27] There is no record of efforts by the individual denominations to discuss with other church groups building plans and the development of an over-all strategy for the city.

Near the end of the century, the Protestant churches sensed that they were abandoning the working-class areas of the city and several efforts were made to establish religious education societies and services below High Street. In 1892 a group of volunteer workers from the Second Congregational Church who had established Grace Chapel aided in securing friends for a resident pastor and a church edifice. The building, described by the new pastor as a "workers' institutional, religious center," became Protestantism's major effort to penetrate the most highly concentrated Roman Catholic and working-class area of the city. Today, aside from the work of Grace Church, the major Protestant activity in the lowest income districts is being carried on by the sect groups.

Summary

What can be said in summary about the relation of the churches to the classes and social areas of the city? There is some basis in fact for the widely held belief that Catholicism is the religion of the working class and Protestantism the religion of the well-to-do. The question asked in various forms, "Are the Catholics or Protestants gaining more ground in the city?" has been in the past a convenient way of alluding to a contest with wide economic and social implications. However, over the years less clear distinctions could be made between the religious groups in terms of class differences and less neat identification of social cleavage with religious tension. For example, in the past two generations many Roman Catholics have joined Protestants in the upper income brackets. They express much the same interest as the Yankee in maintaining interfaith relations that do not encourage serious public debate of fundamental differences. In many areas of thought, economic and class associations appear more important than experience in the church.

Nonetheless, habits of thought and loyalties developed in the churches persist through changes of class rank and ethnic assimilation. Distinctions can be made between Catholic and Protestant apprehensions of the realities of social class. These viewpoints are not mutually exclusive, but they vary in emphasis, and they help explain the actions of religious leaders. They become, at certain times and on certain issues, fundamental sources of tension and conflict in the community. They have ramifications in the approaches of the church leaders to labor, recreation, politics, as well as to ecological areas of the city.

The Catholic leaders tend to see society arranged according to a structure written into the universe. The role of the religious leader is to see that the programs and the territorial arrangements of the church (parish lines) correspond to the natural order that God has already given us. The Catholic pastors, looking at Paper City, see that men have different vocational tasks, belong to different social classes, tend to live in different residential areas according to income and national origin. They conclude that it is natural for men to be ranked and arranged according to the economic function they perform and the house they can afford. The central administrative problem for the clergy is to see that all men are reached by the sacraments of the faith. If adaptation to the social order aids this, well and good, for there is no religious or moral issue at stake in the adaptation. The central problem in social ethics is to make society correspond to the natural order promulgated by God, to make sure that good Catholics become active in all aspects of the social structure, and to rearrange the parts of the social structure periodically in the interests of justice (for instance, by giving labor a more active role in industry). The fundamental theological problem is to discern and interpret the system of natural law known by all reasonable men and to add to this law the divine law given in Christian revelation.

The extent to which this law is interpreted in terms that are static or dynamic, abstract or concrete, will depend, in part, upon the Catholic leaders' view of God and His action in the world. Is God conceived as beyond capacity for change in Himself, or is God involved in the working out in history of His eternal purposes? The interpretation will depend also upon what is happening in the community itself, in its social life.

It is clear that enforcement of and conformity to the social ecological areas of the city is more deliberate, precise and extensive in Catholicism than in the Protestant churches. The Catholic parish system is a rational and systematic placement of churches and grouping of members according to the residential areas of the city. The divisions of class are reinforced, parish lines being a more accurate index of the actual social areas of the city than the boundaries drawn by any other institution. But discernment of social reality is not so static that the leaders of the church are unable to adapt to the growth and change in the city. They have developed a parish system that has reached in time all of the areas of the community.

The Protestant view of society is, like that of Catholicism, a compound of theological and social aspects. In comparison with

Catholicism, Protestantism places less emphasis upon class, social area and ethnic group as parts of a structure or order and more emphasis upon viewing the social structure as itself an aspect of process. To say this is to give the Protestant view more of an explicit theory than its leaders actually express. The liberal Protestant leaders are reluctant to face the existence of class stratification within the churches, so strong is their desire to acclaim the uniqueness of each individual and the possibility of all men living in harmony in the sight of God. They have developed fewer norms for guidance of church strategy than the Catholic hierarchy has; they have less knowledge of the actual social composition of their church membership than the Catholic pastors do. Some Protestant pastors, influenced by theological views recently developed in the seminaries, try to express God's relation to society not so much as one in which He has promulgated immutable laws or orders as one in which He is at work within the changes and interactions going on in the community.

The total impact of these varied theological perspectives has been to give Protestantism more of an openness and a quick sensitivity to the movement of the dominant groups in their membership than present in Catholicism. Note, for example, the rapid shift of location of most of the Protestant churches when the residential patterns of their major lay leadership changed. But the social adaptations of the Protestant churches reflect the one-class nature of Protestantism's most influential lay leaders. Protestantism, unlike Catholicism, had no center of responsibility for making over-all, rational, strategic decisions. Once it became evident that the Protestant churches had abandoned important areas and social classes of the city, the leaders then sought to overcome or circumvent the class divisions of the city by the great evangelistic and sentimental gesture of the Grace church mission. The Protestant leaders show a much greater sympathy than Catholic pastors with upper and middle class reluctance to identify men by class, and with the desires of their members to use the church for movement upward in the class structure. This can be understood as a reflection of the greater middle and upper class composition of Protestantism, but it also appears to express fundamental theological orientations.

The faith groups have their differences of perspective, but they are involved in a common social reality which has both structure and process. The relations of both Catholicism and Protestantism to the classes and social areas of the city reflect this fact.

Chapter 13

The "Foreign" and the "Native"

When you speak of Catholics in Paper City it is important to know whether you mean Irish Catholics, French Catholics or Polish Catholics. The major ethnic or "foreign" groups in the city are Roman Catholic; the Yankee host or "native" group is Protestant.

Paper City was begun largely in the Yankees' image. Representatives of powerful textile interests in New England had conceived the city in 1849, blocked out its streets, canals, mill and tenement sites, persuaded manufacturers to establish firms in the city and recruited the labor force. But within twenty-five years of its founding, a majority of the city's laborers were foreign born.[1] This growth of immigrant people in Paper City was part of a larger population movement of Canadians and Europeans to the United States during the latter half of the nineteenth century, a movement which concentrated its settlement in the northern and eastern industrial cities. By 1875 Paper City had the largest percentage of foreign-born people of any community in the state; by 1890, only two cities in the United States exceeded Paper City in this respect.

From the first years the Yankees owned the mills, the mill sites, the biggest stores—as they do today. The native Yankees who manned the mills were replaced by the Irish, who yielded to the French Canadians, Germans, Scotch and English, and these groups were by the turn of the century making room for Polish workers.[2] By 1920, Paper City had ceased to be the community of foreign-born people it had once been; only a third of the population was foreign born and of this third about 49 per cent were naturalized or had first papers. By 1940 the foreign-born population composed less than a fourth (22.5 per cent) of the people in Paper City. Of these 25.5 per cent were French Canadian; 18.8 per cent Irish; and 16.7 per cent Polish.[3]

The Yankee mill owners and managers remained dominant in their economic positions, and the Yankee ethos continued powerful in its impact on the immigrant groups. Yankee roots were deep in the past of the region. Prior to the establishment of Paper City by the General Court in 1850, the community was first known as "Ireland," the place taking its name from a Protestant Irishman who was assigned land in 1665 by Springfield proprietors; it was later called "Irish Parish" when the area was thought by the Congregational Church officials to be capable of supporting a ministry of its own in 1792. The area was populated by Congregationalists and Baptists in 1845 when Boston Yankees began to develop the area into an industrial center. The strong Catholic influx in the city began approximately five years later.[4] As the Yankee owners became more and more surrounded by immigrant groups and their wealth increased, they developed a self-contained social life, comfortably but not ostentatiously withdrawn from the life of the majority of the people. Spacious houses were built on the hill overlooking the mills of Paper City. Fortunes were accumulated which would command power for at least three generations. A feeling of proprietorship and of long, selective lineage was expressed in the organization of Protestant charitable organizations and feminine ancestral cults and in the withdrawal of the Yankee male from the political life of the city.

Irish immigration into Paper City took place chiefly in the period from 1850 to 1875. The Irish were the first "newcomers" and first "foreign competition" to the native workers. The poorest of the Irish settled at first in "the Patch" above the dam, where they built crude shelters, half board, half dug out holes in the ground, comprising one room and a loft, without windows. So clearly was this understood to be an Irish Catholic area that a Congregational minister being interviewed for the most prominent Protestant church in the city considerably shocked the leading elder who was taking him on a tour of the community when he asked if the people in the Patch would become his parishioners.[5] Here the Irish lived in the communion of the poor, several families sharing a pump, an oven and the firewood gathered by the men from the riverbanks.

Other Irish settled in an area which had by 1860 been labeled "Tigertown" (Map I) for the rough men who lived there and worked in the brickyards and mills close by. Within a decade "Tigertown" had become polyglot with French and German as well as Irish. The Irish became the old settlers, resisting the inroads of the "Canucks," who lived, according to the Irish, like "mackerel packed in a barrel" and "worked cheap." Feelings were so intense between the groups and cohesiveness so great that they maintained largely separate neighborhoods in Wards 1 and 2 from 1870 to 1890.[6]

The Irish held a middle position in the social strata of the city. Their religion, their illiteracy, their lack of experience with popular government and their poverty gave them some affinity with the French Canadians and Poles, while their English-speaking background and their early arrival in Paper City set them apart from the other Catholic immigrant groups and gave them a decided advantage in social mobility.

The variance in the social mobility of the Irish produced three major class levels within the ethnic group which have been termed, by a *Catholic Mirror* writer, the "shanty Irish," the "lace-curtain Irish" and the "venetian-blind Irish." The distinctions between the three types were described as follows:

> Lace-curtain Irish means cultivating the [Yankee] people who despise you, and condemning in turn the pipe-smoking women and whiskey-drinking men who live in Kerry Patches, Shanty Hills and Hell's Kitchens in New England. . . .
>
> When a mother stops her husband, or her son, or her old father from being himself with the horrified whisper, "What will the neighbors say," that's lace-curtain too. The lace-curtain Irish children go to fancy schools, make respectable friends and marry the financially elect, unless they are "Polacks, Frogs or Dagoes."
>
> The lace-curtain Irish are midway between the shanty Irish from which they sprang and the venetian-blind Irish who live next to the people on the hill, the rich and respectable families with whom they wish to mingle and whom they hope eventually to replace. If there were no shanty Irish or venetian-blind Irish, there would be no lace-curtain Irish. The lace-curtain Irish are stiff and prudish, frugal with their charities, ashamed of their traditions, whether they are the noble heritage of the storytellers or the ignoble superstitions of the ignorant poor. . . . Lace-curtain Irish never acknowledge they are lace-curtain; in their own words, they are successful, industrious, decent. They are not like the rest of the Irish at all.
>
> The lace-curtain Irish families have rebellious sons and daughters,

children laid waste by the war of nerves waged by their ambitious parents against their tendency to relapse into shanty Irish.[7]

These distinctions belong more accurately to Paper City's past than to its present. The shanty Irish who dug the canals and tended the spindles have become lace-curtain Irish—the straw bosses, the foremen, machinists, toolmakers, ward chairmen, teachers, policemen, firemen, union organizers, construction engineers, doctors. The fact of wide-scale social mobility has reduced the intensity of the drive.

After residential consolidation in the Patch and the Flats with their ethnic businesses and churches, the closely knit colonies disintegrated as the Irish scattered throughout the city. They formed new associations through lodges closely related to the Roman Catholic church. The church itself became an institution under Irish leadership, able to maintain the ethnic system in spite of the loss of the groups' homogeneous residential and economic base.

Religious and economic persecution in Ireland, hard economic treatment by Paper City Yankees, opportunity for social advancement more favorable than that of competing immigrant groups, faith in the superiority of the spiritual life of the Catholic church—these forces forged a militant cohesive ethnic group, motivated to press for opportunities of social and religious leadership. It had a threefold bond of unity.

First, economic deprivation. The local daily newspaper on the seventy-fifth anniversary of the Ancient Order of Hibernians suggested that the "sweat of the Ancestors of many of those who celebrate the jubilee is a part of the very foundations of industrial Paper City, the dam, the canals, the older mills, the railroad, the bridge piers." [8]

Second, the group had common nationality. At the Lenten series of the Paper City Council of the Knights of Columbus members were told by the speaker that "the Irish erected and defended a great nation in the new world dedicated to liberty and freedom, and swept from America the tyrant who had for centuries with dreadful cruelty oppressed them in their own fair land." [9]

And third, the Irish had a common religious loyalty. A Saint Patrick's Day issue of the official diocesan magazine recalled in its lead editorial the "tragic Penal Days of Ireland" when "'twas treason to love her and death to defend her; when the Catholic Faith was under the English law; . . . when Catholic educators were hunted like wolves and treated like wolves when captured."

It is difficult to distinguish the Irish drive to advance the cause of the church from the drive for social status. Attitudes of aggressiveness and watchfulness acquired during past periods of insecurity are maintained to some extent after comparatively high economic rank has been achieved. Irish leadership with the reputation of aggressiveness appears to be mainly located in the middle-class rank, where religious and nationality ethnocentrism possibly compensate for a sense of inferior social status.

The French Canadians, who came to Paper City chiefly during the period from 1870 to 1890, have their own distinctive ethnic characteristics. Settling in the wards below the canals (Map III), they tended to stay on in their original colonies within the city to a greater extent than the Irish did. The French have not shown so great a drive as the Irish for leadership and social status. As the chief historian and novelist of the Paper City French has said, "The part the Franco-Americans have played in New England is not a showy one." [10] They came to Paper City "with largely a peasant background and became the laborers, the small taxpayers, the privates in the Army, the mill workers, the small merchants, the women clerks in department stores, all common people." [11] Their stolid temperament and acceptance of the conditions of work made them more acceptable to the Yankee mill owners than the aggressive Irish. "Work, go to Mass, save money, bear children and return [to Quebec]"—this was long the order of life for the French Canadian. The mill owners in the 1870's and 1880's observed that French Canadian parents put their children to work as soon as possible and kept them there, often evading the state school laws by reporting advanced ages for their children.

The strong control over the children exercised within the traditional French Canadian family and the proximity of the Quebec homeland slowed the acculturation process and the advance in social status of many French Catholics.[12] The French did not seek to create a new Quebec out of Paper City as the Irish sought to create a new Eire out of Paper City. The French sought to live together in the community, to keep strong their national, religious, social and ancestral roots, and then go back to Quebec as soon as possible.

When the French had obtained a French parish with priests and nuns brought from Quebec to teach their children, they were comparatively unconcerned about the rest of Paper City—Catholic or Protestant. Once *"nôtre langue—nôtre foi—nos traditions"* were secured by the maintenance of a national church and parish school, the French desired to live and let live.

The Polish people were the last of the Roman Catholic ethnic groups to establish enough of a colony in Paper City to form a national church (in 1900). The Poles in their first decade in the community, 1893-1903, made little impact on the city. Their poverty and late arrival made it necessary for them to take the most menial jobs. The Polish women replaced the French, who had replaced the Irish, in the mill rag-picking rooms. A few Poles were able by the end of the century to invest in tenement blocks and to buy farms vacated by Yankees near the city, having been urged on by the Polish priest with the call that "land can never be taken away from you." [13]

The German people, who colonized in the southern part of the city, were the largest Protestant ethnic group. They came with the founding in 1863 of the Germania Woolen Mills by two devout Lutheran brothers who encouraged German artisans to settle near their mills. The colony was composed of skilled workmen with considerable culture and education who isolated [14] themselves from what they considered were "uncouth Paddies" and poverty-stricken French Canadians about them. Through the Lutheran Church and its parish schools, the Turnverein and the German Benevolent Society, this ethnic group has maintained a comparatively independent life.[15]

Ethnic lines do not run as sharply or as simply through the community's social structure today. Social mobility has been so general that the longer an ethnic group has been in the city, the higher is the over-all level of social status achieved by its members. However, the degree of mobility has been so varied for individual members of the ethnic groups that the cohesiveness of the groups, particularly the Irish, has been reduced by economic differences.

On the other hand, the ability of the Yankees to maintain a generally superior economic position in comparison with the Catholic ethnic groups, and their resistance to further distribution of power and privilege, have been strong factors in the attempt of the Catholic groups to continue their existence in the city and to search for some unity under the religious symbols of the church.

The Catholic church responded to each of the national groups in a different manner, for their needs and interests varied greatly. The church was willing to adapt to the varied ethnic patterns as "natural" and without conflict with the supernatural goals of the church, so long as the adaptations aided in holding the allegiance of the people to the church. But the Irish and the French leaders differed as to whether support of national language and traditions strengthened the church; so a serious and protracted struggle to maintain areas of influence over the church's ethnic policy went on.

The French and the Poles sought to use the resources of the church to maintain national mores and manners within the parish and neighborhood since it was more difficult for them to adjust to Paper City's host culture than it was for the Irish.

It is significant that when the first French church celebrated its seventy-fifth anniversary, the event was commemorated with a parish history written by the pastor lamenting the decrease of church-centered activities which accompanied the "Americanization process" and appealing poignantly for preservation together of Catholicism and French culture:

> We are Catholics, we wish to live as Catholics, but we desire to be Catholics of the French language. Why, in fact, anglicize ourselves, why become "Yankees," when our French culture, so abundant and so varied, can contribute to the cultural enrichment of the United States. The development of the American people needs the artistic and scientific support of each nationality. . . . The founders of the parish, occupied as they were in earning their daily bread, were not able to interest themselves in things of the mind. We, beneficiaries of their toils and of their battles, shall we neglect our beautiful language? [16]

The Irish sought less than the other groups to maintain their ethnic cohesiveness through the church. When they did, it was by devices other than the national parish and preservation of a national language.[17] The pastor of an English-speaking parish observed:

> The French priests are making a tragic mistake in trying to keep their national parishes in which they can all the time talk French, French, French. They are losing their people by it. They have the mistaken idea that if the French language is lost the people will lose their faith. That's just not so. The Irish don't talk Gaelic and they haven't lost their faith. The Polish church is making the same mistake of talking the Polish language all the time. This is America, not France or Poland, and it's time the priests talked the English language.

There were a variety of reasons for the Irish position. Economic advancement and dispersement to the suburbs occurred first among the Irish. Their native language was English rather than Gaelic; so the English-speaking parish, led by an Irish priest, was no threat to their national heritage. By the time of the French and Polish entrance into Paper City the diocesan and community clergy was dominantly Irish. When laymen broke away from French or Polish parishes, it was to become members of English-speaking, but largely Irish-led parishes. The pastor of one of the French parishes acknowledged this by saying that the French priests

> . . . keep the French language in our churches and schools more to keep the Irish clergy out of our French parishes than we do to keep alive national loyalties. If we had English Masses, then the bishop would send in Irish priests. This is what the Irish have done in the West in French parishes that ceased to use the French language.

The Irish leadership had apparently sought to develop the church into an institution uniting the various ethnic groups in a strong and militant alliance capable of holding its own against the Yankees and of securing recognition and advancement of the faith throughout the community.[18] This was to be done largely under Irish Catholic leadership and through use of instruments of the church to weaken various cultural ties of other groups which appeared to the Irish to hinder the religious alliance. In response the French and Poles developed strong defensive tactics, and the Irish compromised: they established ethnic parishes when flagrant disaffections from the faith occurred and found a place in city-wide Catholic activities for ceremonies and social events renewing memories of national traditions.

Ethnic rivalry and tension, although decreasing over the years as a result of the processes of assimilation, continue to weaken attempts at united action on matters of faith. One evidence of ethnic competition is the fact that each of the ethnic groups in the clergy rates its own members as "better Catholics" than the others—i.e., more observant of religious practices and precepts. The Irish clergy rate the Polish people as "better Catholics" than the French; the Polish clergy rate the French as "better Catholics" than the Irish; and the French priests rate the Polish people as "better Catholics" than the Irish.[19]

The ethnic composition of Paper City is different from that of many New England cities. Most noteworthy is the fact that it has almost no Italian people. In New Haven, Providence, Boston, and many other New England cities ethnic conflict has been between Italian and Irish. In these cities the forms of ethnic rivalry differed from those in Paper City, for the national traditions and characteristics in conflict differed. Yet the effect of the rivalry upon the religious leadership was similar: it used much of their energy for the resolution of internal problems rather than for influence upon the society outside the churches.[20] Paper City has differed also from cities further west in the high percentage of its foreign born. The presence of large numbers of people from French Canada, Ireland and Poland has made possible the extensive perpetuation of ethnic traditions and loyalties, and this has kept the Roman Catholic leaders more absorbed in nationality rivalries than clergy located in cities where immigrants have been more dispersed among the native population. There has been some reduction of internal Catholic tensions in recent years with the inevitable assimilation of ethnic groups, and church leaders are turning their interests somewhat more toward the life of the city.

The Ethnic Parish System

The bishop's incorporation of ethnic divisions in the parish system appears to have been made after clear resistance by French and Polish groups to the English-speaking "Irish parishes" and ethnic-inspired disaffection from the church was evident (Map II). The French colony would have little to do with the first Catholic parish in the city.[21] A French priest writing the history of the first Franco-

American parish in the city observed, "The French people cared very little about the Catholic church of the region. They gave 'poverty and ignorance of English' as excuses for not attending the religious services of St. Jerome's parish." The final event precipitating the establishment of a French parish was the discovery by Irish Catholics in 1869 that several French girls were receiving instruction in English in a Protestant church. Today three French parishes divide up the French Catholics in the city—two in working-class areas and one among the French who have moved "up the hill."

The establishment of the Polish parish followed a pattern similar to the beginning of the French national parish system. The Polish people were attending Mass at "Irish" St. Jerome's in 1895 when an unfrocked priest from Poland arrived in the city and established an independent Polish church. It met at first with some success, but the priest, according to an official Catholic history, was driven from the city soon "for drunkenness and worse." [22] His work caused confusion and dissension among the Polish people, and they ceased to go to any church. In 1896, the Roman Catholic bishop established a Polish pastor in the community. When the priest arrived, he found only 9 among 500 Poles loyal to the Roman Catholic church. In four years he had 370 members and began the erection of a church building to be known as Mater Dolorosa, Mother of Sorrows, for the troubles created by the independent Polish religious venture.

While Paper City Catholics were wrestling with the question of whether to encourage ethnic parishes, a circular letter was issued, in 1897, by the Apostolic Delegation seeking to clarify church policy on the question for the entire American church. The letter gave unmistakable freedom to Catholics wishing "emancipation"—the word is that of the letter—from national parishes in order to join parishes in which "the language of the country, that is, English, is used." [23] The letter strengthened the bishop's obvious policy, supported by most Irish Catholics, of established English-speaking parishes as widely and as rapidly as possible.

A variety of devices have been used by pastors, particularly the more elderly clergy located in parishes "down the hill," fighting to hold ethnic parish membership. They have shifted times for masses (an 11:00 A.M. Mass at Mater Dolorosa, the Polish church, was attracting late Sunday risers among the Irish in St. Jerome's parish;

so St. Jerome's also instituted an 11:00 Mass). They have imposed religious sanctions (such as the denial of a high Mass when a death has occurred in a family which has constantly crossed parish lines). Financial penalties have been levied ($10 a year for each child not observing parish lines in attending parochial school).[24]

But the priests know that general processes of assimilation are changing the parish patterns built upon ethnic loyalties. A French pastor in a very candid statement recently indicated his role in a losing battle for ethnic survival:

> The clergy does all it can to solve the problem [of French ethnic survival]—it builds schools, exhorts the parishioners to send their children there, goes to see the parents. What else can we do? We can't force the people to educate their children in the parish school. Do you see what I mean? The whole problem has always rested with the public, and not the leaders. If the Franco-Americans want to maintain their identity, they'll have to take the necessary steps. The clergy has done all in its power. . . . For my part, I will always preach in French, and I prefer to read in French. On parish business, however, I often have to speak English. So do my parishioners. They cannot escape assimilation where the clergy can. In time, I suppose, we will all be assimilated, and apart from a few societies, and a nucleus interested in the problem as a cultural one, there will be no Franco-Americans.[25]

Close attention is still paid by most pastors to the patterns of church attendance by national groups. Many individual deviations are known to them: the elderly French lady who crosses ethnic parish lines to attend a church which does not have so many steps up to its entrance; the wife of an Irish fireman in Ward 5 who goes to the French parish because it is three blocks nearer than Sacred Heart. When interethnic marriages occur, the family is not usually pressed by most priests to attend a particular ethnic or English-speaking church according to an arbitrary rule. The decision is left to the family. Most pastors believe that families attend as a unit, and when they have made attempts to force each parent to attend the church of his nationality, the family often attends no church to avoid conflict. A substantial minority of the parents in mixed ethnic marriages continue to attend their national church, but for the younger people particularly convenience of time and location of Masses are often as important as the nationality of the parish.

Ethnic Groups and Catholic Societies

Most adult and youth organizations sponsored by the churches are parish-centered and reflect the degree of nationality isolation within them. The city-wide Catholic laymen's organization, the Knights of Columbus, has contributed little to association of ethnic groups. The Irish Catholic priests and lay leaders insist it is intended for all Catholics; the officers have tried to enlist Polish and French Catholics by donating funds to their organizations and holding worship services in a variety of ethnic parishes. But the French priests and lay officials of French organizations continue to call the Knights "an Irish organization," charge (correctly) that it has never had a Frenchman as Grand Knight and that its official publication *Caravel* and its celebrations favor the Irish.[26] The French priests recommend that their laymen belong rather to the French Catholic Society of St. Jean-Baptiste, a fraternal organization also with authoritative commendation from the church.

A few youth activities such as parochial school sports and Catholic Girls' Association have produced interethnic activity.

Each ethnic group witnesses to its tradition and loyalty within the life of the church but largely through separate organizations and activities. Each group holds its high Mass on the feast day of its patron saint, when the priests of its national parishes speak of the ethnic group's great past and future and exhort the people to model their lives on their patron saint. Then the group parades through Paper City with drum corps and drill teams of its own national societies and parochial schools. The priests of each group issue pronouncements on the trials of their own homeland in war and peace.[27] The official press gives space to the glory and troubles of all ethnic groups seriatim, granting space most often to the Irish, then to the Poles and finally to the French.[28] The real unity of the church is attained on the level of common doctrine, sacraments and ecclesiastical polity. The "unity" of peoples within Catholicism as encouraged by the program of the church is the kind achieved by adding up or recognizing the various traditions rather than by deliberate encouragement of programs and discussions involving men of different backgrounds.

Protestant Churches and Ethnic Groups

No special adaptation to ethnic loyalties and culture has appeared necessary to Protestant pastors through most of Paper City's history. The majority of their members were natives, and the ethnic newcomers who joined were English, Scotch or Scandinavian, so similar in culture to the Yankees, and so few in number, that assimilation was much less difficult than for the Catholic ethnics. German Lutherans were the only Protestant group to colonize in the city.

However, deliberate efforts were made in two of the Protestant churches (the Missouri Lutheran and Grace Congregational) to adapt to or to utilize ethnic loyalties for the maintenance of church membership. The early German leaders isolated their people from the rest of the community as extensively as had the French and Polish leaders, whose culture probably differed from the host culture more sharply than the Germans'. Services were conducted in German until the 1920's, when an English service was introduced in addition to the German and soon became the more popular. In 1888, control of the German church was taken over by a group which represented the Missouri Lutheran synod and opposed further assimilation of the group into American culture. A group desiring further assimilation (such as English services) and less dogmatic theology left the German Lutheran church to establish the Reformed Church.[29] The avowed policy now of both churches is to "encourage assimilation as fast as possible," but the German Lutheran church will not co-operate in the interdenominational agencies for clergy, lay adults or youth.

At about the time the other churches had begun to shake themselves loose from strong ethnic appeals, the Grace Congregational Church, located in a working-class area, embarked on what the pastor hoped would develop into "a mighty cosmopolitan church" through deliberate appeals to Protestant British, Scotch, Scandinavian and German immigrants and their children.[30] "It was realized," the minister noted in 1916, "that scores and scores of incomers of Protestant training and tradition were being lost to the Church of Christ through their removal to America. If Grace Church were ever to become the strong 'people's' church which the city so sorely needed, its increment must come from the ranks of the incomers, no other recruits being available."

Grace Church for over thirty years held a series of services, planned with special appeal to particular nationalities, on days commemorating important historical events or personages in the history of the groups. "Preaching was upon such themes as Henry Drummond's Bible, England's Modern St. George, Luther's Hymns, . . . The Soldiers that Saved the Reformation." Organizations of the particular nationality were invited to attend the service and "all the legitimate methods of the politician (were) used to make the invitation effective," according to the minister. The organizations marched in a body to church. "In a city where Roman Catholics parade, it is a fine sight to see Old Scotia's forces marching to the house of God," the pastor observed.

During World War II the programs were abandoned reluctantly by the church staff because of lack of interest. "The people want to be called Americans," the assistant pastor recently observed. "If I say, 'Let's have a German *kuchen* at a church supper,' the women say, 'Why call it German *kuchen*? Let's just have *kuchen*.'"

Grace Church history alone indicates that no neat identification of Roman Catholics with retardation of ethnic assimilation and Yankees with encouragement of assimilation can be made. Further evidence is given in the conflict over teaching the French language in Catholic parochial schools. In 1876 laws were passed in the city which required all public and parochial schools to instruct in English; and the French parochial school was rejected as a part of the educational system of the city under pressure of English-speaking Catholics, lay and cleric. Within a short time, however, the opposition was silenced and the French school was accepted. "How can one explain this change?" a French priest asks in a local history. He answers: "The civil authorities came to realize that the French schools taught English as well as French. And the industrialists, fearing the wholesale departure of the Canadians who furnished such precious manpower, brought pressure to stop the movement against the French schools."[31] The industrialists also contributed funds to the French parochial schools to indicate their support and to aid in their continuation. The Protestant clergy were silent during the controversy in so far as public statements reported in the local press are concerned.[32]

In summary, the tensions between Roman Catholic and Protestant peoples are only in part based on religious differences. Under Protestant and Roman Catholic symbols intense class and nationality loyalties often find expression. Both religious movements are molded by social cleavage in the city and in varying degrees isolate groups through their own adaptations—particularly the parish system of the Catholics and the class-oriented, "planless" location of church resources of the Protestants.

Neither nationality nor church interests have been uniform, fixed or simple. Within Catholicism, for example, the Irish priesthood had a tremendous stake in resisting French ethnic loyalty even while preserving some of their own national habits of thought. The Irish stressed the importance of distinguishing faith from a particular culture, while the French sought to conserve "the natural order" already established. Ethnic rivalry in the Catholic church and serious disagreement over the strategy which would best hold the loyalty of the immigrant affected relations with Protestants chiefly in that it reduced the cohesiveness and unity of Catholicism and turned the attention of its leaders inward toward their own nationality cleavages.

Chapter 14

The Churches and Recreation

Paper City is giving more and more attention to its leisure time and recreational activities. The long week end and the shorter work day leave time and energy for active participation in a number of fraternal and social associations. These associations, like the rest of Paper City's organized life, reflect the particular approaches to society of the churches and the religious tensions of the community.

The Catholic church, sensitive to the structure of the community, seems to regard the social and "booster" clubs as, in many ways, the most important nonchurch activities in the city. At least it has formulated its simplest and most distinct associational policies toward these groups, and has sought with considerable diligence to relate leisure-time activities in some formal way to the life of the church. The Protestant churches have, on the other hand, more generally tended to regard the fraternal and recreational organizations as associations which are to develop their own programs, with Protestant influence being carried informally through individual members or families. Protestant fears of Catholic influence have altered this approach in recent years.

One item from the annual activities of the Catholic Girls' League and the Protestant Girls' Association symbolizes differences in Roman Catholic and Protestant approaches to recreational associations. The Catholic Girls' League has as its most important annual meeting a communion breakfast. The meeting is held in one of the parish houses with a priest as speaker, usually on the relation of the organization to the church. The Protestant Girls' Association, for its part, has as its most important annual event a mother and daughter breakfast held at the Masonic Temple, seldom with a minister as speaker.

The Catholic concept of a parish, as indicated in Chapter 12, is a geographical area of a community whose organized activity centers about the church. The church has either founded itself or encouraged the establishment of parish societies to express the varied "natural" and "religious" interests of the laity. Many benevolent, ethnic, recreational, charitable, educational and special-interest parish societies (Catholic Hospital Alumnae Association, Catholic High School Athletic Association, Catholic Polish Veterans and others) have been established by the laity and none have been condemned by the church so long as their activities have been in church terms at least partially religious. The clergy have, however, permitted none of the societies to operate without a religious program and have directed some, such as the scouts, increasingly toward religious ends. The canon law recommends that Catholics belong to those societies or associations which have been erected or commended by the church.[1] Heretics, schismatics and infidels are forbidden membership in all ecclesiastical societies and in most cases in lay parish societies.[2]

The Roman Catholic church approaches the various social and occupational organizations as "natural" associations to which it is always, when permitted, "adding the supernatural," to use the subtitle of an official Catholic pamphlet on scouting. To add the supernatural requires, for the church, some objective relationship of the natural association with the institution of grace.

The church hopes, insofar as the culture permits, to have new natural interests expressed as societies of Catholics (for example, Catholic Veterans, Catholic Scouts) in order to give more readily a religious aspect to their programs and to channel "natural" interests more directly into the church.[3] In areas such as labor, where Catholic societies cannot be organized and effectively meet the natural needs of Catholics, the church sees the necessity for Catholics to join mixed organizations, but has special policies for exercise of Catholic influence within them.

The latent, if not manifest, result of many of these church policies is to isolate Catholics from non-Catholics. This isolation of Catholics in their "natural" associations has usually been accompanied by programs utilizing these associations for development of religious indoctrination and identification with the church. The church has not sought withdrawal of its members from society, but the disciplining and unifying of members within associations so that they can better advance the world-view of the church.

The closer a "natural" association comes to the development of a philosophy or ideology, the stronger is the Catholic church's opposition to lay membership, the more serious is the sin of participation, the more willing is the diocesan press to accept the worst reports of its activities, and the smaller is the percentage of Catholics in the association.

The Catholic clergy has experienced considerable resistance to its associational policies among laymen in Paper City. The church has been confronted by the influence of well-organized groups, particularly in labor and business, competing for the time and loyalties of Catholics and unrelated to parish life.[4] The upward social mobility of Catholic members has been accompanied by increasing participation in social organizations outside the parish societies. The reaction of some of the pastors (particularly in French parishes) toward such social trends has been to confine parish societies more and more to what they term exclusively religious objectives.[5]

The sect leaders represent the greatest contrast with Catholicism in attitudes toward recreation and religion. They have few social or recreational activities in their sect meetings. They bitterly denounce Catholicism and regular Protestantism for engaging in so much social activity as to be "indistinguishable from the world."

Protestant clergy and laymen have carried on little discussion of the fundamental theological issues at stake in the relations of churches with associations. In general the old-line Protestant churches expect laymen to belong to many autonomous associations, as they also belong to the church. This can be seen in part as an expression of Protestant support of a highly pluralistic culture and perhaps some awareness of the limited guidance general religious and moral principles can give lay action.

The ministers believe that their people, in the words of one pastor, "would not permit church organizations to be developed along class, occupational or political lines. This would be too divisive and rigid a relationship of the church to the community." Yet inevitably some of the educational organizations of the church reflect "natural" class lines, even when policy is not deliberate. (For example, the pastor just quoted had for a number of years a study group of college-educated young people, largely well-to-do, who met at his home. The lower middle class and mill worker young people in his congregation had their own Sunday Nighters' Club which met at the church.)

Most of the clergy consider the development of "fellowship," "sportsmanship," and "clean recreation" as the proper and inclusive functions of leisure-time associations under Protestant auspices. Closer participation by most of the Protestant clergy would not involve any additions or changes in their programs.

The Protestant clergy has not sought to link the church formally with these associations either through special worship services or by their regular attendance at meetings. A Protestant Girls' Association and a Protestant Junior Girls' Association—both recreational and social organizations—exist in the city, but they have no "official" relation to the churches. There are no Protestant Veterans' Association, Protestant Hospital Alumnae Association and Protestant Businessmen's Association corresponding to Catholic organizations in the community with chartered connections with the churches.

The Protestant pastors have no plans for sharing responsibility for participation in major associations developed by laymen with the hope of in some way understanding and illuminating their true nature. They have almost no programs encouraging their laymen to engage in the church in study of the meaning of their faith in relation to specific decisions made in associational life.

City-wide Lay Organizations

The Catholic church has been successful in relating several ethnic fellowship and recreational organizations to its parish structure. The largest and most active ethnic association, the French Catholic St. Jean-Baptiste Society, has authoritative commendation from the church. However, other French ethnic societies—Cercle Rochambeau and the Beaver Club—which are increasingly diverting younger men from the St. Jean-Baptiste Society—have no formal relation to the church, have no Catholic priest as chaplain, and have been organized largely to represent social and political interests. The Protestant churches, in contrast, have developed no formal relationships with ethnic-fraternal groups, although some of these groups occasionally attend church services in a body.

The most important city-wide lay Catholic society in Paper City is the Knights of Columbus, organized to serve as the "strongest lay force at the command of the Church" to be used "for her defense against her enemies." [6] The Knights of Columbus in Paper City number over 1,200; it is the major association for uniting leaders in various parishes and occupations as Catholics and for urging them to work as Catholics in community activities. The Knights are encouraged by the clergy, as the Grand Knight expresses it, to think of their role as militant Christ-bearers taking "Catholic philosophy into the community to aid in the solution of industrial, political, social and educational problems of the day." [7] The chaplain of the Knights is present at at least half of the meetings and is invariably called on for a short speech giving the Catholic viewpoint on current social issues.

The Protestant churches have no city-wide men's organization intended to provide laymen with regular opportunity to exchange interpretations of moral and religious issues. Men from a number of Protestant churches hold annual or semiannual fellowship suppers with an "outside" speaker. Half of the Protestant churches have over the past two decades abandoned attempts at men's religious organizations or Sunday school.[8]

Protestant and Catholic attitudes toward recreational associations are most clearly contrasted in the Catholic Girls' Leagues and the Protestant Girls' Associations.[9] The Catholic church began recommending in 1936 a Catholic Girls' League and a Catholic Girls' Junior League "to unite young women for religious, social and charitable purposes." At present, half of the formal programs of the leagues include discussion of such topics as fashions and home economics; half are on religious themes. Each meeting begins with a worship service. A chaplain is usually present and speaks briefly on Catholic faith and morals. A literary guild in each club gives an opportunity for a few of the members to study Catholic literature. Members chiefly support church social work institutions, but some funds are also given Community Chest and Red Cross.

The Protestant Girls' Associations are the result of a decision of a few young people to develop or sponsor "Protestant social organizations" in reaction to the Catholic program but have no aid from the clergy in clarifying the objectives of the associations. The Protestant Girls' Association was organized five years after the parallel Catholic society was begun and the Protestant Junior Girls' Association nine years after its Catholic equivalent.

Leaders of the Junior Association (girls from fourteen to eighteen years) prepared an "organizing" letter but never sent it out, according to a member, "because we were afraid it would raise too much of a stink among Catholics." The letter began as follows:

> Have you, as a young Protestant girl living in a Catholic city, ever wished that you could meet more girls of your own faith? Most of us wish just this. But you say, "I've met girls of my faith in church." Of course you have, but just how many of you have put yourselves out to meet these girls on a friendly basis?

The letter then described the activities of the organization, stressing the recreational aspects of the program.

> We do not intend to have only religious speakers but also dramatic speakers, speakers from different beauty houses, fashion speakers and so on. We are supported by the ministers of the city and the Senior Protestant Girls' Organization. Our social functions also vary but regardless of this we have our annual semi-formal dance every February, usually on or about Washington's birthday. We do have bowling or ice skating parties, small social parties, and strive to have a square dance and a hayride each fall. This fall our prospects look good as we have a hard-working and diligent slate of officers. . . .

The Protestant Girls' Association (for young women from eighteen to thirty) has developed a program content more explicitly religious than that of the Junior Association. Approximately a fifth of the meetings include such events as talks by a Protestant minister on the history of the Christian church and by a Protestant professor on the relation of psychology and religion. During a recent year attendance at programs announced as "religious" averaged eleven, while attendance at the other programs averaged fifty.

The association's symbols and programs are not as church-centered as those of the Catholic League; sporadic attempts are made to encourage Catholics to join, but its membership is largely Protestant. The officers of the Protestant Girls' Association have suggested on two occasions to the officers in the Catholic Girls' League that a joint meeting be held, but approval from the Catholic clergy was not obtained. The sponsoring ministers of the Protestant Girls'

Association have seldom been present at meetings, coming only when specifically invited to speak or to attend an annual social affair such as a dance or tea. The programs of the association have included speeches by lay Catholics on religious themes (for example, a Spanish Catholic student at a neighboring college spoke on the Catholic church in Cuba). No Protestant speakers have appeared on the Catholic Girls' League program.

Scouts

The scouting program is a good case study of Roman Catholic and Protestant approaches to potentially "mixed" faith associations. The Catholic church has integrated the scout movement into the life of the parish and used it to build loyalty to the church and to Catholic doctrines much more thoroughly than has the Protestant church. Mixed faith troops have been avoided by the Catholic church whenever possible. The national scout movement permits churches to sponsor either of two types of troops—types which in Paper City are referred to as "open" or "mixed faith" troops, and "closed" or "one faith" troops.[10]

The Catholic church looks upon the scouting movement as it does upon many other "worldly associations" as having gone as far as it could "without grace," and in need of the church to "provide the spiritual attributes." The chairman of the Bishop's Committee for Scouting observes that the man who founded scouting: "stopped giving only when the world's treasury was exhausted; and he had not the treasury of the spirit at his command. . . . The Catholic Episcopate of these United States . . . have heard the challenge to spiritualize the Scout Program for our own boys."[11]

The Catholic Committee on Scouting suggests a variety of activities for "adding the supernatural" to scouting: Conduct of an Investiture of Tenderfoot Scouts with Catholic and scout ceremony in the church following the Holy Hour, open and close scout meetings in the spirit of reverence, recommit the scout oath and recite prayers for departed scouts following Communion Mass, begin all hiking and camping projects from the church after prayers for guidance and protection, receive Holy Communion on the second Sunday of every month in uniform and in a body, see that "members practice their Catholic faith, believing that good Catholics make good scouts." Formal religious instruction in scout meetings is not suggested.[12]

The approach of the national Protestant Committee on Scouting is not so much that of adding the supernatural to scouting as in Catholicism (a "Christ above culture" position) as the identification of the program of the church with that of scouting (a "Christ of culture" position). The objectives of the church and scouting are "mutually inclusive and should be fulfilled in the comprehensive program of Christian religious education." [13]

The Protestant Committee on Scouting proposes for integration of the scouts into the life of the churches that they:

> Participate in worship services of the church, provide specific services to the church such as distribution of church bulletins. Pastors or scoutmasters can utilize situations which arise in scouting activities to discuss ethical and religious questions or to provide "more or less informal religious programs." [14]

The policy of the scouting movement is not to permit its program to detract from the opportunity of each church to give its own members religious instruction according to its own principles. The movement will not compete with the churches for the loyalty of boys.[15]

The only limiting national policy actually imposed upon the churches is that in "no case where a Scout troop is connected with a church or religious institution, shall Scouts of other sects or faiths be required, because of their membership in the Troop, to take part in, or observe a religious ceremony distinctively peculiar to that institution or Church." [16]

These national approaches to religion and scouting are representative of basic assumptions held by the scout leadership in Paper City. The Catholic pastors who have co-operated with the scouting movement have all organized "closed" troops with boys and girls from one parish. The clergy have appropriated most of the proposals of the national Catholic committee for "adding the supernatural" to scouting. The local scouting officials have co-operated in this, objecting only to the use of troops in uniform to sell Catholic lottery tickets and to the insistence of one French Catholic pastor that the troop speak French.

When a Catholic Girl Scout troop leader married a Protestant, scout leaders were prepared to ask her to resign, "since," as one noted, "the Catholic church would ask her to leave the troop."

The few non-Catholics who have joined the Catholic troops have found the activities so closely organized about the religious life of the parish that they have soon withdrawn. The Catholic troops answer all calls by the scout officials for community services and attend annual city-wide meetings which are alternately held in Catholic and Protestant church properties. The Catholic pastors desire that the Protestant churches cease operating "mixed troops" and integrate their own scout members into Protestant church life.

Half of the troops sponsored by the Protestant churches are almost entirely attended by Catholic young people. In all but two of the Protestant churches, the troops have little relation to the activities of the church other than meeting on the property and having the church supply funds and a leader for strictly recreational activities.[17] The single exception is the Lutheran church troop in which scouts are entirely of that denomination, and regular attendance at the Sunday school of the church is required for membership. Catholic priests have made efforts to withdraw Catholic scouts from only one church—the Presbyterian. In this instance, the pastor was an active leader in the national scout movement, had spent considerable time with the troops, had encouraged attendance of parents at a special "Parents' Night" in the church, and had made comments on moral issues on a few occasions to the scouts.

Each Protestant church has usually had too small a number of young people interested in scouting to develop a one-faith troop within its parish or neighborhood closely integrated into the life of the church. Most Protestant pastors have publicly praised their "mixed" troops as an aid to interfaith relations. "I'm for maintaining anything like that," one observed, "that will bring us together so we can talk and exchange views." [18]

The Churches and Other Mixed Associations

The Catholic church has worked out more than one kind of arrangement with associations in which Catholic laymen participate in large numbers with people of other faiths. The ecclesiastical authorities may seek (as in scouting) to form groups with programs comparable to those of the other units in the association; though under Catholic leadership, the groups are still a formal, co-operating part of the larger association. In other cases the ecclesiastical authorities may encourage Catholic laymen to form a sub-group within the association itself; this group may meet regularly to plan the kind of program which it will encourage the total association to adopt and which best expresses Catholic aspirations and needs.

In both of these approaches the church is seeking to avoid having "a religious element entering into [mixed associations] without ecclesiastical supervision," and to avoid having the mixed association become a place for the exchange of religious ideas.[19] The basic aim of these Catholic actions, according to the clergy, is a "guarantee of full liberty of conscience to the Catholic members and 'a thorough religious and moral training' and subjection to the mandate of the Church."[20] One effect of the policy is to discourage Catholic and Protestant laymen from discussing religious convictions within the social organizations where they have greatest contact. One Catholic lawyer observed about his recreational and professional associations:

> The Catholic's religion remains a thing apart from mixed groups. It is not polite, it is bigotry for non-Catholics to try to talk religious issues in them. But the Catholic influence and discipline developed by the Knights of Columbus and other Catholic educational groups is always there as a factor in the life of the mixed organization. If the non-Catholic persists in talking religion, then Catholics are withdrawn.

The self-consciousness of the Catholic group, heightened by many themes of the church press, makes it tend to interpret criticism from another religious perspective as a "bigoted attack." Protestants in Paper City are put on the defensive in associations with Catholics, and do not often express their own religious position in social or recreational gatherings for fear of creating tension or of being exposed to the charge of intolerance. The difference in the Catholic and Protestant associational context is pointed up by the answers of leaders in the Catholic Girls' League and the Protestant Girls' Association to the question whether their groups discussed likenesses and differences in the Catholic and Protestant religions. The Catholic leader said it "had never occurred to her" to have such a discussion; the Protestant leader said her group "would not dare to carry on such a discussion." The situation increases the opportunity for social and religious control by the institutions which have the greatest programs for authoritative indoctrination of members.

The Catholic official position is that the nature of societies is specified by the avowed ends.[21] If the society "has an essentially spiritual end," then it is a spiritual society and "is dependent upon the supreme ecclesiastical authority." If the society tends to promote some temporal good, then it is dependent upon the civil power. The church decides what are temporal and what are spiritual ends. Where a society has both temporal and spiritual ends, even if the "temporal seems to predominate, insofar at least as the religious end is concerned, the society is dependent exclusively upon the ecclesiastical authority." [22]

More specific insight into what this official policy may mean for a "mixed" association can be gained from the approach the pastor of the Holy Rosary parish took to a decision of the Paper City High School Alumni Association to cease holding its annual dinner at the Holy Rosary parish house. The pastor announced at Mass:

> I have withdrawn my support from the annual party of the High School Alumni Association. If you want to know why, ask the high school alumni people in charge. I withdrew my support when I found out their plans for the banquet. I had at first supported it, but I did not know their plans. They are still going to have the banquet.

The next day in an interview the pastor explained his action as follows:

> The reason I withdrew support from the High School Alumni Association was this. They used to have meetings at Holy Rosary parish house in past years. Now they say they want to go to a restaurant uptown. I asked, "Why there?" They wanted to have drinks, they told me. I said I was against this. They said they had drunk down at Holy Rosary parties. So I said I didn't know this and that I was against it.
>
> I decided that I would not antagonize them too much now. A lot of them are veterans and they have been a bad lot. They have a tendency to disobey their religious superiors and not show the proper respect. I'm going to discipline them, but not now. I'll need their help in putting on the Carnival [Lawn Fete] down here in June. So at Mass I just said that I opposed the banquet. I did not say I forbade them to participate in it. I'll wait now and see how many go. If

a lot do, I'll start my own alumni association and break off from the other organization.

The high school alumni leaders expressed in interviews a desire to "get some freedom" from the Holy Rosary pastor so they could do what they want. They indicated that the pastor was quite aware some of the people at the banquet drank, since facilities were provided, and that the pastor merely used the drinking issue in order to get the association back into the parish.

The Protestant churches neither develop formal associations alongside of "mixed" groups nor discourage religious discussion in them. Much Protestant energy and leadership have gone into the establishment and maintenance of organizations in the community serving Catholics and non-Catholics—chiefly Catholics when they are city-wide. Efforts of Protestants to get Catholic laymen to take greater responsibility for the conduct of these organizations, such as YMCA, YWCA, Community Chest and Red Cross, have become more extended over the past two decades.

Both the Young Men's and Women's Christian Associations have been moving away from the explicit religious content of their early programs toward more purely recreational activities.

The "Ys" are largely led by Protestants and attended by Catholics. The membership of the YWCA is 83 per cent Catholic, 17 per cent Protestant and Jewish. The membership of the YMCA is 75 per cent Catholic, 25 per cent Protestant and Jewish. The attendance at the "Y" boys' camp in 1947 was 90 per cent Catholic. The board of directors of the YWCA has at no time been composed of more than 10 per cent Catholic membership. The by-laws of the organization now permit one-third of the board to be non-evangelical, although it was not until the 1920's that non-Protestants could be voting, office-holding members. Not enough interested Catholic laywomen have been found to fill the quota, although persistent efforts have been made. The YMCA does not have a non-Protestant quota for its board, but few Catholics have been active members of it. The secretarial staffs of both "Ys" are entirely Protestant.

Religious sources of funds for these organizations are difficult to estimate since operating expenses come from membership, Community Chest, and corporation and private donations. Most "Y" leaders, both Catholic and Protestant, estimate that no more than one-third of the financial support for current operations and for a new building program come directly from Catholics. The estimate if not accurate, at least reflects leaders' beliefs.

The local YWCA when first affiliating with the national agency in 1903 was confined to women professing an evangelical faith. The present "Y" directors, staffs and most of the Protestant clergy generally believe that the "Ys" "have not given up any religious activities or relations with the churches during the past decade in order to secure Catholic co-operation." The "Y" secretaries believe they have no demand from the boards for more religious or church-centered activities.[23]

The professional leaders regard their function in Paper City as one of providing recreation for young people, and feel this function should not be jeopardized by attempting to sponsor religious activities better conducted by the churches.

Speakers of Protestant background at classes or forums on current events and life problems are warned, as a policy of the "Y," not to say anything which would offend the Catholic members. During Lenten meetings, when devotional programs have been planned, Protestant leaders have taken outlines of what they wished to say to a priest for approval. During a period in the 1930's, when Bible classes, worship and prayer circles open to members of all faith were held in the "Ys," objections were raised by Catholic board members and in one case, a Catholic laywoman resigned from the board after consultation with her priest, because of the YWCA's sponsorship of religious discussions led by laywomen. The YWCA and YMCA advertisements of activities make use almost entirely of such social symbols as "etiquette can point the way to success," "social dancing," "modern dancing—streamline your figure," "bridge."

Applicants for the secretaryship of the YWCA, vacant in 1947, were screened in part on the "basis of their religious aggressiveness." One girl from a mid-western Protestant city, with a record of many church activities, was rejected by a member of the board with the remark: "I'm afraid the girl will be too religious for a strongly Catholic community like this. She might lead us into trouble."

The Roman Catholic clergy has evidenced less antagonism toward the "Y" Associations over the years, as the "Ys" have stopped sponsoring discussions on religious themes and have consulted Catholic leaders more about policies. The "Y" was regarded in the 1920's by the diocesan hierarchy as "a great Protestant organization, admirable for Protestants for whom it was intended" and by its nature not capable of an "honest above-board spirit of co-operation marked by equal privilege for all." [24]

The Catholic leaders correctly understood the Protestant character of the "Y" at this time. In Paper City, as in most communities of the United States, the pioneer leaders of the "Y" and its directors of the early 1920's were distinctly cool toward the Roman Catholic church. Few if any of them appear to have been involved in the notorious anti-Catholic movements, but they clearly regarded the "Y" as evangelical in character.[25] From the late 1920's until the present the leaders have in the main seen the "Y" as a movement fighting sectarianism, offering a program in which each person can become a better adherent of the church or synagogue which meets his needs, and at the same time grow in the attitudes toward life that are essential in all religions.

Most priests still regard the "Y" as a "Protestant organization," but they recognize that its evangelical intentions have changed considerably. Their approach and that of most lay Catholic leaders is neither to support nor to oppose the "Y" actively. YMCA clubs do not exist in parochial schools; few Catholic public school teachers will serve as leaders of the clubs or recommend them; Catholic laymen willing to serve on the boards are difficult to find; the diocesan press makes no comments upon the "Y"; the priests neither supported nor opposed the recent YMCA building fund campaign. On one occasion, eight years ago, when a very careful program of instruction on the physical facts of sex was presented by a doctor in the YWCA, the Catholic girls were not withdrawn by the priests, but no Catholic physician (four were approached) would give public support to the program. In recent years, the Catholic girls were asked if such a program could be sponsored by the YWCA and were so certain their pastors would object that the proposal was abandoned. The impact of Catholic associational policy upon the "Y" has been to make possible the continuation of a recreational program and to restrict Protestant discussion of religion among Catholics.

The service clubs of the community, such as Rotary, Lions and Kiwanis, have adjusted their programs so that no controversial discussions involving use of Christian doctrine or terminology will take place. Their constitutions (reflecting national policies) contain no references to religious belief or practice apart from the expression of willingness, in a few of the clubs, to support the work of the churches and to encourage members to attend religious services. The leaders and members believe that to permit religious controversy to enter the life of the clubs would endanger their continuance.[26]

The Rotary has never had a program discussing the relations of the religions. For the past fifteen years an annual talk has been given by a Protestant minister upon a nonreligious topic, with the exception of one year when a minister reviewed Bruce Barton's book about Christ, *The Man Nobody Knows*. After this talk, it was announced that members who wished could come to the speaker's table and discuss it, but no discussion was permitted from the floor. Several years ago the officers decided not to have blessings before meals, since, according to the present president, "the club could not have priests in the organization." [27] Two Protestant ministers are members, filling the quota for that profession. The charities of the Rotary are purposely nonsectarian, funds going either to community-wide organizations or to specific Rotary projects. In the past fifteen years, the club has had two Catholic presidents; the remainder were Protestants. The club has 142 members: 15 are Catholic, one is Jewish, and the others Protestant.

As the Knights of Columbus represents the organization of Catholic business and professional and semiprofessional leadership in the community, the Rotary Club is the closest to being the men's club of the most influential Protestants.[28] Present Rotarians are predominant on the boards of directors of the major community service organizations—Paper City Hospital, Community Welfare League and Chamber of Commerce. The Rotary Club, with enough pretensions of an explicit philosophy or theology to make priests caution laymen against belonging, is viewed by many upper-income Protestants as doing, with an assist from the Masons, most of the city-wide work of the Protestant church.

The major service activity of upper-income Protestant young

women is focused in a Junior League. Until 1942 it did not enroll any Catholics; now it has ten Catholics in a membership of ninety. At meetings there is no mention of religion. "No volunteer service is rendered to churches," according to an officer of the Junior League, "specifically to avoid controversy." In 1949 a Catholic Junior League was formed. It places more emphasis than the Junior League upon participation in church activities. What little social service work it does is confined to Catholic welfare agencies.[29]

The secret societies, such as Freemasonry and Odd Fellows, encounter greater opposition from the Catholic church than any association except the Protestant churches themselves. The Catholic church believes, for example, that Masonry regards itself as a religion, "teaching as it does doctrine and morals and offering worship to God." [30] The *Catholic Mirror* recently reported that a source "well acquainted with the general run of members of the Masonic lodges in Massachusetts, the mid-west and south" found the lodge "taking all comers, regardless of how ignorant they may be." It reported that men forsaking their families and living openly with women as man and wife, were welcomed, and that most Masons were reading communist literature, and being educated in communism.[31]

Paper City Masonry numbers 800; officers claim 12 per cent are Jewish, 4 per cent nominally Catholic. Neither the Odd Fellows (whose membership is 100 per cent Protestant) nor the Masons have sponsored discussions of religious relations or tolerance in the past fifteen years. Only the Lutheran church among Protestant churches forbids or discourages membership in the Masons or Odd Fellows. Two Protestant ministers are Masons.

It is difficult to know all that is at stake in the different religious approaches to recreational and fraternal associations; the widest consequences of associational policies are apt to be seen in labor, business and politics. (See Chapters 15 through 20.) But the patterns of relationships are clear.

The Protestants have encouraged a prolific growth of associations emphasizing their freedom of action. The associations have often developed either rival religious ideologies or a very vague and honorific use of Christian symbols. The Protestant churches have made little attempt to keep informed of the concrete activities of these associations or to help laymen understand more adequately their meaning and significance in light of the Christian faith. On the other hand, there has been no general Protestant church attempt to control the discussions of religious and moral themes when they arise in mixed associations.

The Catholic church has not encouraged the growth of these associations so much as it has attempted to form Catholic ancillary groups after new associations have emerged, and to limit the discussion of religious ideas apart from ecclesiastical guidance. The Catholic approach has stemmed largely from widespread Catholic belief that the direction of man's redemption is always outward from the church to the natural association; hence such groups as the scouts must be brought as much as possible into some formal, direct and dependent relation with the supernatural institution. This contrasts with the widespread Protestant belief that God redeems man within the interaction of groups in the whole common life, the church responding to the action of God in other associations as men within these associations respond to the action of God through the church.

The Protestant churches, without explicit norms of their own to guide them in their relations with recreational groups and in a minority situation, have increasingly accommodated to the Catholic program. The Catholics have in recent years been undergoing some reappraisal of their policy, not from Protestant church pressure or witness, but from the revolt of the younger Catholic men and women against ecclesiastical control of their activities. The people sense the profound pluralism of American culture and have in the newer ethnic fellowships and school alumni associations been asking for less church direction of their activities. The Catholic church has been able to continue its traditional associational policy most successfully with the children (for example, in the scouts) and with the older folks (in the St. Jean-Baptiste Society).

The real troubles of the Catholic and Protestant churches over associational policies in the area of recreation lie ahead. The old religious controls over leisure time activities are breaking down. So much of the layman's time is spent not in fraternal groups but in mass leisure—TV and movie viewing—produced from New York and Hollywood. This is becoming in many ways the most productive source of images of self-understanding. The content of this popular culture is highly standardized and conventionalized, and it greatly influences the layman's interpretation of the church's message. It is not being interpreted by the clergy in the associations the churches have developed for social and recreational activity. Its content is being rated in very moralistic terms by the church publications and by the reviews of the pastors at women's clubs. What more is to be done, the leaders of the churches do not yet know.

Chapter 15

The Churches, Business and Industry

A new manager of a paper mill is introduced to the director's board of a bank first as a "Congregationalist" and then as the "new mill supervisor." A new laborer in a textile plant, a Protestant with an Irish name, finds himself identified as a Catholic until he eats meat on Friday in the mill cafeteria and then notices that some of the men—one of them his foreman—who formerly ate with him no longer do. No matter how marginal the formal relationship of the individual may be to a church in Paper City, he often finds himself identified in his daily work by religious terms—as a Catholic, a non-Catholic, a Protestant—and he discovers that these identifications have some importance in his relations with other people in his vocation.

Religious differences are of some importance to laymen in their achievement of economic satisfactions and in their pursuit of higher personal status within the businesses and industries of Paper City. This can be noted in general historical terms and also in the present situation.

The Historical Situation

Paper City began as a company town established by Yankee "cotton interests" in Boston anticipating a great New England industrial expansion. In the depression of 1857, the financial group which had promoted the city and the water power development went bankrupt after an expenditure of over $2,500,000. They had been premature in their anticipation of the demand for water power. The promoting company's assets were purchased by local manufacturers. With the aid of the national industrial expansion of the 1860's, the new interests were able to develop a prosperous city. By 1865, the paper mills, owned largely by Yankees, became the dominant industry, utilizing the combination of cheap and ample power and the ready supply of chemically pure water. The descendants of these original Protestant families continue to own and operate many of the mills.[1]

The ruling dynasty of Yankee paper mill families were able to ride affluently through the periodic depressions—until the debacle of the 1930's—with the great profits accumulated during the boom years. In the 1870's one of the oldest of the Protestant family paper firms was earning at least 50 per cent on its $60,000 capital stock. Another paper firm provided a Yankee family in the same decade with a steam yacht, an exotic greenhouse and an American baronial castle with crenelated turrets. The constituency of Second Congregational Church in the 1920's included seven millionaires in its ranks.[2]

The Irish and French Catholics began their rise from economic conditions typical of the mid-nineteenth century. In 1867 the city's wages in the paper and textile mills were rated by a trade magazine as slightly higher than those elsewhere in the state; yet children were working for 35 to 80 cents a day and adults at an average of $1.52 a day for 12 hours of labor. Women's wages in the paper mills sorting rags were $2.98 to $3.00 a week. In such industries as cotton, manufacturers were dominated by pools of finance capitalists seeking to manipulate prices and production for speculative gains, and workers suffered the insecurity of great fluctuations in demand for labor. In 1871, as a result of periodic unemployment, the average yearly wage for workers in one cotton mill was only $163.63.

The insecurity, long hours and meager pay were endured because the conditions were on the whole less trying than the immigrants had known before in Ireland or Canada.[3] And some money could be saved with a promise of better housing and better education for the children if everyone in the family worked.

Directors of the Water Power Company, controlling most of the city's land, encouraged the building of tenements high and close together in order to leave room for industrial expansion along the canals.[4] Within twenty-five years Paper City was one of the most unhealthful dwelling places for workers in the nation. In 1856, the board of health reported after a study of housing: "Many families are huddled into low, damp and filthy cellars, and others in attics which are but little better, with scarcely a particle of what might be called air to sustain life. And it is only a wonder (to say nothing of health) that life can dwell in such apartments." [5]

By 1878, the death rate in Paper City was 21.67 per thousand. During the four census years, 1860-1890, the period when the most rapid rise of Roman Catholic ethnics to new social and political power took place, Paper City had the third highest mean death rate in the state. Surveys made in 1880 and 1910 indicated that only two cities had as crowded tenements as Paper City's—New York City and Hoboken, New Jersey.[6]

This social history is interpreted by Catholics in different ways in Paper City today, depending in part on the economic position of the speaker. A Catholic social worker remembers, "My mother worked in the mills at night through to 7 A.M., then rushed home in order to have a half hour to get breakfast for us kids and see us off to school. All of us worked and saved so the children could go to school. We can remember those days and we see the mansions on the hill and we know how they got there."

A successful Catholic "merchant-Knight" recalls in *Caravel,* the Knights of Columbus paper how "all the leading Catholic business men in the present life of Paper City started by putting their feet on the lowest rung of the ladder," and how "the successful Yankee businessmen have always been an inspiration for Catholics to try to come up through." [7] A Catholic labor leader of a paper workers' union recalls how "in the depression we got a good bit of talk from workers about wealthy Protestant owners, and the Catholics' always having had to do all the work in the city, but in prosperous times you don't hear much of that kind of talk."

The militancy which characterized the drive of many immigrants for status beyond labor in the mills may, in part, have grown from their awareness of the great economic power and interest aligned against them. An Irish Catholic clothing store owner noted, "My father used to tell me about how some mills had on their doors 'No Catholics Hired,' and then he would say, 'The only way to get anywhere is to keep bucking, keep bucking the line.' So that's what we did."

In 1879 the local newspaper published an exchange of letters which indicated the mood of some of the more articulate Protestant Yankees and Catholics. The first letter complained that the Irish were trying to run the city, while holding no property to make them responsible. An Irish Catholic answered:

> You say we rule or ruin, and own no mills . . . You could not run your mills except we did the work from which you realize your profits. You say we own nothing, yet try to rule the city. This is another lie, and for evidence I refer you to the books of the City Clerk Delaney and Collector Andrews for evidence of the truth of this statement and you will see we pay more than you have any idea. . . . In conclusion let me say we have not ruled Paper City, but in the future, we shall endeavor to do so.[8]

Economic competition was felt and antiforeign sentiment was expressed first among the native American workmen. The attitude of well-to-do Yankees toward the Catholic workers was at first chiefly indifference and unawareness of any challenge to their position. Then with the increase of Catholic political and economic power in the 1860's and 70's, hostility spread upward in Protestant ranks. Strong Protestant hostility lasted into the late 1890's and then slackened when the social power of the Catholics became obvious, when Protestants began to believe that they could accommodate successfully to a situation which did not destroy their own economic and social interests though it expanded social opportunities in the city.

The construction industry is the only area of large-scale business (over two hundred employees) in which ownership and control are predominantly Catholic.[9] The four largest building contractors in the city are Catholic, all their companies having begun with the organization of gangs of Irish and French laborers to build the new factories and tenements. Chief Catholic industrial or wholesale ownership has been in small machine shops, printing, engraving and building supplies.

Catholic business ownership is most widely represented in real-estate holdings (chiefly "block houses," three or four story tenements) and retail stores (mainly clothing, grocery, liquor). Today half the real-estate agencies and approximately 55 per cent of the business is Catholic managed. Reliable estimates are that fifty years ago less than 10 per cent of the retail establishments were owned by Roman Catholics. Today, 90 per cent are Catholic-owned.[10]

Paper and textile manufacturing and processing have either remained in local Protestant control or been purchased by absentee interests. A dozen paper manufacturing and processing plants employing approximately 2,500 workers and owned by Paper City families, a silk and satin mill employing over 500 workers and a thread mill employing 150 workers make up the core of Protestant industrial interests. Local Catholics own stock in several paper and textile companies, but do not have controlling ownership in any.

The banking interests of Protestants are centered in the major commercial bank in the city which is entirely Protestant-owned. Fifty years ago no Catholic was on the board of directors of the two other commercial banks; now Catholic families, chiefly representing building-construction fortunes, almost control one bank and have bought an important interest in the other. The three savings banks are all Protestant-dominated. The upsweep of Catholic economic interests in the past twenty-five years is reflected in the fact that in 1920 only two Catholics were members of the Chamber of Commerce; today out of 32 members, 10 are Catholic, 22 Protestant.

The major avenues to higher economic status for Catholics have been the legal and medical professions and the managerial or engineering skills demanded by industry. Law and medicine, which at the turn of the century had less than one-fifth Catholic representation, are now dominated by Catholics. Out of 66 lawyers, 46 are Catholic, 11 Protestant and 9 Jewish.[11] The city has 68 physicians and surgeons; 41 are Catholic; 12 Protestant and 13 Jewish.[12]

The industries of Paper City are increasingly recruiting their managers not from the ranks of labor but among college-trained young men showing high intellectual and personal aptitude and possessing special engineering or managerial skills.[13] Advancement from the rank of wage earner usually stops at the foreman level. Only in the past generation have considerable numbers of Catholic families been able to send their children to college to learn a particular business or skill and to compete with Protestants for managerial jobs.

The emerging pattern of education and employment in Paper City is symbolized by the case of the son of one of the oldest Yankee families recently graduated from Rensselaer Polytechnic

Institute. Three of his classmates were Catholic boys from Paper City. The father of one of the Catholics was a janitor; the son is now city engineer. The father of the second was a journeyman plumber; the son is now manager of a Catholic-owned Paper City plumbing supply company. The father of the third student was a gas and electric meter reader; the son is superintendent of the municipally owned Gas and Electric Company. But the Yankee graduate—no longer attracted to the small family firm—soon left Paper City for a position as aeronautical engineer in a New York factory.

The high economic mobility for some people over the past few decades must be placed against the slight mobility of perhaps the majority of the people who with their children have remained in the social class in which they entered Paper City, although they have improved their absolute standard of living. Approximately 62 per cent of the people are now in the laboring class in the community.

General trends in economic mobility and industrial expansion have tremendous implications for the relations of the major religions. Group conflict appears to be not so much a correlate of differences in status as of *changes* in status; for ours is a society in which comparisons with others greatly affect satisfactions with one's own achievement. The greatest tension between Roman Catholics and Protestants over the pursuit of wealth and power did not come in the first two decades of the city's existence, when there was little conspicuous change in the economic status of the Catholics and the city's industry was having a hard time getting established. (One of the oldest Yankee mill owners in the city recalled: "When the Catholics came into Paper City and worked, and left the governing of the mills and the city to the Yankees, feelings were friendly between Protestants and Catholics. There was a clear division of responsibility. Each group had its own area and type of work.")

Nor did the greatest religious tension occur in the decades from 1910 to 1940 when the majority status of Catholics had been definitely established and the economic growth of the city had leveled off.

The great tension came in that fabulously rapid period of economic growth in the city from 1870 to 1910 when new opportunities opened up so fast for the Catholics.[14] The new wartime and postwar expansion of the 1940's and 50's did not equal the previous rate of growth, but religious tension was again highly evident.

The Relation of Religion to Advancement Within Present Business

Intensive studies were made of eleven companies in Paper City as to the relation of religious differentiation to employment and promotion patterns on all levels—from top management to wage earners.[15] The studies included the major types of firms in the city: absentee-owned, large corporations; Protestant family firms of various sizes; Catholic family firms, representatively small in size; firms of various sizes which are locally owned and controlled by people of "mixed" religious background.

Two general observations emerge from these studies. First, when religious identifications or symbols are used in business or industry they are employed largely to advance personal status within the social system. This is so even for management. General inquiries about religious relations in the factory are associated immediately with the issue of religious discrimination in hiring, firing and promoting. And this is in the judgment of most workers, managers and owners the only area in which Roman Catholic and Protestant religious differences "really and consciously matter" in the specific decisions men make in the factory. The nearest approach to "religious" groups within the factory system are organizations for the advancement of the social status of members. (These "religious" cliques will be discussed in detail later.)

This situation bears careful examination. The managers of business have been placed, many of them without greatly seeking it (particularly in old family-owned firms) in positions of tremendous social power and responsibility. The designation of "manager" is appropriate, for these men make decisions requiring considerable personal resources and exhibiting great discretion and autonomy of action. One of the most important tasks of the businessman, as he sees his relations to other associations, is to protect the freedom and morale of an organization so that it can perform its basic economic functions: create consumer demand for goods and co-ordinate the skills of man in their production. This does not mean, however, that the businessmen of Paper City are unaware of the fact that they direct organizations which are deeply involved in the whole social system of the city and nation.

The serious attempts of businessmen to understand and interpret their role as managers in this complex setting have proceeded along several lines. The managers have made self-conscious attempts to give all the people in a firm a sense of common interests and friendly co-operation. The family image is most often used by Yankee owners —the "Palmer Mills Family" and the "Hazen Paper Family." The managers have made extensive efforts, through Rotarian and Kiwanis club activities, publicity programs and other devices, to place the relations of their company to the community at large on different grounds than "the profit motive" and the "cash nexus." Even Yankee businessmen who still operate with their grandfathers' old roll-top desks in their offices attach great importance to an up-to-date "public relations" program. The accent, particularly among the younger men brought in from the business schools to manage the old family firms or the new factories of the great national corporations, is increasingly on "service" to the consuming public.

The churches—Catholic and Protestant—have only begun to fathom the moral and religious significance of the developing business ideology. No groups of businessmen have been encouraged by church leaders to reflect critically upon the considerations that go into their policy decisions on pricing of products, public relations programs, employer education, the position of their trade associations on national economic issues (tariffs, economic stability and growth). The businessmen stress their sensitivity to what the public wants, but there are few associations in their lives, not even the church, in which they come into some intimate and sustained discussion with men of different perspectives and experience than business.

The top-level business leaders, whether of Roman Catholic or Protestant faith, when queried about the religious and moral dimensions of their economic and administrative decisions are usually quite uniform in their assertions that business could not be conducted in "the American Way" if managers did not seek to live out the great principles and verities of the Christian religion. But the discussion of what these are rarely proceeds beyond affirmation of faith in "some kind of God," adherence to "the Golden Rule," and such spiritual values as "honesty" and the "inherent dignity of man." These principles are so nebulous that they give little insight into the habits and patterns of thought which really influence decision-making, and the businessmen have had little experience in their church life of trying to make more explicit the assumptions which do operate in their action. Businessmen are conscious of exercising their "churchmanship" chiefly through the practice of personal virtues, through acceptance of responsibility for support of "church activities," through philanthropic and charitable duties, and through conscientious attention to the economic welfare of their firms.

On first reflection, most businessmen claim that decisions affecting their firm's welfare are largely made in response to cues of the market. On further reflection they recognize that even in highly competitive situations they both influence the market and respond to it. They are also aware often that moral and religious issues are at stake in the type of interpersonal relations employed in firms and in the relations of firms to the community.

The preachers reflecting the early "Social Gospel" movement in the Christian churches aimed their greatest criticism at the "profit motive" or principle of "economic self-interest" on which they believed the business leaders were basing the relations of industry. They argued that "service" and "co-operation" with the community should replace such a principle as the foundation of the economic system.

In the past two decades another movement, particularly in the Protestant churches, has had its influence on a few pastors in Paper City. This movement, called by some "Neo-orthodoxy" has stressed the Christian understanding of evil in the world and sin in man as well as a renewed sense of the dependence of man upon the grace of God. These pastors have in some of their sermons begun to criticize business leaders for not seeing that their "service" ideology obscured the way in which managers' interests were often distinct from other interests in society. But such interpretations have been very general and occasional and have not affected the fundamental situation in business—in which "religion" is consciously employed chiefly in maneuvers for personal advancement, and not for illumination of one's human situation in the society.

The second general observation to be made about religious relations and the modern industrial system is that jobs or positions in industry represent to the worker much more than wage claims, even though in a money-economy these are highly important.[16] The job is a composite index of general social status. Whether the job is a "good one," or better than others, depends upon a whole series of often subtle and subjective distinctions—such as opportunity for better "social connections," acceptance as a likable fellow worker, the "friendliness" and openness to suggestions of the foreman and of superiors, the amount of freedom to move about and to determine one's speed of work, the importance and quality of the product produced. These noneconomic and nontechnical factors are made more important by the fact that in many basic industries in the city—such as textiles, and (to a lesser extent) paper processing—there are for most workers no important distinctions to be made between one another in terms of skill.[17]

Many of the differences in pay in jobs below foreman are based on what appear to be minute, largely subjective criteria. Therefore, promotion to the better jobs does not come often through learning a new and more difficult technical skill, but through "skill" in selling oneself, in being liked by the right people.[18] The subjective or nontechnical criteria for favoritism by superiors become important—ethnic background,[19] religion, lodge affiliation.

Many of the jobs in paper and textiles in Paper City have been made highly routine and so standardized that there is little the worker can do to increase his interest in the product or to improve the quality of it. Capital has been lacking or not advanced by management for introduction of further automation in the factories for the more unskilled work. Thus, the pay for the work, in order to pursue leisure-time interests, not simply the doing of the work, is highly important and small gradations in pay and the factors that lead to higher pay take on great significance.

Moreover, in Paper City's economic system, even in prosperous times, Protestant and Catholic workers periodically lose jobs or fail to achieve advancement for reasons—such as production and demand cycles in the industry, regional competition for industry—which have nothing to do with what they as individuals do or are.

Many workers find it hard to accept this and sometimes seek to explain their personal defeat to themselves or to their associates on the basis of religious prejudice operating against them.

The factory system has some characteristics which encourage religious tension between men. It has some characteristics which lead to subordination of religious differences. The content of church thought and experience also produces cross pressures. Therefore, a variety of patterns of behavior emerges in industry.

Most Catholic laymen, for example, whose church associational policies tend most to divide and isolate men, will still reflect a tension of claims. One claim is the triumph of the true faith. Another is the demands of this faith that one's fellowman be loved, be understood, be given the opportunity for earning of a livelihood adequate to his needs as a person and that he be rewarded for meritorious performance of functions necessary to society.

Religious Relations in Eleven Firms

In the eleven firms studied, the greatest religious uniformity among owners, top managers and foremen was found in the Catholic family-owned firms (Table XXIX). The Protestant family firms also employ their own religious group almost exclusively for top management positions (board of directors, company officers, superintendents and department heads). However, all the Protestant family firms employ some Catholic foremen. The more employees a Paper City firm hires, the greater is its tendency to employ Catholic foremen; thus, 75 per cent of the foremen are Catholic in a Protestant company employing 780 people, while 25 per cent of the foremen are Catholic in a Protestant paper processing company with 120 workers.

In the larger firms, and particularly in the absentee-owned subsidiaries of big corporations, the top management is more mixed in religious background than in the smaller, family-owned plants, but the majority of the managers are Protestant. In these firms, the foremen tend much more to be of the same religious background as the wage earner than in the small family-owned firms. The farther one moves down the managerial structure toward the rank of foreman and supervisor, the greater becomes the proportion of Catholics. In the textile firm of "mixed" religious ownership, and in the paper manufacturing firm of mixed religious and absentee ownership, managers and foremen are from all three major faiths and from religiously unaffiliated ranks.

In the Catholic and Protestant family firms, a fairly definite pattern of ethnic and religious position-expectancy has developed for top level (above foreman) managerial recruitment and is widely recognized in the community. Certain firms are assumed to be family concerns with relatives or friends of the owner—usually of the same religion and social background—being given the top rank positions. In most family firms, the top managers have arrived at a highly homogeneous ethnic or religious management staff chiefly by conscious attention to factors with which religious cleavages are highly correlated, that is, hiring of men in one's own social circles and industrial contacts. The managers and owners disclaim vehemently any conscious effort to secure top-level associates of one religion, but the established patterns of recruitment have accomplished this.

The most active and conscious manipulation of religious differences in order to gain status in managerial ranks occurs in large corporations in which present personnel of management is of mixed religious affiliation, where no long established and regularized patterns of promotion and recruitment have been developed on the basis of rationalized and "objective" standards. The general and diffuse character of the job requirements for junior executives and administrators and the emphasis on men skilled in personnel and public relations provide conditions for informal and unofficial cliques to thrive.

The bases of these informal cliques seem in great part to be that of religion and lodge affiliation. The cliques reduce individual competition for jobs or promotions in which several men could qualify by substituting group action. Although the operation of these cliques presents, from the managerial point of view, one of the gravest evils in industrial organization, "Square clubs" of Protestant Masons and "K. of C." factions are highly influential in two of the firms studied and have been powerful in at least one other in the past.[20] Neither the "Square clubs" nor the "K. of C." cliques are official, recognized units of the Masons or Knights of Columbus.

They are usually described by the participants as informal clubs of men for "social purposes," for "passing on information as to job and promotion opportunities," and for identifying members of one's lodge or religion in the organization ("to make new friendship easier").

Apparently such religious-social factionalism feeds upon itself. Moves by one group of managers to decrease the power of another group usually produces bitter counterpressure. In a few plants within the past three decades, such factionalism has contributed to the inefficiency and financial instability of the firm. In both a textile and a paper company, it was necessary for the controlling interests to hire outside managers (in one case a team of Catholic and Protestant managers) to get rid of men who had come to the top more through social and religious contacts than ability. The most extensive reorganization occurred in a firm where Yankee nepotism had dominated managerial recruitment. Widely circulated stories of high living and poor management by some Yankee mill families have contributed to Irish and French Catholic belief that a little "circulation of the elite"—to use a non-Paper City term—was long overdue.

The Role of Foremen in "Religious Promotions"

The foreman in the factory status system is probably more crucial to wage earners than any other managerial rank in the determination of the importance that religious differences will play in employment and promotion. The foreman is the focus for most of the laborers' maneuvering for preferential position, since he stands between them and top management.

The foreman under the usual hiring system in the mills can, when a wage earning position is open, hire whomever he wishes so long as the person can do the work.[21] Opportunity for favoritism based on religion is often great. The firing of men is checked more closely than hiring by management for possible discrimination, but here also the foreman has great power.

Despite this great influence, less than 10 per cent of the foremen in the firms studied had developed a reputation among top management for deliberate religious and ethnic favoritism in hiring and promoting or were thought of by a majority of the employees of a different religion from the foremen as engaging in such discrimination.[22]

The foreman's degree of religious favoritism is affected by the policies of top management in regard to hiring and promotion, since the foreman ultimately maintains his position through management's acceptance of his practices.

The managers of the small family-owned firms usually adopt a laissez-faire policy, permitting foremen to hire and promote as they wish. Sometimes the managers have even acquiesced when workers harassed a foreman so that he would resign or be fired, and a foreman of their own religious or ethnic background could be hired. Managers rationalize such an attitude by claiming that it reduces ethnic and religious friction and earns good will in the community.

This policy by management invites maneuvering by religious and ethnic groups and promotes the development in some firms of departments of one nationality or religion. In the nineteenth century some of these departments were predominantly Protestant—Scotch, English or German. Now the "homogeneous" departments are almost entirely Catholic. The ideal of the small Protestant family-owned firm, as one president noted, "is to be known as a friendly company, with a plant whose workers are like a happy family. I know these phrases have a bad connotation now of paternalism, but we try to give work first to the friends and relatives of the people who have been with us longest." In most of the Protestant family-owned firms, the tendency is, in the words of one president, to "let the natural course of events [the foreman's recommendations and the worker's recommendations to him] take care of hiring." These firms display on the levels below foremen the general shifts in positions of power and status of the various ethnic groups. Those who arrived last in the city are confined to the poorest jobs. Managers seldom hear minority complaints against discrimination by the few foremen who set out to develop "homogeneous" departments. The foremen and superintendents act as buffers or shields for management against such complaints.

In the large, absentee-owned corporations, the policy is for managers to discourage the growth of departments dominated by one national or religious group and to prevent discrimination against any group. The policy is based on the belief that when one nationality begins to predominate in a department, it feels its strength and agitates for hiring more of its own group and for preference in advancement.

Some managers with these policies argue that the state fair employment practices law makes it difficult for them to check discriminatory practices, such as a group monopoly within a department, since the religion of a worker is not recorded and trends in foremen's recommendations cannot be checked. However, the names of employees are used as a general indication of group affiliation and in some instances employment agencies receive and fill oblique requests indicating religious preference.[23] Enough people with potential skills for most mill work are available so that some balance can be kept if the employer wishes. In one instance where a department had become entirely Catholic under a Catholic foreman, the foreman was kept on and the department broken up, so that some workers could be placed under a Protestant foreman. The Protestant foreman had difficulty for a while in securing the cooperation of workers.[24]

The question of religious discrimination in the relations of leaders in a factory is usually considered so delicate that elaborate care is often exercised not to mention religion specifically, even though the parties involved are aware of its importance. (The factor of religion was not mentioned by the managers to the foremen involved in the department changes just mentioned.)

The general manager of an appliance company recently asked the assistant general foreman, a Catholic, which of two foremen to lay off as a result of a shortage in materials. The assistant general foreman suggested that the company keep the man who, according to the general manager, had clearly shown less efficiency and ability by objective standards. The foreman recommended for retention was a fellow Catholic, the other a Protestant. However, the manager hired the more efficient man. He then told the assistant general foreman, the manager recalls, that "his advancement in the plant depended on his ability to judge men solely for their ability. I had his promise that he would never let other factors enter in his selection again. I never said that religion was an important factor in his choice, but he knew it and I knew it."

Many Protestant foremen, in departments where the majority of workers under them are Catholic, harbor a variety of fears about the cohesiveness and antagonism of "certain Catholics" in their work force. Some of the most evident prejudice and indiscriminate hostility toward Catholicism is to be found among these men in the middle class who have great inner doubts about their ability to handle the duties of foreman and about the variety of pressures from both management and workers that accompany their middle rank in the factory system. These Protestant foremen feel that their jobs "are constantly being gunned for by Catholics." Some claim that they discover coteries of workers in the plant who become ominously silent when they approach. They are convinced, often correctly,[25] that particular departments are brought under rumor barrages begun by cliques seeking to create bad morale among workers to discredit the foreman and to undermine his self-confidence.

Protestant foremen believe that the workers can easily create, if they wish, incidents which could lead to their foreman's demotion or dismissal. In such a situation, personally insecure Protestant foremen exaggerate the cohesiveness of Catholic workers. They talk to friends secretly about "Catholics moving into key positions of influence." For example, one foreman reported that all the foreman positions in his plant were gradually being filled by Catholics because the new personnel director was a Catholic named O'Brien. O'Brien, however, is a stanch Episcopalian.

In factory situations where religious factionalism has become an important element in the status system, the protective devices developed by Protestants and Catholics do not vary greatly. When either group is in a minority, the representatives usually seek to avoid acts or talk which will heighten identification, and even welcome ethnic or religious misidentification. Thus many Protestants who work in situations where only two or three other workmen in their department are Protestant report that they "never advertise their Protestantism," or "don't declare themselves." Some Protestant laborers work for years beside other Protestants, never knowing the fact until engaged in some private discussion. The Catholics often use devices to identify Protestants who have Irish or

French names. A Baptist Downie becomes "Deacon Downie" at the shop. And in Protestant-dominated shops, Catholics with Protestant-sounding names are often given similar identifying labels.

Labor Unions and Religious Discrimination

Labor organizations, particularly in firms with "hands off" approaches to religious discrimination, have been major agents of rationalization and standardization of recruitments, promotions and layoffs. The unions have introduced machinery for weighing grievances against discriminatory practices. The fact that major tension over religious discrimination exists chiefly on the white-collar, salary level in Paper City firms, may be related to the fact that little union organization exists on this level.

In the early years of unionism, 1935-38, religious and ethnic discrimination was a major grievance in the textile and paper mills. In textiles, the unions have been able to regulate the hiring of workers sufficiently to break up departments where such discrimination existed. Several other unions, without control of hiring in their contracts, have been able through bargaining and consulting with management to end such departments. The unions have consistently advised management to make all departments multinational and multireligious, and if necessary to remove foremen, since they are the key figures in perpetuating discriminatory patterns.

The unions at first, since they were dominated by Catholic members, found complaints being directed principally against Protestant foremen. The union leaders for a few years followed through on these cases, often securing removal of the foremen. In time they learned to sift out workers' complaints which were based upon foremen's job policies from those based upon religious prejudice of the workers. "The job policy of a man your union can help you change, but the religion of a man your union can't and won't help you change," a textile labor leader recently told a group of workers. Both religious groups, when they have become majorities in industries, have used their position to discriminate. The union mechanisms for handling workers' complaints that they are being discriminated against religiously are now being used principally by Protestant laborers in a city with a Catholic majority.

An example of a case dealt with by a textile union is as follows:

A French Catholic was promoted to foreman in a silk mill. He was not familiar in his new position with the way in which workers use the foreman's power to discriminate against other laborers on ethnic and religious terms. He complained to the union executive secretary that a Swedish Protestant girl was too young to work on the night shift. The union investigated and found this was not true. Then the foreman complained to management that the girl was hurting production by talking too much to people around her. Management called the union executive secretary who then talked with the girl. She reported that she scarcely talked to people around her since the noise of the mill would not permit conversation. Moreover, the other workers were French and she knew little of the language. The union official then called a meeting of the foreman and all workers on the shift. In the discussion, it became clear to the foreman that the girl had a difficult job and stuck at it, speaking little to anyone. All the workers agreed except a group of French Catholic women who had been complaining to the foreman about the girl. The foreman had taken their word on the girl's behavior. He apologized to the girl at the meeting and they shook hands. The agitation at the mill over the girl stopped.

In summary, when religious identifications or symbols have been used in business, they have been employed chiefly to compete for preferential treatment within industry. The business associations probably represent the most powerful, cohesive and self-conscious groups in the city. In most churches little attempt has been made to challenge or to understand the deep loyalties, defenses and formalized norms of behavior in the business community. When attempts have been made, the churches have had great difficulty encouraging a self-critical consideration of the religious significance of cherished business assumptions: for example that the content of all the Judeo-Christian historic faiths may be expressed adequately in vague and general spiritual values or moral principles, that "troublesome" noneconomic issues are to be avoided in business so that accord and harmony will reign among workers and managers, that the broad demands of the market and the high "service" motives of businessmen make it impossible for serious conflicts to occur between the actions of business and the best interests of society.

In modern industry distinct technical skills (such as mastery of machinery) are usually less important in achieving comparative advancement and job security than skill in interpersonal relations, ability to make friends and to persuade others. Some factory settings become fertile ground, on the one hand, for exploitation of religious loyalties where management opens its organization to such maneuvering, or on the other hand, for the development of a vague business ideology—of "service," "family-type industry," "harmony" and "spiritual concern"—which glosses over serious interest conflicts and religious differences.

Chapter 16

The Churches and the Labor Movement

The Catholic church has made many high-level pronouncements on modern economic organization, encompassing business and the professions as well as labor. But, in the Paper City area, Catholic programs educating leaders in the implications of this theory have been developed only for the labor movement. Therefore the labor movement has provided an even more fruitful focus than industry for analysis of Roman Catholic and Protestant interaction in the economic order.

In broad retrospect it appears that the Protestant clergy responded more quickly and sensitively than the Catholic leaders to the early demands of organized labor, but Protestant pastoral concern for "the underdog" led neither to formulation of a general theory of economic order, nor to an intensive educational program such as is now represented in the Catholic church.

Catholic concepts of "corporatism" and proposals for industry councils to deal with the relations of organized economic groups contain many principles and attitudes expressed also by Protestant leaders. Both religious groups have rejected naturalistic and mechanistic assumptions about society represented in classical liberal and Marxian economic theories, taking, as we shall see, a more historical and organic view of the emerging industrial order. But there are also important differences in approach reflecting doctrinal and organizational characteristics of the two Christian movements.

Labor, as a minority movement, responded ambivalently to the approaches of the churches. It welcomed support on specific issues but was suspicious of ideologies and broad programs of social reconstruction. Labor's achievement of greater acceptance in the city was accompanied by fundamental changes in the power structure and group relations of the community. A society emerged bearing many of the group characteristics described in the thought and literature of the churches.

Development of the Labor Movement

Trade unions established themselves more slowly in Paper City than in most industrial communities of comparable size in the state.[1] Contributing factors were Paper City's comparatively high percentage of foreign born, the ability of the companies to bid well for new workers with the promise of company housing and association with relatives already in the community. The labor movement confronted unusually strong competition among individual workers in the labor market. The immigrant female workers, of whom there was a high proportion, proved difficult to organize. The rapid growth of the community convinced many workers that great opportunities for individual advancement were possible without labor organization.

While capital and labor fought bitterly in neighboring cities at the turn of the century, Yankee-owned Paper City newspapers pointed to the "peace" and "brotherly accord" within the local mills. In the 1850's the Yankee owners broke the first strikes of workers for an eleven-hour work day in the textile and paper mills where women and girls were chiefly employed. Unsuccessful strikes were also conducted to raise spinning room wages 12 to 15 per cent so that they would be equal to wages for comparable work in neighboring cities. In the 1860's and 1870's, the owners, then largely Protestant Yankees, raised wages to meet those of neighboring communities whenever labor organization threatened. The early history of the labor movement was mostly one of poorly organized and poorly supported strikes, locally fought and lost.

Yet organization of workers in the community continued, particularly in the building and typographical trades. By the last two decades of the nineteenth century the paper industry press,[2] the occasional labor publications,[3] and the local daily newspaper[4] reflected a shift in attitudes of owners and laborers. Among workers, even among highly skilled paper machine tenders, the hope to travel the road to foreman and perhaps to stockholder and manager was fading. The mobilization by employers of the local police and the hiring of "scab" labor to fight union organization drove home to the workers the differences between managerial and worker power and interest. The owners were now less sure that "Christian love," "forbearance," and "good fellowship" ruled Paper City. A social gulf grew between laborers and owners, and therefore, between Catholics and Protestants, since the divisions appeared to many of the workers in the nineteenth century to be parallel. A sense of social guilt, a withdrawal from political life of the city, a new self-consciousness about the distinct interests of a capitalist group, expansion of private social welfare work—these were related phenomena to appear in the owner-management class in the first decades of the twentieth century.

The formation in 1890 of a Central Labor Union to pool the resources of the local labor movement aided organization. Then a disastrous strike in the paper mills during the depression year 1903 almost broke the local movements. The paper unions were of little importance again until the 1930's, open shops prevailing generally in the industry. Textile unions were organized in the major mills in the 1920's, but many of the companies remained unorganized marginal firms, largely employing French and Polish women, and threatening to close or move South if the unions attempted organization to bring wages to the general level of the industry. During the depression, short strikes for union recognition and slight wage gains were held in two textile mills, but no protracted strikes occurred in the decades from 1920 to 1950. Today Paper City is thought of by labor leaders as a "weak union town."

The Catholic Response to Labor

Many of the religious and ethical directives for the economic order formulated in Catholic papal encyclicals and ecumenical conferences of the Protestant churches represented responses to broad labor developments considerably in advance of union growth in Paper City. These concepts were to appear radical, or at least, strange to many Paper City laymen in both managerial and labor groups. However, by the middle of this century, some of the churches' principles had become part of a common frame of reference.[5]

The response of Paper City Roman Catholic leaders to the rise of the labor movement, both before and after the issuance of the major social encyclicals, was cautious and conservative.

The first strike in Paper City was instigated in 1848 by Irish day laborers constructing the water power dam on the Connecticut River. They protested a pay cut from 75 to 70 cents a day and also opposed the work pace set by the bosses. A Catholic priest hurried to the scene and with the arrival of militiamen persuaded the men to return to work.[6] A second demonstration of workers which threatened to become a riot against a cotton mill which had sold its stores of cotton during the Civil War at top prices in the market and then shut down was also quelled by a Catholic priest.[7] The priests in sermons in the 1880's paid homage to the "men of vision who developed the water power" and the industry of the city, and preached against labor associations which would augment the development of class feeling.[8]

After the issuance of *Rerum Novarum,* and also *Quadragesimo Anno,* the local priests continued to refuse to participate in the efforts of the workers to establish a stable and secure labor movement in the city.[9] Labor leaders seeking to organize the textile and paper unions in the early 1930's met with the local Catholic pastors before intensive campaigns were begun in the low-income parishes of Wards 1, 2, and 4, but the pastors were unwilling to make public statements on the rights and duties of union organization.[10] The labor leaders were able to secure public statements from a curate in Holy Rosary parish. He spoke to several labor and civic meetings advocating union membership, and conducted classes in schools to train local leadership, particularly shop stewards. A president of a local union recalled recently:

> The only Catholic clergyman—or any clergyman for that matter—who ever came in here to our office and offered to help was a curate from Holy Rosary Parish. He was good to make speeches to the people when we were having trouble explaining the purposes and principles of the union. Also, he would explain national legislation and social movements for us. It is a lot better to have an outsider, a minister or priest, come in, because then it's not a paid union man arguing his case. The curate used to spend a good bit of time explaining to me why it was difficult for the clergy to come out in

> the pulpit on specific issues. But he would come to meetings and speak straight out to the people.

The curate was, after a few years of such activity, transferred from Paper City to a small parish in another county with few industrial workers.[11]

Public support of the labor movement by the Catholic pastors has been more restrained in Paper City than the editorial positions of the diocesan journal [12] and the statements of the clergy in charge of diocesan institutes or schools for labor leaders. This difference is attributed by the local priests in part to the comparatively weak economic and political role of the labor movement in Paper City. The pastor of one of the oldest parishes, for example, commented:

> The people who are working for the cause of a decent living wage and for labor's right to organize are basing their action on Pope Leo XIII's encyclical [*Quadragesimo Anno*]. The Catholic church stands for these things, but the church today has to be darn careful. There is a lot of opposition to labor now, particularly in this community. I'm for the poor man who's worse off than ever with inflation. But the bishop is a conservative bishop, and this is a conservative city. I haven't, and none of the priests here have, taken public stands on labor's rights in the city.

The local pastors have usually waited for the bishop to take a position on a labor-management issue before speaking in a concerted manner. The only public position on a labor-management issue taken in 1947 by the bishop of the diocese was opposition to the Taft-Hartley bill when it was under consideration in Congress.[13]

The Catholic church's program of education for labor leaders is rarely participated in by the parish priest. The traditional role of the pastor has been to teach the principles of the social encyclicals in general terms, with little reference to the particular problems of labor-management relations. The regional and national publicity given to the activities of the Catholic labor priests has obscured for the general public the limited contact of the local pastors with the labor movement and its problems.

The labor leaders generally have a realistic understanding of the labor education programs of both Roman Catholic and Protestant churches. They are impressed both by the interest in labor problems of some of the young curates and by the apathy of the older priests. "Some of these young Catholic clergy know the score. At present they are moved so much by the church you can't develop a real friendship with them," a president of an American Federation of Labor paper union observed. "When these younger men come on, the church will have something."

The most effective diocesan agency for reaching organized workers is the Catholic labor school or institute. These schools, extensive as they now are, did not begin as well-financed and carefully organized efforts of the Catholic church to mold or penetrate a great social movement. They began as the struggling, spontaneous attempts of a few dedicated teachers and parish priests to reduce the conflicts that raged between labor and management in varying areas of the state.[14] The pioneer efforts were meagerly financed at first through the priests' solicitation of unions and companies. In time the priests were to become "labor specialists," through course work and study done "on the run." The bishop gave them a good deal of freedom in this activity.[15]

The first Catholic labor school in the state was established in 1941 at Holy Cross University in Worcester, after Father Thomas E. Shortell, a local priest and teacher, "began," as he recalled recently, "to look around for some way to bring labor leaders and management together to talk over their problems and to train them in the ways by which other industrial leaders had developed harmonious relations." The church leaders sought to create occasions characterized by trust and intimacy between clergy and laymen to open minds to new thoughts and commitments. The Catholic schools attempted to fill gaps in the traditional educational programs of the unions and to disseminate Catholic social and moral principles to Catholics and non-Catholics.[16]

The Catholic church now provides the major opportunities for labor leadership training in the city and diocese. Unions and other groups in the community have until recently shown little initiative in providing a broad and intensive educational program for workers. The last effort by groups other than the Catholic church to sponsor a labor school in Paper City was made by an Amherst college professor from 1920 to 1930.[17] The Central Labor Union co-operated with the school but the Catholic church would not.

The Catholic labor schools have varied widely in their sponsorship, the formality of instruction, subject emphasis, and level of leadership participation. Paper City workers and union officers, several of them Protestant, have attended informal schools of ten or twelve men meeting in a local parochial high school with a priest from a neighboring city, as well as diocesan-wide labor schools in nearby Springfield. The usual curriculum for local and diocesan schools includes elementary courses in labor economics, responsibilities of shop stewards, public speech and parliamentary order, and Catholic social principles, each offered in six to ten sessions during the year.

In the local schools, potential leaders are encouraged to take more advanced work at Holy Cross. The Holy Cross Institute of Industrial Relations, directed during the 1940's by Father Thomas E. Shortell and assisted by the faculty of Holy Cross University, is one of the leading Catholic labor schools in America, offering such technical courses as grievance procedures, contract negotiation, union administration, labor law, and current social problems.[18]

The Catholic program of labor education was not the first in the state. In 1939, Wellesley College began the first institute for labor leaders. At the fifth institute at Wellesley occurred an incident that indicates the difficulty of dealing explicitly in such general adult education with differences in religious approach to the social order. It also indicates the necessity to provide for genuine confrontation and discussion by representatives of the various faiths if such matters are to be mentioned at all. Some labor leaders believe that the incident aroused the Catholic church to extension of the Holy Cross program of labor education begun in the 1940's.

A Protestant lay officer in the New England Council of Churches spoke to the Wellesley institute, giving his appraisal of the history and current role of the labor movement. In the speech he said that the labor movement could not be described apart from its relations to "a Christian church which did not stick to the approach of Jesus."[19] This church, the speaker charged, had sought:

> clerical and social power in order to enforce its moral laws and to govern the daily lives of its people. Yet it has talked of being for general liberty. This Christian church has sought to place its leaders in positions of power to which they have had no rights. They have

tried to become the ones who bargained for the masses. But we look back on the record of such religious leaders, and we find that they have operated chiefly on the policy of centralizing more and more power in their own hands. . . . What all of us need now is less action after the fables of Aesop and more after the parables of Jesus.

Several Catholic labor leaders tried to obtain transcripts of the speech. The next day, several priests were conspicuously present at the Wellesley institute. Two priests from Holy Cross University were invited to speak. They explained that Holy Cross had 210 working people enrolled in evening classes sponsored by Catholic educational groups and that an extended training program was planned. The priests then gave a brief survey of Catholic labor colleges in America.[20] After the incident several Catholic labor leaders from Paper City who had previously participated in non-Catholic programs sent members to Holy Cross for training.

For most Holy Cross labor institutes there is considerable joint planning by university and labor representatives. Catholic social doctrine is related to the major areas of the curriculum, with almost all courses organized in the categories of union activities rather than of theology or ethics. Priests teach some of the courses, and syllabi indicate the chief Catholic books, periodicals and other resources in the field.[21] Speeches in general sessions deal with the social encyclicals and the role the Catholic church has played in the various social and political movements. Elective courses are offered in Catholic social doctrine. In a typical session of the institute—that of 1945—there was no reference to Protestant literature in bibliographies; there was no presentation by Protestant interpreters of labor problems or the role of the Protestant churches in society.

A sampling of twelve major unions in the Paper City in 1947 indicated that one-fourth had sent delegates to Holy Cross Catholic labor schools and had paid their expenses.[22] A few key unions such as the Textile Workers have sent no officials to Holy Cross Institutes, but have sent them to Harvard University labor schools, which have no formal religious affiliation.

Catholic clergy closely associated with the labor schools appear more receptive than parish priests to lay inquiry into the nature of moral law and more resilient in debate with laymen over the practical implications of moral and religious principles. At least many labor leaders feel this is so. Such men as Father Shortell seem to appreciate more deeply than the local priests the complex and dynamic nature of labor-management relations. Father Shortell often requests correction of judgment or insight from labor leaders as to the nature of the problems confronting labor and the implications of moral principle. Study materials for the institutes often contain summaries of articles in Catholic journals presenting a variety of interpretations of the implications of Catholic moral principles for specific situations.[23] This contrasts with the lack of genuine debate on basic political and economic issues in the diocesan journal and the general, exhortative preaching of the parish pastor. Yet it must be observed also about the action of the "labor priests" such as Father Shortell that the debate with laymen is over the practical application of the moral law, not the content of the law itself.

There are many Catholic leaders in New England, particularly the "intellectuals," the editors of Catholic publications and scholars in the universities, who forecast a decreasing role for the Catholic labor schools in the work of the church in the economic order. They feel the unions desire more and more to operate their own programs of adult education. They also predict that as the Catholic church extends its social base, out into the suburbs, laymen and clergy alike will be less happy with the concentration of the church upon the labor schools. They see them as responses to a period of labor weakness and severe industrial conflict that is passing. They see now an extension of the church's influence out into a variety of professions and vocational groups through conferences, retreats, institutes and schools.[24]

The Response of the Protestant Churches to the Labor Movement

Protestant response has been distinguished not by a corporate educational program for leaders but by the crusading efforts of a few ministers to encourage the growth of the unions, to initiate private welfare activities and to support the intervention of the government for improvement of working conditions. The pioneer clerical support of specific labor causes in Paper City came from the pastor of the Grace Congregational Church. *The Artisan,* Paper City's only labor newspaper able to survive for more than a year, observed in 1914 that only two pastors in the Christian churches were to be seen in attendance at public labor meetings, both of them Protestant.[25] The only sermons quoted by this labor paper during the five years of its publication are those delivered in Protestant Grace Church by the pastor or by visiting preachers of "Social Gospel" fame, such as Charles Stelzle and Washington Gladden. The "special Labor Sunday services" at which the editors urged attendances were conducted at Grace Church.[26] In 1914, *The Artisan* observed:

> Labor men in large numbers should turn out Sunday to hear Rev. Charles Richardson of Grace Church preach a special Labor Sunday sermon. Rev. Charles Richardson is a fraternal delegate to the Paper City Central Labor Union and he has always taken a deep interest in the cause of the workingman and does not hesitate to assist labor at any time during the year. He does not save his friendship for a sermon of words on Labor Sunday. He would be pleased beyond measure to receive the encouragement of a large labor attendance on next Sunday morning at 10:30. Bill Clements, president of the Eagle Lodge of the Papermakers, is chairman of the committee on arrangements, and the union label is on the cards announcing the services. As you will not be asked to take part in any other labor demonstration try to be present at this service. It will be profitable to you. We owe it to ourselves to encourage those in the ministry who are willing to preach Labor Sunday services by attending the services in larger numbers. Let's go.[27]

The Grace Church pastor, during the first decade of the twentieth century, made strong public statements on the importance of expanded labor organization in the city, appealed often for workmen's compensation, fought "to make Sunday a genuine day of rest for all workers," participated in the raising of funds for the defense of labor leaders arrested during organizing drives of unions, and often preached to congregations of four hundred to five hundred people in a worship center intended for two hundred fifty persons.[28]

Most of the Protestant church pastors, who occupied middle and upper class churches, conceived of their principal role as that "of interpreting the labor movement to those who habitually misunderstood it."[29] The most sustained and controversial effort of a minister to interpret to mill owners and managers the relation of Christian love to the demands for union recognition occurred in the

Second Congregational Church during the early 1930's. This church has the largest representation of Protestant businessmen in the city. The pastor preached, one businessman recalls, "as a man who felt entirely free from the economic pressures of the congregation. He tried to keep from offering blind resistance to the labor unions. He tried to produce some sense of guilt about our domination of industry."

The pulpit was for the pastor his chief means of communication. Many laymen complained that the pastor did not give ample opportunity for laymen to express their positions on labor-management controversies, but none took the initiative to organize sustained study and discussion programs on Christian faith and economics, although a few evening forums were held on social issues. The largest donor (one of his gifts was a $500,000 memorial chapel) threatened to withdraw his membership from the church because of the sermons, walked out during one, and then ceased participation in church activities while the pastor remained leader of the church.

The approach of most Protestant churches to labor-management controversies during the 1930's and 1940's was similar. Labor-management relations were viewed as social problems which the pastor should preach about, and members should discuss occasionally with due decorum in adult education programs. Neither union nor business leaders were approached by the Protestant churches as groups to be organized into schools or institutes.

In the discussions by Protestant congregations today the whole membership is invited to participate and the topics are much more likely to be directed toward a general theme, rather than action of one group—labor or management. Almost none of the practices of the Catholic labor schools for guidance of discussion are used: speakers are seldom briefed as to the issues that concern those who attend; the laymen never study particular literature prior to the discussions; there is almost no confrontation of experts and representatives of major special interests involved. Despite Protestant claims that they oppose directing social education toward a particular group, labor leaders have only rarely been asked to participate in discussions held in middle-class churches over the past decade. Confrontation of laymen with a "different point of view" comes chiefly from the pastor—a pattern characteristic of the personal, "prophetic"-type ministry.

The Protestant pastors have over the past two decades become increasingly isolated from local labor leadership. The pastors are, particularly because of the occupational composition of their church boards if not of their general membership, commonly associated in church activities with business and professional people. Protestant pastors belong to Kiwanis, Rotary, and other service organizations, with a membership largely professional and business, more than to any other type of association outside the church. None are now members of unions; two have been in the past. One of the sect leaders was once president of a baker's union but withdrew from the office when he established Gospel Hall. "I'm not working for temples in this life, but for the Gospel that goes beyond this life," he explained. Two-thirds of the pastors have not attended a union-sponsored meeting in the past decade or sought out a union officer to talk with him about social problems in the community. None attends labor-sponsored conferences in the state.[30]

The Protestant pastors generally believe that the labor leaders and union members are overwhelmingly Roman Catholic, so that there are no Protestant union people to involve in their church programs. Actually Protestants comprise approximately 11 per cent of labor union membership.[31] A study of the Central Labor Council indicated that, of 112 presidents and secretaries in the fifty unions, 14 are Protestant, 96 are Catholic, 2 are affiliated formally with no religious group.[32] Eight of the Protestant officers are presidents of locals. Protestants are chosen to be stewards of unions more than any other office, expressing a desire of varied Catholic ethnic groups to have a non-Catholic represent them before management.[33] In six representative unions, 32 per cent of the stewards are Protestant, while 17 per cent of all offices are held by Protestants. There is evidence that a much higher proportion of Protestant union membership has become labor leaders than the Catholic membership, and that there is considerable involvement of Protestant laymen with union activities.

Protestant churches in the Paper City area have developed no leadership with special responsibilities and competence for educational programs on the relation of Christianity to labor or business decisions. For at least three decades the chief reputation for Protestant expertness on labor problems centered in the pastorate of Grace Church. This church was by 1906, according to the press, the "most successful institutional church in Western New England." [34] Most of this ministry was, in the pastor's reflections, directed toward "the survival of my parish." (The Catholic labor priests are by contrast responsible for their role in the labor movement to sources of support and direction beyond local parishes or congregations.)

The relations of the Grace Church pastorate to the labor movement during the past fifty years provide a bold paradigm of the social and religious forces that tended to isolate the Protestant pastors (and many Catholic parish priests) from the new economic organization in the society. Almost every Protestant minister experienced some of the difficulties faced by the Rev. Charles Richardson in shifting—in his words—from "a simple ethical decision" to back an "underdog" movement to the "complex application of Christian experience" to a power movement "affecting the destiny of many local mills" and the economic stability and growth of the nation.

The Rev. Charles Richardson was attracted to the Grace Congregational Church as a place to begin his ministry, after a B.D. from an Eastern seminary, because the church was a "labor parish." The pastor felt himself to be on the frontier of the Protestant "Social Gospel" movement at the beginning of this century. He had learned in a brief survey of the community that the other Protestant churches had moved out of the working-class area, following the press toward suburbs of middle-class and upper-class members. He had also seen that the laboring people were not coming to the Protestant churches now located geographically and culturally away from them, even though all the Protestant pastors professed a strong desire to minister to every man—bank president, spindle tender, and rag picker.

In the early years of labor organization in the community Richardson had believed that he saw the relevance of the Christian gospel with clarity and concreteness. The God revealed in Jesus Christ willed that love and justice govern the relations of men. What chance would a local church have to witness before man to that will if the church were indifferent to oppression and tyranny? When members of the first unions were refused the right to work, the young pastor proclaimed from his pulpit and by tracts distributed from door to door that this action was un-Christian, and an affront to God. The pastor was welcomed at labor meetings and was invited to speak to the meetings whenever he appeared. The pastor saw his role then chiefly as that of giving morale to the movement, to help men see their part in developing a just and free society.

After many years of organizing, the unions gained a more accepted position in many of the large firms and industries of Paper City. Leaders of labor and management settled down to making the day-to-day decisions involved in regularized contract negotiation and administration of them. As the years passed, the decisions became increasingly specialized and complex. For a while the pastor tried to keep up with the technical discussions of the relations of wages and profits, the new competition of Southern, unorganized firms, the issues of job evaluation and seniority, and the alleged "reforms" of unions by state and national legislatures. He believed that Christ was the Lord of all of life. He believed that loyalty to Him could transform the basic attitudes toward one's vocation.

But the pastor could no longer feel that he saw as he had in the old days the specific relevance of the Gospel to what went on among the labor unions which served his church members. He confided to friends, with genuine sadness, that the union people "no longer need me, or want me to advise them." And then, more bitterly, he added, "The union people are riding high; they know they can go it alone."

Richardson sensed that deep religious problems were involved in these technical discussions. He sensed that unless he had some knowledge of the meaning of the technical issues confronting the labor movement in its new position of power he could not aid leaders in deciding which values deserved priority in policy making. He could not aid in interpreting the moral and religious issues at stake in too easy identification of union interests with the welfare of the whole community. To some extent he sensed an inadequacy in his past interpretations of his faith to workers primarily in terms of the affirmation of general ideals such as justice and freedom unrelated to the concrete decisions faced in the associations to which they belonged.

Over the years, Richardson watched many of his own church members who were union members withdraw as did he from positions of influence in their labor organizations. The educational life of the church provided no opportunity to examine in a sustained or disciplined way the decisions facing the movement, and to seek to illumine them out of the experience of the Christian faith.

In the later years of his ministry, Richardson shifted the emphasis of his statements to the press and of his speeches on the relationship between Christianity and community problems. He ceased to talk about labor economics, which had become too complex for his type of Christianity. He concentrated on a few social issues that still seemed simple to him, such as the liquor problem; or on issues that seemed to him more directly involved in the maintenance of the Protestants' own institutional life, such as opposition to gambling activities of the Catholic churches.

The pastor's experience represented a development in many of the Protestant churches: a withdrawal from the concrete, specialized activities of society as too "temporal" or "technical" to be interpreted by moral and religious insight. This led to ministerial concentration upon more narrowly defined "church issues."

The labor movement has seldom in recent years pressed the faith groups to commit themselves on specific issues. In 1946, one attempt was made to "put the clergy on the spot," as the president of the Central Labor Union termed it. The response of the clergy points up the slight interaction between the churches through the labor movement.

The state legislature in 1946 placed before the voters a referendum on a proposal known as the "Barnes Bill." Proponents claimed the bill would make unions more responsible by requiring labor officers to register information with state authorities about their organizational affiliations—and their expenditures of union funds.[35] Union leaders in Paper City looked upon the Barnes Bill as discriminatory, requiring information from labor not required from management. The Central Labor Council of local unions (A.F. of L.) directed its president, a Protestant, to write letters to all the clergy and rabbis in the city, asking "their attitudes toward the bill, the moral principles involved" and inquiring if they "thought as labor does about the Barnes Bill."

The council received three letters: two were from Protestant pastors, one from a rabbi. The only response from the Catholic clergy was a one-sentence note from a French pastor saying "I do not enter political arguments with anybody." [36] One of the Protestant letters arrived too late to be used in public discussion before voting on the referendum (requests for opinions had been sent six weeks before vote upon the bill). In this letter the Presbyterian pastor criticized only a provision in the original bill outlawing political contributions of unions which had in principle already been declared unconstitutional by the United States Supreme Court. The other letter from a Protestant clergyman, the pastor of the First Congregational Church, arrived only in time to be read to a labor meeting and a veterans' organization before passage of the bill. This letter opposed the bill as having a worthy objective but using means which would simply reduce labor's power rather than contribute to making the movement more responsible.

The request of the unions was discussed in a Ministerial Association meeting. The First Congregational Church pastor tried to convince the Protestant pastors to write letters to the labor leaders giving their judgment on the Barnes Bill. The pastor argued that the request gave the Protestant churches an obvious opportunity for leadership. They could express to Catholic working people genuine concern for their social welfare. They could offer to cooperate with the Catholic clergy in common moral and social concerns, and perhaps, he argued, influence the parish priests to assume more responsibility for the social problems of working people.

The Ministerial Association decided, however, to invite the managing editor of the *Transcript*, a conservative Republican newspaper, to explain the Barnes Bill to them. The association did not invite any labor representation to discuss the bill. It attempted no formulation of the issues in the bill, but left the decision to each pastor as to whether he should write a letter to the Central Labor Council.

The reaction of the union leaders to the response of the clergy was varied. Catholic leaders expressed on the floor of the meeting surprise, disappointment, even anger that the Catholic clergy gave less attention to the union's request than the Protestant pastors. The president of the council reported to the meeting that he personally had anticipated replies from most of the Catholic clergy, and little, if any from the Protestant pastors.

Christianity and the Social Order

The relations of the faith groups within the labor movement reflect much more than educational tactics or agitation on current events. At some point in the labor schools Protestant and Catholic laymen are encouraged to assess not just the present position of labor but the significance of its past and future in American culture.

The Paper City labor leaders who have participated most extensively in the Catholic labor schools generally believe that the schools are seeking to work out for industry the implications of a few basic ideas to be found in the medieval guilds and the social encyclicals. The basic ideas of Social Catholicism, as these leaders understand them, can be paraphrased as follows:

We are moving slowly and steadily in America toward a corporatist society, a society in which the major decisions are made and the major roles defined by the leaders of associations of men formed to carry out common economic functions. In the truly Christian social order, *all* men would be functionally organized by their place in their occupational, industrial or professional group. Today the worker in America improves his standard of living over the years, but always within his particular economic association or order. To leave this is to risk the loss of accumulated benefits (for example, seniority), the sense of belonging, of having a recognized status in society. The Catholic labor schools are seeking to encourage the growth of a corporatist structure in America—the organization of unions where they are not now present, the development of codes of conduct for the guidance of professional associations and industries and so on.

The second thing the labor leaders learn from the schools is that the Catholic church is trying to help the leaders recover the religious spirit that dwelt in the medieval guilds at their best—the desire of men to live together in harmony, seeking the good of one another. Social justice or the common good, the leaders of the schools argue, ought to be the "overarching norm" to which a Christian society conforms. A basic reading in the schools is the Papal encyclical *Quadragesimo Anno,* which observes:

> Because order, as St. Thomas well explains, is unity arising from the harmonious arrangements of many objects, a true, genuine social order demands that the various members of a society be united together by some strong bond. This unifying force is present not only in the producing of goods or the rendering of services—in which the employers and employees of an identical industry or profession collaborate jointly—but also in that common good, which all industries and professions together ought to achieve, each to the best of its ability.[37]

Thus, if the unions conceive of their interests in the right spirit, their demands will be for the good of the whole of society as well as for the good of the unions.

Most of the union leaders who have been involved in the Catholic schools see the Catholic concept of corporatist society as standing somewhere between the extreme individualism of the "free enterprise" talk of some of their employers and the "class conflict" views of socialism and communism.[38] Catholic social thought stresses the necessity and the naturalness of class harmony and cooperation. There is an impassioned simplicity in the practical admonitions of "labor priest" Father Shortell to union leaders "to keep in mind that harmony is always a higher value than tension and conflict." The tensions between labor and management are not to be interpreted by the labor leaders as serious, irreconcilable conflicts; the workers of Paper City, in the teaching of the schools, are to keep in mind that both labor and management "belong" to the textile and paper industries. The industries are organic wholes, common possessions of worker and employer, incapable of existence without the contributions of both groups. One labor leader recalls that Father Shortell said, "If more men would become good Catholics and desire the common good, then serious differences in society would end."

Yet this does not mean that the various groups within an industry do not bargain and negotiate with strength and vigor. The Catholic labor priests generally advise each union to concentrate on working out problems of justice within each industry. The workers are advised to bargain as hard as they can to get their due from their own industry. Problems of justice involved in the impact of union and management agreements upon the price stability, growth and employment of the economy are seldom raised by the labor priests.

Some Catholic leaders have attempted to formulate, with the aid of these general principles, proposals for structuring the American labor movement and the economy as a whole. They are often known as *industry council plans*.[39] The proposals have had several versions in the history of Paper City and the diocese, indicating the efforts of the Catholic leaders to adapt their proposals to changing conditions in the economy, and to anticipate the concerns of different groups in the economy.

In some statements the plan is chiefly a proposal for correcting the evils of "managerial despotism" and "rugged individualism" through the extension of labor's participation in the economic and social life of America.[40] In most versions, however, equal emphasis is given to the plan's contribution to maintaining the "freedom of the economic areas" of society against "encroachment by the state." [41] Lack of precision in the proposals has led to varied interpretations by labor leaders and business. The former tend to see the plan as a proposal for greater industrial democracy, and the latter as an antistatism program.[42]

Thoughtful union officials have been able to obtain little clarification from the labor schools and Catholic literature about many crucial aspects of the proposals. What is the actual relationship of the proposals to the present economic structure in American society? [43] In some statements the industry councils are referred to as "autonomous economic legislatures, executive and judiciary." [44] Apparently the decisions of these boards in some plans are to have legal status, but there is no discussion of the radical revision of the American legal structure that would be required by such new legislative-executive-judiciary aggregates.

There is considerable confusion as to what economic decisions are to be made by the councils proposed. Some Catholic statements have commended labor-management committees which deal *only* "with production and morale and avoid such matters as wages, hours, and grievances." [45] Other statements commended by Catholic leaders in Paper City propose giving to the industry councils "power to administer quantity of output, quality, prices, steadiness of works [*sic*], wages, salaries, hours, training, social insurance, capitalization, interest, profits and credit." [46]

The values that emerge from most statements of Catholic leaders about labor-managerial relations are fairly clear, although the action suggested for specific situations is ambiguous. A few proposals tend either toward managerial corporatism in which big business interests dominate the economic scene, or toward laboristic corporatism, egalitarian and socialistic in ideology. But most proposals seek a diverse economic and social structure in which neither management nor labor dominates the other, and where both are checked by the activity of a variety of noneconomic groupings.

Over the past two decades even such socially conservative leaders as the editors of the *Catholic Mirror*—who opposed most of the New Deal welfare measures—encouraged the growth of labor power, the expansion of union organizing activity, and union efforts to obtain greater job security, higher wages, and a fairer share of increased industrial productivity. The drive of labor unions for greater industrial democracy—conceived as the expansion of the workers' participation through union representatives in decisions made in industries—has been supported by conservative Catholic leaders when not infringing directly upon more traditional and basic managerial functions such as pricing of goods. In many instances these developments have been interpreted by the church leaders as effective alternatives to the expansion of the state's influence in the economic order—an influence that otherwise seemed inevitable.

Perhaps the most fundamental unanswered questions asked by laymen about the proposed industry councils concern the relation of the councils to American political institutions.[47] The most common question—where does ultimate authority rest for the general welfare in the industry council system?—is either not faced directly or given very different answers in the various plans, indicating a lack of serious and sustained attention to the problem. Most of the plans appear to assume a democratic political ethos and a pluralistic social structure in which they will operate. The various economic groups and councils are generally assumed to be subject to the sovereignty of the whole nation as expressed through representative institutions of government and politics. As one proposal notes, the government is "the guardian of the general welfare" in a way not equaled by other institutions in the society, and therefore "supervises the system, not in the role of dictator, but only to direct, watch, urge or restrain." [48] The private economic associations are neither to absorb the state nor to be absorbed by the state.

Although broad principles of corporatist thought have taken on little concrete meaning for most Paper City participants in the labor schools, the church has managed to give the impression that it has a specific proposal for the solution of deep economic ills in American society, even though the union leaders do not themselves know the details.

Protestant Response to Corporatist Developments

Protestant attempts at interpretations of general trends in the economy, which originate from ecumenical gatherings and from denominational social education programs, are, in many essentials, in agreement with Catholic thought. Most of these statements by Protestants reveal a greater reluctance than among Catholic social educators (not the parish priests) to wrestle with the concrete economic controversies at least broached in industry council plans. They have represented, as has Social Catholicism, a revolt against the excesses of industrial and finance capitalism. They have supported, as a partial corrective, labor organization and government intervention for the welfare of the individual. These positions have been looked upon as expresisons of traditional Protestant or Christian desires that the needs of all persons in the community should be met, that men should be free to form a great variety of associations, and that groups tending to coerce other people should be actively restrained.

Some Protestants, on the other hand, disagree significantly with Catholic economic thought. Some Protestant clergymen voice fears that Catholic or Protestant efforts to give meaning to work through discovery of the "natural orders God has set for men in society" will result in a too easy compliance of men with divisions of labor or stations into which they are born. They fear these adaptations to natural orders will ignore the need for keeping open channels of social mobility and of developing new work functions so that men may discover freely the work they are best suited to do, and may make improvements in their job conditions.

As an example of a Catholic approach to daily work which fosters too rigorous an acceptance of economic arrangements, one Protestant pastor cited the fifth meditation in a *Double Novena to the Holy Family* prepared by the director of social welfare work in the diocese. This meditation upon "St. Joseph, the Model of Working Men," reads in part:

> St. Joseph's work was a labor of life, seeking not merely wages, but spiritual benefits. He was not a clock-watcher. Time to him was God-given gift to be used profitably. He worked carefully and zealously so that he was recognized as an expert in his occupation.
>
> St. Joseph experienced the unfairness, the injustices, the uncharitableness of fellow-workers and associates; yet he was ever calm and charitable. He was never resentful or revengeful but always kind to his oppressors. When he was told that there was no work for him, he remained hopeful and patient. . . .
>
> St. Joseph, my foster-father, you are my model and friend. . . . Hence, when my daily tasks displease and exhaust me, when my work is a burden, when my fellow-workers bore and irritate me, I will think of you St. Joseph, and find courage in the example that you have given me.[49]

Thus, Catholic corporatist statements appear to some Protestant leaders to put too much emphasis upon social structure and orders, and too little upon dynamic group interaction, upon response in daily work to the changing demands of other human beings.

A few Protestant pastors, influenced by the renewed theological examination of classical Christian beliefs such as sin and forgiveness, express misgivings that many Catholic and Protestant proposals do not take seriously enough the self-preference of man, the inevitable tensions in a society of free men. These pastors fear that many church statements ignore the fact that pleas for harmony between social groups may serve best those who have the greatest stake in the *status quo*. The pastors note, for example, that management and labor have sometimes engaged in "harmonious," collaborative action which first raised wages and then passed the cost of them on to the consumer in higher prices, contributing to inflation which seriously hurt people with fixed incomes. They maintain that an adequate social theology would need to focus not simply upon harmonious labor-management action, but upon conflicts of interest in the whole economy, and upon the responsibility of government for policies in which the interests of many groups in inflation, economic growth and price stability would be weighed.

The most fundamental criticism these Protestant pastors have against the Catholic church is that, although its American social thought prefers a variety of social organizations common to a democratic society, it does not provide the *religious* grounds which maintain this pluralism. The introduction of the concept of infallibility at one crucial point in the social structure—the church and its discernment of correct religious thought—cuts the ground from vigorous nonconformity of all kinds, economic as well as religious. The dominant themes of most of the Catholic church's economic proposals characteristically become those of order, hierarchy of function, and harmony. On the other hand, the principal themes of this kind of Protestant economic thought characteristically become the importance of fostering vigorous diversity of activity, the creative benefits from mutual interaction of persons and groups, and the fruitfulness of group tension (if it does not originate in anxiety over group survival or find expression in coercion of others).

There have been a few exchanges between Catholic and Protestant laymen in the labor schools which reveal some appreciation of these clerical attitudes. Protestant uneasiness has been expressed occasionally with Catholic "strained efforts" to guide labor into "right acts" deduced from the "natural laws" enunciated by the church. "Must we always start with the encyclicals in these discussions of social order?" asked the Protestant president of a large A.F. of L. union in one session. "Why can't we begin with what is happening to the unions in Paper City and the United States? Can the Pope, way over there in Italy, really know what kind of business system we work in here?"

This kind of query finds supporters among Catholics who want to get at the moral law in the only way that seems truly meaningful to them in a world of process and change. The query often comes from men imbued with the pragmatism and day-to-day improvisation experienced in labor's fight for survival with other groups. It often comes from a fear that the flexibility and movement within the "American free enterprise system" is not adequately appreciated.

But it also may stem from interpretations that Protestants have received in their churches of a creative God whose action cannot be adequately encompassed in "basic principles."

The thought of these Protestant labor leaders focuses on the action and reaction of Christians and non-Christians within the unions and industries of Paper City, rather than upon the precepts of the Christian faith. They are interested not so much in attempts to formulate the essential moral principles of the Christian faith and to apply them in objective fashion to social problems, as to understand more adequately how they and the men they confront actually make crucial decisions. ("What made the company representatives fight the seniority clause of the new contract so hard? It was coming to us. The other unions have it. The industry is making money. It's what the company is already doing in effect.") What the church is asked to do is to deal with moral principle in the only way these men experience it—in the real world, in the complex confluence of principle with technical fact, of new demand with past practice. This struggle for opportunities to engage in ethical and religious inquiry that concerns the concrete decisions and actions of men runs through the life of Catholicism and Protestantism.

Chapter 17

The Morality of Politics

No group of contemporary leaders faces the problems of community more squarely than the politicians. There are fundamental and important conflicts among them as to what politics is all about and as to their actual or expected public role. The debate centers about their attempt to achieve necessary governmental action or policies without loss of vital freedoms and the rich variety of associations which distinguish American society.

Some men see their role primarily as brokers of the demands of interest groups, as manipulators of single issues and blocs of votes—religious, ethnic, or economic. The task of the politician, in this view, is to add up the demands of the organized electorate, to deal with each separately. There are no public interests which cut across or reconstitute these private interests. Or, if there are public interests, they do not have to be actively discovered; instead, private interests merely happen to converge on some issues.

Other politicians stress, at least in public, that good politics deals only with public interests, that men of high principle in politics live above personal or group interest, that they formulate public programs on behalf of every citizen.

Still others see contemporary politics as an attempt to discover ways of sustaining, reconciling and coordinating diverse private and personal interests in such a way as to encourage action for the general welfare. These men see a great need for over-all public policies in such areas as education and recreation, the maintenance of healthy and free labor and business organization, the resistance to the spread of communism and fascism, the encouragement of economic growth and stability at home and abroad. They see the political and governmental institutions as the chief centers for coordinating and channeling the use of the vast resources of the various private power groups. They view man's capacity for justice and freedom as making possible public policy; they view man's capacity for injustice and tyranny as making necessary democratic ways of changing and checking leaders seeking to achieve such policy.[1]

There are aspects of the history of Paper City politics which are grasped at least in some part by each of these views. Which is most adequate for understanding the public life of the community? Historically it appears that the people of Paper City and of the nation have evidenced greater and greater interest in the public policy roles of leaders in government, the major parties, the private interest groups, and the mass communication media.[2] Nineteenth-century civilization centered in the market mechanism through which independent, private pursuit of economic interest, as if guided by an invisible hand, was considered to produce the greatest possible good of the society. Twentieth-century civilization concentrates much more upon political institutions through which private interests are to be actively revised and reconciled for the public good.[3]

Paper City participates in these tremendous controversies as to the requirements of a free society in the modern world. On a state and national level the stakes are usually greater than on a municipal level. But the problems of policy and power to be seen in the broad sweep of national and world history have their local dimensions and structure. Business and labor press for various action from the local government and seek the support of politicians and church leaders in expression of creeds and objectives of their national organizations. Municipal, state and federal governments are in continuous interaction in development of programs of regional industrial expansion and social welfare. Local politicians debate the possibilities of activating a "religious vote," particularly the Catholic ethnic vote, at the same time that similar calculations are being weighed in the counsels of national party leaders. The quest for unity amid diversity, for common cause amid a variety of interests, dominates the historic political struggles in Paper City as in the nation.

Paper City Political History

Protestant Yankees have gradually retreated from direct participation in Paper City's municipal government and political parties as the activity of Catholics has increased. The Protestant retreat has been marked by occasional flurries of activity chiefly to restore "fiscal prudence" in the local government when Irish mismanagement or excessive patronage challenged the Yankee mill owners' interest in low taxes and efficiency in government. Organized Protestant Yankee political activity has been more a restraining than a formative type—concerned chiefly to check the expenditures of the local government rather than to use the power of the municipal government for meeting city-wide social problems. This has been true particularly when the Yankees have been out of power. They have been more willing for tax funds to be used for specific community projects when in political control than when out of office.

The Irish Catholic efforts to gain political power have been directed largely toward the control of patronage and jobs available through the city's largest business—its government. The Irish Catholics have not seriously challenged the chief political concerns of the Yankees, since the Irish have not sought to reform the government's structure or expand its expenditures for meeting health, housing or other social needs of the people in the city.

The first municipal government in Paper City, organized in 1874, was dominated by Yankees.[4] They ruled for the remainder of the decade. The period from 1873 to 1878 was one of business recession and of great population expansion. The Yankees were anxious to stay in political power to maintain low taxes.[5] By 1878, however, business was on the upturn and the mill owners were more willing to have money spent for badly needed streets, schools, water and sewage facilities. With prosperity and the lure of large economic gains, the "Brahmins" again lost interest in politics.

Diversion of Yankee interest to money-making occurred at the time that the Irish were becoming aware of potential political power in the numerical dominance of Catholics in the city. By 1870, the Catholic immigrants outnumbered Protestants and were rapidly achieving naturalization. By 1880, they were ready to back the Irish ward politicians in their rise to control of the city government and the Democratic party. By 1882, the city council and board of aldermen, which in the previous decade had been composed chiefly of wealthy and influential business and professional Yankees, were preponderantly Irish; the men were little known outside their own wards. In 1883 the first Catholic mayor was elected. The government remained in Irish Catholic control until the end of the century.

This phenomenon of the rise of the Irish people to control of city politics was common to municipal areas throughout America in the last two decades of the nineteenth century. The limited access of the impoverished Irish to dominant positions in business demanding large sums of capital channeled into politics the energies of ambitious and gifted Irish leaders.[6]

Political battles over the use of the municipal government have been waged chiefly on fiscal matters—the size of governmental expenditures and of taxes to be permitted in the community.

The tax rate was highest during the rule of the Yankees and lowest under Irish control. The Yankees obviously have been more willing to accept higher taxes when they have had more direct involvement in management of the local government. The Irish came into control of the government after the tax rate had been increased by the Yankees to meet the great need in the city for trunk sewers, fire prevention equipment, sanitation facilities in low-income areas and macadamized main roads.[7] Under Irish control, the government began in 1885 to accumulate a sizable debt and by this device to shift the burden of payment to future years. Yankees, no longer bearing the responsibility of the city government, and absorbed in the production of wealth, either acquiesced in the policies of the city government or used their corporations' influence to encourage the continuance of the low tax policies.

During the 1890's, battles in the city government over the aldermen's power to grant licenses for the sale of liquor overshadowed all other political issues. For six years a young Irish cigar salesman, named James Connelly, was able to control the city's politics as alderman and boss of several other aldermen who vetoed all reform action. The Yankees sought to offset his power by securing the adoption in 1896 of a new city government charter shifting major political power away from the board of aldermen to the mayor. Connelly had himself elected mayor and from his new powerful position he increased the price of a liquor license or protection. While the mayor was on a triumphant visit to his home town in

Ireland, the scandal of a $65,000 embezzlement by the tax collector broke.

Nothing then, as now, aroused the Yankees to political activity so much as the cry of personal corruption in government office. A new political machine was organized, headed by B. E. Hall, a wealthy Protestant paper manufacturer. The "reform" administration went into office in 1898 with Hall's brother-in-law, also a Protestant, as mayor, and five newly elected Protestant aldermen.[8] A "rigid economy" was instigated in city expenditures; a new liquor commission was established; a few new schools were built.[9] Money was not forthcoming, however, for improvements in public health requested by the Board of Health—particularly house-to-house sanitary inspection, and closer public control of distribution of milk to decrease the high infant mortality rate.

By the end of the century, the Yankees in the new machine had gone as far as they wished to go with municipal reform. The flush of popular disgust with Paper City's "Tammany regime" and of popular enthusiasm for the reforms instituted during the first year of the new machine's rule ran their course. If the Hall machine was to stay in power and introduce no other popular issues, it had to seek alliance with the Irish Catholic politicians who had access to votes which could be delivered on the basis of personal favors and ward patronage. The major Irish political alignment which the Hall machine made was through the retail liquor business.[10]

Dealers were given free reign, so long as they kept license squabbles peaceful and conducted their business without arousing public indignation. Hall extended capital to men wanting a start in the liquor business. These men bought their barroom fixtures from the Yankee dealer who sat on Hall's liquor commission granting licenses to bars. The political machine was well financed by contributions of the liquor dealers, by Catholic-owned construction companies given street and building contracts, and by wealthy Yankees grateful for low taxes. Hall also gave jobs in his mill to Catholic political leaders who supported him. He became important as a national political figure when he spent large sums for the election of Calvin Coolidge to the presidency of the United States and was given a position in the Cabinet.

This political machine maintained mayors from Protestant mill-owning families in power until 1910. It was the last sustained effort of the Yankees to operate within the municipal government. After 1910, Yankee political influence was chiefly exerted through economic pressure from outside the government, by such special interest organizations as the Taxpayers Association, and by the supply of financial backing for popular Catholic candidates in order to secure favors for certain mills.[11] Such influence was directed not so much toward the achievement of general government policies or programs, as to the securing of exceptions to policies.

By 1908, a new Irish-French Catholic coalition machine developed in opposition to the Hall faction. It had the support of organized labor and also the important patronage base of the municipally owned Gas and Electric Company which had been established by a referendum vote in 1900.[12] The municipal company had been supported as a popular reaction to the high rate policies of the Yankee-owned Water Power Company.[13]

The new Irish Catholic machine was not long in establishing rapport with Yankee mill-owning interests which financed its campaigns; it secured lower and lower city government budgets and taxes.[14] The familiar pattern appeared again of Irish concentration upon patronage, the withdrawal of Yankee leadership interested in using the city government to meet community problems, and the resurgence of Yankees interested simply in inexpensive government.

The "Gas and Electric" machine remained in power until the depression of the 1930's. Yankee industrialists again entered politics with a crusade to reduce the cost of the city government and the tax load of the mills. This time the general economic collapse of the mills was so severe, the reduction of municipal salaries and jobs such a serious threat to city employees, and the tensions that resulted so great, that the political action was directed by an outsider. He was a business "trouble-shooter," named Clarence Randolph, brought to the city in 1930 by the largest paper mill in the city to carry out extreme measures to save the mill from bankruptcy.

During the two years previous to Randolph's arrival in the city, unsuccessful attempts had been made to organize a Taxpayers Association to fight for reduction of city government costs; but many businessmen, particularly retailers, claimed that they were afraid to join the association for fear of economic boycotts by the employees of the city government and their friends.[15] Randolph became president of the association and sought to induce several Irish and French Catholic businessmen to become officers, so that the association's attack against the Catholic-manned government could not readily be interpreted as a religious issue. The association was able to persuade only the Catholic owner of a construction company to serve on the first executive committee; the other members were Protestants.[16] Although in the first year of the association only two members were Catholic and today the membership is only 30 per cent Catholic,[17] the association is primarily a union of common economic, not religious, interests.

The extreme tension between upper-income groups and city officeholders was related to the progressive nature of Paper City's property tax and to the comparatively high and stable level of municipal salaries in comparison with the wages paid in local industry.[18] In 1931, 96 industries and firms paid 47 per cent of Paper City's local taxes.[19] So great was the mills' cutback in production that the salaries of municipal employees totaled half of what the city's mills paid out in wages.

Taxpayers Association leaders took their position to women's church groups, ethnic societies and service clubs throughout the city. The fear of an organized city bureaucracy claiming control of 5,000 votes could be overcome, Mr. Randolph told a Protestant women's group, "only by faith. Faith will some day win this battle in Paper City. . . . With heads erect, let us say with St. Paul—'Watch ye, stand fast in faith, quit you like men, be strong.' "[20] The Taxpayers Association speakers also indicated that "five industrial firms and less than one hundred other taxpayers in the city by calling a taxpayers' strike could force Paper City into the hands of a receivership, or to use a more polite term, a commission."[21]

The campaign was successful in the municipal elections. Five Protestant businessmen were elected aldermen; a former supervisor for a Yankee mill—also a Protestant—was elected mayor.[22] Additional Polish and French aldermen indicated an ethnic support of the businessmen's crusade to break the Irish control of the city government. Within a few weeks, a reduction in tax valuations of over $10,000,000 was made and a tax rate decrease of $3.59 per $1,000 of property.[23] Also a 20 per cent salary cut was passed for city employees. Paper City's tax rate soon became and has remained the third lowest in the state for all communities, and the lowest for any city over 25,000 population.[24]

Direct participation by Yankees in local politics reached its lowest ebb in Paper City history during the prosperous years of World War II. Cynicism about the corruption of politicians and the pettiness of local politics is now widely expressed among leading Protestant laymen. These are typical comments of businessmen:

> If you can pay the Irish politician, you don't have to go into politics to get what you want.

> It doesn't matter who is in politics here—Catholic or Protestant. They're all a cheap lot. A fifty-cent piece will buy them.

> I once ran for alderman—back when I was younger and more foolish. Got the worst beating of my life. My opponent was an Irish Catholic who went around the lower wards calling on all his relatives and their friends to come out and vote for good old Mike. I knew nobody, so I talked about the need for lower taxes. I had the right issues but the wrong name.

> You know what's wrong with Paper City's politics? The Protestants have all the money and the Catholics have all the votes.

The Protestant businessmen confine their political activity largely to "pressure" through such groups as the Taxpayers Association. Republican leaders who have the major party contact with Protestants report great difficulty in persuading Protestants to run for local office.[25] The chief impact of Protestant leadership in local politics now, as throughout most of Paper City's history, is directed toward the limitation of government activity, not the use of government for meeting various community needs which cannot be met through private welfare resources.

The predisposition dies slowly among businessmen, particularly among Protestant businessmen—who have more often than Catholics inherited family mills, and who manage firms that do business less directly with government people—that politics is the area in which narrow interests compete with one another for power, whereas in business men seek only opportunity for creative service. What is "response to demands of the market" in business is "grubbing" for votes in politics; what is "bargaining" in business is "making deals" in politics. Protestant "reform" leadership, its "socially conscious" well-educated young people, have directed their energies almost entirely into private social welfare and nonpolitical activity. The Highlands Junior League, for example, composed of college-educated Protestant young women (alumnae of such colleges as Vassar, Smith, and Mt. Holyoke) has assiduously built files on various social problems needing "urgent attention," but has developed no knowledge of the *political* channels for getting attention directed to the data. No League of Women Voters exists in Paper City. The Catholic dominance of politics and the Protestant dominance of private social welfare foster and reflect the isolation of the two religious groups in Paper City.

Government Structure and Political Control

The governmental and political structure of Paper City hampers greatly the responsible formation of public policy. Most reforms were instituted "to get the government out of politics" or to change the governmental structure to meet some immediate abuse of office. The mayor was given tremendous power, but he operates in a nonpartisan setting, without strong competition between the two major parties to assure majority control of the office. The Board of Aldermen has little effective control of the mayor, since only a two-thirds vote can override his veto. This means that a minority of aldermen interested in avoiding government action can easily support a "do nothing" mayor.

Nonpartisan elections were adopted in 1913 mainly, according to present-day Republican leaders, through the insistence of business leaders, largely Republican, that too many people were voting for the party rather than the man, and that better candidates would be elected without party labels. Republican party leaders believe that a Republican cannot be elected to a local office, so strong is loyalty to the Democratic party in the community. There are religious angles to the nonpartisan structure. Since most Protestants, the

Republican party leaders observe, are Republicans, and most Catholics are Democrats, a party system operating on the local level would mean that no Protestants could be elected.

Party organizations are weak in the city, since their functions are limited; they do not successfully and actively compete for support of local candidates, nor discover and define issues in the community which will appeal to great numbers of voters.

The local political scene, particularly the crucial mayoralty race, is dominated by personal factions and by the most articulate interest groups. The mayor usually exercises the power of his office to build his own personal machine out of amorphous factions with narrow patronage or economic interests.

Paper City's nonpartisan system gives Republican leaders, the most influential of whom are business leaders, the low taxes they want, and it gives the Democratic leaders, most of whom are Irish Catholic ward politicians, the jobs and patronage they want. The system keeps in power a Republican mayor in a city which votes generally Democratic in state and national elections. The mayor uses the influence of his office to fight for Republican positions on crucial state policies against the positions advocated by local Democratic politicians.[26]

Religious Composition of the Present City Government

Control of the city government is more widely distributed in the community than is that of private business. The personnel of municipal offices has reflected more sensitively the shifts in numerical power among the various religious groups in the community than has corporation management. The religion of the officeholders is overwhelmingly Catholic.[27] The 24-man board of aldermen in 1947, for example, had a president and fifteen members who were Irish Catholic, four members who were French Catholic and four who were Protestant. All but one of the Protestant aldermen were elected at large.[28]

The municipal officers elected by the voters, appointed by the mayor or elected by the aldermen are 80 per cent Catholic; about 65 per cent of these positions are held by Irish Catholics. The only commissions or boards which the Protestants control are the Child Welfare Commission and the Fire Commission, reflecting Yankee concern and leadership in social work and in securing an efficient fire department for low insurance rates. An equal number of Protestants and Catholics are on the Parks and Recreation Commission. No Protestants hold full-time non-civil-service positions in the city government except the secretary to the mayor who is also leader of the women's division of the Republican party. The ranks of the firemen and policemen are approximately 90 per cent Catholic.[29]

The mayor, when this study ended, was nominally a Protestant, but participated regularly and equally in both Protestant and Catholic religious activities, and the affiliations of his immediate family were with both major religions. The mayor's wife, recently deceased, was a prominent Catholic, "the sweetest little Catholic I ever knew," the mayor often noted, on public occasions. This anomalous, ambireligious position is characteristic of a number of the top-level Protestant figures in the city with community roles demanding strong support from both Catholics and Protestants.

The mayor attended retreats conducted by the Catholic church for laymen, at the invitation of church officials. One Catholic official in the city government stated in an interview that he had been so suspicious of the mayor's motives in attending a Catholic retreat as an honored guest of the church and quartered in the bishop's suite of the retreat house that he had anonymously called an insect and rat exterminating company; he had had it send a crew to the bishop's quarters during the retreat under instruction to rid the quarters of rats. The mayor regularly attended the annual Knights of Columbus communion breakfast.[30] The fact that Paper City had a Protestant mayor was often alluded to by the mayor and by Catholics as an indication that "Paper City is a friendly little city with no religious prejudice."

Political Parties and Religious Alignments

The Republican party organization represents a coalition chiefly of French Catholics and Protestants. In 1947 the Republican party committee in the city had a religious composition as follows: of 78 members, 35 were Protestant (8 of German descent, the remainder Yankees); 41 were Catholic (23 French descent, 10 Irish, 8 Polish); 2 were Jewish. The Democratic party committee was controlled by Irish Catholics: of 60 members, 51 were Irish Catholic, 5 were

French Catholic, 2 were Polish Catholic and 2 were Yankee Protestant. In more recent years the proportions of ethnic and religious affiliation have remained approximately the same.

The Irish Catholics began this strong attachment to the Democratic party in the 1870's, as a minority ethnic group attracted to an "out" party. The Republican party was dominated by Protestant Yankees, but the Democratic party, as a minority party, welcomed Irish leadership.[31] The Irish, as the "intermediate" ethnic group between the Yankee and the non-English speaking French and Poles, acted successfully for almost two decades as spokesmen of the "newer elements" against the Republican, "old" immigrant, Protestant stock.[32]

However, as early as 1873 influential French leaders were arguing that the French must not rely upon the Irish to represent their political interests and that a party dominated by them might prove a poor vehicle for ethnic interests.[33] The extent of control over the Democratic party by the Irish and over the Republican party by the Yankees has been slowly but steadily reduced over the years.[34]

By the turn of the century the social mobility of the Irish produced some break into Republican party ranks, particularly among upper and middle classes. But party leaders generally observe that upper and middle class Irish today are still not as active in Republican party work as Protestants and French Catholics in the same economic group.[35] The opportunities for French leadership have always been greater within the Republican party than in the Democratic party, since the Yankees were withdrawing from politics at the time the Irish were becoming highly active.

This is not to say that the French wards have regularly voted Republican simply because the party was more open to French leadership. Positions of the parties on public issues mattered also. In 1892, the vote in the French wards was overwhelmingly for Cleveland, the free-trade principles of the Democratic party appealing to a people who had been forced to emigrate from Canada in part because of the effect of American high tariffs.[36] A national depression and the free silver campaign of Bryan contributed to a shift in French voting to the Republican party, a shift which lasted until the Al Smith campaign in 1928 when Wards 1, 2, and 5 went Democratic. From 1928 until the present, registration in the wards with highest French representation has been strongly Democratic, approximately three Democrats to each Republican in all three wards and in both presidential and off-year elections until the 1952 presidential election, when Democratic strength was reduced slightly in Wards 1 and 2, and considerably in Ward 5 (Tables XXX and XXXI). The lower the level of income and housing in the ward, the higher the Democratic registration.

In 1946 the enrollment in both parties dropped and the independent vote increased significantly (Table XXX), indicating the presence of considerable cross pressures within the Catholic people in the city. They were being torn, it appears, between traditional Democratic party loyalties based largely on domestic economic interests and the mounting criticism of Democratic foreign policy, such as evidenced in the *Catholic Mirror* (see Chapter 19). The Polish people were particularly influenced by the argument that Poland had been "sold out" at Potsdam and Yalta. The Polish ward 7 from 1940 to 1946 increased its independent vote more than any other ward. In 1952 and 1956 it showed the biggest swing from Democratic to Republican presidential candidates. The inner suburbs in the upper middle class Ward 6 show the next greatest shift toward the Republican president.[37]

The Republican party has clearly in the last two presidential campaigns attracted Catholic votes on all class levels and in all ethnic groups; the lowest income, French Catholic wards (1 and 2) remain the most heavily Democratic. There is indication that the Eisenhower vote is still largely a personal rather than a party vote, even though a vote for him may be for many Catholics the first exploratory step toward Republican affiliation, particularly among the middle class Catholics. However, the vote in 1956 for Eisenhower was 13,214 to 13,041 for Stevenson, a plurality considerably below that given Democratic candidates for the rest of the offices. The major affiliation of the Catholics is still Democratic, and of the Protestants, Republican.[38]

In Paper City a great number of voters are unenrolled in party ranks.[39] The apathy toward the parties cuts across every ward and income group, but the highest percentage of unenrolled people is to be found in the low-income Catholic wards where those who do indicate party affiliation are largely Democrats. Political inactivity is also revealed in the failure to register to vote. This tendency is deepest in low-income, Democratic, Catholic areas.[40] The Democrats apparently benefit more than Republicans from large registrations.

Voting for specific candidates does not necessarily follow the religious and ethnic patterns of early party leadership. Ethnic and religious lines are crossed in response to various other factors—the personality and character of a candidate, the type of campaign waged, positions taken on economic, political and social issues that matter greatly to voters, and personal associations established during a public career. There seems to be little validity in the concept of a "hyphenated vote" (Franco-American, Irish-American, Polish-American, Yankee-American) that can be manipulated en masse simply by the choice of a candidate of a particular faith or nationality.[41]

Religious affiliation is in Paper City a very general composite symbol of voting patterns, party affiliations, income, interest in local government jobs, economic attitudes, and so on.[42] The Protestant tends to be Republican, middle or upper class, lives "up the hill," has little interest in local politics so far as getting a job is concerned, and is against an active and expensive local and state government. The Catholic tends to be Democratic, lower or lower-middle class, lives more often in the working class wards, has more interest in the positions and social services provided by the local and state government. The French Catholic candidate for state senate carries Ward 2 not so much because he is French or a Catholic but because he is a Democrat, because he stands for certain social beliefs strongly held in Ward 2, and because he is known in the area and is able to conduct a forceful campaign. A Protestant Yankee who had these other characteristics would probably run well in Ward 2.

When the convergence of such factors does not occur, religious and ethnic factors are usually not influential enough of themselves to control an election. In the instances when ethnic and religious lines have been crossed, candidates have waged vigorous campaigns highlighting issues and made personal appeals which subordinated factors of ethnic and church affiliation. The politics of the New Deal-Roosevelt era sharpened economic and class divisions and subordinated in politics the loyalties of nationality and religion which had formerly divided lower-income elements in Paper City as well as in the nation.[43]

This is not to say that there is no ethnic and religious vote in Paper City. The ethnic religious vote takes on greater importance as a factor for marginal manipulation when parties and candidates are competing successfully and elections are expected to be won only by narrow margins.

The fact that the Catholic population has since 1928 usually supported Democratic party candidates has had other bases than simply religious or nationality loyalties. The support of Democratic candidates in dominantly Catholic, French, Polish and Irish wards has been uniform regardless of the candidates' ethnic or religious affiliation.[44] The local candidates who have won in Paper City since 1928 have generally been Catholic, and Democratic, but this has been because of the convergence within ethnic groups, religion and party of a wide range of common interests and historical developments. One factor in the large Democratic vote has been the early party recruitment of leaders from low-income, "out" groups who took a position on issues such as taxes, distribution of patronage, and extension of social welfare which appealed to the economic and social interests of the people among whom they had risen to political influence.

No major break in the strength of Paper City support of Democratic presidential and congressional candidates occurred until 1952, when Eisenhower was able to win 13,035 votes to Stevenson's 16,590. (In the 1948 elections, Dewey had been given only 9,394 votes to Truman's 19,281.) Some shift from Democratic presidential candidate ranks to Republican ranks took place throughout every ward, but the greatest inroads into Democratic support were made in the upper and upper-middle class wards, 6 and 7. The slightest shifts were in the lowest income wards, 1 and 2 (Table XXXI).

Obviously great numbers of Roman Catholics in suburban areas of the city were convinced in this election that their interests were not better served by the Democratic candidate. The shift was, however, too dramatic a break from the 1948 presidential vote to be regarded as yet as the kind of basic party regrouping which occurred in 1928 and 1932.

The second major aspect of the religious-ethnic vote in Paper

City is this: there are several factors in the *local* political situation that make ethnic and church loyalties more important here than in state and national campaigns. The nonpartisan structure minimizes discussion of social issues and contributes to party inactivity. Voters tend to select candidates on the basis of familiar affiliations when important public issues are not involved. The mayor noted recently, "When it comes to distributing offices and attending events in the city, I watch the Irish most, then the French, and then it's a toss up between Poles and Protestants." The distribution of jobs according to nationality representation becomes a major political concern.

Political leaders in arranging campaigns for state and local candidates often have the men devote more time to visiting ethnic social clubs, raffle and beano games sponsored by the Catholic churches than to any other public contacts. (At these affairs a priest usually invites the candidate to "come forward and draw the winning numbers.") Candidates always state, when possible, their parochial-school attendance and arrange for advertisements of support by representatives of all ethnic groups.[45]

There is a third basic aspect to the bloc voting in religious or ethnic lines. Such voting has become an important factor in Paper City politics only when a group has felt that its status was being menaced by the candidacy of a particular individual, or that a campaign had been posed unmistakably and predominantly in religious or ethnic terms. The Alfred Smith-Herbert Hoover campaign took on such religious attributes in Paper City. The dramatic shift of French Catholic Wards 1 and 2 from Republican ranks in 1924 to a vote of 3,401 for Smith and 360 for Hoover must be attributed in part to the religious connotation the campaign assumed.[46] Hoover carried only the strongly Protestant precinct 7A in Paper City (355 for Smith and 608 for Hoover).[47]

In Paper City the conduct of a campaign so that religious affiliation becomes an issue works to the disadvantage of representatives of the minority religion. The temptation deliberately to raise religious issues is greatest in this community for the Democratic, Catholic politicians. However, the practice has not been widespread. The occasions when Catholic bloc voting against a candidate of another religion was necessary to win the election have been few.[48]

The introduction of religious affiliation of a candidate as an issue cannot usually be done with effectiveness unless the opponent can be identified, not merely as of another faith, but as actively opposed to the majority faith. The evidence must be at least an "adverse" position on what is in the public mind a "religious" issue affecting the welfare of the faith. The range of these issues is not great—centering about such concerns as public support of parochial schools and birth control.[49]

The question of the religious affiliation of candidates has arisen most recently in Paper City politics over the issue of whether certain municipal boards whose decisions affect the interests of all the churches should exclude the minority faith entirely from representation. The issue was raised by both Catholics and Protestants in a school-board election. Influential French and Irish political leaders lined up enough Catholic members of the board of aldermen to vote a Protestant into the school board to replace a vacancy made by a deceased Protestant member—the only Protestant on the board.

The supporters of the Protestant candidate against an Irish Catholic argued that the school board should not be entirely Catholic and that the Protestant candidate had supported the school lunch and child aid programs strongly approved by Catholics. The Protestant candidate wrote all of the aldermen of her desire for the position, and talked to all but two of them. Junior League representatives followed up her contacts with telephone calls. The Protestant was elected. Several of the Catholic aldermen who voted for the Protestant informed her that they had done so in order that all the major religious groups would be represented. The policy of avoiding a complete exclusion of Protestants from the school board and the board of aldermen appears well established in Catholic political circles.

One of the few issues treated by the churches as a religious issue was the referendum for legalization of the right of doctors to disseminate birth-control information. This issue was voted upon in the state in 1942 and in 1948; both times the referendum lost in the state, in the Paper City diocese, and in Paper City. A crucial factor in the voting in response to the referendum drives is whether they are conducted in "off year" or presidential years.[50] The Democratic vote has in the past decade gone to the polls more strongly in presidential elections, and this vote tends to have a higher proportion of

Roman Catholics than Protestants.[51] Therefore, increased opposition to the referendum comes in the presidential year.

How strongly did Catholics oppose the birth-control referendum? The number of eligible voters in Paper City in 1948 was 33,293; one careful study estimates 22,489 were Catholic and 10,804 non-Catholic.[52] In 1948, 17,606 people voted against the birth-control referendum; 8,529 for it, 3,363 voters did not indicate a position, and 3,795 did not vote. A "bloc voting" of Catholics against the amendment did not occur. However, the general tendency for opposition to the referendum to grow with the increase of the Democratic vote and the high Catholic percentage of this vote probably indicates considerable religious alignment on the issue.

A comparison of the pro-birth control referendum vote with the Republican vote reveals that the Republican vote for governor and for president was considerably greater than the vote for the referendum.[53] Opposition to the referendum and indecision of voters is so great that a party or a candidate would probably contribute to defeat if it or he became identified with support of the referendum. Republican party candidates who strongly supported the referendum would run the risk of being interpreted as anti-Catholic and might contribute greatly to the solidification of Democratic support around a religious issue, since the referendum's opponents are already strongly predisposed economically and politically to the Democratic party. A candidate cannot substitute manipulation of a "religious issue" for wide economic and social appeal.

Summary

Some politicians still practice in Paper City, with some success in maintaining themselves in office, a kind of political bartering, a bloc vote manipulation and a cultivation of parochial interests. These men think of local politics in terms of manipulating various interests in society; they see the church as having a single interest of its own—religion, morality, and so on. These men try again and again in Paper City to activate the "Catholic vote." They believe that a person's religious affiliation has a determining force in his actions, in that his religion can somehow be isolated from the influence of his age, occupation, residence, family tradition, economic status or national origin.

People acquire such beliefs in part because of the way church leaders describe the jurisdiction of the ecclesiastical authorities (see Chapter 18) and the way they claim that the content and principles of a religious area can be made known, defined, learned and acted upon so that one's action is then Catholic and Christian (Chapter 19). The Catholic church probably encourages this kind of bloc-voting thought and strategy to a greater extent than Protestantism does. As we have seen, the social forces of ethnic identification and defensiveness have, until recent years of nationality assimilation, strongly reinforced talk of bloc-voting.

These people who talk of the "Catholic vote" assume that enough people vote on the basis of religious identification so that the inclusion of a Catholic on a ticket will be a successful political maneuver. They assume also that the candidate makes his appeal to voters in separate groups or blocs, in that he keeps adding on appeals to one group and another until he obtains a majority.

In regard to the first assumption, there is evidence that most Catholics, like most Protestants, are deeply affected politically by a number of factors, which converge in complex fashion, and which include their social and economic positions in the community. Issues or situations which are thought to be purely religious are rare in American life; on most political issues the church leaders have not reached wide agreement as to the religious commitments at stake.

The second assumption envisages a kind of politics in which appeals to one group can be made without affecting the voting of other peoples. This mechanistic view of politics ignores the actual complexities of American life.

The activity of Protestant Yankee business leaders in Paper City politics gives the same evidence as the Catholic record. The Protestant Yankees at times developed important common interests, such as frugal efficient government; and they sought political power to have those interests recognized. But their interests shifted—toward higher taxes, for example—with the experience of governing and with new awareness of community needs. They could achieve and maintain power, even in the factional politics of Paper City, only if they were sensitive to the changing interests of many people outside business. Yankee claims to leadership above interest and partisanship were not long maintained in the thrust and counter-thrust of groups, the elemental dynamism of Paper City politics.

In looking at Paper City's past and anticipating its future, it seems likely that politicians who have the best chance of survival in politics have some appreciation of the powerful institutional loyalties that operate in men's lives as well as the essential dynamism in public life. They are aware of the increasingly city-wide character of the problems people face in improving suburban living and in expanding their educational opportunities. They understand the deep relationship of local, state and national politics.

The political positions they support are neither simple deductions from moral principles nor efforts to achieve some ideal or perfect society. They are responses to demands and proposals for action from a variety of persons and groups. They are efforts to find the public interest, the general policy direction, that cuts across or brings into some significant relationship these varied demands. In these demands and in the politicians' response, facts, moral principles, drives, lusts, past memories, future hopes—all the varied loyalties and patterns of thought which have become the creative core of personal identity and freedom—are brought to bear.

Chapter 18

The Politics of the Churches

The religious leaders of Paper City are more concerned with the politics of morality than with the morality of politics.[1] Their discussion of politics is more largely a way of corroborating their own or their church's doctrinal and ethical system than an attempt to discover the actual situations confronting men in the formation of public policy. Most of the religious leaders believe that their Christian faith and philosophy of life have given them a system of religious truth and moral principle with which they may proceed to interpret politics. Their task, as they see it, is to engage in those activities which will bring people into an understanding of Christian morality, and will, as one Catholic priest observed, "define the spiritual authority of the church." Or as a Baptist pastor said, "the task of the church is to encourage the politician and the citizen to pursue the great ideals of the Sermon on the Mount."

There are differences to be observed in Catholic and Protestant approaches to politics, along lines already observed in other areas of the community; but most leaders of both faith groups assume that they are making judgments about politics from the perspective of an established and assured system of natural and divine laws or ultimate ends. The substance of these ends and laws is known prior to one's involvement in particular political problems. They are not conditioned by political events.

The Catholic ethic rests much more than the Protestant ethic upon an explicit metaphysical system. The truth and inclusiveness of this system are thought to have been demonstrated by reason; its validity is not dependent upon empirical verification within the political events of a particular society. To the demands of reason the Catholic ethic adds the demands of faith. In Protestantism the emphasis is much more upon an ethical system thought to have been derived from an established and assumed faith that transcends politics, upon Christian objectives and principles, such as the "brotherhood of all men under God," the "love of neighbor as oneself." These are held to be not simply the requirements of reason, but the teachings of Christ.

These differences between Catholicism and Protestantism are expressed in the more precise, formal and detailed development by Catholics of rules of conduct leading to "right policy." They are expressed also in the greater preoccupation of Catholic leaders with setting strict spiritual boundaries for church concerns in public life.

These are matters of emphasis. Most religious leaders begin with actions which they believe are simply the defense and expression of religious principle; but, in the effort to do this, they become involved in decisions about how to accommodate the real interests at stake in a situation and about the tactics to be pursued in achieving their objectives. They discover that their interpretations of moral law have partisan implications for politicians. They discover tensions between clergymen who stress, in their interpretations of politics, the importance of deducing correct action from moral principles and those who stress responsibility for knowing the facts of the situation and the meaning of the whole of Christian belief as well as of moral principle in the concrete. Within Protestantism particularly there are great tensions between men who act as if they are making judgment about politicians from a politically transcending religious ethic, and those who proceed in their political activity from a faith that on its own admission is at once politically conditioned and politically transcending. Most of the action of the religious leaders can be understood as efforts to reconcile the demands of their ethic of natural law and ultimate ends with the concrete requirements of the situation.

The Moral Concerns of the Roman Catholic Church

Since the Roman Catholic leaders start their interpretations of politics from the most systematically and precisely developed metaphysical and ethical position of all the religious groups, they give the greatest attention to efforts to define the "religious and nonreligious issues," and the "moral and technical aspects" of problems faced by the politicians. Even though the Roman Catholic leaders differ at times in their demarcation of the boundaries, they are diligent in their attempts to maintain and observe distinctions between the spiritual and political spheres. Most parish priests have a fairly simple confidence that they can designate the boundaries between the moral, the spiritual and the political. This confidence rests on the equation of the spiritual order, for all practical purposes, with the Catholic church, its concerns, and its claim to have captured the truth of reason and revelation in a system of universal doctrines, principles and laws. The parish pastor also tends to use the terms "political," "temporal" and "secular" interchangeably, in distinction to the "sacred" and the "ecclesiastical"; the church is spoken of almost as if it is neither in time, nor time in the church.

The Catholic priest views man as by nature having a certain character and structure rooted in the cosmos. Man has a mind which will grasp basic principles of right and wrong, and will discern the broad purposes written for him into the universe. Man can act contrary to nature; he can violate its laws—but he will pay dire consequences. Man has achieved knowledge of some ultimate ends and laws which are eternally and universally valid. Some of these are known by reason, some have been revealed in faith. Through these, men can be guided to right conduct in the practical or concrete situation. The application or deduction from the law varies with the situation. The natural-law ethic of the priests is not an entirely static one, but it assumes that the church has in its keeping some perennial and immutable truths.

Man is to adjust his politics to these truths—not the truths to politics. Men may vary somewhat in their ability to do the good they know, but the role of the religious leader is clear: it is to exhort men to fulfill the requirements of divine and moral law. Men are to be urged to do the right thing and to leave the results to the Lord. Resistance to compromise of high moral principle is the primary concern of the priests' ethic. The task of the clergy is to propound this system of truth and to help men apply it. The system of truth is in the keeping of the church.

Catholic leaders, although they may differ over the boundaries of the church's authority, are in close agreement that the church has a "prior," "independent" and "superior right" in politics over all secular powers.[2] The Catholic church has been founded for supernatural ends, the noblest of all; so "its authority is the most exalted of all authority." God has appointed the ordering of the human race between two major powers, the ecclesiastical and the civil; "one is set over the divine, the other over human affairs." Each has its limits which are defined by the special province and ends of each. One has for its chief object the everlasting joys of heaven, the other the well-being of this mortal life. God has "marked out the courses of each [power] in right correlation to the other," so that instead of conflicting they work in correct relation for the common weal. Each power respects the autonomy of the other.[3] Where disputes arise as to the boundaries for the "autonomous" areas of faith and politics, the church claims ultimate jurisdictional authority.

The system of principle and law the priest applies has a validity and existence independent of any political powers or events in history. In reply to Protestant charges that the Catholic church introduces an authoritarian, "foreign" influence in American politics by the Pope's assertion of superior judgment in all moral issues, the editor of the diocesan journal has observed that "the Pope does not control what Catholics think politically, only morally, so why should Protestants be fearful of the Pope's political influence?"[4]

The church has sought to establish a clear doctrinal basis for wide application of the ethical system to public affairs.[5] Moral and spiritual issues could conceivably arise within any of the major areas of governmental and political activity in the city. Copies of papal encyclicals such as *Rerum Novarum, Quadragesimo Anno* and *Ubi Arcana Dei,* which propound a wide definition of moral and religious concerns, are distributed throughout the church—in book racks in the vestibules of the churches, in the Catholic lending library, in Catholic high school libraries.[6]

Catholic leaders proclaim the church as the "authoritative spokesman" which can "bring order out of chaos" in economics and politics.[7] "Today it is generally conceded," the *Catholic Mirror* notes, that the church "alone has a constructive economic program."[8] Or again, "Every wholesome pronouncement on faith, on morals, on Christian education, on the family, on social reconstruction during the last decade has come from her."[9] In light of this, the editor of the *Catholic Mirror* has, while asserting that the Pope controls morals, not politics, also stressed "the impossibility of a complete separation between religion and public life for anyone who is trying to live a Christian life." [10] But the "application" is always of immutable principle to changing fact.

The materials relating Catholic doctrine to social and political issues which are the product of "top level" activity (the work of diocesan experts, Catholic journalists, priests in charge of work with the labor movement[11]) deal with a much wider range of issues than the statements or program emphases of the parish priests.[12] The Catholic pastors agreed unanimously that the following public issues are the kind that directly involve citizens of the community and contain matters of faith and morals demanding action by the church:[13] attacks upon parochial schools; religious and irreligious content of instruction in the public schools; controversy over public financial aid for parochial schools; the activity of the birth-control movement; growing communist influence in the community (particularly in certain unions) and in the world; excessive consumption of alcoholic beverages; legitimacy of gambling.[14] In these areas the pastors have often acted quickly and efficiently. They have no doubts as to the moral principles involved. And they have developed enough disciplined lay support of the church's position to make an impact in the community.

At least 80 per cent of the Catholic pastors regarded the following areas in the public life of the city as presenting no moral issues of concern to the church: housing for low-income people; tax policies and welfare expenditures of the local government; collective bargaining of labor and management in the city; extension of union activity; expansion of political participation in the community; reform or change of the political and governmental structure of the city; economic instability of an inflationary or deflationary nature in the community.[15]

Typical statements made by pastors and curates in seeking to differentiate temporal political, economic and social issues from moral or spiritual issues reveal the wide range of public problems considered to be outside the church's concern:

> The Holy Father means for the priest to enter the political field for the improvement of moral well-being and for saving souls. He can act to prevent attack on the parochial schools, or oppose birth con-

trol because they are in themselves moral issues. We certainly decry poor housing, but housing is a material concern, and the priests' first aim is to remedy things of a moral nature.

The church is not concerned with political matters as such—only with political matters that have moral and religious issues involved. Better housing and higher wages are political issues, not moral. Birth control, refusal of public transportation of parochial students, antireligion or atheism of candidates are moral and religious matters and the church must fight them with all the power at its disposal. On moral issues, we ask our people to go all out, to do all they can for the cause of religion.

When I first came to Paper City from a largely middle-class Irish parish, I felt I wanted to see people tear down the slums and build new houses. But Father Duval [the pastor of a French church where this priest served] told me that Paper City would never have money to do that. It would cost too much. He helped me see that the church cannot press for such things as better housing. The church's task is to prepare men for life in the hereafter through living a spiritual, clean life now. The Protestant churches emphasize social and political reform and they are too utilitarian. They are going the way the rest of the world is going—materialistic, interested in filling their bellies and having a bigger time. The church wants a man to look after his soul now. . . . Will better housing help a man's soul? I don't think so.

A majority of the pastors acknowledge that such issues as improvement of local housing and the loss of real income because of inflationary or deflationary tendencies in the national economy or because of seasonal layoffs in Paper City firms could conceivably involve moral or spiritual principles, such as that of distributive justice. (By "distributive justice" they mean that form of justice which directs the community through governmental action to share burdens and benefits among individuals and groups in accordance with the proportionate equality implicit in the common good.) But they explain that the Catholic clergy have *not* taken a position on such issues in recent years because in Paper City no injustice has existed. The pastors say: "The people receive good wages." "They have their housing well taken care of." "The government of the city is efficiently operated and the political instruments are adequate for the people." "Catholic workers are well treated and prosperous."

These views of the pastors influence greatly the parish educational activities and local Catholic Action. Reports of the political leaders of the city as to the concerns expressed to them by the Catholic pastors confirm the generalization that action by the priests is confined almost entirely to a few issues which directly affect the traditional worship and educational life of their parishes.[16] In no instance could the principal politicians of the city recall that they had talked with pastors concerning Catholic moral principles involved in what the politicians generally considered to be the major issues for the electorate in Paper City politics—tax rates, the level of governmental expenditures, and the maintenance or change of local political party structure.

The contacts of priests with politicians are chiefly in connection with immediate favors such as "the silencing of work in a garage on Sunday to stop disturbance of a religious service," the "refusal of a liquor license to a bar making trouble in a parish," "contact for service from a department of the state or federal government such as the hot-lunch program," "the tearing up of a parking ticket," the "running of a lottery game." A leader in the city Democratic party committee observed: "The only time I converse with a priest about politics is when I do him some favor to help the parish." The politicians of the city generally expect the priest (and the Protestant pastor) to be a "promoter" of his institution or his "religious causes" identified with it.

In the past decade the Catholic pastors have indicated to their members their position in two public referenda in elections. One dealt with birth control and another with the outlawing of beano or bingo. The priests did not indicate any moral issues involved in the Barnes referendum (affecting the rights of labor to organize a closed shop, and to keep secret certain data about union finances) or in a referendum on World Government.

The political problems of Paper City must somehow become deeply involved in the traditional church activities—the parochial school system, the financial support of the church—before the pastors become actively concerned, to engage in the working out of the detailed implications of the moral law, to study the actual choices of action open to the politicians. The role Catholic priests took in Paper City's public housing and public health programs over the past decade indicates how traditional church concerns become intimately involved with the expanding political activities of the local government, and how moral concerns sometimes are redefined.

The only initiative taken by the Catholic clergy in the controversies surrounding the establishment of two public housing projects for low-income people was the holding of a meeting in an Immaculate Conception parish hall after funds for the project had been assured. The chief purpose of the meeting was to arouse public interest in having the first project located in Ward 1, where Immaculate Conception and Holy Rosary parishes are located. The Catholic clergy remained silent on the moral issues in the controversy and did not indicate their position to the leaders of the movement for public housing or to the opponents of the projects.[17]

The deterioration of public health service of the city government in the 1940's and particularly during World War II did not arouse the church to use its influence for reform until 1947, when the public health department was faced with responsibility for supervising the health of parochial school children.[18] Before this time the health needs of the parochial students were met by the public school system and its medical staff. In 1947 the public school superintendent, a Catholic, and several members of the school board became alarmed at the controversy aroused over the transportation of parochial students in public school buses. They were concerned whether a state law enacted in 1917, providing that no public school department should provide for the health supervision of parochial students, was being adequately observed. This service was held by the law to be a public welfare function belonging to the public health departments. The public school officials therefore asked that the public health department in the city take over the responsibility of caring for parochial students.

When the public health department was given this function, the Catholic leaders were faced with the problem of what to do about a department which they believed lacked the knowledge and the will to organize a program for the parochial schools. The director of the public health department was in their view a man without adequate professional training and too elderly to guide his department vigorously in meeting the new health needs of the community. Health surveys indicated that the department faced one of the highest death rates in the country for tuberculosis,[19] and that unprofessional public health work and poor conditions for public education had contributed to the low health indices. The chairman of the public health commission was a chiropodist, highly concerned with improving the department, but without great influence in the medical profession or the community. Leading Protestant and Roman Catholic physicians had been asked to serve as chairman; but they had refused the position—"eschewing," as a leading Protestant physician noted, "the smoke-filled room, the political atmosphere in which you have to operate in such a position."

Once the Catholic leaders saw a clear-cut institutional interest—the welfare of the parochial schools—at stake in reform, they acted with considerable awareness of the political realities. They persuaded both Democratic and Republican party leaders to visit the public health department offices and inform the director and staff that they could be assured that funds would be available for "a good cause." When a year passed with only study of the situation, the Catholic clergy took the initiative to have set up a committee to supervise the parochial school medical program, and to gain control of it so that action would be taken in the interests of the parochial school system. The church sought to obtain a three man committee to consist of a representative from the public health department, the superintendent of public schools (a Catholic), and a local priest (the pastor of Sacred Heart parish). The public health department fought for a five man committee with three representatives from the department, the superintendent of schools and the priest. The issue was not resolved when this study ended, but the church had clearly seen its stake in the department's reform and was involved in all the hazards and issues of practical political action.

These events illustrate the fact that when the Roman Catholic clergy say they do not discern spiritual or moral issues at a particular time in an area of political life, this does not mean that the church will necessarily continue to regard the area as outside Catholic concern. The way in which an issue is posed by a group in the community, the pressure of another religious group, the infringement of a social issue in a new way upon the life of a parish—any or all of these factors may arouse the clergy to action in behalf of moral principles not previously applied to a certain area. But if past institutional practice is an indication of future action, the expansion of active Catholic concern will take place chiefly within the areas which become directly and intimately associated with the educational, sacramental, financial and membership recruitment activities of the church.

The Moral Concerns of the Protestant Churches

The conduct of the Protestant leaders in politics may, like that of the Catholic clergy, be interpreted very largely within an ethic of natural law or ultimate ends. The ministers are attempting to expound a system of ends and principles which they believe expresses the "content of the Christian faith," and in some way transcends politics.

The sect leaders and the ministers of churches comparatively conservative in their theology (Lutheran and Reformed) profess a certainty and a precision as great as that of any Catholic leaders in defining spiritual and political boundaries. These distinctions, particularly for the sects, are roughly correlated with the categories of "individual" and "social." The province of religion is the "personal life." As the Polish Evangelistic Assembly pastor observed, "Christ came to save souls, not politics." The person's faith may strengthen him to withstand the trials and tribulations of life in society, but his faith is involved in no other significant way in politics.

The scope of religious concern in public life is narrower for the Protestant sect leaders and for the "fundamentalist" pastors than for any other religious leaders. Political judgments center, not upon the consequences of public policies and upon those who support or oppose those policies, but upon the estimation of the relative personal piety of the candidates.[20] The "good" and the "evil" men are known by their personal virtues and vices—virtues such as church participation, regard for family, honesty; vices such as irreligion, sensuality, alcoholic intemperance, dishonesty, profligate expenditure of public funds for personal gain. These corruptions require personal salvation for correction, not "political solutions." The Gospel Hall leader observed: "Our task is to have people become conscious of their sins, and to seek the forgiveness of God and His assurance of life in the future. When a man is saved, he will lead a clean, holy life. Leading such a life has nothing to do with a man's politics."

This concern for personal purity, this attempt to make political judgments in terms of the good will and intent of the politician rather than in terms of the consequences of action, is a strong motif throughout Protestant political ethics.[21] Protestant leaders have a strong belief that personal conviction and purity of motive can overcome limits imposed by group interests and institutional structures. The Christian ideal can be achieved by the spontaneous and free acts of love, kindness and honesty. Political issues are chosen for action which can be interpreted within the maxims.[22] Among pastors of a liberal theological persuasion an emphasis upon the "sanctity of the individual" underlies an uneasiness about collective action and mass movements, and a tendency to avoid involvement in political issues that are interpreted by politicians in such terms. The Protestant pastors of a liberal theological point of view are predominant in the Ministerial Association. They see themselves principally as cheerleaders in the great game of politics, encouraging men to fight on for such general and universal goals as brotherhood and justice. Such a role, it is assumed, does not require much knowledge of the limitations or possibilities in concrete situations nor does it run the risk of placing too great confidence in a particular political solution or movement in history. The Ministerial Association resolved, after a day's study of the "Minister's Responsibility in the Present Crisis":

> As a messenger of the Kingdom of God, he dare not be a spectator; he must lead. And no class is better equipped as a thinker and spokesman for the Kingdom of God which he is commissioned to usher in, and which creates a condition in which peace, justice, and righteousness prevail supreme.

The nature of the conditions of "peace, justice and righteousness" are more vaguely stated than in the ethics of Catholicism, the Catholic system carrying its rational discernment of natural laws into more detailed areas of political action. Yet pastors of the Methodist and Second Baptist churches believe that the validity of Christ's teaching is demonstrated in the "practical experience" of their laymen and of mankind. The problems the pastors describe in the world and in individuals range widely from international war to personal anxieties. There is not much description of the church as a community of believers who wrestle with the various involvements by laymen in these problems. There is rather the comforting assurance from the pastor that none of these problems is so formidable that a greater effort to pursue God's purposes cannot alleviate or resolve them.

The Christian gospel in some way stands complete and apart from all inferior secular alternatives; if one is persuaded of its reasonableness and its truth, "the way out" will be clear. In the midst of the difficult days of economic depression and rapid change in our structures of political power in America during Franklin Roosevelt's first term, the ministers met to discuss "modern 'isms' as a remedy for the present crisis." They asked, "Is Communism, Fascism, Socialism, or Capitalism the way out? If not, why not? Or is Christianity the way out, or is Christianity plus some ism the way out?" The "conclusion" the pastors reached was that "to Christianity and to it alone we must look to lead us out of the dilemma." [23] The acceptance of Christianity instead of other "isms," as a vision in itself of a fuller life, removed the necessity of an extended study of competing faiths in the economic and political world of the twentieth century.

Almost every current major issue in Paper City politics has been discussed in adult forums of the churches of these liberal pastors.[24] This wide concern has the value of opening up new areas to the laymen where issues of great religious and moral significance are involved. On the other hand, most Protestant attempts to influence the actions of politicians lack the depth and cohesion of the Catholic defense of a few basic institutional interests.

The Protestant leaders tend more than the Catholics to conduct spontaneous, spasmodic "one-shot" crusades on a variety of unrelated issues. The educational programs of the adult women's organizations of the Protestant churches are characteristic of the tremendous variety, and at times almost random selection, of activities, and an unwillingness to choose a few crucial social and political areas for concerted study and influence. This annual report of the Women's League of the Second Baptist church is typical of Protestant adult groups:

The different departments have been active through the year and good work is being done. The Surgical Dressing Group has held regular meetings. A box of clothing was sent to Mather Negro School, four boxes of clothing for World Relief, and our White Cross quota was filled. We cooperated in the Northern Baptist Campaign against alcohol advertising, sent over 200 cards against Pari-Mutuel betting, signed petitions and gave out literature in behalf of World Government, and signed a petition against the use of public funds for buses to private schools.[25]

Many of the issues chosen for greatest political activity by the ministers have a distinctly Protestant flavor; they reflect the long history of Protestant anti-saloon crusades, the support of planned parenthood, worry over personal status and authority in the profession, and deep involvement in family events.

Throughout the life of the Ministerial Association, the liquor issue has received the greatest attention.[26] During a four-month period in 1947, three-fourths of the time spent by the association in discussion of political-economic areas involved (a) planned parenthood and (b) police favoritism in the city toward Roman Catholic pastors in over-time parking. A typical exchange of views between two pastors on this issue was as follows:

Pastor of one of the smaller Protestant churches: I almost got a tag for parking at a place where Father McMichael parks every Monday as long as he likes while he takes in his swag from the lotteries. And I was on a call. I told the mayor if the police ever tried to tag me when I'm on a call, I'll raise holy hell about the police favoritism in this town.

Pastor of large Protestant church: Is it true that the police play favorites? I don't know. Anyway I don't think we should ask for special favors.

Pastor of one of the smaller Protestant churches (aside to researcher): Just because he has a big town church and is one of the people who the police know not to give a ticket to, he wants no stink raised when I get tagged.

The preaching and educational activities of the Protestant churches concerning the social implications of Christianity are much more the projection of the pastor's personal interests than is true in the Catholic parishes. This is partly because of the differing types of authority represented by the minister and priest, as previously noted in Chapters 7 and 8. The tendency of Protestant ministers to interpret the relation of Christianity and politics in private or personal terms is most starkly illustrated by a pastor who regularly summarizes the life of his church in an annual report. This report is perhaps the most extreme Protestant symbol of widespread tendencies of the clergy to portray public life in terms of a series of unrelated, unpatterned events, overshadowed by private and family concerns. The annual report during the period from 1930 to 1939 devoted only three lines to the economic depression and the experience of unemployment for laymen: "The year long inactivity of the United Wool Company and the second year of inactivity of the Paper City Hosiery Company made the industrial background rather grim." [27] The pastor's college reunion got more space.

The records of the Ministerial Association also indicate the great absorption of the Protestant clergy with their personal relations with one another. The items of business receiving the most extended and frequent attention in the minutes of the association have been resolutions of appreciation of the services of fellow ministers, and records of condolences and flowers sent to sick ministers and their wives. Fewer motions are recorded and less space given to social problems of the depression of the 1930's, World War II, and the religious relations of the city than to the personal relations between the Protestant clergy and their families.

Another group of Protestant ministers, led by the First and Second Congregational church pastors, are often in considerable disagreement with other churchmen whom they believe ignore many areas of politics that are deeply significant morally and religiously. These ministers stress that religious leaders should concentrate upon understanding Christians in action, in the process of making political decisions, and not upon the tenets of Christian belief as such. They say they "are trying to minister to the whole man" and that when men act in politics they are not confronting "boundaries between religion and politics but other men with specific programs and demands."

Here are two statements from sermon manuscripts of Congregational ministers:

> There cannot be two Gods in the life of men—one who created the world and entered it to redeem it, and another who rules public affairs.

> A man's life cannot be neatly divided into those elements which are private and unaffected by interaction with other people and those which are social. All life is lived in community in the sense that every decision is made in relation to the decisions of others. . . . A man's new understanding of God through Christ affects the whole of his being; acceptance of Christ means accepting a new orientation, a new direction to life, a turning of the whole self, not just the part of man labelled the "soul."

These pastors speak of moral experience which other religious leaders have also known in political action but have not been able to express within the thought of their natural law ethic. To indicate the distinctive emphases of these men, their approach might be termed a "situational ethic" or an "ethic of cultural responsibility."

These pastors are impressed by the way in which issues that appear on the surface to be merely technical or political become, when the deeper implications are known, entangled in profound moral and religious problems. They refuse to view Christianity as a code of behavior, a set of principles, an area of life. They see Christianity as the faith of men in a living God and the church as a community of persons who have faith in Christ. The attempts they discern in the church to define neat boundaries of the supernatural and the natural lead, they believe, to man's assumption that these divisions are finally real for God. The inevitable distinctions become efforts to segregate God, to assign Him to certain places, people, situations, and to claim that God is guided by our distinctions.

In a "situational ethic" the stress is upon the social and relational character of principles of conduct. According to the religious leaders with this point of view, men cannot talk in a meaningful way about ultimate ends and natural law prior to actual involvement in a concrete moral decision. We come to know what men mean by the principles they profess through their specific acts. In the moral act, men confront, not laws, objectives, values as such, but other persons confronting them with conflicting needs, and bringing to bear their faith and experience in problems they face. Men cannot carry into a political situation an ideal model or an infallible law to indicate the will of God for a particular situation. Love, for example, is not an ultimate ideal or law, but a relationship of God and man, man and man. Men do not compromise love, as if they know its demands in full before entering a situation requiring a decision. A person who believes that he has such knowledge of an ultimate end or moral law becomes obstinate, rigid and defensive in his acts.

The Christian, according to this point of view, does not depreciate the part that norms and principles play in our lives, but rather insists that speculation about their meaning cannot be abstracted from the real world, from the interactions of persons and institutions. God is working when people face each other's needs in faith, when different perspectives are freely and openly discussed, when men expect good to emerge out of the experience but have no illusions that an infallible solution to their problems will result. The role of the religious leader in politics, then, is to ask men to be concerned not so much for their personal righteousness as for what they can accomplish in the world. It is to help men understand the actualities of sin and of anxiety in politics, to face the fact that there are problems in politics which are not solved once and for all—but that we can, with God's grace, live with them courageously and patiently. It is to ask men to seek in the community of the church the understanding of the nature of their political acts with all the resources at their command.

The pastors of the First and Second Congregational churches have engaged in some serious debates with their colleagues in the Ministerial Association over the question of whether the Association was refusing to discuss ministerial responsibilities in a number of areas, such as party politics, considered to be unusually "dirty" or "compromising." They sought to get the Association to choose certain issues of particular interest to the Protestant laymen in Paper City politics and to "stay with the issue long enough actually to face the practical questions of how to get some political changes for the better."

The decisions these two pastors have made as to what they personally will concentrate upon for systematic study and for sustained work with lay members of the church have been influenced by many factors—their deep involvement in professional responsibilities to advance the traditional activities of the church, their concern over the impact of Catholicism in the city and their desire to find issues that would be supported to some extent by fellow ministers with less broad social interests than their own. For example, the First Congregational pastor has for the past fifteen years concentrated his political action upon advancement of the birth-control movement in the city. The fires of the Sanger incident forged in him, and many other ministers, a powerful identification with this cause. This concern is shared by the upper and middle class women in his church, but little by the business and professional men. The pastor has therefore made some attempt to organize discussions among laymen about taxation policies of the local government—a leading issue among his churchmen. The pastor had mastered the range of technical and ethical problems involved in the birth-control issue, but he was unable to do the same in the area of taxation. He felt the discussions in his church were unsuccessful, the laymen all agreeing with the position of the Taxpayers Association that "the tax rates are exorbitant in Paper City in comparison with other communities of comparable size and should be lowered." The pastor said he could only agree with the laymen and could offer no position that raised any serious questions that would lead to a rethinking of lay responsibilities in politics. He learned, he said, after the meetings in his church that the city's tax rates are among the lowest in the state.

The Protestant pastors differ in their approach to political issues. But when one considers the actual issues the pastors communicate with government officials about, it becomes clear that all the Protestant pastors are drawn into action almost entirely on the same issues that agitate the Catholic clergy. These are the issues that most directly involve the traditional institutional interests of the churches —birth control, gambling, public aid to parochial schools. On many of these issues the Protestant ministers, absorbed in preparing sermons, finding leadership for educational programs, keeping up the physical facilities of the church, are not as likely as the Catholic pastors to be brought directly into contact with government officials and with the tough requirements of political reform.

There are two important consequences of the narrow range of public issues that actively involve the church leaders in politics. One is that the deepest concerns of the churches in politics are so predictable that the politicians can easily manipulate the church leaders and avoid arousing lay protests. The politicians tend to look upon either Roman Catholic and Protestant moral interests chiefly as those of one more organized group to be anticipated, managed and met. The church interests are almost as clearly definable and predictable as the interests of the Taxpayers Association or the Central Labor Council of the A.F. of L. Second, Catholic and Protestant divisions are intensified because the church leaders always come into the political arena over an issue on which the other religious group already has taken a different, well-formulated and intransigent position. The church leaders do not seem able to search out new areas of action where there is a chance of common agreement and support.[28]

Summary

In the efforts of church leaders to define boundaries of "the religious" and "the political" there has still been a concern to make clear the relevance of Christianity for all of life and to accept responsibilities in public life. Both Catholics and Protestants want to make sure both that Christianity does not become vulgarized by too much and too casual a contact with the world, and that the church does not become inflexible and irrelevant by being too remote from politics. The safeguarding of these concerns is no easy task, and the religious movements are the scene of continuous debate over the balance to be maintained.

The proponents of natural law and of situational ethics have different emphases—but these are more supplemental than exclusive. The advocate of natural law fears that the drive of men to be free to respond to the demands of each new political situation will make impossible any ultimate meaning for practical problems, whereas the situationally oriented leader fears the submerging of the individual in some body of forced dogma. The approaches are attempts to appreciate both the church and politics.

As noted in the next chapter, the church leaders find their tensions heightened and clarified when they attempt to engage in political reform. Sometimes in these moments of decisive action the leaders sense that the major elements in each of the ethical approaches are united. Their most creative action occurs when they are aware, on the one hand, that, if they pursue their ultimate good with a pure ethic of absolute ends, then in their zeal they tend to ignore the consequences of their action and make impossible any constructive change; and, on the other hand, if they allow their political view to become determined by immediate demands, they risk the danger that no new aspirations for the future will give meaning to acts of the present.

Chapter 19

The Churches and Political Reform

In the past decade, the Protestant and Catholic clergy of Paper City have each been stirred by a particular issue to unusual efforts at political reform. At the start, at least, of their activity, the clergy have felt themselves to be in a proper and comfortable role for church leaders. They have felt that they were exhorting the politicians to forsake "expediency" and to strive for higher ends. They were challenging men to bring their political conduct into line with moral principles or natural laws. As one Protestant minister said about a public statement he had signed, "We were in effect saying, 'Here we stand. We can do no other.' And we were asking the politician to have the courage to take a similar moral stand." In these attempts to change political behavior, the religious leaders have revealed something of the strengths and limitations of an ethic of ultimate ends or natural law which lies back of most of their political statements.

The Protestant leaders, interestingly enough, were stirred to their major concerted effort at political reform by the issue of widespread gambling in the city. The choice of issue symbolized their absorption with the affairs of the local congregation and of individuals in it and their preoccupation in a dominantly Catholic community with the power of the Roman church.

The Catholic clergy were stirred chiefly by the spread of communism in the world. They took up the fight of the hierarchy and the diocesan journal to get a "stiffer national policy toward communism." The priests of Paper City supported the effort in sermons, in speeches to parish societies and in informal conversations with laymen in politics. There were some reservations among the priests about some aspects of the position laid down in the *Catholic Mirror,* but they were not publicly expressed. The choice of issue reflected the Catholic pastor's great sense of involvement with his church in a world struggle, and the power of the hierarchy to give clear priorities of action to local leadership.

The Protestant Attack Against Gambling

The incident that precipitated a concerted public protest in 1947 by the Protestant ministers was a story told to the pastor of Grace Congregational Church by a woman in his congregation. Her husband, a textile worker, had lost all of his last pay to a local race-track gambling syndicate and owed gambling debts totalling $820. The family, the woman reported, was destitute. The pastor, who believes that he has a state-wide reputation for his "two-gun crusades against gambling and liquor interests," took the woman to the probation officer of the city to describe her situation. The pastor also called the local manager of the gambling syndicate, told him the woman's story, and informed him that "he was in for trouble." In a half hour a representative of the gambler was at the home of the woman, had cancelled the debt and given her fifty dollars for food.

The probation officer, long a political rival of the mayor, went to the local newspaper with the incident, and used it as the occasion for a "sweeping denunciation of the freely operating horse race bookie racket in Paper City." [1] He accused the mayor and police department of "laxity in smoking out crime and bookies" and added as a final charge that he knew of "some 300 people in this city who are living in cohabitation and nothing is being done about it." The police department and the mayor at once issued "clean-up" orders to the police; the gambling centers and bookies ceased open operations, some moving their operations while "the heat was on" to nearby cities where no public campaign against gambling was being conducted. The police made no arrests and no reports of violations of gambling laws. The state district attorney met with the mayor and chief of police in a private session. The mayor and chief of police for three days made no press comments on their plans or on the accuracy of the probation officer's charges. They then admitted the existence of the bookies in the city and said they were doing everything in their power to "operate on them and keep them out of here." A full investigation by the local police department was promised.

The following day six Protestant clergymen issued a statement urging a public hearing on charges made by the probation officer that "gambling and other forms of vice are allowed to operate in the city without restraint." The statement was interpreted by the local newspaper as support of the probation officer, an Irish Catholic, against the mayor. The reaction of the pastors to this political use of the statement varied. An Episcopal, a Baptist and a Congregational minister who signed the statement were highly surprised and angered by the efforts of contending groups in the controversy to direct it at each other, when the statement, they said, was meant to be nonpartisan—"simply a statement of moral principle—the evil of gambling." The Episcopal minister, who was also president of the Ministerial Association, made a statement from his pulpit before his sermon: "The clergymen's pronouncement indicated our great displeasure with gambling. It was not directed against any person or for any person. We are not backing anyone. We are opposed to gambling, whether it bears the blessing of the city hall, the police department, and ecclesiastical authority or any other authorities. We are just against gambling."

The newspaper editor, a member of the pastor's congregation, published the statement but in the published version no reference was made to ecclesiastical authority. Two of the ministers, on the other hand, stated privately that they had anticipated that the statement would be used in a political battle, and were of the conviction that issuance of statements of moral principle could never be kept neutral. The ministers, they said, were obligated to act upon the implications of their principles as they understood them in terms of support of particular reforms or groups sponsoring the reforms, just as they expected other people to use the statement as a clarification of a position to be taken in a political controversy.

The mayor meanwhile, as he recalled, was "on the spot on an issue that could get the Catholic church down on my neck, as well as the Protestant clergy." The mayor was convinced that the "Protestant clergy had pulled a mean trick in the way they handled the issue. They had gotten excited about the statements of an irate, unstable probation officer that had been shooting off his mouth that way for years." Instead of coming to the mayor and talking the situation over, "they rushed into print with a statement for a public hearing just when we were getting things calmed down. I'll tell you what it looked to me like—a case of getting at the Catholic church pure and simple."

The mayor astutely recognized the political value of appearing to the Catholic clergy as a defender of the church's interest in gambling against a religious attack, and avoiding the strong pressures from secular gambling interests against a sustained effort to close them down.[2] He talked in the midst of the crisis with the pastor of the Holy Rosary parish, which operates a lottery. The pastor assured him, according to the mayor, that the Catholic clergy felt "the mayor had things in pretty good shape on gambling and vice in the city. Of course, there were some abuses as in all cities." The Catholic clergy have never protested to the mayor in any way about the extent of gambling in the city, but at one time or another all but one of the ministers of the Protestant churches have done so.

The mayor had co-operated closely with the Catholic church in its gambling program particularly since 1945 when a referendum in the state eliminated beano or bingo from the legal forms of fund-raising activity specifically permitted when the proceeds were for educational, charitable, fraternal and religious purposes.[3] The mayor states that he gave assurances to both the Immaculate Conception and Holy Rosary pastors that the state laws against beano, bingo and lotteries for raising funds for religious authorities would not be enforced by the local police. The mayor made available rooms in the city hall for the Immaculate Conception church to conduct its beano games, when the attendance overflowed the store room rented on the main street by the church for the games. The mayor said of his decision to offer the facilities of the city hall to the Catholic church:

> The priest of Immaculate Conception—an exquisitely beautiful church by the way—is a dear, hard-working fellow. He came to me one day and said, "Joe we have a debt of $450,000 on our church, and our people are poor. They can't even now meet the interest on it. We have to get funds by a beano program." He wanted to know if it was all right to run a game. Well, I knew there was a state law

on the books against it, but "who," I said "is going to enforce it? I'll help you all I can with police and fire department aid." So he said that he could rent a storeroom on High Street. They soon had so many playing we had to open up rooms in the city hall to accommodate them. The first summer, the church cleared $11,000.

Paper City Catholic clergy say that they asked the opinion of the state district attorney and the governor in 1945 if they had approval to conduct beano and lotteries, and that they understood they had permission, if they did not advertise the games on a state or regional level or publicly state they had official approval. The local Catholic clergy have often expressed support for the mayor. The pastor of Holy Rosary parish said that "the mayor has been like a father to me since I've been here." Both the Immaculate Conception and Holy Rosary pastors publicly supported the mayor's candidacy from the pulpit in two campaigns before 1947 and planned to in the future.[4]

It was within this pattern of political alignments that the mayor asked two of the Protestant ministers who had signed the statement requesting a public hearing on local gambling and vice to meet with him. When they arrived at his office, he explained to them that they could continue their demand for a public hearing, but that if they did, he was going to be present. "I bet that I will break the hearing up with some of the things I can tell about the Protestant clergy's support of vice and gambling. You know I know them too," the mayor recalled saying. The mayor said, for example, that he could document the fact that a local Protestant minister had been arrested in a nearby city for molesting a woman on the street.

The two ministers said they would think over what the mayor had said and departed. On the way home from the interview one of the pastors expressed a strong disgust with becoming involved in politics, where one might expect such dirty tactics to be used. He was "more strongly convinced than ever of the need to keep church and state separate." Neither minister knew if the mayor's specific charge was correct, but they decided that they did not wish to test the mayor further. They also believed that another specific act alluded to by the mayor was the sale of lottery tickets for a veteran's organization by one of the Protestant pastors the same week that he signed the public statement against gambling.

Meanwhile, the ministers were receiving numerous complaints from their church members about raising a troublesome issue which would accomplish nothing, and which, as most businessmen saw the problem of gambling, "could not be solved by laws any more than could intemperate drinking."

The ministers did not press further for a public hearing. They did not report a decision back to the mayor about the hearing. The mayor told newspaper reporters the next day that "if the ministers think a hearing should be held, that is up to them." The mayor felt that his and the ministers' attention ought to be centered chiefly on "the 300 cases of cohabitation in the community, which if they existed were the worst disgrace." State police officials surveyed the city's liquor establishments and found no violations. Within a month, the police pressure on local bookies was eased.

The only arrest made by the police for gambling violation during the controversy was of a Protestant woman in a local Smith College alumnae association who was selling lottery tickets for the association. (The prize was a trip to Bermuda.) She was fined $25. (Her young daughter at the same time was helping several Catholic girls sell lottery tickets on a doll raffle at Holy Cross parish.)

The ministers' public statement became an issue again for a brief time in an unsuccessful candidacy to defeat the mayor in the 1948 election. The alleged breakdown of public morals under the present mayor, as evidenced in the charges of the probation officer and the ministers, became the single cause on which the campaign was waged. "When the Ministerial Association went on record for a public hearing in an attempt to get Paper City on a HIGHER MORAL STANDARD, their plea was denied," the mayor's opponent charged in advertisements. The minister who was the most insistent of the Protestant clergy for a statement and hearing on the gambling situation sought to secure a statement from the clergy repudiating the advertisements. The ministers decided to remain silent during the campaign. One Protestant pastor did, however, telephone the campaign headquarters of the mayor's opponent and rebuke an assistant for seeking to involve the clergy in a political campaign. Another pastor observed that "the whole fiasco of political action has convinced me that I and other clergymen ought to concentrate in the future upon personal counselling."

The activity of the church leaders in this incident follows some characteristic patterns in the two religious movements. The Protestant ministers were drawn into the gambling issue and an attempt at political reform by the difficulties of a family in one of the churches. They sought to correct abuses in civic life contributing to the family's problems by a quick, spontaneous gesture, a righteous call to the mayor to clean up the gambling in the town. They made no calculations about the variety of economic, political and religious interests entangled in the gambling activity and likely to come into the fight if changes were seriously sought in the city. This was not necessary, most of the ministers reasoned, for all they were going to do was expound the goals of good government, to lay down the simple moral principle at issue—"the evil of gambling." The Protestant pastors were not going to be dogmatic about this; they merely wanted to encourage public discussion of the role of the local government in support of gambling activity. Hence the request for a public hearing so that conflicting views could be debated and evaluated.

But the politicians would not let the Protestant pastors stay in the role they assumed of expounders of the ultimate ends of politics. The moral principle chosen appeared to the mayor to have partisan implications, to encourage an old political enemy to embarrass and harass him. The mayor proceeded at once to test the seriousness and the unity of the pastors, and the amount of support they had back of them. It was soon apparent to the mayor that the ministers "did not mean business" and that they were interpreting the issue in such narrow moral terms that he could easily manipulate the issue. He was able to use the Protestant clergy's protest so that his reputation for "protecting" the Catholic church against "bigoted" attacks was enhanced. He could act with assurance that the Protestant laymen would feel they had no stake in the issue chosen by the ministers for wide public discussion.

The Catholic pastors' conduct during the incident was also a clear indication of what they understood their natural-law ethic and Catholic faith to require of them in politics. The main Catholic clerical figure entered the controversy when a politician saw the church's stake in the issue and called for assurance that he was interpreting the church's needs properly in the issue. The points of institutional involvement for the Catholic church in local politics had previously been so clearly and precisely indicated that this seemed like the natural thing for the politician to do. The politician knew that when he talked to the priest about his problem, the religious leader would duly consider many of the same things the mayor had considered—such as the groups whose support was essential in future elections and the importance of clerical leadership in Ward 1 and Ward 2 politics.

The Catholic church's natural-law ethic had produced not one ultimate objective—the end of all forms of gambling—as the Protestant position had. The church had elaborated a position discriminating between types of moral and immoral gambling and had indicated the institutional setting (church charity affairs) in which good gambling was to be carried on. The rules were to be enforced with rigor, but they recognized a variety of situations.

When the moral stand taken by the Protestant clergy called for a fight, the ministers, with a few exceptions, knew little about the methods of political influence available to them. They wished to operate only in their traditional role as preachers, with statements to the public. The Catholic clergy made no statements to the press, but cleared what they wanted done with the responsible political leaders. Their relations with the politicians were cordial and informal, the manner of men who had had long experience in such discussions.

The Catholic Church and the Communist Issue

The political problem that became overwhelmingly the most important to the Catholic church in the postwar years was the expansion of Soviet communist influence in the world. Indeed, Roman Catholic leaders claim that the greatest contribution which the church made to American politics in the postwar years was the insistence that all policies of the federal government must have as their primary objective the reduction of communist influence in the world.[5] The greatest alleged failure of the Protestant clergy and most politicians in general was in not making the "fight against communism the dominant and overwhelming preoccupation of the American people."[6] One Catholic pastor noted in 1947, "The lines between the contending forces of good and evil need to be seen as so irreconcilable that none of us will evade our responsibilities to defend the nations of the Western world against Stalinism." The general charge by the Catholic pastors that Protestantism suffers from a vagueness in its ethics was particularly directed at the role of the churches in "the Communist issue." [7]

Catholic clergymen maintain that many Protestant ministers and, some pastors add, "their liberal and pinkish cohorts" made two basic mistakes. "They sought in the crucial postwar years," the pastor of one parish observed, "to operate in international affairs from the same liberal assumption they applied to the relations of groups within Western democracies. This was done even after the tragedies that resulted from the West's slow resistance to fascism." And, the Catholic priests maintain, the Protestant pastors failed to recognize the true demonic nature of Soviet communism. The Catholic clergy widely believe that the Protestant pastors tried to advise their laymen on postwar international relations in terms of a too-simple love ethic, assuming that if we showed trust and regard for another nation—particularly Russia—that nation would respond in trust. This position did not recognize the fact that America had to deal "with the greatest evil in the world," that "concessions were taken as indication of weakness by a movement which operated from absolutely different assumptions than those of the Western nations." The editor of the *Catholic Mirror* expressed succinctly the general interpretation of communism by Catholic leaders: "Communism is anti-God, anti-social, anti-human; that is anti-Catholic." [8]

The Catholic leaders were convinced that there was a great public ignorance of the nature of communism, and that the religious nature of the struggle—the ultimate meaning of it—had to be made clear if the American people were to resist the spread of communism with all the military and economic resources at their command. The drive of the *Catholic Mirror* and the clergy was for public recognition of the policy priorities, and for the general will "to fight for the right."

The following summary of the history of World War II and its aftermath was made at the most widely attended gathering of Catholic laymen in the city in 1946. It gives something of the general mood of the argument which dominated the thought of the Catholic clergy at the time:

Everything since the agreements at Teheran, Yalta, and Potsdam have driven home the point that our partnership with Stalin was a blunder even greater than our war involvements. And only now, with "liberated" nations (like Poland) enslaved, millions starving, and the spirit of hate released—with Russia unwilling to make any genuine move toward peace, American officials have come back to a belief which they could have learned ten years ago by reading Lenin or following the ideology of the Stalinist movement.

It seems like a nightmare to turn back the pages of history. Germany sought Danzig and the Polish corridor. Great Britain, fearing trade competition, urged Poland to resist. With great gallantry, Poland did, but went down to defeat. Poland and the other small nations have been sold into slavery. Great Britain, which in 1939 feared a powerful Germany, today has a greater fear of powerful Russia.

As for the United States, we know our losses in blood and wealth. . . . And what now? A devastated world insists we supply food to keep from starving those we helped make homeless. Nations appeal to us for raw materials, wealth, manpower to guard or free threatened people. And if we are tardy in endeavoring to do the almost impossible, then we are scorned as selfish, isolationist, reactionary, pro-Hitler. It is a sorrowful sight, one which the Pope and many of us foresaw but to no avail.[9]

"Even if agreement were reached that the chief goal of public life is resistance to communism," noted a prominent Catholic lawyer, "there are still the problems of the extent to which resistance is to be carried on in military, economic, social or moral terms, and at what cost to whom. Allies have to be won, interests at home dealt with." The Catholic church's concern for the battle against communism tended in effect to reduce all historical analysis and description to consideration of a simple, single issue—containment of communism. The *Catholic Mirror* reported very little of the debate waged in American politics in 1947-1952 over the means to be used in resisting communism and over the nature of the communist appeal to peoples in other countries. Yet the State Department and other agencies of the national government were seeking to reconcile these positions in concrete policies of military containment, psychological warfare, rehabilitation of war-devastated countries, aid to underdeveloped nations and the like. The *Catholic Mirror* seemed to many people to be saying in effect that, if the politicians were clear as to the moral and religious principles at stake, they would know the nature of communism and the right policies to defeat it.

In some Catholic church discussions of world politics, complex military policy decisions, such as evaluation of the activities of General MacArthur in the Far East, were dealt with, first, by claiming knowledge of the intentions of Russia and, second, by accepting an opposite position as the valid one. Thus the *Catholic Mirror* supported a campaign to get "public sentiment [to react] vigorously against attempts to force MacArthur to resign or to curb some of his activities." [10] The argument advanced was that Russian Communism's "big objective now is to get MacArthur out of Japan so that the Communists can (1) take Korea, (2) organize Japan, and (3) eventually dominate the Orient."

When there is complete assurance among Catholic leaders that certain fairly precise moral principles or laws have been revealed by God to the church, and that these principles are effective in policy-making, then the only conclusion that often seems possible about intransigent political opponents is that their action is the result of personal perfidy, moral corruption or even subversion. One of the major contrasts between the judgments of most Roman Catholic and Protestant pastors is the much greater confidence of the former in evaluating personal integrity in terms of positions held upon specific policy issues.

Much of the argument of the local pastors and the diocesan press does not presume that different policy positions in fighting communism could be arrived at between conscientious men, all likely to make error in judgment in seeking to appraise complex, contingent and ambiguous situations, and in relating a number of interests and objectives. This view contends that the leaders who were in control of the United States government in the fateful postwar years, when the Russian "orgy of rapine and cruelty" was loose in Europe, betrayed, at best, their moral immaturity and ignorance of history, and at worst, their disloyalty to church and nation by their policies which failed to restrain communism.[11] In a few instances, frustration with the intractability of history comes to be expressed in terms of a politics inhabited by demonlike politicians and interpreted in demonologies—hideous, pervasive and inexplicable:[12]

> Thanks to Yalta, the Marshall mission, and Secretary Acheson's stab in the back, China appears to be hopelessly doomed. Except for a miracle communism will soon flank India from East and North. . . . This would be only the newest of a long series of follies, though America's portentous wickedness in China has moved some Catholics to ask in solemn dread whether Lucifer has not picked the United States State Department as his throne room and capital seat.[13]

In this kind of political thinking uniqueness of situations and variety of people in history are given little consideration beyond broad moral distinctions between the "good" and the "bad." Even distinctions within the "good" group, such as distinctions between "conservative Catholics" and "liberal Catholics"[14] are condemned as meaningless. Distinctions between communist party leaders, and men frustrated by social conditions such as colonialism who have formed mass movements and call themselves communists, are dropped in considerations of American approaches to foreign peoples. There is only "Catholicism versus communism."

In making political judgments, the general tendency of Catholic leaders is to utilize a much more detailed system of moral principle than the Protestant leaders. Many Catholic leaders claim that they can deduce correct policies from the principles elaborated and verified by the church. These positions are often sweeping indictments against whole administrations, cultures and generations. The question that some politicians ask as we shall note in more detail later, is whether the kind of literature represented by the *Catholic Mirror* has the precision and flexibility essential even to aid voters choose between the major policy alternatives offered in party platforms and presidential campaigns—to say nothing of illumining the considerations of officials in government bureaus with responsibility for detailed implementation of foreign policy.

The Protestant Clergy and Communism

The Catholic pastors are correct in pointing out that the Protestant ministers in 1946 and 1947 were not attempting to direct their parishioners toward a single-minded concern with checking the communist movement. For one thing, they were generally not able to bring themselves to the kind of bifurcation of the world into good and evil (the church and the Christian West against communism) posed by an influential segment of the Catholic clergy. The discussions of foreign affairs in the Protestant churches were often directed toward achievement of one major objective, but it was more likely to be "world order" or "relief and rehabilitation" than the checking of communism.[15]

Most Protestant clergy had, at least before World War II, been pacifists who had responded to "national jealousy, hatred and war" before Pearl Harbor with statements about the "urgency of Christian Unity" to be brought about by "Group Fellowship through which a clearer and better understanding may be fostered."[16] In 1946 and 1947 they were preaching, as one pastor stated it, that:

> The most stupid thing that can come out of this war is for us to begin another struggle for a balance of power. I am not a prophet nor one's son, but I would venture that if the "peace" eventuates in an effort at balance of power, we shall be into another war in less than twenty-five years, only this time it will be a racial war with certain races getting eliminated and it won't be the colored races either.

Pastors with so little concern for the problems of power and organization in the achievement of political objectives found the sending of clothes and food abroad and the encouragement of friendly contact between racial and social groups more manageable areas of "social action" than development of national policies to contain a communist aggressor seeking to dictate terms on the basis of superior military and economic resources.

In some Protestant women's groups, under the encouragement of the pastors, "World Government" became in 1946 and 1947 the basic reform for international politics. The signing of a World Government petition for "peace through legal and constitutional reforms" took the place of acquaintance with the power structure of the community and the modes by which its political, economic, and educational associations participate in the formation of national policy. The Catholic clergy were right that the most articulate Protestant leaders were seeking in the early postwar period to project to the international scene their own experience of group compromise about the conference tables of American society.

The Protestant pastors generally regarded themselves as anticommunist. The clergy who considered themselves social and religious liberals viewed the "right wingers" in their congregations as using the communist issue to discredit the social action and education departments and movements in the churches which "sought to attack the poverty, loss of meaning in work and racial tyranny on which communism thrives." [17]

Several Protestant pastors saw a deep affinity between opposition to domestic social reforms of the New Deal and opposition to communism in the public statements of many Catholic leaders.[18] The contests being waged between social conservatives and liberals in the Catholic church were not reflected in the diocesan journal, the major public forum for the church in the area and the chief source of information Protestant leaders had of Catholic church activity. Little of the widespread lay and clerical support of New Deal measures was expressed in the *Catholic Mirror,* the organ of a socially conservative bishop.[19]

A minority of the Protestant clergy, whose position was most forcefully stated by the pastor of the First Congregational Church, sought to distinguish their approach to communism and American foreign policy from that of either the Catholic clergy or the liberal pacifist Protestants. These men believed that they were participating in the reformulation of American theology of the 1940's led by such journals as *Christianity and Crisis* and such spokesmen as Reinhold Niebuhr. They agreed in 1946 with Catholics on the need to make a clear choice as to priorities of public policy. They held also that communism posed the chief problem in the relations of nations, and that compromise with the movement offered few creative possibilities since there was no basic common ethos between Russian communism and the Western democracies.

These pastors rejected, however, what they thought was a too narrow and rigid formulation of policy alternatives by Catholics. They held that much of the Catholic leadership in the Paper City diocese had failed to make the extension of economic justice, and of political and religious freedom of commensurate importance with containment of communism. Such a failure, they charged, increased the opportunities for communist expansion. Protestant clergymen of this persuasion broke with both the Protestant liberal pacifists and what they understood to be Catholic assumptions on the profound theological questions of the nature of man. They affirmed that some clergymen had held too optimistic a view of man's capacity to love God and his neighbor, and had, therefore, failed to deal responsibly with the inevitably perplexing and tragic problems of coercion and power in the relations between economic groups and nation-states.

This minority of Protestant pastors also indicated that the extremely conservative laymen of their congregations were backing candidates for political office who were in 1946 running chiefly on platforms of anticommunism, but who were making possible the spread of totalitarian forces by their isolationist foreign policies and reactionary domestic policies.[20]

The Protestant approach to the relation of "personal morality" and "policy positions" does not differ from the Catholic in the stress placed upon the importance of personal morality in politics. The difference is the greater inability or unwillingness of Protestant pastors to establish a neat one-to-one relationship between personal integrity and specific policy positions. The "ultimate end ethic" of most pastors is so abstract and vague that no significant relationship between positions on policy issues and personal morality is possible. For a few pastors, such as the leaders of the First and Second Congregational churches, the religious experience of the God revealed in Christ can influence greatly the decisions they make—widening the range of people toward whom they feel responsibility, making them aware of the possibilities of self-deception, intensifying moral commitments—but the decisions about particular acts in politics always involve *both* Christian experience *and* detailed technical knowledge of the social situation which is not peculiarly Christian.

The Politicians' Response to Church Views on the Communist Issue

The battles within the political parties over campaign strategy in the past decade cannot be understood apart from the approach to public policy of the *Catholic Mirror* and its supporters. The approach became part of the conservative argument—particularly within the Republican party—in the campaigns of 1948, 1950 and 1952. The 1952 Republican pledge of "liberation of enslaved peoples" in countries, such as Poland, taken over by Russia after World War II, and the broad charges of Senator McCarthy and others about substantial communist infiltration of the Department of State had been foreshadowed, in religious and moral terms, in the *Catholic Mirror.*

The logical conclusion some Catholic politicians drew from the *Catholic Mirror's* political ethic was that good Catholic candidates who knew the religious and moral law were the "kind of men you could count on to do the right thing in politics," and that they were to be preferred to men without a firm and well-known religious commitment. If a Catholic candidate was defeated, this was sometimes interpreted as the consequence of a secular or bigoted attack. The attempts to promote Catholic candidates to win back the Democratic Catholic vote were based in part on an awareness of the influence in the church of the *Catholic Mirror* view of public policy formation, and on a belief that the approach had some influence in the shift of Catholic Democrats to Republican ranks. In a strategy meeting of politicians planning a slate of nominations and a campaign, the views of the *Catholic Mirror* were mentioned as an indication of "how a lot of Catholics think about communism" and as justification for a "balanced ticket" with careful religious and ethnic representation.[21]

The approach of the *Catholic Mirror* was supported by many conservative businessmen in the city who did not hold political office or exercise public leadership in any party organizations, and who publicly called themselves non-partisan. These men nevertheless had political power in the community through large campaign contributions (usually to the Republican party) or through support of interest groups, such as the Taxpayers Association, which acted as ancillary organizations supporting the Republican party. These men sought to encourage their own Protestant pastors to embark on an "anticommunist crusade" like that of the Catholic clergy. They regarded the Catholic clergy and the diocesan journalists, in the pointed words of one paper-mill owner, as "more right on communism than the Protestant clergy." A Second Congregational church layman observed: "The Catholic church is wise on political problems. The Protestant ministers don't know anything about the world. The Catholic clergy is anti-CIO-PAC and is anticommunist. But a Protestant minister the other day signed a statement endorsing a CIO candidate."

The position expressed by the *Catholic Mirror* had its importance in the life of the city. Yet intensive study of the responses of the leading politicians to the journal and its supporters indicate that its position did not, even in 1947 and 1948, represent the way most of the Catholic politicians thought about the relations between morality, religion and politics. A minority might be called "moral legalists," deriving a strict "thou shalt" from their religious dogma for political action. But most of the Catholic politicians with heavy responsibilities in the parties (the majority were Democrats) were less prone to believe that a person could arrive at a correct public policy by application of the moral law than the writers of the *Catholic Mirror* and the local clergy most outspoken on the communist issue. Some politicians feel that religious ethics have meaning in their personal life, but less relevance in a discussion of what to do about communism, particularly when the kind of questions concretely before them are how to exploit a number of "gut" issues among the electorate, or how to justify past party actions against charges of immoral political conduct or of softness toward communism.

Most political leaders are conscious of an almost infinite number of causal forces that have influenced their past actions. They appreciate the flux in the world scene ("there's always another election"). They lack assurance deep within themselves that any temporal success, or ultimate approval, will result from what they do. They pride themselves on their "realism," on knowing what is really going on. They say they deal with the tangibles, the evident. But they mix their scattered impressions of the empirical world with bits and dabs of religious doctrine and philosophy. Even the "smart operators" are acutely aware of the variety of associations, including the churches, that affect the people they deal with. Yet they agree with their pastors that political acts are not derived wholly out of situations and relative commitment. Some being becomes sovereign, the basis for evaluation of all others. A fight is made in politics for whatever is too precious to lose—even if it is no more than the honor of one's own political organization against charges that it has sold out the national interest.

Perhaps the most important Catholic politician in Paper City tried to state this confluence of faith and politics in this way:

Part of the difficulties I face in politics arise out of my trying to do something in a certain honest and aboveboard way that other people might not do it in. This is not because they are not as religious as I am, but because they do not know the specific problems I face or the limited range of action open to me. If I understand Christianity right, it isn't that I learn religion and then I get some knowledge of politics and then I try to relate the two. They are already related. Your religion opens up aspects of politics you wouldn't have known or thought about without your religion, and your experience in politics opens up new understanding of your religion.

One of the most active Protestant politicians who is also a businessman, observed:

Now I happen to think that there is an important moral choice involved in whether I work with the Republican or the Democratic party in order to influence the action the government takes. I want to tell you there were a lot of considerations that went into my decision to get into the Republican party and really work. But I never heard the things that were important to me discussed in any church meeting calling us to be Christians in politics.

These laymen, deeply involved in politics, raise serious questions not simply about the action of the church leaders in particular issues but about their general conception of the appropriate role for the pastor in attempting to influence lay action in politics.

Views of Appropriate Means of Church Influence in Politics

Behind the attempts of the clergy to bring about specific political reforms, such as the "clean up" of gambling or the encouragement of greater resistance to communism, are their convictions as to the appropriate means for the church to use in influencing politics. The Catholic leaders, for example, have a theory of "indirect powers." This conception of the clergy's role envisions no participation in partisan political action and no extensive knowledge of the techniques of political action. Catholic clerical influence in the main is to be exerted in politics indirectly, through the education of the consciences of individual Catholics and the creation of a Catholic climate of opinion in the nation which provides the basic premises of action for Catholics and non-Catholics alike. "The church has no political machinery and no political agents," according to a statement often made by Catholic leaders.[22] The pastor of St. Jerome's parish observed, for example:

> We have no political action groups at all in Paper City churches so far as I know. The Catholic Action program is for building up religion in the minds of people, not for political action. As to my own acts, if an out and out rascal ran for office, of course, I would take up the issue. But I feel the pulpit is for religious sermons. Our people do not like to hear politics from the pulpit. I use the pulpit only in this city to stress that Catholic women vote. They are slow to take advantage of their right. It is a civic duty to use the ballot. This is as far as I go. Such a statement is without partisanship. This applies to most priests. Once in a while a priest will go on a tangent, but not often.

Catholic leaders emphasize that the concept of "indirect" action represents the culmination of a long process of transforming the direct political power of the medieval papacy into a form of influence relevant to modern times. The Catholic church is aware that modern democratic governments are controlled by the people, not by "princes" and "kings." Politics is prevented from "touching the altar" in most Western nations not by bulls of excommunication or religious disciplining of top leaders but by the influence of the educational program of the church upon rank and file citizenry and upon many leader groups in the society.[23] The church leaders believe they are sufficiently realistic to recognize that future influence in politics depends not so much upon establishing church power at the pinnacle of government, as upon achieving wide popular support of church beliefs.

Paper City politicians, when pressed for their understanding of the church's conception of "indirect" power, are somewhat ambivalent. Many cannot see that the concept takes the church "out of politics." Moral and spiritual concerns of the church, they argue, must be related to positions men take and organizations they support in politics, if those concerns are to have meaning to laymen. Even the clergy's urging church members to vote, though without partisan intent, takes on for politicians partisan significance. In Paper City the Democratic party clearly has more of a stake than the Republican party in the Catholic church's widespread "get out the vote" campaign.

The theory of "indirect" power apparently has some restraining influence upon the clergy's personal participation in political activity. But when issues develop which deeply concern the priests, they are unwilling to rely simply upon the action of laymen informed by the teaching of the church. In some cases they appear to lack confidence that the position of the church has wide enough support to secure the lay action they desire.

They have waited upon political leaders with specific proposals, advocated particular legislation at public hearings and endorsed particular candidates (in rare instances from the pulpit, more often in personal conversation and at parish society gatherings) for their position on particular moral issues, their "friendship for the parish" and their general moral character. They have aided the political careers of particular candidates by co-operating with laymen in extending invitations to participate in church functions, such a retreats, pilgrimages, communion breakfasts. One priest once became so concerned about public and parochial schools that he sought election to the school board.[24]

The Catholic priests' knowledge of the channels of political influence in Paper City is superior to that of the Protestant leaders. Their personal acquaintance with leaders in the centers of political power in the city is much greater. The Catholic priests have within their parishes most of the aldermen and ward leaders of the city. The Catholic priests express their concern in face-to-face contact with the politicians, while the Protestant clergy tend to make statements to the press and pass resolutions at church gatherings. As the chairman of the Democratic party observed, "the ministers blast away in the newspapers; the priests buttonhole me personally."

Within the Catholic clergy there is an attention to organizational power and to determined and disciplined action that is absent among Protestant clergy. The Catholic priests generally stress the power of the individual Catholic to change the world, but they highly value also the militant and cohesive expression of the faith in a world of determined groups.

The Catholic priests' view of political reform, for all their appreciation of disciplined and organized witness to the faith, rests, as does most Protestant clerical thought, primarily upon making men "good" so they can mold history in the image of a "Christian world." President Roosevelt, one gathers from the articles the priests write, "if he had just stood up to Stalin, could have secured a free Poland." [25] But instead he chose a politics of "cynicism and expediency." Had a Christian prophet been at Teheran, Yalta, Potsdam "the standard of moral principles as the only power of durable peace" would have been held high.[26]

One of the most widely distributed statements on Catholic Action argues that:

> Our country will be safe in another generation if all Catholics would rally round their bishops today and under the guidance of their parish priests, would carry their faith, their religious principles, their church's moral standards, her social principles into the lives of their respective communities. The Kingdom of God will truly come into its own, and the whole world will be enrolled in the "one fold under one Shepherd," if the present generation of Catholics in every country will, besides practicing their faith, quietly profess it and proclaim it and defend it and expound it openly.[27]

At times it appears from the talk of some priests and professional Catholic lay lectures that all the ambiguities, conflicting power structures, and worrisome complexities of history are to be circumvented or overcome by some simple, great spiritual act such as prayer. The Catholic religion is seen as the force which can determine or circumvent all other factors in politics. In an important speech sponsored by Catholic lay organizations in Paper City and enthusiastically received by priests, John M. Haffert told his audience that study of the message of Our Lady of Fatima, who appeared in apparitions to three Portuguese children and to 70,000 persons in 1917, had convinced him that "through prayer Russia will be converted from atheism." There will be a period of great happiness for the world if it "will turn to God and devotion to the Blessed Virgin." In contrast to the turmoil throughout Europe, Portugal, because it has "returned to God," now has "peace and prosperity." The speaker believed that communism, like Saul of Tarsus, the first "Red," will go on in triumph until it is knocked from its horse by God. Then the world will experience an era of peace such as it has never known.[28]

A minority group in Catholic clerical leadership, composed mostly of curates, has considerable criticism to make of these "easy" and "ill-informed" hopes for church influence and reform of politics.

These clerics have strong convictions that the church cannot escape the responsibility for becoming much more intimately acquainted than at present with the facts of political life. They are less anxious to have church leaders "go into disciplined action" on specific issues than they are to find ways for the church to come to some understanding of what politicians do, just as the church has come to some understanding of what labor leaders do through its "labor schools." [29] They are highly sensitive to the "mixed nature" of the judgments which the church's diocesan publications make about such complex areas as foreign affairs; they stress the fact that understanding of the specific political situation is highly important to decision-making, and particularly so in international relations. They believe that the church's strong emphasis upon the definition of moral and temporal boundaries should make Catholics sensitive to the contingent nature of any priest's judgment about a specific political situation.

These men press the church for greater contact with laymen active in politics, for opportunities of politicians to carry on a sustained discussion with priests of the relations of the Christian faith to the most controversial and influential decisions the laymen face in politics.

A start toward such discussion, these priests argue, has been made by Holy Rosary parish with the most extensive educational program in the area of politics carried out by any religious organization in the city. For several years, Holy Rosary parish has spent approximately $8,000 annually to sponsor a pilgrimage to Washington. The parish usually pays all the expenses for approximately one hundred "pilgrims" and eight or ten priests from various parishes in the city. In Washington and in Paper City the participants are briefed on a number of legislative and party issues. Prominent Paper City politicians are invited on the pilgrimage and gain the opportunity to talk with state and national political leaders.

Such minority efforts at extending the contact of Catholic church's religious leadership with political realities should not obscure the dominant patterns of clerical relations with politicians. The priests minimize the importance of extensive knowledge of public policy or exposure to political controversy.

Back of the day-to-day, informal, private contact of priests and politicians are impressive occasions when the church has made available its traditional facilities for worship and education to non-Catholics and Catholics alike. These are occasions when no efforts are made by priests to direct theological discussions to specific issues. The laymen are free to raise whatever questions they wish—personal or professional. A description by the mayor of Paper City, an Episcopalian in church affiliation, of his attendance at a Catholic lay retreat sponsored by the Passionist Fathers, illuminates the importance of such an experience:

> I didn't know whether I should go to the retreat or not, because of my not being sure if I could genuflect and all that business at the right time. But the priests told me that I was just to act natural. So I went.
>
> When I got to the retreat house, I was met at the door by a priest who picked up my grips. I told him I should carry them, not he. Here I was 62 and 220 pounds, and he a slender man. But he insisted. He escorted me into the most exquisitely furnished living room I had ever been in in my life. The priest said that these were my rooms during the retreat.
>
> I realized that these must be the quarters for the bishop when he came, and I said, "But, Father, I'm just Joe Hadley. I want to be just one of the boys and stay where the other men do."
>
> Then the priest drew himself up and looked very sternly at me and said, "The church respects the state, and the state respects the church. When you come here, you are not Joe Hadley to us. You are Mr. Mayor of Paper City."
>
> So I stayed in the suite of rooms.
>
> The other thing I remember most about the retreat was that they had a question period and each person wrote out a question on a card for the priest to answer. When it was over, the priest said, "Now we've had questions from all but the Mayor of Paper City. Mr. Hadley, do you have a question?" I said I thought I did and that I hoped I could phrase it correctly. The priest said that he hoped he could answer it correctly. I said, "Not many years ago I lost my dear Mother and Father. Each month as I drive by the cemetery I stop and sit down by the car and smoke a cigar in quiet meditation. I feel they would like me to do this. What I want to know, Father, is, do they know I do this for them?" It was so quiet you could hear a pin drop. Then Father said, "Do you think they do?"
>
> I said, "Yes, I believe they do."
>
> "Then that's all that matters. You have faith that they do," the priest said. "That's all the answer you need."

There was no doubt in the mayor's mind after the retreat that his contact with the church had deepened his respect for the Catholic church and his desire to aid its growth in the community. But such contact is a long way from the systematic exploration of vocational decisions carried on for Protestants and Catholics in the "labor schools."

The Protestant ministers make no claim to having a formulated theory of "indirect" power for church action, but they make the same distinctions the Catholics do between appropriate "non-political" methods of the church and non-appropriate partisan methods. However, they are much more given than the Catholics to moralizing about their approach, to identifying the other faith group with "political" methods. The Protestants claim that Catholics "use power and coercion while the Protestants use moral suasion." Most Protestant clergy, say they "are suspicious of religious leaders who talk about power." (The Catholic priests know where power resides but talk little in terms of "power" or "coercion.") They are anxious to see good done in politics but lack concrete knowledge of the relevant alternatives of action available to them.[30] They are eager to counsel laymen on religious and ethical problems in politics, but they rarely know the party affiliation of their leading laymen or the extent of their political activity.[31]

Most Protestant pastors believe that the Catholic clergy mainly rely upon organized group action in politics while the Protestant leaders rely upon individual influence. They view the Protestant clergy as in a superior moral position on this count. Historically the Protestant pastors have from time to time been caught up in frenzied crusades to remove some social problem by a "one shot" solution, and have organized themselves to act as a pressure group. The antisaloon movement of 1915 to 1918 aroused the Paper City Protestant clergy to its most intensive political action. On most issues they have followed their own personal interests, with no attempt at coordinated action. Sometimes the clergy have been confronted by issues that concerned them deeply, but they have found the problems so complex and the moral issues so ambiguous that they felt collective action was not possible. For example, the Ministerial Association in 1936, after long discussion of legislation proposed to remedy labor-management conflict, "concluded that while collective action was not desirable, yet as individuals the members of the association ought to interest themselves in matters pertaining to the welfare of the community." The ministers have conceived of collective action in terms of "pressure," of making public statements and waiting upon public officials—not as cooperative organization of programs of study for laymen utilizing the resources of the whole city or region.

Summary

As one observes the actions of the church leaders on local and national political issues, one can perhaps understand why many policy-minded politicians in Paper City view some of the judgments of the religious leaders about public life as dogmatic in their sweep and inclusiveness, naive in their optimism, and ignorant in their disregard of the ways in which general affirmations can serve partisan and special interests.

Yet these politicians would also acknowledge pervasive and constructive contributions of the Catholic and Protestant churches to discussion of political issues, such as those that arose with the threat of communism. The Catholic church leaders have stressed that political decisions are fundamentally moral decisions, and that man is not without guidance as to what is evil in the world and what is the right course of action to combat it. The Protestant leaders have been worried that the shift from sentimentality to realism about forceful resistance to communism has been short on creative and outgoing elements, such as deep concern for social and economic reconstruction in the world.

Chapter 20

The Churches and Political Compromise

To most Paper City politicians, the very stuff of politics is the formation of a program of government action which represents the reconciliation of conflicting demands and interests of the electorate. The politician lives in the midst of the continuing interaction of the parties, the factions within the parties, the varied branches of the government, the private groups seeking to influence public policies. As noted in Chapter 17, public policy emerges out of the continual redefinition of private interests in this process. Public policy represents the emergence of the common good out of the serious debate, hard negotiation and imaginative reflection of men facing the concrete demands of persons and institutions. In the continued creation of this new reality—public policy—the original demands of groups and individuals are taken into consideration, but in an important sense reconstituted; new unarticulated interests of the people are called forth; obligations are accepted as well as rights demanded, in acknowledgment of an interdependent society.

Our concern in this chapter is to describe the relation of the churches and of the religious leaders to the processes and institutions of compromise which are so much a part of Paper City politics. The appropriate areas for detailed analysis are three: (1) the controversy of Protestants and Catholics over the attempt of two Protestant ministers to support the referral of an issue of great interest to the churches—the transportation of parochial students in public school buses—to a public referendum and debate; (2) the efforts of the churches to formulate a general position on the relation of church and state, within which such issues as the public transportation of parochial students could be dealt with "on principle"; (3) the attitudes of the churches toward the major political parties, since they are American institutions which epitomize the give and take of democratic politics.

At the start a general pattern can be noted in all of these areas: the religious leaders have more difficulty interpreting the relationship of Christianity to political compromise than to political reform. Most of the leaders, as we have seen, attempt to conduct themselves according to an ethic of natural law or ultimate ends. The role of calling men to bring politics "into line with" the principles of the Christian ethic seems, at least on the surface, more appropriate to the church than actual involvement in the rough and tumble of political debate and negotiation. There are, however, in this area of community life, as in all the areas we have examined, significant distinctions to be made between various Protestant and Catholic leaders in their relations to society.

Referral of a Church-State Issue to Public Discussion and Referendum

The public transportation of parochial school students has been the issue which, in the past decade in Paper City, has occasioned the greatest debate between Protestants and Roman Catholics as to whether there should be a test of public sentiment in the city. The dispute over "city-wide gambling" also involved an attempt of the Protestant leaders to arouse public discussion of a moral issue on which the churches differed; but the public transportation of parochial students produced a more thorough statement by some of the Protestant pastors of the religious concerns at stake.

In a lengthy statement widely circulated among Protestants in the city, two Baptist ministers stated their reasons for support of a petition to have placed on the ballot the question of whether the people wished to repeal a state law providing for the public transportation of private-school pupils to and from school.[1] The appeal in the statement was made primarily on the basis that the issue should be decided as directly by the voters as possible, and that the petition would ensure public discussions of an issue which, the statement implied, the Catholic church and other supporters of the present transportation arrangements had not wanted debated by the rank-and-file electorate.

The statement then affirmed that the "petition is not an anti-

Catholic proposal," and that the authors of the statement were not motivated by "prejudice or bigotry, but by a sincere regard for the future of religious freedom in America." The ministers privately interpreted this part of their statement as an effort to anticipate charges which they were certain would be leveled against them by Catholics, and which would tend to close discussions of the issue. The charges would pose the question purely as one of Catholics versus anti-Catholics, tolerance versus bigotry.

The statement prepared by the Baptist pastors reviewed the history of New England Protestant deprivation of political rights and religious freedom "of Catholics, Jews, Baptists and other groups." The pastors stated that oppression of others is possible by any group of men inadequately checked by a community with a genuinely pluralistic social and religious structure. "Such a tragedy may some day be ours, if we do not oppose every inroad upon the principle which guards our liberties" (the principle of separation of church and state). The authors observed further:

> Public appropriations for private school transportation may seem to be a small matter. However, the undermining of great principles usually begins with apparently minor violations. Moreover, there are indications that the present transportation law is just part of an extensive movement towards much wider public appropriations for private sectarian schools. Of course, such a program cannot be enacted without breaking down the separation of church and state.

The pastors were in part correct in their prediction of the statement's reception. The daily newspaper of largest circulation in the diocesan area reported the statement as "anti-Catholic" in origin.[2] The statement was widely interpreted by Catholic pastors to laymen as bigoted and prejudicial against Catholics. Almost all of the Catholic pastors believed that the Protestant pastors should not have sought to have the transportation issue submitted to a referendum.[3] An economic boycott was instituted by a Catholic priest against a Protestant businessman who had signed the Protestant statement, and several Catholic laymen instituted boycotts against other signers.[4]

The fundamental assumption of the Catholic leaders most vocal in their opposition to the statement was that the church does not enter a controversy in politics unless the moral and spiritual implications are clear and therefore the position is surely the "right" one. The position is not to be submitted to the "give and take" of the political process, and the clergy or hierarchy is not much interested in public debate or discussion of its position. The position is seen as a moral and spiritual one, and should therefore, as the pastor of Holy Rosary parish noted, "in a good Catholic community enjoy immunity from criticism or compromise."[5]

In the controversy over public transportation of parochial students, politicians noted that the protest of the Protestant pastors was based on a principle they believed to be right, and to be essential to "guard our liberties." The ethics back of the position taken by the Protestants did not appear to some politicians as distinguishable from that of the Catholic leaders. However, they did note that the Protestant position emerged in a different institutional context. The position of the pastors was viewed by Protestant laymen as a statement of a personal moral position of the clergy, and not as a position whose defense involved the protection of the authority of an institution. The Protestant pastors, for all their attempt to deliver what one pastor termed a "high-level" pronouncement on a moral issue, and for all their defensiveness about political rebuke, live within churches representing much more variety and ambiguity about the relations of religion to specific political decisions than do the Catholic pastors. The politicians know this, and the knowledge influences their assessment of the responsiveness of religious leaders to criticism and compromise of their public position.

During a discussion of the Protestant pastors' statement on the petition, a prominent leader in Republican politics, a "nominal Protestant" by her own definition, sought to introduce the subject of the referendum into a Republican women's club discussion. The group would not discuss the issue. "One can easily tell which of the girls in the club have been to a parochial or public school," she noted in recalling the incident. "One can tell by the degree to which they are willing to discuss an issue. The public-school graduates who have been under less Catholic influence have a greater liberality on issues. This is important in politics where conditions change rapidly."

Most politicians are of the opinion that the strong public presentation of a position on a moral-political issue by the Catholic church can, more than any other factor in the community, stop efforts at discussion and compromise of contending positions.[6] When the Catholic church introduces an eternal law or sanction for a position in a controversy, the issue becomes "frozen." "If you want an issue to stay fluid," a Republican political leader from Ward 7 said, "then try not to get it interpreted as a religious or moral issue."

The Catholic approach to the relationships between morals and politics makes it particularly difficult for the church to deal with the political processes and associations of compromise. The Catholic church has, in its own attitude toward public debate, often sought immunity from criticism of its moral position on the basis that it is not politically partisan and that its judgments are not to be submitted to the political process.

The Protestant moralistic approaches to political judgments have also contributed to the freezing of public discussions, but apparently to a lesser extent than Roman Catholic influence. This fact is due to some extent to the less authoritative claims of the Protestant churches and their greater appreciation of the importance of discussion among people of varied interests and background in discovery of the "right" thing to do in public life. But it is also related to the often vague character of Protestant affirmations in political matters and to the lack of power represented in a minority—and a highly diffuse one at that.

"The Separation of Church and State"

In the controversy over the petition on public conveyance of parochial students, the Protestant pastors appealed to the "principle of separation of church and state." There are several aspects to the disputes of the churches over the kind of general recognition and aid which the state is to grant the churches as institutions in the society. At stake is the question of whether a genuinely independent religious organization is to exist in the society, free to criticize or support the activities of the state.

One aspect of the dispute has been over the question of "equal status" of the various religious groups before the state. This question historically has involved two issues: (a) whether the state is to grant formal and legal recognition, in the present or at an ideal future time, to a particular church's superior spiritual or moral offices; and (b) whether actual preferential use of the powers of the government has occurred.

Politicians in Paper City are quite certain that none of the churches are asking for the first of these. The difficult problems center on the second. The politicians generally use the phrase "equal status for all groups" as a nice-sounding description of what they do. In practice, equal status may mean the government's acceptance of formidable pressure from one religious group (unchecked by claims from other groups) to use certain resources of the state accompanied by announcement of the availability of the same facility to other religious groups.[7] Such a grant, even though available to all religions on equal terms, may actually increase the comparative advantage or power of the group wanting the favor, and may antagonize other groups which do not have the kind of church activities that are enhanced by such government aid.

On the issue of the state's legal recognition of religious groups, the Catholic diocesan press and local Catholic pastors have never speculated publicly on whether they felt the Roman Catholic church needed, desired, or could achieve in the community, or in the nation eventually, the kind of formal status for the church known as the "confessional state." The confessional state, as defined by the senior priests, is one in which the state publicly professes the superiority of the Roman Catholic church's judgment as to the nature of God's will in moral and spiritual matters, establishes Roman Catholicism as the only official religion and uses its temporal power to limit in varying degrees the public presentations of other faiths.

For a minority of the Catholic pastors in Paper City[8] (approximately 40 per cent), it is not mandatory within Catholicism that the confessional state be pursued as the proper end for the Catholic church in every society. For them, the most practical general policy for the Catholic church in Paper City and in the United States now is to avoid religious discrimination by the government and to adhere to the goal of equal treatment in civil affairs for all religions.

These men differ with Protestant leaders on what is equal treatment in many areas—for example, whether equal treatment means use of government funds for transportation of students to parochial schools. But these priests—they tend to be the younger men—see the development in America of a lay state without religious pretensions and with no claim to control the internal activity of the churches. They see the Catholic church as a voluntary association influencing the state principally through the religious beliefs of individual Catholic citizens. They can envision a political system of separation of church and state which gives many opportunities to the Catholic church to use state funds and services not utilized by other church groups. They hope for a moral union of church and state in which the state observes the laws of God which the church discerns. They believe that the achievement of moral union does not necessitate a mixture of state and church organization, or the use by the church of state power to enforce conformity to certain laws and to ideas that the laws implement.

These priests hold that this separation of church and state has been the position of the Catholic church in America in the past, that it has not been rejected by the Holy See as a satisfactory solution for the church in America, that it is the generally held position of the Catholic church today on levels above the priesthood of Paper City (for example, the bishop of the diocese and the *Catholic Mirror*).[9] These pastors stress that they do not know, any more than anyone else does, what will be the nature of relations between the church and political forces in America in the distant future. They do not exclude on religious grounds the possible desirability of the confessional state (any more than they exclude on religious grounds the present American separation of church and state), but only on grounds relative to the requirements of a vital church and faith within a particular political situation. They do not expect the American political system to change in the foreseeable future, and they are not working for its change.

For a majority of the pastors, the confessional state is an authentic Catholic thesis, the ideal end to be worked for as a long-term goal for all Catholics in all countries.[10] The pastors who hold this position do not differ greatly from the men who reject the confessional state as a mandatory objective in their views as to the practicable action for the church to pursue in the present American situation. Finally, it should be noted, none of the Catholic pastors believes that a confessional state is incompatible with the politics of a democracy.

For the Catholic pastors the supreme issue in a debate over use of government resources by a religious group is always "the freedom of the church to declare the divine and moral law" and not whether equal status has been given all religions or separation of church and state maintained.

For example, in a dispute between the churches over whether the municipal government was to aid the gambling activities of the Roman Catholic church, the Catholic pastors almost uniformly favored aid for the project from the state. The Catholics believe they have the correct moral position for the government on this issue—gambling conducted under proper auspices can be a recreation which serves worthy causes. The Catholic church is not claiming a special privilege for itself in having the state aid in implementing this moral position. The church is not asking for formal recognition from the state. The other churches may make similar use of the resources of the state if they wish. But the decision of what resources of the state are available to the Catholic church and to other churches cannot rest upon the least common denominator of desires of all churches, or upon the position of another church which may claim right to veto proposals for co-operation with the state.

The Catholic leaders assert they are as concerned as the Protestants that the church remain strong and vigorous, separated structurally from the state, able to contract and expand its functional co-operation with the state to assure its freedom to carry on its work.

The degree of aid from the state sought by the Catholic church depends primarily upon the hierarchy's estimation of the effect it will have upon the church's freedom and influence. This decision is never made apart from calculations as to the actual social, political and religious context of the community, region and nation in which church policy is projected. In Paper City the clergy concentrate mainly now upon the constructive possibilities in expansion of the church's use of state resources. But such expansion is always with a keen eye to the possibilities of future state interference with the church's freedom.

The ways in which the Catholic pastors make judgments are illustrated by their discussion of state aid to parochial schools. One pastor observed:

> The doctrine of church and state was not planned by our forefathers to keep religion out of our public conscience or to prevent provision of religious instruction for the people. The provision of bus transportation for parochial students is not mixing church and state. It has nothing whatever to do with mixing of the two institutions. We are just asking for some use of the tax money we pay. That is all the government aid we want.
>
> I am against any more state money than that, for it would endanger state control of Catholic education. The state gives money and it wants to control you. The church is made too dependent upon the view of the state. Therefore I'm opposed to financial aid beyond bus transportation.
>
> But this is a different use of the idea of separating church and state than the Protestant doctrine. The Protestant doctrine would mean that all medical care for parochial children, all police and fire protection would have to be denied. And this would be against the general welfare.

Another Catholic pastor is more confident of the ability of the church to protects its freedom. Note the importance he attaches to the religious composition of the citizenry and of the government itself:

> Of course, the church will ask for more tax funds after it receives transportation aid. The church should in time ask for money to build school buildings, to employ teachers. We pay taxes the same as anyone else. We think the government, if it's a Christian government, should want the young people taught religion and be willing to pay for it.
>
> We need not fear state interference in Catholic schools. It hasn't happened in Quebec. We feel that the basic problem is one of getting honest, religious men elected and we are working for that. It has been done elsewhere. Why can't it be done here? We feel that if we have the right kind of men they will not interfere with the way we run our schools.
>
> There won't be any problem of control. The Catholic people will be influential enough in the state to secure the church against interference from the state.

The Catholic clergy interpret the Protestant positions on "equal status for all religions" and "absolute separation of church and state" as having the real goal not of equity and freedom, but of limiting the Catholic church. "If the Protestant churches were interested, for example, in equal status," a priest typically contends, "they would support the Catholic church's present attempt to secure public funds for parochial schools, since Catholics wish only to use their own tax funds for the kind of schooling they believe in."

The Protestant ministers, for their part, reject any relation to the state in which formal and legal recognition is given to the churches. They want no state church in America. For all pastors a minimal requirement of the state is that no denomination is to enjoy a privileged use of the resources or power of the state not available to all religions.

For a majority of the Protestant pastors, but not for most laymen, "equal status" is the slogan for a radical demand that the state make no general use of resources which are rejected vehemently by any one denomination in the society. These Protestants seek severely to limit the use of the state's resources to maintain their view of the church as an agency supported almost entirely by "voluntary" financial contributions. They are for the greatest possible restriction of the state's financial establishment and maintenance of religious activities. The more the church has to rely upon the powers of its own persuasion, rather than the coercive power of the state, the greater, they argue, will be the churches' vigor and independence.

A corollary of this "equal status" position is the advocacy of an "absolute separation of church and state," and the "containment of every attempt to break the wall between them." A sermon by a Presbyterian pastor on "The American Way of Life" is representative of the manner in which the majority of the pastors talk:

> The church is primarily an institution of worship. The state is society policed. Both institutions should be kept absolutely separate and neither should restrain the other. . . . We can find the basis for separation of church and state in the scriptures as well as in the wisdom of the founding fathers. Jesus said, "My Kingdom is not of this world. . . . Render unto Caesar the things that are Caesar's and unto God the things that are God's." This is the scriptural basis of our great American doctrine of separation of church and state. As Elihu Root said to William Howard Taft when he was going to the Philippines, "There is one controlling principle of our government: the complete separation of church and state. It is basic and there can be no shading of that separation. . . ."

In such issues as the public transportation of parochial students, no distinctions between "indirect" and "direct" state aid to the churches are generally accepted as valid. (Indirect aid is given by the government in carrying out welfare functions such as the school-lunch program; direct aid is aid intended for such purposes as providing instructors for parochial schools.[11]) The pastors have not dealt with the implications of their position for a whole series of Protestant activities now carried on in America with at least indirect use of tax funds—subsidization of activities of church-related hospitals, student scholarships and research grants for private colleges.

The chief problem in church-state relations for the Paper City Protestant pastors is the discouragement of the growth of the Catholic church's influence—not, as in the Catholic church, the expansion of the church's freedom to influence the life of the society. The principles for church-state relations are formulated always within the immediate exigencies or tactical problems of Catholic-Protestant relations. In politics, perhaps the chief point of focus for the Protestant clergy is resistance to the Catholic church's efforts to expand its use of the resources of government.

A minority of Protestant pastors speak also of a society in which public judgments will emerge out of the interaction of a rich variety of religious and social institutions. But they believe that a vital voluntary church can be achieved while permitting some indirect aid from the state for certain church functions, in recognition that too rigid interpretation of church and state separation may merely reflect conceptions of politics bereft of profound ethical and religious insight, and religious activity bereft of a sense of political responsibility.

Yet, on such highly charged issues as use of public funds for transportation of parochial students, all of the Protestant pastors (except for the Lutheran, who is uncommitted) are opposed to state aid. The different theoretical positions have not made for significant tactical differences under the exigencies of Catholic-Protestant relations in the city.

The slogans of "equal status for all religions" and of "absolute separation of church and state" represent a vast fabric of truth and fantasy about politics and religion. It is a fabric which hides from the religious leaders their actual involvement in political life; it also hides from the general public the narrow tactical considerations for checking the power of the other religious group which have gone into church action—particularly the recent improvisations of some of the Protestant leaders. The leaders of the Catholic church have struggled more with practical and long-term problems because of their responsibility for the parochial school program. However, both church groups have been severely limited by suspicion of each other and by inadequate ideologies in the task of developing programs that could aid laymen and clergy in a real understanding of the crucial and difficult decisions to be made in public life.

The Significance to the Churches of the Political Parties

The political institution given the least attention by Catholic and Protestant religious leaders alike is party organization. This is a significant omission, particularly perhaps for Catholic social thought, so systematic and comprehensive in its analysis of society.[12] To many practical politicians the major parties when competing well and enthusiastically represent very fundamental institutions in an "open society." They offer to the electorate the over-all, general policy choices. They compromise and reconcile group positions until majorities are formed. They provide the majority with organization for some minimal co-ordination of the executive and legislative branches of the government.

Leaders in the Catholic church, by their close relation to the labor movement, were confronted in the 1940's by a very profound trade-union attack against worker apathy toward the major parties. Catholic debate over the democratic role of the parties was precipitated (chiefly in the labor schools[13]) by the formation of the Political Action Committee of the Congress of Industrial Organizations during the presidential campaign of 1944. The CIO-PAC had the announced purpose of aiding the re-election of President Roosevelt and the election of what it termed "liberal" congressmen and senators.[14] This development provided some indication of Roman Catholic difficulties with making their religious and moral principles relevant to the party system. The development is not so helpful in indicating responses of the Protestant leaders, since they had much less direct relation than the "labor priests" to the labor leaders who were conducting the debate.

The Catholic pastors of Paper City's parishes and the diocesan paper[15] dealt with the rise of the CIO-PAC almost entirely in terms of whether communists controlled the movement. At least, the impression gained almost unanimously by the executives of the local CIO unions in the schools and in talks with their pastors was that the one crucial moral or religious problem to be faced by the Catholics was the communist role in the PAC movement. The CIO leaders became so concerned over conservative comments of the popular press about CIO-PAC and the approach of local clergy that they published a large advertisement in the daily newspaper giving selected quotations from Catholic publications and Catholic leaders approving activities of the PAC ("Read the truth and testimony, then condemn those who bear false witness against the Church and PAC.") [16]

The Protestant leaders, in contrast to the Catholic church, took little or no part in the controversy in the labor movement over the role of the political parties and of the groups who work for them. Only one or two Protestant leaders have enough contact with the labor movement to become involved in searching out the religious or moral dimensions to the issues to which the PAC drew attention. The chief contact of the Protestant churches is with the business and middle class community, and in the 1930's and 1940's the problems of partisan politics did not stir the leaders of this segment of Paper City's social structure.

The pastors of a liberal theological position were guided in their approach to politics, as we have noted, by an ethic of natural law or ultimate ends. Their concern with personal piety and with avoiding compromise of moral principle led them to draw the line of political involvement at the level of the "independent citizen" who remains aloof from the ambiguities, the scraps, the shady dealing associated with partisan politics. To an "independent" the vision of the ultimate objectives remains clear, and his ethical position is not shattered by the hard choices of "appropriate and possible means." The pastors who pressed publicly for a referendum on the parochial transportation issue wished to take moral concerns to the voters by the direct means of petition, where the clear choice could be posed; but they offered no speculations upon the religious stake in the controversies over the function of the political arm of organized labor—an issue faced by some of the Catholic clergy.

The pastors of the First and Second Congregational Churches, with their greater orientation toward a situational ethic, represent partial exceptions to these generalizations about the Protestant clergy.[17] The pastor of the First Congregational church believes that the Catholic church's preoccupation with industrial and economic councils further perpetuates Marxian and classical liberal views of *homo economicus*.[18] He observes that the political parties in America unite and divide men in society about great public policies and interests that are not narrowly defined within economic groupings.

Both Congregational pastors feel that many prevailing views of party politics in America rest upon inadequate understanding of the implications of Christian views of sin and grace. Most local Catholic statements, one pastor observes, are too optimistic and rationalistic in their hopes that strong moral leadership can lift group demands to the level of national and common needs. One Protestant minister cited a speech by a Roman Catholic editor to the Knights of Columbus, in which the editor said:

> Last Sunday a man in a hotel [in Paper City] asked if we ever thought the country would get to the love of independence, of worship of God, of unity, and good will, and honesty and virtue in social life on the scale that these ideals were followed years ago. We said we believe it will if a new type of leadership comes forth—a type of leadership which will consider the country as a whole and not a group of blocs and if the citizenry had enough interest in preserving what had been the greatest experiment in the history of governments and the widest liberty any nation has ever enjoyed. Our friend said of one thing he was convinced and that is the Catholic church never had a better or greater opportunity to preserve the nation and its institutions and to supply the masses with the truth and order which will help preserve society.[19]

Doctrines such as the sovereignty of God, the sinfulness of man, the possibilities of social reconciliation through the activity of God in history, as interpreted by this pastor, favor the kind of continuous contention and shifting agreement found possible within a responsible, competitive party system.

Public Policy and the Churches

There is little evidence that the local leaders of either religious movement understand adequately the nature of public policy formation. Politics is the social area in which Roman Catholic and Protestant churches seem most limited by cliches, outmoded ideology and deep suspicions of one another's motives. Yet the churches can and do contribute to the search of people for a better understanding of the nature of public policy formation.

The church leaders have all strongly condemned the special-interest type of politics as bereft of ethics or high principle. But when it comes to the promotion of financial, education or other traditional institutional causes of the churches, the leaders have used their influence in such a way as to encourage a special-interest kind of politics. Indeed most politicians feel that they are usually approached directly only for these purposes.

The churches have sensed the need that people feel to be governed in the public interest, not just in the interest of a few private concerns. They have known the hunger for agreement in America on the fundamental beliefs which distinguish our nation from totalitarian forces; the churches have contributed to that hunger. The church leaders of Paper City have at times been so happy with the endorsement by influential men of their own beliefs that they have failed to see that politicians and political organizations most narrowly confined in their interests—class, economic, sectional, racial, ethnic—have often in Paper City been the most devoted to talk of unity above all partisanship, harmony without rancor, and moral integrity and religious piety which knows no selfish interest. Both Catholic and Protestant leaders have by their general attitudes toward politics and the Christian life provided a climate of opinion that fosters the easy and successful manipulation of religious symbols by narrowly interested people.

The Catholic leaders have sought to express in the city something of the medieval Western ideals of organic and the common good. These ideals are to be inculcated in men in the educational programs of the church so that they can then apply them in their every-day life; the church only rarely assumes responsibility for having the various concrete political interests of men explicitly discussed within the life of the church and for having clergy and laymen together seek to comprehend and reconcile these interests in a way that reflects serious consideration of the theological and social meaning of the Christian faith. Much of the Catholic talk about unity and the common good does not prepare men to understand the genuine struggle with diverse points of view and interests that goes on within a truly city-wide or truly national political organization; they do not illuminate the processes of give and take, of compromise that are at the center of democratic policy formation, processes which by their very nature never quite let any man have his way.

The Protestant churches have contributed their own brand of confusion to the political scene by their obsession with the pious, good, independent man in public life—a man who seems to be able to stride over or circumvent all the ambiguities, power temptations and institutional rigidities of history. This hero type—dear to men in both movements, but especially dear to Protestants—can, because he has a "pure heart" and is "active in the church," achieve harmony and unity where reason and organization fail. The unity may be nothing more than agreement on vague general principles and the idealization of a likable personality; but it will appear good and real in a period when the problems of the world have been shorn of their deepest political dimensions.

The business community first learned to take over the moral concepts and vocabulary of the churches, in an effort to meet the criticism of the social gospel movement in Protestantism and Catholicism. Public service was to be pursued in place of profit; "harmonious teams" of employees and "industrial families" were to replace warring labor and capital. This ideology provided only a slight instrument of self-criticism because of its platitudinous, self-righteousness and individualistic nature. The basic distinctions between the Christian movements in their historic interpretations of these symbols were lost or ignored. The politicians, particularly those recruited from business and mass communications, used the same concepts in interpreting public life.

Both in Protestantism and in Catholicism, new insights are being developed as to the meaning of the Christian faith; these insights will help the churches to appreciate the kind of politics that is neither a mechanistic manipulation of interests to keep power, nor a claim to achievement of unity and harmony without contention and strife.

The Protestants have, at least within their own church life, appreciated the sources and strengths of diversity of belief, of the kind of attitudes that keeps all viewpoints under criticism. If Protestants understood more adequately the implications for American politics of their own church polity, they might contribute to public life a healthy suspicion of easy talk about harmony and unity. They could call attention to the fact that genuine alternatives of action are made possible only by genuinely competitive parties, by diverse centers of power, by clear focus of responsibility, by serious and respectful attention to positions different from one's own. Perhaps the Protestantism of Paper City will continue to underestimate the number of areas where the public interest must be actively sought, and to overestimate the possibilities of uncoerced agreement and voluntary emergence of policy proposals. But it has the resources to give ultimate meaning—the meaning of a faith in God who loves all men in their weakness and freedom—to a political activity which hears out and reconciles, not just the interests of the few, but the aspirations of the many.

The Roman Catholic tradition makes its most characteristic contribution to public policy formation by its attention to the establishment of clear priorities and preferences of action necessary in achieving large-scale organization. Catholic leaders have known the tragedy that always stalks policy decisions, when the demands of some groups must be preferred over others.

The Protestants have sensed more often than the Catholics the way in which rigid actions, ignorant of the concrete needs and possibilities of people, are produced by attempts to make a particular objective (such as victory over communism) or a preconceived "hierarchy of values" (such as "spiritual over material goals") the absolute or sole guide to policy. But both groups have in the history of Paper City politics—for example, the *Catholic Mirror's* fight against the Truman foreign policy in 1946, and the Protestant anti-saloon movement—taken on crusades that either turned politicians into simple manipulators of "single issues" or froze political action so that the discovery of viable and freely supported policy became impossible or extremely difficult.

Democratic politics is actually a continuous process of compromise in which leaders must formulate for themselves "sound" and "just" policies, but always with respect to the possible restraining or corrective insight of others. Men live in America in a political system which is always unsettling their calculations of their own true interests and of the public good. Value judgments and moral experience occur in common life, but not as entities divorced from fact, from the contention of persons and groups in the social and religious structure.

Both Roman Catholic and Protestant leaders, in their isolation from political decisions and in their desire to appear as keepers of the public conscience, have contributed to popular stereotypes of politics as a "dirty" area of life, devoted to expediency and to "deals" with private interests. The clergy have played the role chiefly of correctors of the "stark realism" of politicians in their exhortations to follow the vision of the transcendent ideals of the Christian faith. The Protestant leaders have been particularly vague, sentimental and abstract in their public statements about local policy; they were often attracted to the "reforms" and "crusades" of the upper-class Yankee businessmen, whose drives for fiscal prudence in municipal government were accompanied by appeals to the "good people" to become active in politics, and whose drives for more restricted federal, state and local activity were accompanied by symbols of social and religious pluralism dear to the Protestant churches. The Catholic leaders have been more attracted to the political appeals claiming that precise, correct public policies for foreign affairs can be deducted from moral and religious principles, such as for the liberation of ethnic groups (e.g., Poles) from communist dominance, and that in politics the good men can be separated clearly from the evil men. The diocesan press has particularly contributed gross caricatures of the "enemy" and the "faithful" in world politics.

The churches have had to discover over and over again that there is no fruitful way for them to understand policy judgments apart from recognition of the concrete and historical nature of public life and of the Biblical Christianity which affirms a transcendent God who yet reveals Himself in world events and supremely in the person of Christ. Speculation about the ideals and objectives to be supported go on among the laymen as they became involved in public life, but this speculation is seldom divorced for long from the elements of the real world. Actual decision-making of persons is always related to specific claims—perhaps an alderman seeking to reconcile the demands of parent-teacher groups that a new school be built with the insistence of the Taxpayers Association, "the voice of over a thousand home owners and retailers," that public school expenditures be reduced next year. When men try to give freedom and justice abstract definitions and to relate them apart from "the facts" or the "technical situation," they pave the way for illusions about the ease with which the various demands of organized groups can actually be reconciled, and for intransigence and rigidity of position as to the nature of the good life.

Many practicing politicians look to the churches for some faithful interpretation of a profession which must inevitably deal in interests and must give careful attention to the concrete implications men see in the moral principles they profess. For many old-time Paper City politicians there was a greater sense of freedom to carry out the functions of negotiation and compromise in the more secular politics of an earlier day, when the politician was widely accepted as practicing a "dirty" profession, dealing in deeply felt interests, and not expected to give continual evidence of being in favor of religion, brotherhood and harmony. Politicians have seen real issues avoided and positions frozen by the introduction of a type of religion that encouraged self-righteousness and the appeal to doctrinal and moral precepts as if by them alone one could judge character and resolve tensions. The policy-minded politicians look for support from the churches in developing a kind of politics that recognizes the need to see special interests for what they are, to make hard choices, to have the courage of conviction, to compromise when necessary, to work through to common ground, to find solid support for a program because it has been fought out in earnest. In our world, agreement that matters does not come quickly or with slogans; it is discovered in the hard wrestling of consecrated men with specific problems.

Conclusion

For almost a century in Paper City the Roman Catholic and Protestant faith groups have conducted a profound dialogue. The principal subject has been the nature of Christian community—as expressed in the corporate life of the churches themselves and in the society or political economy.

The broad sweep of the data of such a study as this cannot be reduced to some simple affirmation about the content and structure of this dialogue, or about the rightness of one movement compared with the other. The study has been directed at understanding the actions of all the participants. But one may perhaps arrive at a perspective within which the whole dialogue can have deeper significance.

The chief problem of community is how to achieve "creative mutuality"—how to discover and strengthen common interests and action while at the same time encouraging the development of the unique potentialities of each person and group in the community. At times the interaction of the religious movements has been narrow and destructive, the product of fearful and anxious men. At other times the interaction has enriched the experience of the churches and the city, the product of confident and trusting men.

Within the perspective of this study, the truth known by the various groups in Protestantism and Catholicism is always partial or fragmentary. Only the object of faith is one. The action of each religious group is a necessary or potential supplementation and correction of the other. The whole of Christianity is not to be captured or synthesized in one organization or one system of thought; its expression is to be found in the continuing interaction of the various movements in the church, each carrying out its task in its own way and in its own time, always aware of the limited nature of its witness and always confident in the whole life of the church which makes the partial work important. If real Christian community is to be achieved, no one organization or group of men within it can be thought to represent the universal; nor can one time or one generation of men—but only all times and generations—reveal the total meaning of living in truth and the likeness of God. Public policy within such a community will emerge bearing the stamp of no one dominant and overwhelming faith group, but the molding, strengthening action of men who have come to appreciate different, but complementary aspects of their faith.[1]

Recovery of the experience of Christian community depends upon recognition by both Protestants and Catholics of the dynamic character and the rich continuity of the Christian movement. This recognition is essential if men are to cherish and understand another aspect of Christianity than their own, if they are to avoid all neat schemes for dividing people into the "good" and the "bad" men. This recognition protects men against self-righteousness, while encouraging them to act vigorously within the truth they know, finding unity of thought and action in the frank, unsentimental and non-coercive contention of men who share faith in a God who sustains, judges and redeems them all.

As to the approaches to community by each religious movement this can be said in conclusion:

Roman Catholicism has conceived of community primarily in terms of the acceptance of the church's authority in areas of life it terms religious and moral—not through the discovery of common interests in the give and take among diverse associations. It has assumed that these moral and religious areas can be defined with a great deal of precision and that they determine the actions of men; and it has had high hopes for public unity in Paper City, because of the predominance of Catholics in the population. Most Catholic leaders have viewed religious relations on all important and substantive matters as involving victory, defeat or temporary compromise for the church's correct position, rather than as the continuing reformulation of the meaning of one's faith for men's changing experience out of the fires of criticism and witness from other faith groups.

The most persistent search of Protestantism, on the other hand—and we are speaking here in broad, general terms—has been for clear evidence and assurance that a vital diversity of religious and social groups will be maintained in the structure of the city. It has been somewhat more impressed than Catholicism with the inextricable connection between religion and other aspects of life, and with the difficulty of identifying Christian revelation with religious doctrine and moral law, of identifying God's grace with a particular institutional form and space. It has been less concerned with agreement on the precise issues of public debate and on the principles involved than with the conditions that would permit a creative and respectful interaction among diverse movements.

The Catholic leaders believe that Protestants have not faced up to the requirements of disciplined moral action and that they do not appreciate the rigorous nature of the encounter of men in the modern world. They believe that Protestants often cannot state clearly what they stand for and cannot bring adequate resources to the support and defense of a correct position. They press Protestants to face the tough problems of organization: of power and status of members, of placement of responsibility. They ask that sentimental affirmations of good will be supplemented by rigorous reasoning and by a sense of the importance of precision and detail in religious expression. What they see as dangerous Protestant diffusiveness is, for the Catholics, the end product of a refusal to face the problems of authoritative definition and expression of religious truth.

The Protestants believe, on the other hand, that the Catholic church misunderstands the way in which men come to know truth and to give assent to the truth discovered by others. Catholic leaders, in the Protestant view, make too pretentious claims to precise knowledge of correct moral action in complex situations, and to certain control of the efficacious channels of God's grace. Such misunderstanding is the major source, Protestants assert, for coercive group action harmful to a vital religious and cultural pluralism. Most Protestant leaders see in Protestant organization a greater tolerance of variety, a greater appreciation of the importance in social change of strong personalities, a greater sensitivity to social mobility of members, a greater tentativeness and ambiguity about the action of God in a particular situation. For Protestants these are the characteristics of a community open to new truth, flexible in action, responsive to process and motion.

The Protestants, unaccustomed to a minority position, have in recent years been so absorbed with the Catholic problem, with the influence of a movement that rejects its theology and denies its values, that they have not been able to look away from it, and to turn resolutely to those actions and affirmations that would need to be done and said, even if Catholicism were not a very powerful religious force.

The clergy, privately and publicly, speak more often as strangers to one another than as men sharing deep ultimate loyalties and common historical situations—so great has been Catholic disregard of all that is not labeled as Catholic, so thorough has been the Catholic separation of its leaders from other people, so complete has been the Protestant absorption in the problem of minority survival, so sensitive have Protestant clergy been to the Catholic charge of bigotry. Protestant leaders, while disagreeing with many of the assumptions of Catholicism, at least respect the movement. But most Catholic clergy, in contrast to their less critical laymen, could be said to look upon Protestant doctrinal and institutional expressions largely with pity and with impatience at restraints placed upon their action by the Protestant movement. The leaders of both sides betray ignorance of theological and social developments. And everywhere laymen are apparently indifferent to many of the issues that most concern the clergy—not because of the layman's lack of concern for religion, but because of his involvement in problems that seem more difficult and crucial to him.

This situation has its tragic elements and may be a reflection in part of the kind of religious structure in Paper City. "America's most Catholic city" has a Protestantism that often acts scared and ineffectual because of the unusually strong position, for America at least, of Catholicism. Paper City has in many ways a comparatively rigid and conservative Catholicism because of the state of Protestantism there. The most healthy society would be achieved where Roman Catholic and Protestant movements were both vitally represented and interacting in candor and mutual trust. This is not possible where either faith movement has become so powerful as to threaten the existence or vitality of the other.

The leaders of many of the most influential economic and political organizations of Paper City have come to view the impact of the churches on some social issues as divisive and emotional. Thus they wish to exclude religious discussion from the conduct of important affairs, particularly affecting those matters in which there are known differences of interpretation among the faiths. At best, many civic leaders give ritualistic observance to outward worship forms and honorific reference to general and vague principles—such as the "dignity of man," the "importance of individual morality and integrity in public life," "spiritual values above material ones"—thought to be favored by all the traditional religions. The sacrifice of profound religious conviction has been the price of social harmony. The chief use of religious identifications in economic enterprise has been to advance personal status amid strong competition on those levels of industry and business where technical or objective criteria of performance are not readily available.

The forebodings of the minority, as well as the confidence of the majority, can be overemphasized. We are not likely to be confronted in Paper City or in America with either a "Protestant culture" or a "Catholic culture" in any future that has continuity with the past we know. Paper City—like the rest of our nation—reflects the influence of the continuous dialogue of the faith groups. Catholicism, even in so favorable a climate as Paper City, is not increasing its comparative hold on the popular culture or on the policy-making centers; and it is comparative, not absolute, achievement that matters, particularly in a rapidly changing and growing society such as America's.

The interaction of Roman Catholics and Protestants in Paper City has led to serious re-examination of the nature of Christian community. Protestants have been brought by Catholic contention in the Sanger incident and other encounters to increased inquiry about the relation of organizational strength to love of God and man. Roman Catholics have been brought by Protestant witness to a greater understanding of the voluntary and fraternal aspects of their faith.

There are men in Paper City who are aware of the continuing contributions to community of both faith movements; they attempt to work out programs and policies on the basis of the dialogue between the religions. These are not men without faith, but men who are enabled by the kind of faith they possess to understand what is going on in the whole life of their city. These men sense, as this study has noted, the great stress of the Catholic church upon order, status, law, reason, discipline, organization, precision of religious expression. They sense that Protestantism brings to the dialogue a greater emphasis upon diversity, mobility, flexibility, sentiment, and individual freedom.

These are broad contrasts between the faiths. Americans should have no illusions that the contributions of Roman Catholicism and Protestantism to American culture are the same. There are significant differences, as there are significant likenesses, in the movements. It is also important that men see that these movements are not monolithic structures. Within Catholicism and Protestantism are groups with varying aspirations, and individuals who live with serious tensions between their own way of life (derived from exposure to a number of associations) and the faith group to which they belong. This variety makes possible a great range of involvement and action by men in their respective religious movements.

Terms such as "order" and "freedom" are symbols of relationships between institutions and people; their meanings are known only in the specific and comparative judgments men make about concrete situations, such as have been the subject of this book. There are no values or disvalues monopolized by one faith or the other. Much of Paper City Catholicism will appear to Catholics of other countries to be highly flexible, pluralistic and rapidly changing. Only in comparison to certain aspects of American Protestantism will it appear as more concerned with stability, permanence and status. And Paper City Protestantism will appear to Protestants in other sections of our country—sections where the faith is in a majority position and given to more easy talk of unity and harmony—as possessing an unusual concern for religious diversity and civil liberty. In both Protestantism and Catholicism there is an abundance of self-righteousness, of illusion and sentimentality about what is going on in the world.

There are no ready-made issues in which the clear lines of order and flexibility, status and mobility await their religious advocates. Each new issue in the common life of the city demands from all the hard search for facts, prayerful study of the relevant moral and religious insight, the creative decision which unites the continuities of the past and the aspirations for the future. For example, there are no neat denominational lines for the debate being waged in Christendom over the nature of Christian ethics and the manner in which religious convictions actually enter the decisions of men in public life.

In the life of Paper City there is evidence, fragmentary though it is, that collaborative and fruitful action among Protestants and Roman Catholics can and does occur on many public issues. This is possible both because men bring to public issues varied and complementary contributions out of their religious and social experience, and because they are wrestling with issues that are not denominational but must be faced by all movements and men.

In the debate over the nature of moral acts, those who stress an ethic of "natural law" or of "ultimate ends" and those who stress an ethic of "responsibility" or of "the situation" need not be regarded as supporters of positions that are "right" or "wrong." One position cannot be understood without the other; they do not exist in isolation. The emphasis on natural law and the emphasis on the situation both reflect the experiences of men in decision making; men fear the loss of personal structure and identity in the flux of experience as they fear the loss of responsiveness to new evidence and ideas in the concern for principle. The controversies between men holding these positions have at times been between Catholics and Protestants and at other times between men within the same religious movement.

There is no real understanding of Protestantism in Paper City without understanding of Catholicism, and no adequate meaning for Catholicism without knowledge of Protestantism. The leaders of these movements are often speaking in response to what they see in others, and out of understanding of themselves gained from the responses of others to what they say and do.

The spiritual arrogance which has afflicted Catholics and Protestants alike in their relations with each other and with non-Christian people has theological, historical and sociological roots, as we have seen in concrete detail. The certitude of ecclesiastical authorities about religious doctrine, present in both movements but more evident in Catholicism, has been carried over into philosophical and political assumptions.

The historical reasons for the arrogant vehemence of many Catholics may be found in the formative years of American Catholicism, when the faithful fought a difficult minority battle for recognition and independence from the majority, for a chance to hold onto heartfelt traditions and convictions as strangers in a new land. The majority Protestant faith has had to adjust to a change in its status and to the great influence of a movement which clearly rejected much that it held dear.

The sociological reasons for Catholic sensitivity to criticism have been centered in the frustrations of a movement aspiring to be the *ecclesia*, the church of all people, while torn by ethnic, national and class divisions. The Catholic church's defensive actions have often been born of an internal sense of weakness, not of power. They have been desperate measures of leaders to make good in America, which many saw as the last great stronghold of the faith against the spread of Communism. Many of the clergy have felt and acted like men who have little time to reflect, to study, to plan anew for the future, driven to put out the fires of secularism among their people and to plug up the gaps in leadership. The labor schools, although they may seem to result from grand strategy, were in reality the improvised and scattered efforts of a few men to do something about labor-management strife; they are now in need of revision toward a broader and deeper approach to lay vocational and social interests. The Catholic priests who ran the economic boycotts against the nonconformist Protestants were men who rightly sensed that their kind of ethnic-centered city and their kind of minority Catholic witness was passing. A superficial common front of Catholic leaders was maintained during such action, but the private reactions of suburban parish leaders indicated the beginning search for new modes of lay action.

The Protestant churches knew well that they were confronted by a movement which, despite its changing forms of action, represented tremendous power, discipline of organization, and a desire to provide the basic assumptions of the culture. The intentions and power centers of this fervor have often been misjudged, and nowhere more clearly than in the Sanger incident, when Protestant leaders failed in the midst of very real pressure to appeal effectively to forces within Catholicism that were unsympathetic to the direct action being taken by some Catholics. In a majority position, Catholicism has put to severe test the sociological expression of Protestant faith. Protestant fears that the power of this movement could be or would be directed to the elimination of Protestantism have not been borne out. But the price of its liberty of action, like that of any minority, has been clarity as to what are the reasons for its existence and courage to act upon them.

The theological sources of much abuse of doctrinal and moral principle will remain. Many are inherent in the kind of Christianity each movement represents. But there is evidence of renewed inquiry into the rich resources in the traditions of both religions for more adequate approaches to relating faith and culture. Many of the historical and sociological sources of Catholicism's decision to wall itself in from the intellectual and popular currents of American life are disappearing. The new generations of ethnic groups seek wider social and religious contacts, greater mobility of persons and ideas. Catholicism stands between old and new ways of relating herself to the world.

Protestantism is actually now the faith movement which faces the greatest challenge to its hopes for society and its understanding of the organization of the religious community. As Catholicism broadens its activity in the nation and looks less defensively on its minority status, Protestantism is having to decide whether it will fight a rear-guard action with tactics calculated simply to keep down Catholic influence in the world, or whether it will erect new organizational forms and policies—not to oppose another faith but to express its own genius.

Some of the Protestant churches have shown evidence of evolving an institutional form that makes the pastor more of a leader of a community of believers than a lone prophetic voice; here the congregation seek the religious meaning of its common life, rather than listening periodically to a charismatic leader who speaks the "truth." The importance of the pastor's personal leadership is not diminished but directed toward the corporate inquiry of the faithful.

Leaders of both faith groups have wanted, almost desperately at times, to speak with conviction and clarity to the ambiguities and intricacies of current events; but their routine professional responsibilities have so consumed their time and energy that they cannot do so. This is one of the terrible frustrations of the local clergy. Their morale suffers because they have not worked out with their congregations a satisfactory concept of the ministry, which would enable them to guide laymen in a serious grappling with the significance of the Christian faith for their vocational and public life. The laymen will not tell them about the actualities of professional and public life, or the laymen cannot find a setting within the life of the church in which these actualities are intimately and consistently faced.

Much of the talk of the ministry and the congregation about the church's role in public affairs has little to do with reality. There is talk, as we have seen, about "direct" and "indirect" means of church action, as if men can take faith and contemporary American politics seriously without involving themselves in partisan considerations of what party programs and activities are to be supported. There is talk of "spiritual" and "temporal" areas, as if the principles and dogmas of the theologians are developed outside history, their meaning known apart from the immersion of men of faith in political problems, in scientific data, and in the specialities of the professions. In the decisions of leaders of both movements there is a confluence of theology and politics, doctrine and organization, moral principle and social status. The important judgments of men in public affairs involve considerations of many factors—the popular climate of opinion, their own moral principles and values, technical data, and the demands of various groups and persons upon them.

There is a tremendous need for both religious movements to develop organizations and situations in which men experienced in theological inquiry, in the various behavioral and social sciences, and in the institutions of public life can explore together the significance of their faith. Such enterprises will not be possible if there is an excessive reliance upon dogmatic principles or if representatives of Christianity have a prideful scorn for the sincere search for truth of non-Christians. It is consonant with both Catholic and Protestant faith in God who is Lord of all to see serious criticism as an instrument for bringing Christians to an examination of their historical conscience and to an understanding of their teaching task in the contemporary world.

Many people will perhaps be dissatisfied with the conclusions drawn from this study. They will want—as did many persons in Paper City—simple solutions to such problems as whether Protestants should oppose Roman Catholicism and try to keep the movement from becoming bigger, and whether it is a bad thing for Protestantism and America when Catholicism achieves a dominant position.

It would be a distortion of the social and religious actualities of Paper City—and, in so far as this community is representative, of our American culture—for a person to decide that he must now be *for* or *against* Catholicism or Protestantism. The choice to be a Protestant, at its best, need not be a choice against Catholicism; and the choice is a very imprecise one, for there are many kinds of Protestantism, as there are kinds of Catholicism. There are significant choices to be made within one's own faith as to the nature of the Ultimate Being and as to the kind of religious relations one desires. There are important choices to be made as to which groups will be encouraged in other faiths by action taken within one's own religious movement.

The dialogue between the faith groups can be affirmed as a significant source of truth, something to which a man contributes his own fragmentary and partial religious knowledge with candor and humility; or he may shun the places where the dialogue most forthrightly occurs, viewing it as a threat to faith. A man may confess what he knows within one movement as a contribution to the Great Conversation, accepting the necessity of corporate study and discipline, of independent and serious reflections; or he may come into a community of faith as a ritualist, looking for a superficial conformity to a popular means of social identification.

Television, radio, movies, magazines, business, political parties and the popular press all use as never before the moral and religious symbols and phrases of our churches. The clergy have greater audiences than at any time in the nation's history. Financial support for serious religious inquiry is more readily available than ever before. Perhaps the central issue now before religious leaders is whether this opportunity will be used to illumine the nature of the whole Christian movement, with its significant differences, tensions and harmonies, or whether the content of our historic faiths will be further reduced to vague, sentimental creeds endorsed by everyone, the symbols not of national unity and conviction but of national drift and complacency.

Appendix

The Point of View

There have been many inquiries into the faith and power of religious groups in American society by men with little evident appreciation of the importance of their own point of view in selection of facts and interpretation of their meaning. This I hope to avoid. A rational and scientific approach to a subject as controversial as Roman Catholic-Protestant relations begins with a consciousness of one's own point of view and an appreciation by the people to whom one speaks of its profound importance in a study. No claim is made that this study achieves full knowledge of Roman Catholic-Protestant relations as they actually are in a community, but a serious claim is made that objective relations of the faiths are being portrayed, basic relations of men analyzed and genuine empathy for the various positions expressed by the leaders achieved.

The discipline which most informs the methods and theories of this study is the sociology of religion. This is a field which has as its purpose description of "the interrelationship of religion and society and the forms of interaction which take place between them." [1]

The assumptions made in such a field as to the nature of society and the relation of religion to it are crucial. Every man has certain assumptions about these which have been formed from previous observation and reflection. A sociologist of religion formulates these assumptions more consciously perhaps than some other men and looks upon them more tentatively as operating hypotheses which aid description of the world, and which may be restated or abandoned if additional facts make them appear to be inadequate generalizations.[2]

The term "society" as used here points to the existence of a system of human relations in which persons, groups and institutions have some authentic autonomy, as well as some ordered, meaningful and mutually conditioning relationships. The Protestant and Roman Catholic movements which are the center of attention cannot be accurately described simply as aggregates of individuals with an entirely private, separate and static life of their own. Nor can the religious movements or the society in which they live be understood as monolithic wholes, determining the character of the individuals and groups within them.

The book in every phase of its analysis gives attention to the *structure* of the whole community and of the religious movements, so that distinctive characteristics and arrangements of the basic social units are noted. It seeks to describe accurately the *patterns of meaning*, the aspirations and purposes by which the groups identify themselves, interpret particular situations and deal with others. But the principal emphasis is upon society and history as a dynamic process in which Protestantism and Catholicism are most significantly studied at those points where *interactions* and interrelationships occur. The persisting structures and patterns of meaning are important, to be sure, and they in large measure transcend the process, but the priests and preachers who provide the chief dialogue of this book, and the Catholic and Protestant churches which provide the major institutional focus of the study, have their effects in their actions and interactions. In the relations of Protestants and Roman Catholics, beliefs are tested and more adequately understood; positions are clarified and reconstituted; power drives are reinforced, checked and molded; differences and common concerns are discovered.

The fundamental problem of society as seen from this perspective is the determination of the manner in which various interests and vitalities in human existence are to be integrated and related to one another and to the whole of social life. This problem may be summarized in the phrase "the quest for unity-in-diversity." It is in the context of this central problem of society, as faced by a particular community in America, that the relations of Roman Catholic and Protestant churches are dealt with here. What are the conditions of autonomy which each religious institution demands for itself and grants to others, and what are the terms of its co-operation and association with other groups? What do Protestant and Catholic leaders identify as disintegrative forces in American culture, and how do they seek to deal with them in the reintegration of society?[3] What are the contributions or hindrances of the churches to the attempts of laymen to reconcile various interests in the achievement of policies in business, labor and politics?

The resources of the classic or basic works in the sociology of religion in Western society can be utilized to the greatest possible extent in dealing with such questions, since they have usually seen the theme of cultural unity and pluralism as the central one.[4]

As to this book's approach to the relation of religion to society, we are assuming here that what men identify as religious experience and seek to express in worship, doctrine and organization can and does have some force, dynamics and autonomy of its own. It is not to be dealt with as inevitably or entirely a reflection of social and economic events. On the other hand, Protestantism and Catholicism, it is clear, cannot be understood apart from their social contexts as movements which somehow transcend culture. We are deeply concerned with social classes, ethnic cleavages and economic and political interests in their relation to the Roman Catholic and Protestant churches. For example, church memberships are analyzed as to their ethnic and class nature and the bearing of this on the finances, the parishes boundaries and the educational programs of the churches noted.[5]

It should perhaps be pointed out that the approach to religion used here need not involve the author as a sociologist of religion in trying to prove the claims of the churches that their action has its sources, in part at least, beyond or outside society, or that their particular understanding of God's action in the world is more adequate than that of other religious movements. I may live these assumptions as articles of faith and in some roles and settings confess them freely, but while working as a sociologist I am seeking primarily to describe other men accurately as to whether they live by such beliefs or not, and what importance these and associated beliefs have in the understanding of the situation investigated. It is difficult to determine the line, if ever one can, between what one derives from the reason and discipline of a science and what from the consecrated wisdom of a religious faith. They are not utilized in tandem fashion but transform each other at once. The religious convictions of the researcher aid in calling attention to data which he might have ignored without experience in at least one of the faith groups—in my case, Protestantism—involved in the city; and these convictions and experience also may serve as a source of distortion of the reality one seeks to describe.[6] But there is no way really to abandon the discipline of a science or the faith of a religion once they become a part of a man. They can only be utilized for what strength there is in them in giving meaning and significance to what one does and made explicit in so far as one understands himself and his subject.

The people of the city described here, like you and me, make decisions day after day about the kind of society they want and the kind of faith and church which is most satisfactory to them. Even the failure to make deliberate and conscious decisions or to understand the alternatives of action available constitutes a choice. These decisions are not made in one big moment, but in a whole series and combinations of acts over time. They reveal, as we have seen, some continuity and pattern expressive of the basic character of the person and institution. These habits of thought and preferences are developed always within some community of faith; acts affecting the church and society are never taken by men apart from loyalties, predispositions and social experience that matter deeply to them.

Few people are converted out of one faith group into another by some great rational and emotional act. Men, by and large, are reared and nurtured in a faith and in a society to which a number of faith groups have contributed, and in which a number of faith groups continuously interact. In time the interpretations of reality of a particular faith group become more meaningful to them than the symbols of other faiths. They can hold this preference not as some purely subjective whim, but as an expression of the deepest reality outside themselves which they know, and as a guide to their understanding of other people. They may live within their community of faith aware that theirs is not the final or sure wisdom as to God's purposes, and that His actions are not confined to one people, nor His words to the aspirations of one institution.

Notes on Methodology

Sources Used in Securing Data on Church Membership (Chapter 3)

This study has relied upon three major sources for church membership data. First, the United States Census of Religious Bodies for 1916, 1926 and 1936 have been utilized. Reports are available for the total membership of Paper City Roman Catholic churches reporting in these three years, but not for individual churches. Reports are also available for all "old line" Protestant denominations in Paper City, but are lacking for four small sect groups: Jehovah's Witnesses, Polish Evangelistic Assembly, Polish Bible Students and Gospel Hall. The membership of these groups at no time in these three census years totalled more than 150 (Tables III and VI).

Second, the Roman Catholic information on individual churches in Paper City for 1936 and 1946 is based upon the data supplied by the diocese chancery, its data having been obtained from annual reports sent by Roman Catholic pastors to their bishop (Table V).

Third, data is utilized from Protestant denominational yearbooks for the years 1926, 1936 and 1946. The Protestant yearbook information for 1945 (data for 1946 was not available at the time this aspect of the study was done) is supplemented or revised somewhat in light of interviews with pastors, consultation of church records and reports to state associations (Table VI).

The data from these three sources cannot be regarded as derived from entirely the same categories for each church. The Roman Catholic data is fairly uniform; it is composed of those who have been baptized Roman Catholics or have been converted to the faith and practice the Roman Catholic religion. The minimum requirements for "practice" of his religion, according to the chancellor of the diocese in which Paper City is located, is that the Roman Catholic member perform his Easter duties—the confession of sins and participation in communion. This data, therefore, includes children born to Roman Catholic parents or parent, baptized but not yet confirmed. It does not include Roman Catholics who have been confirmed but have not performed minimum religious duties for the year. (There are minor discrepancies in the Roman Catholic data. The 1936 census data indicates five Roman Catholic churches reporting out of ten in Paper City. The Greek Roman Catholic Church reports to another diocese. But the total of these five churches is only 432 less than the figures of the chancery for the same year with all Roman Catholic churches reporting.)

The Protestant church membership data appearing in the census and in denominational yearbooks is not exactly comparable to the Roman Catholic, although interviews with ministers indicate that in most cases the data represents the pastor's or clerk's effort to include in the total: (a) children in the church, whether simply enrolled in Sunday school or baptized into the church; and (b) the adults who at one time by letter or confession of faith joined the church, even if they *are not* residents in the community and attend church activities only once or twice a year. Such data is roughly comparable to Roman Catholic data. In cases where the researcher collected church membership data directly, rather than from yearbooks or the census, he sought to utilize the same categories which had been used by the church in previous reports. This was so that 1926, 1936 and 1946 data would have some comparable characteristics. In cases where no clear precedent existed in past reports, the researcher sought to make the data as comparable as possible to Roman Catholic criteria of membership.

Obviously none of the source of religious membership data used here is wholly satisfactory for research purposes. Perhaps no area of sociology of religion is more time-consuming and less productive of accurate results.

The Role of the Churches in Man's Salvation

In Chapters 4, 5 and 6, the areas of agreement and disagreement between Roman Catholic and Protestant religious leaders and laymen over doctrines and rites are described. The inquiry was largely concerned with the theology expressed in Paper City by the leaders to laymen through sermons, instruction, popular pamphlets, comic books, periodicals and conversations rather than with statements originating outside Paper City in centers of theological scholarship of the various churches. This emphasis did not exclude the use for background information of official and scholarly doctrinal statements prepared outside the community. The doctrinal statements by scholars within the national or international religious institutions have great precision and balance but they do not necessarily reflect the doctrine which the laymen receive in Paper City from their religious leaders and from the literature recommended by them.

Data was, therefore, chiefly secured from lengthy interviews (formal and informal) with pastors and laymen, from attitude questionnaires, copies of sermons, observation of religious services, and popular pamphlets, leaflets and periodicals recommended by pastors in the community to laymen. All Roman Catholic and Protestant pamphlets quoted in this chapter were recommended by the pastors and distributed to laymen through the churches.

The content analysis of literature undertaken here is what Bernard Berelson (*Content Analysis in Communication Research,* Glencoe, Illinios, 1952, p. 18) terms a qualitative study of the substance of religious literature. There is little attempt to measure space given to various themes or to describe the precise form they were given. Rather the intent is to describe what was said by various publications upon a limited number of themes over an extended period of time.

Methods Used in Study of Socioeconomic Class Structure of the City and Churches (Chapter 13)

The occupational structure used in Chapter 13 is very similar to the one developed for purposes of another type of research by Raymond Pearl. See his article, "A Classification and Code of Occupations," *Human Biology,* Vol. 5, p. 493. Pearl grouped all occupations under three headings: (I) Owners, managers, officials and professional men; (II) Skilled and semiskilled professional workers; (III) Laborers—unskilled and semiskilled.

The nine occupational groupings of the 1940 census are not satisfactory for the class and occupational alignments recognized by community and religious leaders. The census categories are as follows: (1) professional and semiprofessional (reported separately); (2) proprietors, managers and officials; (3) clerical, sales and kindred workers; (4) craftsmen, foremen and kindred workers; (5) operatives and kindred workers; (6) protective service workers; (7) service workers except protective; (8) laboring, including farm: (9) occupation not reported.

The first two categories are too broad to be included in the upper class as Paper City people conceive of that class. The semiprofessionals and the small proprietors, minor business and government officials ranked in these first two census groups lack the income, prestige, and community leadership to be considered upper class.

OCCUPATIONS OF EMPLOYED WORKERS IN PAPER CITY
(U. S. CENSUS, 1940)

	Total		*Male*	*Female*
Population	53,750			
Total Employed Workers	19,136		12,711	6,425
Professional	1,342		549	793
Semiprofessional	343	White	143	200
Farmers, Farm Manag.	36	Collar	34	2
Proprietors, Managers, Officers, Ex. Farmers	1,641	37.0%	1,457	184
Clerical, Sales, Kindred	3,726		1,983	1,743
Crafts, Foremen, Kindred	2,444	Indust.	2,374	70
Operatives, Kindred	6,351	46.0%	4,150	2,201
Domestic Service	612	Service	17	595
Service, Ex. Domestic	1,610	11.6%	1,070	540
Laborers, Ex. Farm	794		763	31
Other, and Not Reported	237		171	66

The categories of semiprofessional, clerical, sales, craftsmen, foremen and protective service workers are roughly similar to Paper City's middle class, comprising 43. 7 per cent of the employed workers. The other categories (manual operatives, service workers other than protective, and laborers) comprising 40.6 per cent of the employed workers serve somewhat satisfactorily to indicate Paper City's lower or working class.

Objective economic criteria of occupation, income, material possessions, place of residence and type of dwelling were employed chiefly in locating a church member's economic class in the community. Occupation was the principal index. The organization of these criteria in relation to class groups and evaluation of their relative importance was worked out by the researcher with twelve representatives of all the major occupation, religious and ethnic groupings in the city. Families widely known in various areas of the city as representative of various class positions were indicated by this group. This work served to guide a group of 62 raters of the membership of all the churches and sects in the city.

In each church the pastor (in a few cases a curate or religious worker) and at least two laymen were involved. The laymen chosen were men and women who appeared stable in their economic position, who had been at least ten years in residence and who had knowledge of many, if not all, of the families in the membership of their respective churches.

For the data of this chapter, ethnic and religious criteria of class were not introduced deliberately by the raters, in an effort to arrive at a socioeconomic structure. The raters were for the most part rating people of their own religion and ethnic affiliation.

In the very large churches the first and last one hundred names arranged alphabetically on each church roll were rated and then the remainder sampled (one in ten) for any significant variations. In one Roman Catholic parish only an estimate of the pastor from general observations, with criteria provided by the researcher, and random sampling with aid of laymen were possible. In another parish, the pastor gave no guidance at all in development of the class structure of the church. In all the churches, the ratings were largely done internally, that is, by members and leaders of a church estimating the class position of their own members from criteria provided by the researcher and the board of twelve described above. These ratings were checked with raters outside the church in each case. Rankings were not relative to other members in the church but to the people in the entire community.

Methods of class analysis with characteristics similar to this study's have been used by or recommended by a number of sociologists: August B. Hollingshead, *Elmtown's Youth: the Impact of Social Classes on Adolescents* (New York, 1949), pp. 26-30. G. Wilson, "A Qualitative Study of Rural Depopulation in a Single Township: 1900-1930," *American Journal of Sociology*, Vol. 33 (1933), pp. 210-221; George A. Lundberg, "The Measurement of Socio-Economic Status," *American Sociological Review*, Vol. 5 (1940), pp. 29-39.

CHART OF DOCTRINAL CHARACTERISTICS OF THE RELIGIOUS INSTITUTIONS

Roman Catholic Church	*Protestant Churches*	*Protestant Sects*
	SALVATION	
What man is saved from:		
Man is saved from sin, death, hell for life eternal with God. But salvation principally a heaven-or-hell proposition.	Man is saved principally from sin or a continuing tendency to self-centeredness which frustrates his life here and now.	Man is saved from sin, death, hell, but chiefly hell and sin. The latter keeps him from living the law of the Gospel and being prepared for heaven.
The role of Christ:		
The role of Christ is chiefly to win for us the power of meriting eternal reward, to bear the penalty of man's original sin, and to establish His Church.	The role of Christ is chiefly to provide a moral example for man, a source of strength for leading a better life. Other aspects of atoning work alluded to but usually not developed.	Christ did all that is necessary for man's salvation, but chiefly he paid for our sins. Man must only believe.
Extent of Christ's sufficiency:		
Christ established His Church with power to continue His work and to bring spiritual progress through the impartation of grace in the sacraments administered by the priests.	The sufficiency of Christ is asserted, but members are reminded Christ has no hands but theirs and that the church is the place where the Word of God is preached.	Christ has the power to save man. He needs no institutional instruments with sanctions and special works. No one need come between man and God but Christ.
Means of salvation:		
The act of faith in the church which sets man on the way to salvation is God's gift. But man must do his part in receiving this gift. He can increase grace by good acts which will merit eternal reward. Man does good works in part because he knows they will earn him salvation.	Several affirmations are made. Salvation is by faith, not works; man must show a moral determination to follow Christ's example; if man does good deeds he will be rewarded in this life with happiness and peace. Emphasis varies with minister.	Chief assertion: salvation is a gift of God received through faith. Man can never do enough to merit salvation. Personal holiness is a sign one is saved. This may become a form of salvation by works but basic principle is that man acts good out of gratitude to God.
	RELIGIOUS AUTHORITY	
Certainty of knowledge of truth:		
Man may be certain of the exact truth, for it has been given to God's church.	Man's relation to God is precarious and uncertain. God's exact and entire will cannot be known by one person or institution, though he can be certain by faith of God's revelation in Christ.	Certitude of religious knowledge can be found in literal adherence to Scriptures.
Test of truth:		
The ultimate test of religious truth is not the Scriptures, but the infallible teaching of the Catholic church. The Pope when intending to bind the whole church on an article of faith cannot err.	Christ is the ultimate judge and no institution should claim final, infallible truth. The Bible should be freely interpreted by the individual Christian in a fellowship of believers. Literalistic interpretations should be avoided. In practice, independence of individual judgment is valued so highly, a vast variety of religious beliefs is tolerated; little emphasis is placed on institutional resources or discriminating between authorities in discovery of truth.	The Scriptures are the only standard of faith and court of appeal. Verbal inspiration of the Scriptures is affirmed. Interpretation is legalistic and literal with the judgment of the sect absolutized. Too great an independence of interpretation may lead to self-exclusion.

Roman Catholic Church	*Protestant Churches*	*Protestant Sects*
	NATURE OF THE CHURCH	
Norm for religious community: Ideal is a community of sacraments and authority, with a strong, centralized leadership possessing sacramental and teaching powers. Essential polity of the church is also given by God and a matter of deep concern.	Ideal is a community of faith and grace whose cohesiveness and influence springs from individual response to the Word of God, without concern over polity or organization. In practice no instruments for united and disciplined action are created.	Ideal is a community of saints who have evidenced the piety and doctrinal correctness of the founders. Lack of concern for influence on the world outside the sect makes unnecessary development of organization with strong leadership.
Sacraments: The church objectifies possession of religious truth and control of the supernatural through manipulation of the sacraments by the priesthood. In the Mass the natural elements change in order for Christ to be present.	God is present in the church, and its symbols express that presence. Yet no object of the church can be said to be divine, or changed in its essential nature by being an instrument of God's grace. No institution can claim that its works or means are fully divine. This claim belongs to God.	Objectification or location of God's grace in a specific, visible reality is opposed. Faith is always a personal, inward experience. Symbols are used conservatively.
Importance of institution: Chief emphasis of clergy in relations with laymen is the importance of the institutional channel for God's grace and necessity for individual to relate himself to the institution, to forward God's plan of salvation.	Ambivalent position held toward church as an institution. Man's moral obligation to support the church is affirmed (as one supports the family) and individual access to God so esteemed that little balance between community and personal claims is achieved.	The doctrine of justification by faith is taken to have corollary belief in man's sufficient relation to God without need of or concern for institutions.
	CULTUS	
Sanctuary: The church building where men worship contains a sanctuary which is "the home of Jesus." Here men can assuredly locate and find God.	The Word of God is taught and symbolized in the church. The attitude due the worship center is "decorum" and reverence for the Word of God wherever it is voiced.	God is present in a church building in a fashion no different from that of any other place where men who reverence him live and witness.
Responsibility for conduct of rites: The supreme act of the cultus is accomplished by the priest whose procedure is legislated by the episcopate. Highly ritualistic service, with participation by members precisely described. Restrained and passive participation.	Centralization of responsibility for conduct of services in professional leaders, but with their duties carried out with a combination of routine formality and personal warmth. Restrained and passive participation by members whose major responsibility is to listen to what is said.	Mutuality of discernment of religious truth and priesthood of all believers expressed by general participation in service, without professionalized leadership. Fervent and spontaneous participation by almost all members.
	ETHICS	
Standards for membership: Sacramental community embracing all those who participate in the sacraments and people both of perfectionist and of cultural morality.	Community of grace, embracing all who are socially compatible, accepting conformity to culture-centered ethic.	Community of saints, excluding those deemed morally unworthy.

	Roman Catholic Church	*Protestant Churches*	*Protestant Sects*
		ETHICS (CONTINUED)	
Recruitment of members:	Membership recruited largely by birth but with comparatively systematic and careful indoctrination before rituals of acceptance observed.	Combination of ritualistic signing of covenants and confessions of faith with generally casual administered education into beliefs. Recruitment largely by birth and transfer from other "old line" churches.	Voluntary, confessional basis of membership. Recruitment by personal evangelism. Emphasis on religious experience, speaking in tongues, etc. as sign of true membership.
Ethical sanctions:	Major stress on reward of eternal life, but with temporal rewards also part of the moral system.	Interest primarily in a successful, happy, charitable future in this world. Life here is as much a part of the Kingdom of God as life in the hereafter.	Stress on eternal reward, on being prepared for death, "for no man knows the hour."
Moral psychology:	Psychology of dominance and success, of power and certitude, combined with a minority strategy of isolating members in a hostile world.	Mixed psychology—in some areas one of dominance and success and in others of inferiority, restriction and restiveness.	Minority psychology with a sense of being discriminated against and segregated for one's religion.
"Treasury of Merits":	Some men can do more good deeds than required of them by God. These are works of supererogation. The extra merits can be applied to the account of sinners through indulgences.	Men cannot do more than God requires. Before Christ, one knows only humility for his moral failure. No extra merits available.	Men never do enough to build up extra moral credits with God. But they must do what good deeds they can.
Nature of man:	Optimism about nature of man in sense that original sin did not involve all of man. Particularly optimistic about man's reason and ability to discern truth within the tradition of the church and progress in state of grace through properly received sacraments.	Usually exhortation to follow Jesus and progress toward a better life assumes more good than evil in man and ability to grow in grace. Also witness to life-long tendency to sin which in some cases becomes basis of acquiescence in cultural ethic. Original sin involved whole of man.	Deep sense of persistence and depth of sin but optimism about power of God to help believers lead a good life and to forgive guilt.
Power of Christ on earth:	The way of salvation revealed by Christ is already instituted with great power and efficacy by the church.	Claim for Christ's power to draw men to the good life is for many leaders close to the Catholic view. Others feel more strongly the rejection of God's revelation by man.	The eschatological element is strong, with sense of Christ's coming in power as imminent but not yet accomplished.
Moral exactitude:	Church has taken over natural morality and claims knowledge of right and wrong, down to minute details of conduct in both personal and social areas.	Claim of an ethic of love expressed by Christ's life and death which is beyond or breaks through rules and laws of conduct. Uneasy in detailing right conduct for fear of Christianizing particular virtues. Becomes basis for evading discipline of precise statement of position on particular issues.	A precise, legalistic ethic for personal life centering in certain virtues, many of which are class requirements—frugality, industry, humility, temperance, truthfulness, tithing, non-participation in worldly sins of dancing, movies, etc.

ETHICS (CONTINUED)

Roman Catholic Church	*Protestant Churches*	*Protestant Sects*
Levels of morality:		
Two-level morality—one for laymen, one for religious vocations. Also two area morality—natural and supernatural. Revealed, supernatural laws of God in Scriptures are added to natural laws by reason. Love is one of the supernatural virtues. The Ten Commandments and "six precepts" of the church are the major obligations for laymen. With some priests and laymen, morality becomes a simple *quid pro quo* affair between man and God—man does a good deed and God rewards.	All men live under one absolute demand revealed in Christ—to love God and neighbor. Therefore, no dual morality is possible. Laymen must seek to live same ethic of perfection in daily work as minister. The effort to live the ethic of love transforms all virtues and areas of life. However, the application of the love ethic results often in enforcement of cultural and class demands.	Men are bound by the commands of Christ summarized in the Sermon on the Mount. The obligation to perfection is upon all.
Social ethics:		
Church has an ethic for society with specific recommendations for its structuring. Actually, clergy accept the rational ethics of laymen in political and economic areas except for issues closely affecting the institutional life of the church.	Ideal of personal perfection is preached, but no exclusion or censure of members for failure is practiced. Moral standards of upper and middle class are dominant among laymen. Clergy has not developed an ethic for society but efforts are made to relate personal morals to social issues.	Strict Scriptural standards for a perfectionistic, self-centered ethic at odds with the general community mores. No ethic for society and no effort made to relate personal morals to social issues.

Tables

TABLE I

PERCENTAGE INCREASE IN POPULATION FOR PAPER CITY, STATE AND NATION (1910-1950)*

Year	*Paper City*	*State*	*Nation*
1900 to 1910	26.3	20.0	21.0
1910 to 1920	4.3	14.4	14.9
1920 to 1930	−6.1	10.3	16.1
1930 to 1940	−4.9	1.6	7.2
1940 to 1950	1.7	8.7	14.9

* Statistics based on population reports of the United States Bureau of the Census.

TABLE II

SUMMARY OF RELIGIOUS POPULATION DATA ON PAPER CITY (1916, 1926, 1936, AND 1946)*

RELIGIOUS MEMBERSHIP

Year	*Population*	*Rom. Cath.*	*Prot.*	*Jews*	*Others*	*Total*
1916	60,742	34,503	6,694	100	400	41,697
1926	61,249	39,052	8,916	2,000	359	50,301
1936	55,578	35,118	8,891	1,870	268	46,147
1946	56,487	37,264	7,164	1,900	277	46,605

	PER CENT		PER CENT OF TOTAL RELIGIOUS MEMBERSHIP WHO ARE:			
Year	*Rel. Mem.*	*Not R.M.*	*R.C.*	*Prot.*	*Jews*	*Others*
1916	68.6	31.4	82.7	16.1	0.2	1.0
1926	82.1	17.9	77.6	17.7	4.0	0.7
1936	83.0	17.0	76.1	19.3	4.1	0.6
1946	82.0	18.0	79.8	17.6	4.0	0.5

* Data from United States Census of Religious Bodies for years 1916, 1926, and 1936 unless otherwise indicated. Roman Catholic data for 1946 from chancery records. For explanation of Protestant data for 1946, see Appendix. Total population data supplied by "Reports of the Water Board," *Municipal Register of Holyoke*, 1916, 1926, 1936, 1946.

If 1936 data were calculated from chancery records rather than United States Census data the statistics would be changed only slightly as follows: per cent of religious membership 80.6; per cent of nonreligious membership 19.4; per cent of total religious membership who are Roman Catholic 75.8, Protestants 19.3, Jews 4.0, others 0.6.

TABLE II (CONTINUED)

Year	R.C.	Prot.	Jews	Others		R.C.	Prot.
	PER CENT OF POPULATION WHO ARE:				PERCENTAGE INCREASES AND DECREASES IN PROPORTION TO TOT. POP.		
1916	56.8	11.0	0.2	0.7	1916-26	12.3	33.0
1926	63.8	14.6	3.3	0.5	1926-36	−0.9	9.5
1936	63.2	16.0	3.4	0.5	1936-46	3.7	−20.6
1946	65.6	12.7	3.0	0.4	1916-46	15.4	15.5

TABLE III

CHURCH MEMBERSHIP IN PAPER CITY, ACCORDING TO CENSUS REPORTS (1936, 1926 AND 1916)

	1936	*1926*	*1916*
Protestant	8,891	8,916	6,694
Roman Catholic	35,118	39,052	34,503
Christian Scientist	93	83	—
Greek Orthodox	175	250	400
Jewish	1,870	2,000	100
Protestant			
		67 (Negro)	
Baptist	1,153	1,110	1,072
Brethren	38	38	—
Congregational Christian	3,650	3,605	2,684
Evangelical and Reformed	150	—	—
Lutheran	1,600	1,500	677
Methodist Episcopal	459	511	691
African Methodist Episcopal	88	30	—
Presbyterian	650	665	400
Protestant Episcopal	981	1,084	610
Reformed in United States	—	175	165
Salvation Army	104	84	—
Theosophical	—	26	—
Unitarian	18	21	300
All Other	—	—	95

TABLE IV

RELIGIOUS ORGANIZATIONS OTHER THAN ROMAN CATHOLIC AND PROTESTANT IN PAPER CITY (1946)*

Name of Church	*Date of Organization*	*Members 1946*	*1936*	*1926*
Christian Scientist	1912	95	93	83
Theosophical Society	1899	—	—	26
Greek Orthodox	1917	182	175	250
B'nai Zion Congregation of the Sons of Zion (Jewish)	1902	1,400	1,000	1,000
Raidphi-Sholum (Jewish)	1904	500	870	1,000
Totals		2,177	2,138	2,359

* Statistics from the United States Census of Religious Bodies for 1936 and 1926. Data for 1946 from local records of religious organizations.

TABLE V

ROMAN CATHOLIC CHURCHES IN PAPER CITY (1946, 1936)*

Name of Church	*Date Organized*	*Members 1946*	*1936*
English Speaking:			
St. Jerome	1856	3,561	3,379
Sacred Heart	1878	6,519	6,124
Holy Rosary	1887	2,127	1,890
Holy Cross	1905	4,900	5,135
Holy Family	1900	500	360
Blessed Sacrament	1913	2,485	2,100
French:			
Precious Blood	1869	5,011	5,119
Perpetual Help	1890	3,600	3,250
Immaculate Conception	1903	3,456	3,324
Polish:			
Mater Dolorosa	1900	5,000	4,000
Greek:			
St. Michael	1923	105*	100
Totals:		37,214	34,781

* Statistics in this table have been gathered from figures reported by the individual churches to the chancery of the diocese and reported by the chancellor to the author, with the exception of the figures for the Greek Catholic Church which are reported to another diocese and were supplied by the priest of the church.

TABLE VI

PROTESTANT CHURCHES IN PAPER CITY (1945, 1936, 1926)*

Name of Church	*Date Organized*	*Members* 1945	1936	1926
First Baptist	1803	398	347	1,100
Second Baptist	1849	730	706	
Bethlehem Community (Bapt.)	1945	46 (1947)	—	—
First Congregational	1799	528	629	614
Second Congregational	1849	1,172	1,958	1,755
Grace Congregational	1894	1,044	1,076	1,185
Evangelical Lutheran (Mo.)	1867	1,021	969	800
First Methodist	1853	635	358	702
African Methodist Episcopal	1924	—	88	30
First Presbyterian	1885	618	630	885
St. Paul's Episcopal	1863	624	718	660
St. Luke's Mission (Episc.)	1942	15	—	—
Reformed Church in U. S.	1888	134	152	168 (1928)
Salvation Army	1890	30	35	30
Gospel Hall	1923	40	30	40
Polish Evangelistic Assembly	1933	35	5	—
Polish Bible Study Group	1935	15	12	—
Jehovah's Witnesses	1936	79	26	—
Unitarian	1874		18	No record
Totals		7,164	7,757	7,969

* Statistics in this table for 1936 and 1926 have been gathered from reports by individual churches to their denominational yearbooks with the exception of the data for the last six churches and for the Reformed Church in U. S. in 1936 which were supplied by local religious leaders or by local church records. The statistics for 1945 are derived from sources explained on pages 381-382.

TABLE VII

COMPARISON OF DATA FOR TOTAL PROTESTANT CHURCH MEMBERSHIP IN PAPER CITY (1936, 1926)

	1936	*1926*
Total from yearbook reports plus local record for small denominations not reporting to yearbooks	7,757	7,969
Total from census reports	8,891	8,916
Total using highest data for each church from yearbook, census or local record	9,040	9,236

COMPARISON OF DATA FOR TOTAL ROMAN CATHOLIC CHURCH MEMBERSHIP IN PAPER CITY (1936)

Chancery Records	34,781
Census Records	35,118

TABLE VIII

RELIGIOUS CENSUS DATA FOR PAPER CITY AND STATE (1940)*

	PER CENT OF RELIGIOUS MEMBERSHIP	PER CENT OF TOTAL RELIGIOUS MEMBERSHIP			PER CENT OF POPULATION WHO ARE:		
		R.C.	*Prot.*	*Jew*	*R.C.*	*Prot.*	*Jew*
Paper City	85	76	19	5	65	16	4
State	60	65	24	9	39	15	6

* Statistics based on study done by Massachusetts State Council of Churches from reports of the United States Bureau of the Census.

TABLE IX

RELIGIOUS CENSUS DATA FOR PAPER CITY AND NATION (1916, 1926, 1945)*

Year	*Place*	*Per Cent of Religious Membership*	*Percentage of Total Population*	
			R.C.	*Prot.*
1916	Paper City	68.6	56.8	11.0
1916	Nation	42.0	16.0	24.0
1926	Paper City	82.1	63.8	14.6
1926	Nation	46.5	15.8	26.9
1946	Paper City	82.0	65.6	12.7
1944	Nation	52.5	17.0	31.5

* The national percentages are from an unpublished study by the Committee for Religious Liberty of the Federal Council of Churches of Christ in America, based on a study of United States Census data, church yearbooks for 1943-44 and the *Official Catholic Directory*. If the Roman Catholic percentage for 1944 is calculated on the national population data given in the *Official Catholic Directory*, it would be 18.0, since this population data is lower than that of the United States Census. In the table the *Official Catholic Directory* was used only for Roman Catholic data. The year 1936 is not used since it was very inadequate in reporting Protestant church membership, particularly among sect groups.

TABLE X

BIRTHS IN PAPER CITY, STATE AND NATION (1940)*

Place	*Births per 1,000 Women 15-44 Years of Age*	*Births per 1,000 Married Women 15-44 Years of Age*
Paper City	54.8	113.7
State	62.5	121.9
Nation	73.7	121.0

* *Sixteenth Census of the United States, 1940.* Data recorded by residence.

TABLE XI

BIRTHS AND DEATHS IN PAPER CITY AND NATION (1940)*
(PER 1,000 POPULATION)

Place	*Births*	*Deaths*
Paper City	13.5	11.8
State	15.2	11.8
United States	17.9	10.8

* *Sixteenth Census of the United States, 1940.* These figures are based on statistics recorded by residence rather than place of occurrence.

TABLE XII

PERCENTAGE INCREASE IN POPULATION BY AGE GROUPS FOR PAPER CITY AND STATE (1900-1950)*

Period	*Under 5 years*	*5-9 years*	*10-14 years*	*15-19 years*	*20-44 years*	*45-64 years*	*65 yrs. & over*
PAPER CITY							
1900-1910	7.0	14.0	28.0	37.4	27.4	34.4	77.1
1910-1920	3.5	1.0	−4.0	−13.2	2.3	28.2	28.0
1920-1930	−31.4	−13.9	−1.1	−5.3	−10.7	12.9	36.3
1930-1940	−26.5	−30.9	−23.0	−6.3	−5.7	12.5	42.4
1940-1950	61.3	14.2	−22.6	−31.6	−6.2	6.8	30.4
STATE							
1900-1910	16.5	15.1	24.3	24.3	26.5	26.3	22.3
1910-1920	17.3	22.0	17.0	1.9	1.3	28.4	18.0
1920-1930	−9.4	8.6	16.0	21.2	5.5	18.5	32.8
1930-1940	−19.4	−22.0	−8.5	5.2	2.0	12.9	5.8
1940-1950	59.3	19.4	−16.5	−19.9	5.3	9.8	2.1

* Statistics based on population reports of the United States Bureau of the Census.

TABLE XIII

POPULATION OF PAPER CITY, BY SEX (1850-1950)*

Year	*Male*	*Female*
1850	1,753	1,492
1860	2,225	2,772
1870	4,856	5,877
1880	10,308	11,607
1890	16,946	18,691
1900	21,744	23,968
1910	27,671	30,059
1920	28,901	31,302
1930	26,918	29,619
1940	25,831	27,919
1950	25,889	28,772

* Statistics based on population reports of the United States Bureau of the Census.

TABLE XIV

PERCENTAGE OF MARRIED WOMEN, 14 YEARS OLD AND OVER, IN PAPER CITY, STATE, NATION (1910-1950)*

Year	*Paper City*	*State*	*Nation*
1910	47.8	51.2	58.9
1920	49.6	53.2	60.6
1930	50.8	53.7	61.1
1940	50.8	53.3	61.0
1950	57.7	58.9	65.7

* Statistics based on population reports of the United States Bureau of the Census.

TABLE XV

PERCENTAGE OF MARRIED MEN, 14 YEARS OLD AND OVER, IN PAPER CITY AND STATE (1910-1950)*

Year	*Paper City*	*State*
1910	53.5	54.7
1920	56.2	57.5
1930	57.7	58.0
1940	56.3	57.6
1950	65.4	69.0

* Statistics based on population reports of the United States Bureau of the Census.

TABLE XVI

PERCENTAGE OF FEMALE POPULATION, 14 YEARS OLD AND OVER, GAINFULLY EMPLOYED IN PAPER CITY AND STATE (1910-1950)*

Year	*Paper City*	*State*
1910	40.1	31.7
1920	40.2	31.6
1930	34.1	29.2
1940	34.8	30.6
1950	36.5	33.1

* Statistics based on population reports of the United States Bureau of the Census. 1910-30 are for women ten years old and over. The 1940 and 1950 figures include females having an occupation "regardless of whether they were working or seeking work."

TABLE XVII

FOREIGN-BORN WHITE POPULATION IN PAPER CITY (1900-1950)*

Year	*Population*
1900	18,892
1910	23,238
1920	20,255
1930	16,232
1940	12,067
1950	9,464

* Statistics based on population reports of the United States Bureau of the Census.

TABLE XVIII

CONVERTS IN ROMAN CATHOLIC CHURCHES OF PAPER CITY (1936 AND 1946)*

Name of Church	*Year*	*Converts*
English Speaking:		
St. Jerome	1936	2
	1946	2
Sacred Heart	1936	8
	1946	6
Holy Rosary	1936	3
	1946	3
Holy Cross	1936	1
	1946	7
Holy Family	1936	0
	1946	0
Blessed Sacrament	1936	0
	1946	2
French:		
Precious Blood	1936	2
	1946	3
Perpetual Help	1936	0
	1946	3
Immaculate Conception	1936	0
	1946	1
Polish:		
Mater Dolorosa	1936	2
	1946	7
Greek:		
St. Michael	1936	0
	1946	0
Totals:	1936	18
	1946	36

* Data secured from the Roman Catholic Chancery records.

TABLE XIX

CONVERTS TO PROTESTANT CHURCHES FROM ROMAN CATHOLICISM (1946) AND AVERAGES FOR YEARS 1942-46*

Church	*1946*	*Average 1942-46*
First Baptist	1	1
Second Baptist	1	1
Bethlehem Community	0	0
First Congregational	1	1
Second Congregational	2	2
Grace Congregational	8	6
Evangelical Lutheran	3	4
First Methodist	0	1
First Presbyterian	2	2
St. Paul's Episcopal	3	4
Reformed Church	0	0
Salvation Army	0	0
Gospel Hall	0	1
Polish Evangelistic Assembly	3	5
Polish Bible Study	1	2
Jehovah's Witnesses	4	5
Totals	29	33

* Reliable data on conversions not available for 1936, a year for which Roman Catholic data was collected in order to use with United States religious census statistics. Protestant clergy had kept no records and their memories and those of laymen have to be relied upon.

TABLE XX

RELATION OF POPULATION TO AVERAGE NUMBER OF MANUFACTURING WAGE-EARNERS FOR PAPER CITY (1910-1950)*
(1910 = 100)

Year	*Population*	*Index No. of Population*	*Average No. of Wage Earners Employed*	*Index No. of Wage Earners*
1910	57,667	100.0	17,117	100.0
1920	62,286	106.6	18,242	106.6
1930	56,855	98.6	11,470	67.0
1940	54,695	94.8	8,715	50.1
1950	54,661	94.8	11,838	69.2

* Statistics based on population reports of the United States Bureau of the Census.

TABLE XXI

ROMAN CATHOLIC AND PROTESTANT CHURCH PROPERTY IN PAPER CITY (1946)*

	Roman Catholic	Protestant
Parsonages	$154,430	$76,740
Churches—Worship Centers	$1,584,610	$1,479,160
Charitable and Benevolent	$1,020,390	
Educational	$792,270	
Cemetery	$40,000	$68,770
Total	$3,591,700	$1,624,670

* Estimates of value made by tax assessor of Paper City and entered on municipal tax records. Only property owned by church groups as such is included. Protestant property totals include that of Christian Scientist and Greek Orthodox churches, valued at $48,770. Catholic property valued at $1,510,180 is held in the name and office of the bishop of the diocese.

TABLE XXII

RELIGIOUS GROUPS OF PAPER CITY BY PERCENTAGE IN SOCIAL CLASS (1947)

Category	Name of Churches	Number of Churches	Percentage in Religious Group
I. Labor Churches			
Protestant:	Bethlehem Community Baptist, Grace Congregational, Evangelical Lutheran, Reformed, Gospel Hall, Jehovah's Witnesses, Polish Evangelistic Assembly, Polish Study Group, Salvation Army.	9	33% of Prot.
Roman Catholic:	Holy Family, Holy Rosary, Immaculate Conception, Mater Dolorosa, Precious Blood, Saint Michael, Saint Jerome.	7	52% of R.C.
II. Middle-Labor Churches			
Protestant:	First Baptist, Second Baptist, Methodist, Presbyterian.	3	24.5% of Prot.
Roman Catholic:	Sacred Heart, Perpetual Help.	2	34% of R.C.
III. Upper-Middle Churches			
Protestant:	First Congregational, Second Congregational, Episcopal.	3	42.5% of Prot.
Roman Catholic:	Holy Cross, Blessed Sacrament	2	13% of R.C.

TABLE XXIII

CLASS COMPOSITION OF PROTESTANT CHURCHES IN PAPER CITY (1946)

Church	*Number of Members*	*Per Cent in Upper Class*	*Per Cent in Middle Class*	*Per Cent in Lower Class*
First Baptist	398	2	42	56
Second Baptist	730	4	47	49
Bethlehem Community Baptist	46	0	4	96
First Congregational	528	30	56	14
Second Congregational	1,172	55	41.5	3.5
Grace Congregational	1,044	0	8.5	91.5
Episcopal	624	26	56	18
Lutheran	1,021	1	26	63
Methodist	635	2	43	55
Presbyterian	618	2	31	57
Reformed	134	2	16	82
Salvation Army	30	0	6	94
Gospel Hall	40	0	4	96
Jehovah's Witnesses	79	0	6	94
Polish Bible Study	15	0	0	100
Polish Evangelistic Assembly	35	0	0	100
Totals		14.0 (1,015 people)	34.0 (2,400 people)	52.0 (3,583 people)

TABLE XXIV

CLASS COMPOSITION OF ROMAN CATHOLIC CHURCHES IN PAPER CITY (1946)

Church	*Number of Members*	*Per Cent in Upper Class*	*Per Cent in Middle Class*	*Per Cent in Lower Class*
English-speaking—Irish				
St. Jerome	3,561	0	12	88
Sacred Heart	6,519	0	68	32
Holy Rosary	2,127	0	6	94
Holy Cross	4,900	8	90	2
Holy Family	500	0	4	96
Blessed Sacrament	2,485	2	83.5	14.5
French				
Precious Blood	5,011	0	4	96
Perpetual Help	3,600	2	54	44
Immaculate Conception	3,456	0	2	98
Greek				
St. Michael	105	0	25	75
Polish				
Mater Dolorosa	5,000	0.5	3	96.5
Totals		1.2 (453 people)	36 (13,846 people)	62.8 (22,860 people)

TABLE XXV

PROTESTANT DENOMINATIONS IN PAPER CITY RANKED ACCORDING TO CLASS COMPOSITION (1947)

Denomination	*Percentage in Upper Class*	*Percentage in Middle Class*	*Percentage in Lower Class*
Episcopalian	26	56	18
Congregational	24	31	45
Baptist	24	43.6	54
Methodist	2	43	55
Presbyterian	2	31	59
Lutheran	1	30	59
Reformed	2	16	82
Jehovah's Witnesses	0	6	94
Salvation Army	0	6	94
Gospel Hall	0	4	96
Polish Bible Study Group	0	0	100
Polish Evangelistic Assembly	0	0	100

TABLE XXVI

RANKING OF WARDS BY HOUSING CRITERIA (1940)*

Ward	*Per Cent of Owner Occupied Dwelling Units*	*Per Cent of Dwelling Units Built Before 1900*	*Per Cent of Rooms Occupied by 1.51 or More Persons*	*Average Monthly Rental*	*Final Rank*
7	43.7	28.5	0.8	44.25	1
3	45.8	24.8	1.1	30.68	2
6	24.0	24.3	1.7	33.00	3
5	9.2	61.3	1.6	20.61	4
4	9.1	67.3	4.4	33.54	5
2	3.7	33.4	3.6	18.39	6
1	4.5	48.5	4.4	17.46	7
Total				28.51	
City %	20.2	34.2	2.4		

* Source: *United States Census, 1940*, Vol. II, Part 3, *Population;* and *Housing Supplement, Holyoke Block Statistics.*

TABLE XXVII

RANKING OF WARDS BY AGE GROUP (1940)*

Wards	*Per Cent Under 25 Years*	*Rank of Wards*	*Per Cent Between 25-65 Yrs.*	*Rank of Wards*	*Per Cent 65 Yrs. and Over*	*Rank of Wards*
1	45.6	1	48.3	7	6.1	6
2	43.8	2	50.3	6	5.9	7
3	35.1	5	64.9	1	11.0	2
4	39.4	3	53.2	5	7.4	5
5	28.1	7	60.5	2	11.4	1
6	38.7	4	54.6	4	6.7	4
7	34.2	6	55.9	3	9.9	3
City	37.4		54.4		8.2	

* *United States Census, 1940*, Vol. II, Part 3, *Population*. The number of children under one year is given for the city as 574 (1.1%), but data is not given for wards.

TABLE XXVIII

CLASS DISTRIBUTION OF MEMBERSHIP IN MAJOR RELIGIOUS GROUPS IN PAPER CITY (1947)

	Percentage in Total Membership	
Class	*Protestant*	*Roman Catholic*
Upper	14	1.2
Middle	34	36.0
Lower	52	62.8

TABLE XXIX

RELIGIOUS AFFILIATION OF MANAGEMENT AND OFFICERS OF 11 PAPER CITY FIRMS (1947)*

Type of Firm	*Board of Directors and Officers*	*Superintendent and "Top" Managers*	*Department Heads*	*Foremen*
Outside Corporations				
Machine Mfr. 500 Employees	Absentee owned	66% P (6) 34% C	62% P (16) 38% C	41% P (19) 59% C
Machine Mfr. 200 Employees	Absentee owned	100% P (2)	None	24.8% P (21) 65.8% C 9.4% Non-Aff.
Mixed Local Ownership				
Paper Mfr. 1100 Employees	69.6% P (13) 22.8% C 7.6% J	50% P (6) 50% C	75% P (8) 25% C	75% P (4) 25% C
Textile Mfr. 800 Employees	66% P & J (3) 34% Non-Aff.	75% C (4) 25% Non-Aff. and J		25% P (4) 75% C
Protestant Firms				
Water Power 80 Employees	100% P (9)	100% P (7)		50% P (4) 50% C
Paper Processor 780 Employees	100% P (5)	100% P (6)		25% P (12) 75% C
Metal Manufacturer 300 Employees	100% P (5)	100% P (5)		64% P (11) 36% C
Paper Processor 225 Employees	100% P (4)	100% P (2)		91% P (11) 9% C
Paper Processor 120 Employees	100% P (5)	100% P (4)		75% P (10) 25% C
Catholic Firms				
Machine Shop 165 Employees	100% C (3)	100% C (4)		100% C (6)
Machine Shop 70 Employees	100% C (4)	100% C (3)		100% C (6)

* The numbers in parentheses refer to the number of people involved in the total official or managerial category. Data based on material supplied by "top level" officials and managers in each firm or by personnel managers or appropriate company sources of information. Data collected in 1947. All of these companies, except one, are organized by unions. Details that do not affect the picture of religious affiliation of management (such as the number of employees) have been altered to aid disguise of firms that do not wish to be identified.

TABLE XXX

PARTY ENROLLMENT BY WARDS

Ward	*Registered Voters*	*Democratic*	*Republican*	*Unenrolled*
		1940		
1	2,776	1,597	421	758
2	3,119	1,271	574	1,274
3	4,660	1,827	1,191	1,642
4	3,571	2,164	308	1,099
5	4,519	1,985	991	1,543
6	4,751	2,104	1,003	1,644
7	4,583	1,919	1,512	1,152
Total	27,979	12,867	6,000	9,112
		1946		
1	3,262	1,330	348	1,584
2	3,448	1,106	464	1,878
3	5,303	1,803	1,123	2,377
4	4,106	1,970	311	1,825
5	4,924	1,793	887	2,244
6	5,574	1,971	903	2,700
7	4,993	1,838	1,366	1,834
Total	31,610	11,811	5,402	14,442

TABLE XXXI

VOTING FOR PRESIDENTIAL CANDIDATES BY WARDS (1948 AND 1952)*

	1948			*1952*	
Ward	*Dewey*	*Truman*	*Wallace*	*Eisenhower*	*Stevenson*
1	397	2,667	11	754	2,291
2	544	2,686	23	921	2,231
3	2,155	2,563	52	2,899	2,271
4	630	3,041	26	1,059	2,519
5	1,551	2,875	23	1,987	2,288
6	1,785	3,310	51	2,567	3,045
7	2,342	2,119	18	2,848	1,945
Totals	9,404	19,261	204	13,035	16,590

* Data supplied by Holyoke *Transcript*.

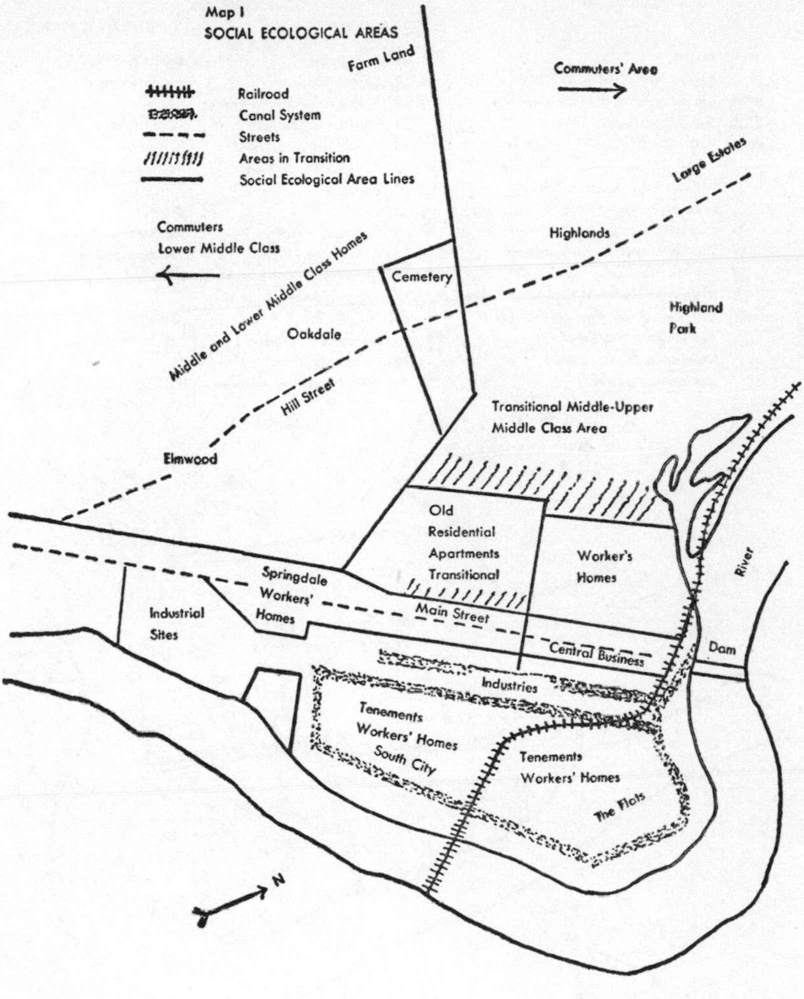
Map I
SOCIAL ECOLOGICAL AREAS
Railroad
Canal System
Streets
Areas in Transition
Social Ecological Area Lines
Farm Land
Commuters' Area
Large Estates
Highlands
Commuters
Lower Middle Class
Middle and Lower Middle Class Homes
Cemetery
Highland
Park
Oakdale
Hill Street
Transitional Middle-Upper
Middle Class Area
Elmwood
Old
Residential
Apartments
Transitional
Worker's
Homes
River
Springdale
Workers'
Homes
Industrial
Sites
Main Street
Central Business
Dam
Industries
Tenements
Workers' Homes
South City
Tenements
Workers' Homes
The Flats
N

Map II

PARISH LINES AND CHURCHES

- English-Speaking Church Parish Lines
- French Parish Lines
- Parish Line for French who wish to attend French Mass at American Parish - line may be crossed to French Parish No. 7
- Catholic Church: English-Speaking
- Catholic Church: French-Speaking
- Catholic Church: Polish or Greek
- Protestant Church with Established Building
- Protestant Church with Meeting Hall

See accompanying list of churches for key to numbers designating location

CHURCHES

PROTESTANT

1. First Baptist
2. Second Baptist
3. Bethlehem Community Baptist
4. First Congregational
5. Second Congregational
6. Grace Congregational
7. Episcopal
8. Lutheran
9. Methodist
10. Presbyterian
11. Reformed
12. Salvation Army
13. Gospel Hall
14. Jehovah's Witnesses
15. Polish Bible Study
16. Polish Evangelistic Assembly

ROMAN CATHOLIC

ENGLISH-SPEAKING
1. St. Jerome
2. Sacred Heart
3. Holy Rosary
4. Holy Cross
5. Blessed Sacrament

FRENCH
6. Precious Blood
7. Perpetual Help
8. Immaculate Conception

GREEK
9. St. Michael's

POLISH
10. Mater Dolorosa

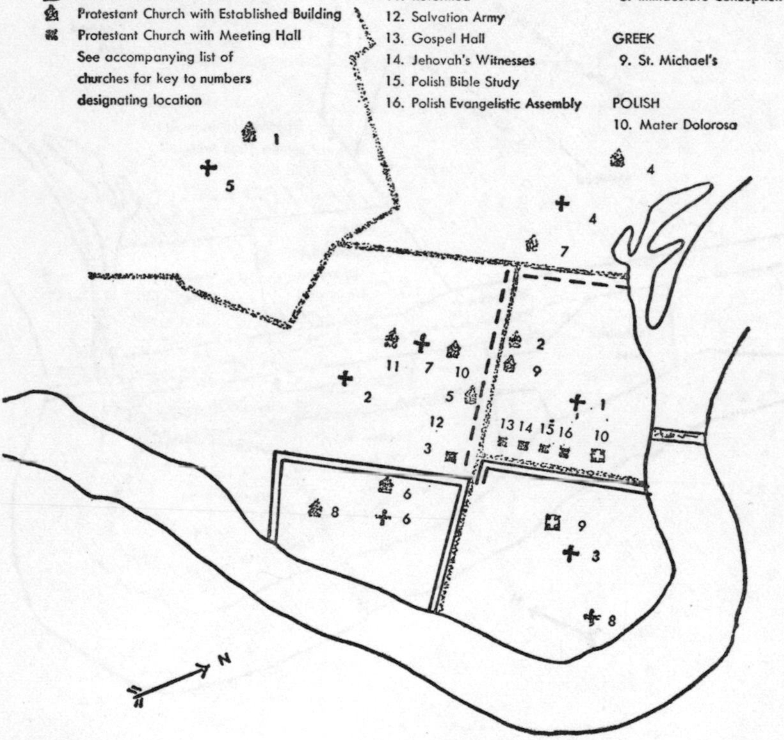

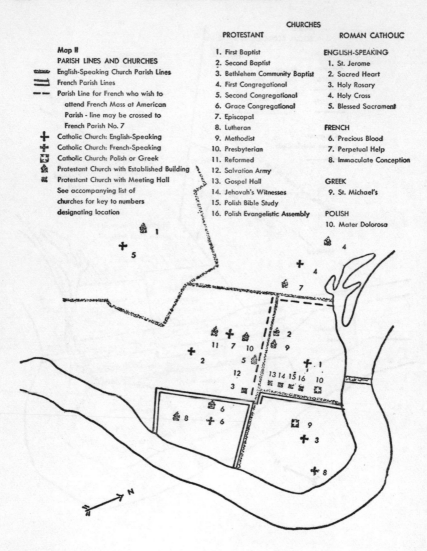

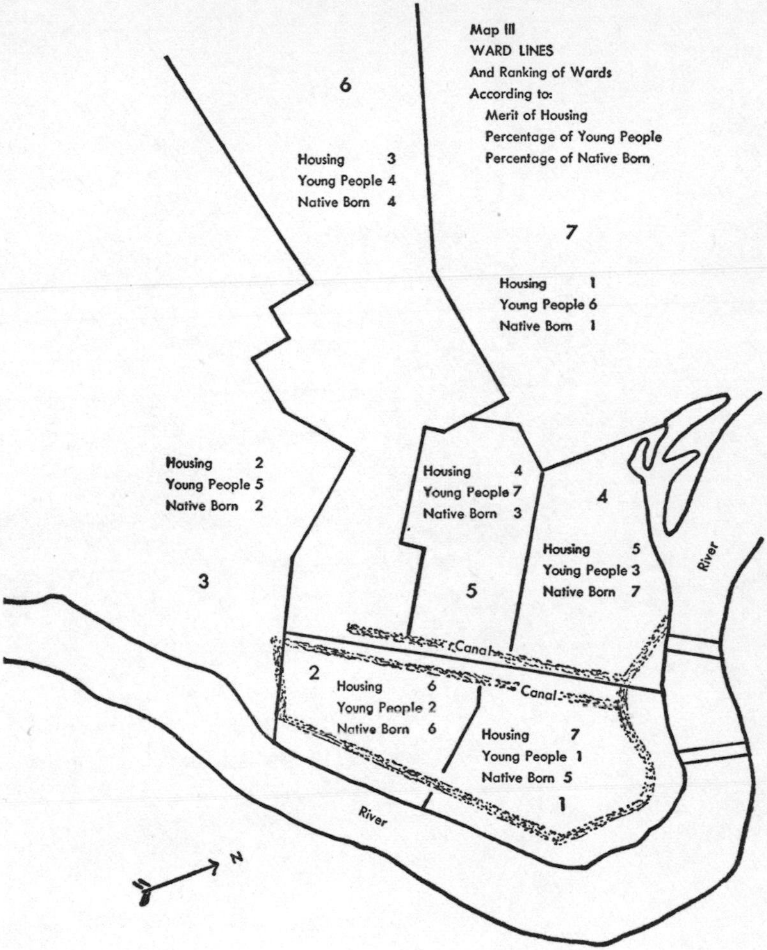
Map III
WARD LINES
And Ranking of Wards
According to:
Merit of Housing
Percentage of Young People
Percentage of Native Born
6
Housing 3
Young People 4
Native Born 4
7
Housing 1
Young People 6
Native Born 1
Housing 2
Young People 5
Native Born 2
3
Housing 4
Young People 7
Native Born 3
5
4
Housing 5
Young People 3
Native Born 7
River
Canal
Canal
2
Housing 6
Young People 2
Native Born 6
Housing 7
Young People 1
Native Born 5
1
River
N

Bibliography

I. UNPUBLISHED MANUSCRIPTS, THESES AND DOCUMENTS

Bagg, E. P., Jr., *History of Second Congregational Church.* Manuscript. In Second Congregational Church offices, Holyoke, 1947.

Chapman, Stanley H., *New Haven Churches, Aspects of Their Structure and Function.* Ph.D. dissertation, Yale University, 1942.

Conflicting Views on P.A.C. mimeographed. Literature distributed to the Current Labor Problems class of the Holy Cross Labor Institute. November 13, 1945.

Constitution, Holyoke Council of Churches. Mimeographed document adopted 1942. In possession of secretary of Council.

Constitution, Holyoke Ministerial Association. Mimeographed document adopted 1914. In possession of secretary.

Department of Economics and Sociology, Mt. Holyoke College. *Population Trends in Holyoke, 1910-1940.* Mimeographed, 1944. Mt. Holyoke College Library.

Department of Economics and Sociology, Mt. Holyoke College. *Recent Trends in Holyoke Schools.* Manuscript, June 1933. Mt. Holyoke College Library.

Freymann, Grace M., *Comparative Birth Rates of Dubuque, Iowa, 1930-1940,* M.A. thesis, University of Iowa, 1942.

Gustafson, James M., *A Study in the Problem of Authority in Congregational Church-Order.* Mimeographed, 1954. Social Ethics Library, Yale Divinity School.

Holy Cross Institute of Labor. *Syllabus* for course on General Economics. Mimeographed. March 1945.

Holyoke Protestant Council of Churches *Religious Census of the Jackson Parkway.* Data in possession of Episcopalian pastor, 1947.

Industrial History of Holyoke. Manuscript. In office of Chamber of Commerce, Holyoke, 1947.

McGuchen, W. J., *Catholic Ways in Education, 1934-1937.* Graduate paper, 1938. Springfield College Library.

Peabody, Alan, *Grace Church in Holyoke: a Case Study.* Religious Education and Field Work Project. Manuscript. Springfield College, 1946.

Questionnaires and data developed for the study of unemployed workers in Grace Congregational Church, Holyoke, 1931. In the possession of Dr. Colston Warne, Amherst, Massachusetts, director of the study.

Report of Tuberculosis Survey in Holyoke. Emergency Relief Administration in Cooperation with Holyoke Tuberculosis Association. January, 1935.

Shull, Gordon, *Post War Issues in International Politics and the Church Press,* M.A. thesis, University of Illinois, 1953.

Springfield Council of Churches, *Study of Population and Religious Census Trends in Holyoke Diocese,* 1948. Data on file in offices of Springfield, Massachusetts, Council of Churches.

Springfield Protestant laymen's study of religious and political trends in Massachusetts, 1950. Photostat copies of basic tables and graphs in possession of author.

Substandard Housing in Holyoke. Manuscript. Holyoke Housing Authority offices. 1938.

II. RECORDS OF CHURCHES AND SOCIAL AGENCIES

Annual Report of the Women's League, 1942-1947. Mimeographed. Second Baptist Church archives.

By-Laws of Catholic Girls' Junior League of Holyoke. Adopted, 1936. In the possession of the secretary of the League.

Constitution, Protestant Girls' Association. Adopted 1946. In possession of the secretary of the Association.

Junior League Statement of Purposes. Archives of Junior League. In possession of the president. Holyoke, 1947.

Minutes, Holyoke Ministerial Association. April 1919—August 1947.

Minutes of Taxpayers Association, July 1932—August 1947.

Reports, Council of Churches. Mimeographed. In the possession of the secretary. Presidents Report, 1942. Minutes, Executive Board, 1947. Report of Annual Meeting, 1942-1947. Report of Women's Department, 1944-1947. Report of Youth Department, 1943-1947. Report of Religious Education Department, 1945-1947. Annual Report of the Ministerial Association to the Holyoke Council of Churches, 1942-1947.

Preliminary Statement of Facts Concerning the Holyoke Affair. Mimeographed report. Issued 1940 by Mothers' Health Council.

Records of the Second Baptist Church, including letters to the Westfield Baptist Association, 1870-1947. In the vault of the Second Baptist Church.

Records of the Second Congregational Church, 1882-1892. In vault of the Second Congregational Church.

Records of First Methodist Church, 1905-1947. Archives of church.

Records, Holyoke Bar Association, 1942-1947.

Records, Holyoke Girl Scouts and Boy Scouts. Offices of Scout organizations. 1947.

Records, Holyoke Medical Association, 1942-1947.

Weekly Calendar, Grace Congregational Church. Grace Congregational Church Archives. 1945-1947.

III. PRIVATE PAPERS, DIARIES, LETTERS

Collection of correspondence, statements and newspaper clippings, diary of events connected with the Sanger incident. In the possession of the Rev. Ronald J. Tamblyn, pastor of First Congregational Church, 1947.

Grace Church Scrapbooks, 1909, 1911, 1913, 1914, 1919. Grace Congregational Church archives.

The Log, 1917-1947. Grace Congregational Church archives.

Papers on the development of the Holyoke Water Power Company. In possession of the president of the company.

Sermon manuscripts and notes for period 1942-1947. In possession of pastors,

First Congregational Church, Second Congregational Church, Second Baptist Church, First Presbyterian Church, Episcopal Church.

IV. PAMPHLETS

Roman Catholic

As an Orphanland Helper. Holy Family League of Charity. Holyoke, 1947.

Betowski, Rev. Edward M., *The True Church,* New York, 1938.

Catholic Action: What is It? Our Sunday Visitor Press, Huntington, Indiana, 1944.

Connell, Rev. Francis J., C.SS.R., *Shepherds of Christ's Flock*. New York, 1940.

Florey, Rev. Myron F., *Commandos of Christ: St. George, Patron of England*. Scranton, Pennsylvania, 1944.

Florey, Rev. Myron F., *Supermen of Church History*. Scranton, Pennsylvania, 1947.

Girl Scouting and the Catholic Girl. Girl Scouts National Organization. New York, no date.

Ginder, Richard, *Prevention and Cure*. Catholic Information Society. New York, 1943.

——— *More Husbands Than Babies*. Catholic Information Society, New York, 1943.

Holy Cross Dedication. Holyoke, 1940.

Lord, Rev. Daniel A., S.J., *Jesus, the Hero*. New Catholic Bible Stories. New York, 1943.

Lord, Rev. Daniel A., S.J., *Let's See the Other Side*. St. Louis, Missouri, 1938.

Lord, Rev. Daniel A., S.J., *Who's Pushing Your Mind Around?* St. Louis, Missouri, 1946.

Malloy, Rev. Joseph, I.C.S.P., *A Catechism for Inquirers*. New York, 1927.

Mueller, Sister Therese, *Family Life in Christ,* Second Edition, Collyville, Minnesota, 1942.

Paroisse du Precieux-sang; 75e Anniversaire de sa Fondation. Holyoke, October 22, 1944.

Poage, Rev. Godfrey, C.P., *Follow Me: A Pamphlet on the Vocation to the Priesthood and Religious Life*. St. Louis, Missouri, 1943.

Secularism's Attack on World Order. Catholic Association for International Peace. Washington, D. C., no date.

Sullivan, Rev. P. Henry, *First Communion Catechism*. New York, 1936.

——— *Double Novena to the Holy Family*. Worcester, Massachusetts, 1942.

——— *My Holy Hour with Jesus,* Birghtiele Institute, Holyoke, 1938.

The Testimony of History for the Roman Catholic Church. The Library Committee, The Catholic Club of the City of New York, New York, 1924.

Protestants:

Brief History of the Evangelical Lutheran Church, Holyoke. Holyoke, November 1, 1942.

Coming to the Holy Communion. St. Philip's Society. West Stockbridge, Massachusetts, no date.

Debt Liquidating Plan. Second Congregational Church, Holyoke, 1943.

Does the Bible Teach Final and Universal Salvation? Evangel Tract, No. 800. Springfield, Missouri, 1945.

The Episcopal Church: Forward Movement. Cincinnati, no date.

Fey, Harold, *Can Catholicism Win America?* Christian Century Press, Chicago, 1945.

Girl Scouting and the Protestant Churches. The Protestant Committee on Scouting. New York, no date.

Guidebook to Social Action. Council for Social Action, 1944.

The Moral Aspects of Birth Control. Majority report issued March 21, 1931, of the Committee on Marriage and the Home of the Federal Council of the Churches of Christ in America.

Niebuhr, Reinhold, *The Contribution of Religion to Cultural Unity.* The Hazen Pamphlets, No. 13. New Haven, 1945.

Holyoke Labor College Classes for Workers. Holyoke, 1930.

The Scout Program in Protestant Churches. The Protestant Committee on Scouting, New York, no date.

V. BOOKS PERTAINING ESPECIALLY TO HOLYOKE AND REGION

Catholic Directory and Family Year Book. Diocese of Springfield. 1913-1914, 1916-1917.

A Century of Catholicism in Western Massachusetts, published by the *Catholic Mirror.* Springfield, 1931.

Ducharme, Jacques, *The Delusson Family,* New York, 1939.

——— *The Shadows of the Trees,* New York, 1943.

Foote, H. L., *History of the First Twenty-Five Years of St. Paul's Church, Holyoke Massachusetts.* Holyoke, 1889.

Green, Constance McLaughlin, *Holyoke, Massachusetts: A Case History of the Industrial Revolution in America.* New Haven, 1939.

Holyoke: *Past and Present, 1745-1895.* Transcript Publishing Co. Holyoke, 1896.

Lucey, Patrick J., *History of St. Jerome's Parish.* Introduction by Father Mc-Coy. Holyoke, 1931.

McCoy, Rev. J. J., Diocese of Springfield. *History of the Catholic Church in the New England States, II.* Two Volumes, Boston, 1899.

Osgood, G. C., *Story of the Holyoke Churches.* Holyoke, 1890.

Thirtieth Anniversary Holyoke Daily Transcript. Holyoke, 1912.

Trask, J. L. R., others. *Fiftieth Anniversary, Second Congregational Church.* Holyoke, 1900.

VI. GENERAL BOOKS

Roman Catholicism, Protestantism and Religious Relations:

Anderson, Elin L., *We Americans; A Study of Cleavage in an American City.* Cambridge, 1937.

Barron, Milton L., *People Who Intermarry.* Syracuse, 1946.

Bates, M. Searle, *Religious Liberty.* New York, 1945.

Blanshard, Paul, *American Freedom and Catholic Power.* Boston, 1949.

——— *Communism, Democracy and Catholic Power.* Boston, 1951.

Bouscaren, T. Lincoln, *Foreign-Born Catholics and Their Children: Parish Affiliation.* The Canon Law Digest, Vol. II, Milwaukee, 1943.

Butler, Dom Cuthbert, *The Vatican Council.* Vol. II, New York, 1930.

Clarke, Rev. Thomas J., J.C.L., *Parish Societies.* Canon Law Studies, No. 176, Catholic University of America, Washington, D. C., 1943.

Cronin, Rev. John F., *Catholic Social Action.* Milwaukee, 1948.

——— *Catholic Social Principles.* Milwaukee, 1950.

Dawson, Joseph N., *Separate Church and State Now.* New York, 1948.

Eisenstein, Ira, *The Ethics of Tolerance, Applied to Religious Groups in America.* New York, 1941.

Finkelstein, Louis; J. Elliot Ross; William Adams Brown, *The Religions of Democracy.* New York, 1941.

Heim, Karl, *Spirit and Truth,* trans. by Edgar P. Dickie, London, 1935.

Husslein, Joseph, *Social Wellsprings.* Vol. II, Milwaukee, 1942.

Johnson, Alvin W. and Frank H. Yost, *Separation of Church and State in the United States.* Minneapolis, 1948.

Kelleher, Rev. Stephen Joseph, S.J., *Discussions With Non-Catholics.* Canon Law Studies, No. 180. (Catholic University of America, Washington, D. C., 1943.)

Maritain, Jacques, *The Things That Are Not Caesar's.* London, 1939.

McKenna, Norman C., *The Catholic and His Union.* New York, 1948.

Moody, Joseph N. (editor), *Church and Society, Catholic Social and Political Thought and Movements.* 1784-1950, New York, 1954.

Murray, Rev. John Courtney, S.J., *Contemporary Orientations of Catholic Thought on Church and State in the Light of History. Theological Studies,* Vol. X, Woodstock, Maryland, June 1953.

Nichols, James H., *Democracy and the Churches.* Philadelphia, 1951.

Niebuhr, H. Richard, *Christ and Culture.* New York, 1951.

——— *The Kingdom of God in America.* Chicago, 1937.

Oberle, Rev. Joseph, *The Association of Catholic Trade Unionists.* Paulist Press, New York, 1951.

O'Neill, James M., *Religion and Education Under the Constitution.* New York, 1949.

Richter, Rev. V. W., *Why Should a Lutheran Not Join Any Sectarian Church.* Streator, Illinois, 1913.

Ryan, J. A. and F. J. Boland, *Catholic Principles of Politics.* New York, 1928.

Ryan, John A. and Moorhouse F. X. Millar, *The State and the Church.* New York, 1922.

Silcox, Claris E. and Galen M. Fisher, *Catholics, Jews and Protestants.* New York, 1934.

Schueder, Rev. H. J., *Council of Trent, 23rd Session.* Sixth Canon in Canons and Decrees of the Council of Trent, St. Louis, Missouri, 1941.

Stokes, Anson Philips, *Church and State in the United States.* New York, 1950.

Tillich, Paul, *The Protestant Era.* Chicago, 1948.

Van Dusen, Henry Pittney; Robert Lowrey Calhoun; Joseph Perkins Chamberlain and others. *Church and State in the Modern World.* New York, 1937.

Ware, Caroline, *Greenwich Village, 1920-1930.* Boston, 1935.

Williams, Michael, *The Catholic Church in Action.* New York, 1934.

Williams, Robin, *The Reduction of Intergroup Tensions: A Survey of Research on Problems of Ethnic, Racial and Religious Group Relations.* Social Science Research Council, Bulletin 57, 1947.

Sociology of Religion:

Durkheim, Emile, *Elementary Forms of the Religious Life,* trans. J. Swain, Glencoe, Illinois, 1934.

Fichter, Joseph H., *Dynamics of a City Church.* Vol. 1 in a series on a Southern Parish, Chicago, 1951.

Malinowski, Bronislaw, *Magic, Science and Religion, and Other Essays.* Boston, 1948.

Niebuhr, H. Richard, *The Social Sources of Denominationalism.* New York, 1929.

Pope, Liston, *Millhands and Preachers.* New Haven, 1942.

Troeltsch, Ernst, *The Social Teaching of the Christian Churches,* trans. V. Wyon, New York, 1931.

Wach, Joachim, *Sociology of Religion.* Chicago, 1944.

Weber, Max, *The Protestant Ethic and the Spirit of Capitalism.* London, 1930.

Society in General—Works in Economics, Political Science and Sociology:

Adorno, T. W., others, *The Authoritarian Personality.* New York, 1950.

Almond, Gabriel, *The American People and Foreign Policy.* New York, 1950.

American Political Science Association, Committee on Political Parties. *Toward a More Responsible Two Party System.* New York, 1950.

Appleby, Paul, *Policy and Administration.* New York, 1949.

Bennett, John W. and H. M. Tumin, *Social Life.* New York, 1948.

Berelson, Bernard, *Content Analysis in Communication Research.* Glencoe, Illinois, 1952.

Brown, Francis James and Joseph Slabey Roucek, *One America.* New York, 1952.

Carr, E. H., *Conditions of Peace.* New York, 1942.

Childs, Irwin L., *Italian or American: the Second Generation in Conflict.* New Haven, 1943.

Clarke, J. M., *Alternative to Serfdom.* New York, 1948.

Gaer, Joseph, *The First Round.* (Contains collection of C.I.O.–P.A.C. pamphlets.) New York, 1944.

Galbraith, John, *American Capitalism, The Economics of Countervailing Power.* New York, 1952.

Gerth, H. H., and C. Wright Mills, ed., *From Max Weber: Essays in Sociology.* New York, 1946.

Herring, E. P., *Politics of Democracy.* New York, 1940.

Holcombe, Arthur N., *Our More Perfect Union.* Cambridge, 1950.

Hollingshead, August B., *Elmtown's Youth; The Impact of Social Classes on Adolescents.* New York, 1949.

Lazarsfeld, Paul, *The People's Choice.* New York, 1944.

Lindblom, Charles, *Unions and Capitalism.* New Haven, 1950.

Lubell, Samuel, *The Future of American Politics.* New York, 1952.

MacIver, Robert H., *The Web of Government.* New York, 1949.

Malinowski, Bronislaw, *The Dynamics of Culture Change.* New Haven, 1945.

Mannheim, Karl, *Freedom, Power and Democratic Planning.* New York, 1950.

——— *Man and Society in an Age of Reconstruction.* New York, 1949.

McConnell, John W., *The Evolution of the Social Classes.* Washington, D. C., 1942.

Meade, J. E., *Planning and the Price Mechanism: The Liberal-Socialist Solution.* New York, 1949.

Merton, Robert K., *Social Theory and Social Structure: Toward the Codification of Theory and Research.* Glencoe, Illinois, 1949.

Mills, C. Wright, *White Collar.* New York, 1951.

Moore, W. E., *Industrial Relations and the Social Order.* New York, 1949.

Myers, Charles A., and MacLaurin, W. Rupert, *The Movement of Factory Workers.* New York, 1943.

Ortega y Gasset, José, *The Revolt of the Masses.* New York, 1951.

Parsons, Talcott, *Essays in Sociological Thought Pure and Applied.* Glencoe, Illinois, 1949.

Pearl, Raymond, *A Classification and Code of Occupations. Human Biology,* Vol. 5, New York, 1933.

Polanyi, Karl, *The Great Transformation.* New York, 1944.

Riesman, David, *The Lonely Crowd.* New Haven, 1950.

Schattschneider, E. E., *Party Government.* New York, 1942.

Schumpeter, Joseph A., *Capitalism, Socialism and Democracy.* New York, 1942.

Shevsky, Eshref and Marilyn Williams, *The Social Areas of Los Angeles.* Berkeley and Los Angeles, 1949.

Tead, Ordway, *The Art of Administration.* New York, 1949.

Truman, David, *The Governmental Process.* New York, 1950.

von Wiese, Leopold and Becker, Howard, *Systematic Sociology.* New York, 1932.

Warner, W. Lloyd and Leo Srole, *The Social System of American Ethnic Groups.* New Haven, 1945.

Warner, W. Lloyd and J. O. Low, *The Social System of the Modern Factory.* New Haven, 1947.

Warner, W. Lloyd and Paul S. Lunt, *The Social Life of a Modern Community.* New Haven, 1941.

Watson, Goodwin, *Action for Unity.* New York, 1947.

Weber, Max, *Methodology of the Social Sciences,* trans. by Edward A. Shils and Henry A. Finch, Glencoe, Illinois, 1949.

Weber, Max, *The Theory of Social and Economic Organization,* trans. by A. M. Henderson and Talcott Parsons, New York, 1947.

Wilson, Logan and William L. Kolb, *Sociological Analysis.* New York, 1949.

VII. OFFICIAL PUBLICATIONS

The Catholic Directory, 1940, 1947, 1953.

Housing Supplement to the First Series, Holyoke, *1940 United States Census.* Housing Supplement, Holyoke, *1950 United States Census.*

Massachusetts Department of Labor and Industries, *Annual Report,* 1910-1942.

Massachusetts Department of Labor and Industries, Division of Statistics: *Employment and Pay Roll Earnings in Fourteen Leading Cities, 1943-1947; Employment and Pay Roll Earnings in Manufacturing, 1947; Census of Manufacturers, 1932, 1942. Municipal Employment, 1947.*

Holyoke Town Records, 1850-1873, Holyoke Public Library.

Municipal Register, 1873-1947. Holyoke Public Library. Report of the Board of Health, Report of the School Committee and Report of the Water Board are bound with the Register.

National Catholic Almanac, Paterson, New Jersey, 1952.
Sixteenth Census of the United States, 1940. Population, Vol. I, II, Part 3. Housing Vol. I, Part 3.
Seventeenth Census of the United States, 1950. Population, Vol. II, Part 21. Housing Vol. I, Part 3.
United States Religious Census: Religious Bodies, 1906, 1916, 1926, 1936.
Yearbooks, 1946, 1947, 1953, of the following denominations: Northern Baptist, Congregational Christian, Episcopalian, Methodist, Presbyterian, U.S.A., Lutheran (Missouri Synod), Evangelical and Reformed.

VIII. NEWSPAPERS AND PERIODICALS

America, 1947, 1952.
The Artisan, 1910-1914, Labor newspaper, Holyoke.
Awake, 1947. Publication of Jehovah's Witnesses.
The Banner, 1944-1947. A parochial high school paper, mimeographed, on file in archives of Sacred Heart parish.
The Caravel, 1924-1947. Official organ of Holyoke Council No. 90, Knights of Columbus.
Catholic Comics, 1946-1947. Published monthly in Holyoke. Unofficial.
The Catholic Mirror, 1918-1954. Official monthly journal of the Roman Catholic Diocese of Springfield.
Christian Science Monitor, 1940, 1946, 1947, Boston.
Massachusetts News, Missionary Herald, 1940, 1946-1947.
News Letter, 1940, State Civil Liberties Committee. On file in Boston offices of the Committee.
New York Times, 1940, 1946-1954.
The Pilot, 1947, 1953.
Orphan Light, 1945-1947. Monthly newsletter of the Roman Catholic League of Charities, Holyoke.
Holyoke *Transcript*, 1882-1954. Only daily newspaper now published in Holyoke.
Holyoke *World*, published in Holyoke, 1880-1887, in Springfield, 1887-1898.
Saturday Democrat, 1940-1947, weekly newspaper, Holyoke.
Springfield *Daily News*, 1944.
Springfield *Republican*, 1940-1947.
Springfield *Union*, 1940-1947.
Worker's News, 1940, mimeographed. On file in office of Textile Workers' Union, Holyoke.

IX. SPECIAL ARTICLES

Barron, Milton L., "Intermediacy: Conceptualization of Irish Status in America," *Social Forces*, March 1949.
Cavileer, Jesse, "The Church and Labor," *Social Action*, October 1944.
Colbins, Orvin, "Ethnic Behavior in Industry: Sponsorship and Rejection in a New England Factory," *Journal of Sociology*, January 1946.
Cost, John C., "Nine Years of A.C.T.U.," *America*, April 6, 1946.
Fineberg, Solomon Anhill, "Strategy of Error," *Contemporary Jewish Record*, February 1945.
Holloway, Vernon H., "A Review of American Religious Pacifism," *Religion in Life*, Summer 1950.

"Is There a Catholic Vote," *U. S. News and World Report*, August 10, 1956.
Jaffe, A. J., "Religious Differentials in Net Reproduction Rate," *American Statistical Association Journal*, June 1939.
Kennedy, R. J. R., "Premarital Residential Propinquity and Ethnic Endogamy," *American Journal of Sociology*, March 1943.
King, C. Wendell, "Social Cleavage in a New England Community," *Social Forces*, March 1946.
Landis, Benson Y., "Protestants and Catholics," *Commonweal*, July 27, 1945.
Landis, Paul H., "Religion and the Birth Rate," *Forum*, March 1946.
Miller, William, "Catholic Plan for a New Social Order," *Social Action*, February 15, 1951.
"More About 'Catholic Vote' in U. S. Elections," *U. S. News and World Report*, August 17, 1956.
"A Note on the 1936 Census of Religious Bodies," *Information Service*, Vol. XIX, No. 35, November 2, 1940.
Outler, Albert, "The Problem of Religious Community in Protestantism," *Journal of Religious Thought*, Spring 1941.
Pope, Liston, "Religion and the Class Structure," *Annals of the American Academy of Political and Social Science*, March 1948.
Redfield, Robert, "The Art of Social Science," *American Journal of Sociology*, November 1948.
Robinson, G. K., "Catholic Birthrate: Further Facts and Implications," *American Journal of Sociology*, May 1936.
"Secularism and Cultural Pluralism," *Information Service*, February 9, 1952.
Smertenko, Johan J., "The Emerging Hyphen," *Harper's*, August 1951.
"Social-Economic Status and Outlook of Religious Groups in America," *Information Service*, May 15, 1948.
Stauffer, Samuel A., "Trends in Fertility of Catholics and Non-Catholics," *American Journal of Sociology*, September 1935.
"This Thing Called Secularism," *Information Service*, February 2, 1952.
Whelpton, P. K., "Geography and Economic Differentials in Fertility," *Annals of the American Academy of Political and Social Science*, November 1936.
Wolseley, R. E., "The Church Press: Bulwark of Denominational Sovereignty," *Crozier Quarterly*, August 1946.

Notes

Readers wishing minute documentation of all sources of data, detailed discussion of research methods, and questionnaires used in the study are referred to the author's doctoral dissertation: "Roman Catholic-Protestant Relations in an Industrial Community," 2 Vol., 819 pp. manuscript, Yale University Sterling Library, New Haven, Connecticut, 1954. The statements used in the book were obtained in personal interviews with the subjects described in the text, unless the notes indicate otherwise. The precise citations for quotations from highly fugitive materials which originated entirely in Paper City, such as sermon manuscripts and leaflets, are not given in these published notes but are available in the dissertation. All scholarly studies and authors referred to in the text are listed in the bibliography. The notes chiefly provide substantial material of more specialized nature than the text and references to published material generally available.

Acknowledgments

1. Various devices have been used to protect confidences given the writer. Comments or information given with the request that no attribution be made are placed in their social or religious context simply by identification of a person's social status or vocation. All the names of persons living in Paper City and used in the book are fictional. This has been done, not because all the people desired anonymity, but to aid in the disguise of sources of information when the people involved thought this advisable. In some instances, sources of information cannot be indicated in any way, the information having been given with such an understanding between the writer and the informant.

2. The *Catholic Mirror* was published with approbation of the bishop of the diocese of Springfield and with the statement on the masthead that it was the "official organ of the Diocese of Springfield." It was not owned by the diocese until 1951. In 1955 the *Catholic Mirror* was succeeded by the *Catholic Observer,* the change occurring after the death of the bishop who reigned during most of the period of this study, and symbolizing the beginning of a period of new leadership under a bishop who appears to be more responsive to social changes in the diocese than his predecessor.

Introduction

1. Knowledge of the Sanger incident had some influence upon the choice of Paper City for this study of religious relations. The investigator looked for a locality where there had recently occurred some overt incident which had compelled people to think about religious relations, but had not cut so deeply into the life of the city as to excite them to a distorted view of the importance of religious cleavage in the community. In short, a city was not desired that

had a reputation for religious antagonisms. Actually, most of the leaders in Paper City believe that the community has achieved a satisfactory accommodation to religious differences, even though the community experienced strong religious tensions in 1940.

2. The term community is used in two senses at various points in this study by the writer and by some of the people who speak in these pages. The first has a spatial or geographic meaning; the other denotes the social processes and value concerns by which men form associations to pursue various interests and achieve co-ordinated and common action between these associations. Robert M. MacIver, for example, combines these two meanings in his definition of community as "any gathering, in one fairly localizable place, of people who are sorted out into various kinds of interacting groups and who share consciousness of spatial unity and social and cultural resemblance. . . . (The community) is set off from other communities purely for convenience of analysis and study." Quoted by Bennett and Tumin, *Social Life,* p. 389.

3. A Yale University Ph.D. dissertation was written about the community, using it as a case history of the industrial revolution in America. The city's history serves as a compact example of the influences of the machine age. The dissertation provided a carefully documented historical perspective for this study. Constance McLaughlin Green, *Holyoke, Massachusetts; A Case History of the Industrial Revolution in America* (New Haven, 1939).

4. For example, Elin L. Anderson, *We Americans* (Cambridge, 1937), pp. 82-87; Wendell King, "Social Cleavage in a New England Community," *Social Forces,* March 1946, pp. 322-527; Caroline Ware, *Greenwich Village* (Boston, 1935), pp. 127-129.

5. There has been one published attempt to summarize the factors affecting religious relations in cities across the nation. It was too cursory for thoroughness (thirteen American and three Canadian communities) and does not deal with religious relations in their interdependence with such factors as size of population or the economic, political and social status of religious groups, etc. See Claris E. Silcox and Galen M. Fisher, *Catholics, Jews and Protestants* (New York, 1934). Recent analyses of religious relations in America have been made by Will Herberg in *Protestant—Catholic—Jew; An Essay in American Religious Sociology* (New York, 1955), and by John J. Kane in his *Catholic-Protestant Conflict in America* (Chicago, 1955).

6. New York *Times,* December 29, 1950.

7. The nature of the study was explained to the chancellor of the Springfield diocese and a list of the formal questions to be asked various Roman Catholic clergy presented. The Most Rev. Thomas Mary O'Leary, bishop of the Springfield Diocese, now deceased, requested that the questions at first be submitted with a letter explaining the study to all the priests of the community, and interviews conducted later if the researcher desired. The mailed questionnaire produced few replies. It did serve as a valuable introduction of the study, the researcher and the basic questions to be asked in interview. After interviews had been held with the priests, most of them co-operated in answering questionnaires for certain data.

8. Letter from chancellor of the Springfield Diocese May 1, 1947, to the investigator clarifying the status of the study. In short, co-operation with the researcher was licit on the part of the priests, but it was not obligatory. For distinctions in status see the Rev. Stephen Joseph Kelleher, *Discussions With*

Non-Catholics, Canon Law Studies No. 180 (Catholic University of America, Washington, D. C., 1943), p. 6.

9. See, for example, Michael Williams, *The Catholic Church in Action* (New York, 1934), p. 2.

Chapter 1

The Incident

1. What is called "birth control" by Roman Catholics and Protestants in Paper City is the use of contraceptives to prevent insemination. Abstention from intercourse and advantage taken of fluctuations in the fertility cycle for reasons of health are considered by Paper City priests legitimate moral acts of lay men and women. The term "birth control" is confined to use of contraceptives.

2. Letter from executive director of the Mothers' Health Council to pastor of the First Congregational Church, September 28, 1940.

3. The Grace Church pastor was approached first by the Council, according to the director, because he had a reputation in the state for fearless action when he was personally convinced of the importance of a cause.

4. Interviews, Blanton and pastor of Grace Congregational Church; and diary of events kept by Blanton during the Sanger incident.

5. The signers, as the letter indicated were: a university president, a prominent Negro civic leader, a former president of a bar association, the president of the American Unitarian Association, the director of a famous hospital, a dean of a medical school, a former president of the Federation of Women's Clubs, a Roman Catholic physician and hospital administrator and others.

6. In 1931 the General Council of the Congregational Christian Churches, the denomination of Mr. Blanton, had endorsed the majority report issued March 21, 1931 by the Committee on Marriage and the Home of the Federal Council of the Churches of Christ in America. The report was entitled "The Moral Aspects of Birth Control." This report held that the use of birth under the guidance of the Christian conscience and the direction of the medical profession is moral and right. Both the majority and the minority of the committee agreed that a church, whatever its conviction about contraception, "should not seek to prohibit physicians from imparting such information to those who in the judgment of the medical profession are entitled to receive it." The General Council of the Congregational Christian Churches in 1931 also expressed a belief "in the right of children to be wanted and the right of husbands and wives to assume parenthood. Therefore, we favor the principle of voluntary child-bearing, believing that it sacramentalizes physical union and safeguards the well-being of the family and society."

7. From a statement by the Standing Committee of the First Congregational Church, October 20, 1940, clarifying the role of the minister in the incident.

8. Letter to Mr. Blanton from field director, Mothers' Health Council, October 14, 1940, and the diary of Mr. Blanton.

9. Letter from Mr. Blanton to executive director, Mothers' Health Council, October 16, 1940.

10. The executive director wrote to Mr. Blanton about the sponsor's decision. Letter to Mr. Blanton from executive director, Mothers' Health Council, October 17, 1940.

11. Springfield *Union,* October 14, 1940.

12. Interview, pastor, Holy Rosary parish, May 27, 1947.

13. Holyoke *Transcript,* October 14, 1940.

14. Interview, senior priest who was involved in the incident, May 29, 1947. Msgr. McGuire had died before this investigation was undertaken.

15. The quotation of the statement by Msgr. McGuire is based on a copy approved by him and given to an Amherst College student soon after the declaration was made.

16. Springfield *Union,* October 14, 1940.

17. Holyoke *Transcript,* October 14, 1940.

18. Letter from Blanton to director of Mothers' Health Council, October 16, 1940.

19. Interview, reporter on Holyoke *Transcript* during the Sanger incident, June 10, 1947.

20. Some of the Catholic laymen had been asked specifically by priests to talk with these Protestant laymen and the setting had been planned. Interview, senior priest, May 27, 1947; also interviews with two of the Roman Catholic laymen concerned, July 15, 1947.

21. *Ibid.;* also notes made by Blanton after he had talked with business men approached at the Rotary meeting.

22. Letter from Blanton to Mothers' Health Council, October 16, 1940.

23. Letter from Blanton to director of Council for Social Action, October 21, 1940.

24. Letter from Blanton to Mothers' Health Council, October 16, 1940.

25. Letter from Blanton; interview, senior priest.

26. Interview, senior priest, May 29, 1947.

27. The banker died, three months after the Sanger incident, of a heart attack.

28. Interview, senior priest, May 29, 1947.

29. *Ibid.*

30. Interview, member of the board of directors of the Paper City Savings Bank, May 20, 1947.

31. *Ibid.*

32. Blanton made a special inquiry to verify this fact a few days after the special meeting. Interviews with three laymen on the standing committee also verified this.

33. Minutes of the Standing Committee.

34. The description of the special session of the Standing Committee is based, unless otherwise indicated, on interviews with members present conducted a few weeks after the controversy by Dr. Leland Foster Wood, investigator for the Federal Council of Churches of Christ in America. Dr. Wood also collected some written statements from members of the Committee. "The Free Speech Issue in Holyoke," *Information Service,* March 22, 1941.

35. "Appeasement in Holyoke—A Story with a Strange Ending," *Protestant Digest,* February—March, 1941, p. 73. This article is based on a report made by the Mothers' Health Council of the Sanger incident.

36. Holyoke *Transcript,* October 17, 1940.

37. In most Protestant churches, authority to use property is vested in parish committees.

38. Some Protestant ministers and laymen expressed increasing fear of mob

action against the meeting. A First Church layman, after consulting with Blanton, had called the chief of police, asking for police protection at the meeting. The chief recalls telling the layman, "You're making a big mistake up there, but I'll give you the protection if you want it." The director of the Mothers' Health Council wrote Blanton: "The only dignified procedure to follow in a matter of this kind is to proceed as though we were living in a society where differences of opinion are respected. It seems to me that it will be a definite mistake to ask for police protection."

39. Springfield *Republican,* October 16, 1940.

40. Holyoke *Transcript,* October 17, 1940.

41. Note the description of Mrs. Sanger as a woman "married twice," making her tour in a "convertible coupé," being entertained at tea in Longmeadow, a fashionable suburb of Springfield, etc.

42. "Appeasement in Holyoke—A Story with a Strange Ending," p. 74.

43. Interview, officer in Knights of Columbus, July 15, 1947, and the mayor, June 25, 1947.

44. "Appeasement in Holyoke—A Story with a Strange Ending," p. 74.

45. *Ibid.,* p. 72.

46. Description of the meeting is based largely on accounts in the Springfield *Union* and the Holyoke *Transcript* of October 18, 1940.

47. This story was the culmination of an editorial policy favoring the opposition parties to the birth-control group. On October 15, 1940, the executive director of the Mothers' Health Council had written the edior of the *Transcript:* "I happened to see a report of your speech on freedom of the press in South Hadley, which was carried in many state papers, and was encouraged thereby to believe that the *Transcript* would, after having carried a long story on the attack upon this meeting, give treatment to the point of view which will be represented by Mrs. Sanger and those of us in the state who believe that there can be no harmony in the community until this law interfering with medical freedom and parental rights is changed, and until there is respect and tolerance by each religious group toward the attitudes of other religious groups in the community."

Chapter 2

The Aftermath

1. The editor in an interview with the author said that she thought the meeting had brought about events that set one religious group against another.

2. Note that the editorial makes at this point no reference to any Protestant church pronouncements on birth control. In an interview, July 14, 1947, the editor said that when the editorial was written the Protestant churches had not made any statements of an "official nature" on the subject. As indicated later in this study, Protestant leaders did not present publicly at any time during the controversy Protestant church pronouncements on birth control.

3. Based on the measurement of space allotted to Blanton's personal views and church activities in the Holyoke *Transcript* from October 12, 1933 to October 12, 1947. In the seven years before Blanton's part in the Sanger incident he was called regularly by reporters of the *Transcript* for copies of summaries of his sermons for use in the newspaper. In the seven years following the incident he received no calls from local reporters for press material.

4. Seven years after the Sanger incident when the unity of the community did not seem to him so precarious, he talked about the controversy with more preciseness. He recalled that weapons of economic boycott had been used in the controversy, but confided "they were used only by a few bigoted priests and Catholic laymen." Interview, mayor, May 10, 1947.

5. *News Letter,* State Civil Liberties Committee, November, 1940.

6. As early as 1933, the *Catholic Mirror* was making comments such as this about the birth-control advocates: "[They are] the wealthy class who wish to drag the country down with them by spreading their pernicious doctrines among the poor and middle class who still, as a body, prefer children to lapdogs and babies to best sellers and wine cellars. Is anybody so blind as a wealthy man or woman? The common good means nothing to them, if they can only reduce the families of the poor so that the laborer, with no family to support, will need only a small wage." *Catholic Mirror,* March 1933, p. 7.

7. *Catholic Mirror,* November 1940, pp. 18-19.

8. Priests are unusually defensive on the birth-control issue and Protestant pastors unusually aggressive, as if both groups sense that the position of the Roman Catholic church on the use of artificial contraceptive devices is poorly observed by laymen. See Joseph H. Fichter, *Dynamics of a City Church* (Chicago, 1951), p. 263. Sixty-eight Catholic laymen in a "southern parish" were asked, "Do you think that it is a good idea for persons of limited income to practice rhythm for the first few years of marriage?" Thirty-five disapproved of the practice. Twenty-six approved, while seven did not know what to answer. The church does not approve it, but teaches that it is morally permissible only when there is a grave cause involved. The laymen were also asked, "Do you think it is better to raise two children in comfortable circumstances than five children in decent poverty?" Twenty-two replied affirmatively, forty-six replied negatively.

9. Holyoke *Transcript,* October 19, 1940.

10. Holyoke *Transcript,* October 18, 1940.

11. Leland Foster Wood, "The Free Speech Issue in Holyoke." *Information Service,* March 22, 1941.

12. *Ibid.*

13. Wood, *op. cit.* The *Protestant Digest* in its report on the incident observed that Protestants were a minority acting as if they were a majority, yet too weak to guarantee their own freedom of speech. "Appeasement in Holyoke—A Story with a Strange Ending," *op. cit.,* p. 74.

14. Interview, Leland Foster Wood, February 6, 1947.

15. "The Free Speech Issue in Holyoke," *op. cit.*

16. The senior pastor noted that "the Protestant ministers called in an investigator from their United Christian Council or whatever they call it. I was amused to read that they called him in not to investigate religion, mind you, but the violation of civil liberties." Interview, June 17, 1947.

17. "The Free Speech Issue in Holyoke," *op. cit.*

18. The pastor referred at one point in his statement to the declaration by the bishop of Springfield on birth control entitled "God Will Not Be Mocked!" This declaration, published by the *Catholic Mirror* Press (Springfield, April 27, 1928) reads in part: "Birth control, which would deny the boon of existence to children, defies the Divine Legislator by completely and wantonly

defeating his purpose in establishing and sanctifying marriage. There is no moral difference between denying birth to little ones and robbing them of existence after they are born, though one may be called birth control and the other may be stigmatized as murder."

19. Interview, senior pastor, June 17, 1947.

20. Interviews of thirty-two such leaders on the Sanger incident provided sample of lay institutional leadership.

21. The president of the local chapter of the Knights of Columbus is owner of a printing shop which has displayed prominently in its business office a slogan: "When two men in business always agree one is unnecessary." He does not believe that the slogan applies to religion "where truth is known absolutely by the church."

22. One of the most prominent Roman Catholic lawyers said he told a priest, "It was none of your business what Sanger said to the Congregationalists since they are not your parishioners."

Chapter 3

A Protestant City Becomes Catholic

1. Jacques Ducharme, *The Shadows of the Trees* (New York, 1943), p. 8.

2. *Seventeenth Census of the United States,* 1950, Population, Vol. II; Part 21, Table 4. The trend of the population in Paper City for the period from 1910 to 1950 is different from the trend of the state and of the nation. Both the state and the nation showed an increase of population in each decade although the rate of increase declined (Table I).

3. A number of sources have been used for demographic data. The reports of the United States Bureau of Census on Population are, of course, basic. *The Sixteenth Census of the United States,* 1940, Population, Vol. II, Part 3, and *Seventeenth Census of the United States,* 1950, Population, Vol. II, Part 21 were used most extensively. Constance M. Green, *Holyoke, Massachusetts; A Case History of the Industrial Revolution in America* (New Haven, 1939), reports data from the *Census of State of Massachusetts,* 1850-1900, and other historical records from the nineteenth century. "Report of Water Board," *Municipal Register of Holyoke* is a precise record for non-census years. Analysis of general trends in the city and comparisons with state and national developments have been carefully made in a manuscript "Population Trends in Holyoke: 1910-1940" (Mimeographed, Department of Economics and Sociology, Mount Holyoke College, 1944).

4. For analysis of comparative influence of social and religious factors, see Samuel A. Stauffer, "Trends in Fertility of Catholics and Non-Catholics," *American Journal of Sociology,* September 1935, pp. 143-166; P. K. Whelpton, "Geography and Economic Differentials in Fertility," *Annals of the American Academy of Political and Social Sciences,* November 1936, pp. 48-51; Paul H. Landis, "Religion and the Birth Rate," *Forum,* March 1946, pp. 595-599.

5. In the total national situation the Catholics are confronted with the problem of membership largely in urban areas (approximately 80 per cent in 1936), which have lower birth rate than rural areas. See G. K. Robinson, "Catholic Birthrate: Further Facts and Implications," *American Journal of Sociology,* May 1936, p. 757; A. J. Jaffe, "Religious Differentials in Net Re-

production Rate," *American Statistical Association Journal,* June 1939, pp. 338, 340, 342; Grace M. Fraymann, "Comparative Birth Rates of Dubuque, Iowa, 1930-1940," (M.A. thesis, University of Iowa, 1942).

6. Patrick J. Lucey, *History of St. Jerome's Parish,* Introduction by Father McCoy (Holyoke, 1931), p. 17.

7. Lucey, *op. cit.,* p. 17.

8. *Ibid.* The figures for Roman Catholics were for communicants, with deductions made for children under nine years of age. Protestant figures were for church members and did not include those who only attended Sunday School.

9. A Unitarian magazine published in Boston (*Christian Register*) commented as follows on the first religious census study made public by the Massachusetts Council of Churches: "There is an obvious need in the nation for a carefully planned religious census. Much of the bigotry throughout the nation can be traced to a misunderstanding of the facts. We Protestants in New England have had a definite 'minority feeling' for many years. Actually the only reasons that we have such small groups in comparison with the Roman Catholics is because we have not gone out to invite the overwhelming majority of non-Catholics to become Protestants."

A Roman Catholic newspaper in the state (the Boston *Pilot*) replied: "If the effort were worth the time and money, it should be possible to discern the exact Catholic, Protestant and Jewish proportions in Boston. But is there any general desire for this information? . . . When the *Christian Register* printed the statistics that Boston is 74.3 per cent Catholic, we were not for one instant inspired by a wish to increase 'majority consciousness in Catholic minds—nor to insinuate into non-Catholic minds a minority consciousness'. . . . The atomic bomb seemed much more worthy of worry than this polite disagreement between statisticians—and over a matter barren of all practical significance."

Both editorials were quoted in the *Christian Science Monitor* [Boston], April 16, 1946, p. 4.

10. See Appendix for an explanation of the methods used in securing and evaluating data on contemporary church membership.

11. The total of eleven churches for the Roman Catholics includes one church called the Holy Family Church, which is a religious organization for a Catholic orphanage located geographically outside Paper City's limits, but listed by the diocese as a Paper City church.

The term "church" as used here included all organizations of "persons for religious worship whether under the name of church, meeting, mission station, etc., which has a separate membership, that is, no members of which are included in the membership of any similar organizations." *United States Religious Census:* Religious Bodies, 1936, Vol. II, Part 1, p. x. In later chapters a distinction will be made between sects and churches.

12. Statement is based on a study using 1940 and 1936 United States Census data and church yearbook data and conducted by the Massachusetts Council of Churches in 1942. The accuracy of its use of census data has been verified.

13. The greatest decline in the population of the community since 1920 has been in the group under ten years of age. This change is in the same direction as that in the population of the state, but the decline began earlier in Paper City and is more severe. The only age group which increased proportionally between 1920 and 1950 was that over 45 years of age. The portion of the

population over 45 years of age in 1940 and 1950 is greater for the city than the state. The advancing age of Paper City's population must not be used as a partial explanation of the lower birth rate, since the percentage of persons between the ages of 20 and 44 is slightly greater for Paper City than for the state.

14. A comparison of the deaths of foreign-born in each decade with the decennial change in the number of foreign-born gives an estimate of the net immigration of foreign-born into Paper City. The estimates indicate that foreign immigration to Paper City in recent years has been negative—a loss of 641 from 1920 to 1930, and of 748 from 1930 to 1940. The number of deaths of foreign-born are obtainable for each year from the "Report of the Board of Health," as published in the *Municipal Register of Holyoke.* Interpretation of the results of the calculations must be qualified in one important respect: the statistics of deaths were recorded by place of occurrence. Deaths of persons who had entered the city after a given year would give an upward bias to the estimates of new immigration.

15. The statistics for converts to Catholicism published by the church are generally very similar to figures for adult baptism. Adult baptisms may be for pagans, for converts from Protestantism, or for people who have been reared Catholics but wish to be baptized again since records are not available. See Claris E. Silcox and Galen Fisher, *Catholics, Jews and Protestants* (New York, 1934), pp. 299-300 for discussion of the difficulties that convert statistics present in research. The chancery of the Springfield diocese in which Paper City is located indicated that the convert statistics given for this study are for previous Protestants.

Comparable Protestant data was difficult to obtain, since Protestant leaders do not claim to keep systematic records, as do the Catholics. In most instances, church membership records had to be gone over with the pastors to develop the data.

16. In Paper City the converts to Roman Catholicism averaged in 1940 about one to a priest (33 priests, 36 converts). The converts to Protestantism averaged approximately two to a minister (14 ministers, 29 converts).

17. *Official Catholic Directory* (Washington, 1946), p. 739.

18. *Official Catholic Directory* claims 100,628 converts for 1946 and a Catholic population in the United States of 26,700,000.

19. *Seventeenth Census of the United States, 1950 Population,* Vol. II, Part 21, p. 35.

Chapter 4

The Role of the Churches in Man's Salvation

1. See Appendix for a note about the sources of information for this and the following two chapters.

2. Theological debate in Paper City goes on largely within each institution as leaders tell members and the investigator of their differences with other groups. As other chapters will document, there is almost no direct discussion of doctrine between Protestant and Catholic clergy and very little explicitly between laymen.

3. The terms "churches" and "sects" are used at various points in this study as pointing to distinct realities. The terms are fairly well established in

sociological meaning, while theologically diverse in usage. See Liston Pope, *Millhands and Preachers* (New Haven, 1942), pp. 117-140. Various characteristics of the sect may be listed depending on which sect is being described—emotional, strict and legalistic in ethical standards; views itself as opposed to or separate from contemporary culture in a number of ways; highly inclusive in its demands on members' time and interests; narrow or particularistic in membership; informal, spontaneous, fervent, evangelistic in worship; relatively poor in economic status of members and value of property of the organization; and nonco-operative and suspicious of other religious groups. The sect's characteristics are generally opposed to the church from which it springs or against which it grows, but the relation of church and sect is dynamic, the sect in time tending to become a church and experiencing new fissions in protest against the transition. The church tends toward an acceptance of general cultural standards with ritualistic or social prerequisites for membership; views itself as in no radical opposition to contemporary culture, working with people in centers of power to transform or add to their loyalties; universal in membership, accepting at least all who are socially compatible; formal, traditional, restrained education and worship; membership comparatively well-to-do, possessing church property; co-operative in public relations, often with pity or disdain for other religious groups.

4. Paul Tillich calls this the "central principle of Protestantism": the doctrine that "no individual and no human group can claim a divine dignity for its moral achievements, for its sacramental power, for its sanctity, or for its doctrine," and that when such claims are made, they are to be challenged by the "prophetic protest, which gives God alone absoluteness and sanctity and denies every claim of human pride." *The Protestant Era* (Chicago, 1948), p. 226.

5. It is significant that most of the sect religious leaders, whose members are largely converts from the Roman Catholic church, place greatest doctrinal emphasis upon the "salvation by faith alone" theme, greater than upon personal holiness, Biblical authority, or eschatology. Although the sect group, and its activities, consumes much more of the time of its members than do most of the Protestant churches, there is no developed doctrine of the religious significance of the sect community. This is so of all the sects with the exception of Jehovah's Witnesses. The revolt against Catholicism apparently leads to a re-emphasis upon one of the basic tenets of evangelical Protestantism. The emphasis on personal purity and Biblical literalism are still major aspects of the sects' theological concern, but the most aggressive witness is concerned with the "role of Christ, not the church in man's salvation." 40 per cent of the members of Gospel Hall are former Roman Catholics, 60 per cent of the Jehovah's Witnesses, 92 per cent of the Polish Evangelistic Assembly, and 95 per cent of the Polish Study Group.

6. H. Richard Niebuhr, *Christ and Culture* (New York, 1951), pp. 45-82.

7. No inference should be made that the leaders of churches whose institutional characteristics can be located as closest to the Roman Catholic position are the most co-operative with Roman Catholic leaders. Various scholars have made such inferences. See for example, Elin L. Anderson, *We Americans; A Study of Cleavage in an American City* (Cambridge, 1937), pp. 80-81. The author maintains that there are two opposing doctrinal movements in Protes-

tantism working toward different results in religious relations: (1) a tendency working toward intensification of differences between Catholics and Protestants. "This is growth of humanism away from 'authoritarianism' and 'religion of man's faith in himself.'" (2) A tendency working to bring Protestants and Catholics closer in philosophy. "This is represented by a new demand that the 'church regain its authority' and that people 'return to religious discipline.'" In Paper City, the minister who most epitomizes the first position is the most highly disliked by Roman Catholic priests.

8. Constance McLaughlin Green, *Holyoke, Massachusetts: A Case History of the Industrial Revolution in America* (New Haven, 1939), pp. 322-333, describes the trends in doctrine, cultus and polity of the Protestant religious institutions from 1859 to 1922. See also G. C. Osgood, *Story of the Holyoke Churches* (Holyoke, 1890).

9. This complex tension of faith and institutional form which revolves about the justification by faith principle is so crucial that the sociologist of religion must deal adequately with it in a study of Roman Catholic-Protestant relations. The tension cannot be observed simply in terms of the degree to which a religious institution tends toward elaboration or simplification of doctrine, toward informal or formal worship or toward professional or nonprofessional leadership. The tension is also revealed in the self-interpretation by the religious group of the meaning of form and by what Wach seeks to designate when he talks of the spirit of the religious group, of its sense of breaking with the forms of previous religious experience expressed in such concepts as regeneration, rebirth and conversion. (See Joachim Wach, *Sociology of Religion*, p. 110). The tension is also revealed in the dynamic aspects of institutional analysis, the shifts in form, as Liston Pope observed in his treatment of the processes of sect-church development in *Millhands and Preachers* (see pp. 117-140). A distinctive characteristic in the objectification of the justification by faith principle is the act which breaks with a dogmatic formulation in order to make way for a new interpretation, with a standardized rite in order to express a new sense of the relation of the sacred and the secular, or with the old polity to order a new witness. The sect has most often been characterized as objectifying this protest, but the sect's external form may represent the justification by faith belief simply as static dogma as much as does the church form. A religious group may decide to express its beliefs through a protest against simple sect forms which have become too confining in its life and through development of a more churchlike institution.

10. Parochial Catholicism has been less exact in stating the authoritative Catholic position on the relation of the church to faith and salvation than such statements as the following:

"A necessary condition for the act of faith . . . is that the believer should know what God has revealed; the object of faith must be presented to him as credible on the divine authority. . . . There are undoubtedly many outside the Catholic Church, who, inculpably rejecting or not knowing her claim to be the infallible guardian of divine truth, yet believe some Christian doctrines by a supernatural act of divine faith. . . . There are exceptional cases. . . . 'That we may be able to satisfy the obligation of embracing the true faith and of constantly persevering therein, God has instituted the Church through his only-begotten Son, and has bestowed on it manifest marks of that institution, that it may be recognized by all men as the guardian and teacher of the revealed word' (Vatican Council)." "Faith as Revealed Truth," Rev. George D. Smith in *The Teaching of the Catholic Church,* ed. by Dr. Smith, Vol. I, New York, 1949, pp. 27-28.

"The first element in the great work of Justification is the grace of God—actual grace. No man can have faith in Christ, no man can even have a genuine desire to possess it, unless the grace of God first draws him. It is for man to accept this grace or to reject it. If he accepts it and listens to the voice of God speaking to him, he is led on to make a true act of faith; that is, he is enabled by God to believe what has been divinely revealed, and more particularly the doctrines of the Redemption and of the forgiveness of sins. With this belief in his heart he is moved to hope in God and to love him, and to turn his heart away from sin. Thus, under the influence of actual grace, a soul is prepared for Justification. Hence it is not a matter of faith alone, but of faith which leads to hope and love and genuine sorrow: yet faith is the foundation of the whole process, or, as the Council of Trent puts it, 'the beginning, the foundation, and the root of all Justification.'" "Sanctifying Grace," Rev. E. Towers, in Smith, *The Teaching of the Catholic Church,* Vol. I, p. 566.

11. Rev. Edward M. Betowski, *The True Church* (New York, 1938).

12. Rev. P. Henry Sullivan, *First Communion Catechism* (New York, 1936), p. 9. Sullivan is a priest in charge of social welfare work in Paper City. The catechism is widely used in Paper City parishes.

13. "Editorial Ripples: Nazi or Christian," *Catholic Mirror,* July 1945, p. 11.

14. It should be noted that at the Council of Trent, Session Four (Declarations on the Canons of the Scriptures), tradition is set on the same level as the Scriptures. The Vulgate is regarded as of equal authority with the original texts. Karl Heim, *Spirit and Truth,* translated by Edgar P. Dickie (London, 1935), p. 103.

15. Sister Therese Mueller, *Family Life in Christ,* (Second Edition, Collyville, Minnesota, 1942).

16. The Catholic and Protestant leaders in Paper City have long been in dispute as to whether the Catholic clergy encourage study of the Bible by laymen. As early as 1858, the first Catholic pastor in Paper City was writing to the local newspaper to answer Protestant charges, claiming that "the Bible is in the hands of every Catholic family, even here in Holyoke; for instance, James Talor and Thomas Burns, North Block, possess two splendid Douay Bibles." Patrick J. Lucey, *History of St. Jerome's Parish,* p. 35.

17. Father Felix, "Why—Questions Answered," *Catholic Mirror,* January 1946, p. 46.

18. See Appendix B for a discussion of the methodological problems in connection with content analysis of material in this study. Two years of issues of the *Catholic Mirror* were studied, 1946 and 1947. Sermons were recorded in three Catholic churches each Sunday during April, May, June and July of 1947, the churches being rotated, so that all were included in the sample.

19. "On Who Will Do the Driving," *Catholic Mirror,* August 1946, p. 34.

20. Richard Ginder, *Prevention and Cure* (New York; Catholic Information Society, 1943), p. 6.

21. "Christmas Cards," *Catholic Mirror,* December 1946, p. 42.

22. "As Modern as Eden," *Catholic Mirror,* June 1945, p. 33.

23. Holyoke *Transcript,* May 17, 1947, p. 8.

Chapter 5

Worship in the Churches

1. Rev. P. Henry Sullivan, *First Communion Catechism* (New York, 1936), pp. 10 and 12.

2. Rev. P. Henry Sullivan, *Double Novena to the Holy Family* (Worcester, 1942), p. 47.

3. "God's Gift: Priests," *Catholic Mirror,* January 1947, p. 34.

4. Protestant interpretations of church service as a social act are reported in the diocesan press, for example a speech by Kinsey Merrit before the Chicago Federation of Churches for Greater Chicago in which he is quoted as saying: "The friendly side of church should be stressed, and it must be made a place of welcome. The churches should be comfortable—where people will feel as relaxed and at ease as they do in a movie house or high class theatre." Rev. Frank J. Ford, syndicated Catholic Column, "Miscellaneous Briefs," *Catholic Mirror,* March 1946, p. 27.

5. See, for example, "Newspaper Editors on the Church," *Catholic Mirror,* January 1946, p. 4; "On Our Mass and Our Remembrance," *Catholic Mirror,* November 1946, p. 22. Sullivan, *First Communion Catechism,* p. 11.

6. Gregoria Fede, "God's Most Wonderous Gift—a Child," *Catholic Mirror,* December 1945, p. 24.

7. The *National Catholic Almanac* (Paterson, N. J., 1952) notes that the devotion to the Infant Jesus of Prague "began in the early 17th century in Prague, Bohemia. Princess Polixena, of Prague, presented the Carmelites there with a statue of the Infant which she herself had treasured for many years. Not long afterward, war and persecution befell the city and the statue was lost and forgotten. Some years later it was recovered and devotions were again instituted which have since spread throughout the world with greatly beneficial results" (p. 298).

8. A "pioneer" of the Jehovah's Witnesses on learning from a Catholic layman about the priest's interpretation of the efficacy of the statue commented, "Such a God is my devil." Observation, July 14, 1947.

9. Rev. P. Henry Sullivan, *My Holy Hour with Jesus* (Holyoke, 1938), p. 3.

10. "On Our Mass and Our Remembrance," p. 22.

Chapter 6

The Faith of Laymen

1. Will Herberg in his *Protestant-Catholic-Jew* makes much of religious "identification" and "belonging" in American culture. The nature of this identification needs careful and precise study. Herberg wants to maintain two incompatible theses: (a) that the American creed of "spiritual values" (such as brotherhood and tolerance) is widely accepted among laymen in our churches, and that this creed has become a "religiousness without religion" with little or no intellectual content; (b) that the identification of the American people with their religion has become their most important way of "finding their place" in life and culture. Both hypotheses cannot be correct; much more complex phenomena compose the American religious scene as the summary to this chapter seeks to indicate.

Chapter 7

The Spiritual Authority of the Religious Leader

1. Paul Blanshard, *American Freedom and Catholic Power* (Boston, 1949), p. 6.

2. See A. M. Henderson and Talcott Parsons translators, *Max Weber: The Theory of Social and Economic Organization* (New York, 1947), particularly pp. 358-359, and H. H. Gerth and C. Wright Mills, ed., *From Max Weber: Essays in Sociology* (New York, 1946), pp. 199, 264 ff.

3. Council of Trent, 23rd Session, Sixth Canon in *Canons and Decrees of the Council of Trent,* original text with English translation by Rev. H. J. Schueder, C.P. (St. Louis, Missouri, 1941).

4. Rev. Francis J. Connell, C.SS.R., *Shepherds of Christ's Flock* (New York, 1940), pp. 8, 9. Pamphlet distributed in Paper City parishes.

5. "A Priest of God," *Orphan Light,* diocesan social service bulletin, December, 1946, p. 1. Rev. P. Henry Sullivan, *Double Novena to the Holy Family,* Fifteenth Meditation. Also, "A Truly Great Priest," *Catholic Mirror,* May 1946, p. 23. A novel about a Paper City French Catholic family tells of the parents' reaction to their son's decision to become a priest. They at once began "to feel him a little strange for in a few years he would bear an immense responsibility on his shoulders, that of taking God in his hands." Jacques Ducharme, *The Delusson Family* (New York, 1939), p. 160.

6. Connell, *op. cit.,* p. 8.

7. The profession of faith for the convert in the Springfield diocese, of which Holyoke is a part, reads near the end: "Besides I accept, without hesitation, and profess all that has been handed down, defined and declared by the Sacred Canons and by the general Councils, especially by the Sacred Council of Trent and by the primacy and infallibility of the Roman Pontiff. At the same time I condemn and reprove all that the Church has condemned and reproved."

8. "Private Interpretation," *Catholic Mirror,* February 1947, p. 37.

9. The members are convinced, as a chairman of a pulpit supply committee noted, that "a minister who has a strong personality and is a real mixer can make this church." And the four qualities of leadership most commonly looked for in a pastor are an ability to preach an interesting sermon, high personal morality or character, sociability and good professional training. (Interviews and questionnaires were used for members of two pulpit supply committees in 1947 and 1950.)

Chapter 8

The Organization of the Religious Community

1. The bishop, during the period of this study, had met satisfactorily the standards of Rome, since he held the highest rank obtainable by a bishop, that of "assistant bishop at the pontifical throne." *Catholic Mirror,* March 1946, p. 17; *A Century of Catholicism in Western Massachusetts* (Springfield, 1931), p. 8.

2. The crucial importance of the authority of the bishop in a community is borne out by the fact that the more liberal policies instituted by a new bishop are being reflected in 1957 to some extent in freer association of the clergy, the reduction of fund-raising through gambling, etc.

3. Goodwin Watson, *Action for Unity* (New York, 1947), pp. 93-128, uses this phrase to define organized efforts of several individuals pooling their strength to shift the balance of power in a situation, as distinguished from educational activity to manipulate attitudes.

4. The organization of Paper City business and political life is described in Part III. For a study of the industrial organization of another New England community, see W. Lloyd Warner and J. O. Low, *The Social System of the Modern Factory* (New Haven, 1947), pp. 66-89, 134-158. For general studies of business and labor polity, see W. E. Moore, *Industrial Relations and the Social Order* (New York, 1949), pp. 71-164, 353-372.

5. Interviews were conducted with thirty parish society leaders, ten in French or Polish parishes, twenty in English-speaking parishes. It should be observed that a selection and attraction of laymen who are most favorably disposed to the traditional concerns and organization of the church takes place in the development of lay parish leadership whose views are described.

6. The understanding which the pastor establishes with laymen of his role in his "candidacy" for a church is important. In some instances, a genuine exchange of views of the minister has taken place between the "candidates" and the committees selected by the congregations to review the potential pastors. But in most instances the decision is largely a unilateral one, the searching questions all coming from the lay side.

7. A study was made of the literature used by the churches for educational purposes among adult laymen in 1946-1947. No ecumenical publications were used. A sample study of forty laymen designated by pastors as leaders in their churches indicated that none could recall reading such literature during the past year.

8. R. E. Wolseley, "The Church Press: Bulwark of Denominational Sovereignty," *Crozier Quarterly*, August 1946, pp. 356-358.

9. A study was made of all the minutes and documents of the Ministerial Association, interviews conducted with all the members and its public activities traced in all the local news publications. Supplementary information came from the records of the Council of Churches.

Chapter 9

Bingo and Building Funds: The Financial Problem

1. *A Century of Catholicism in Western Massachusetts* (Springfield, 1931), p. 326.

2. Massachusetts Department of Labor and Industries, Division of Statistics, "Employment and Pay Roll Earnings in Leading Cities," 1947.

3. See Chapter 12.

4. The power of raffles and lotteries to secure the participation of laymen in fund-raising campaigns in comparison with direct appeals is indicated by the fact that *Orphan Light*, a monthly publication of the diocesan Holy Family League of Charity and published in Paper City, in making direct appeals for funds receives about 3 or 4 per cent replies from its membership. When

it announced a raffle of a Chevrolet, the response jumped to 22 per cent. *Orphan Light,* May, 1947, p. 2.

5. *Holy Cross Dedication* (Holyoke, 1940), p. 13.

6. When the question of whether the city wished to legalize beano or bingo for "Charitable, civic, educational, fraternal or religious purposes" was put to a referendum vote in the state in 1944, charitable beano lost in Paper City by a vote of 6,450 to 5,989. The strongest vote for beano was in Wards 1 and 2, the poorest residential wards where the game had been extensively used to support Catholic churches and is now used. In no other ward, however, did beano receive a majority vote. Holyoke *Transcript,* November 5, 1944, p. 5.

7. Many of the Catholic religious and social clubs such as the Knights of Columbus operate monthly drawings costing one dollar to participate (*Caravel,* February 1946, p. 3). So extensive is the use of gambling as a source of income, that companies supplying novelties for prizes and wheels on consignment advertise regularly in the Catholic diocesan magazine. See, for example, *Catholic Mirror,* August 1945, p. 162.

8. Interview, pastor of Holy Rosary parish, May 27, 1947.

9. The statements of pastor of Holy Rosary parish quoted here were made in an interview May 27, 1947.

10. The monthly drawings are held on a Friday evening in Holy Rosary school. During World War II the lotteries and auctions included scarce items such as whiskey and butter obtained through the auspices of the parish. In one year over 10,000 pounds of butter were auctioned off, some of it selling for as much as $2.25 a pound.

11. Interview, pastor of Holy Rosary parish, June 10, 1947, and Holyoke *Transcript,* July 16, 1945, p. 1. The description of the Holy Rosary Lawn Fete is based on personal observation of the 1947 program.

12. Holyoke *Transcript,* July 16, 1951, p. 1. According to a municipal law (Acts, 1936; Chapter 222) in effect until 1944 groups conducting beano games were required to file within five days "a statement of the total proceeds and expense" with the mayor of the city or the selectman of the town" in which the game was held. The pastor of Holy Rosary parish did this and also began reporting then the data to the local press.

13. This estimate, according to one curate in the parish, is high—almost one-fourth higher than the pastor's estimate. The financial figures of the pastor of Holy Rosary parish are sometimes above those of other pastors. Precise details about church finances are difficult to obtain.

14. Interview with pastor in charge of a parish receiving funds from Holy Rosary.

15. Jacques Ducharme, *Shadows of the Trees* (New York, 1943), p. 224, describes the early fund-raising devices of the Catholic Church in Paper City.

16. See Holyoke *Transcript* report on referendum vote on legalizing beano, November 5, 1944, p. 5.

17. Holyoke *Transcript,* August 18, 1912. In a recent Grace Church calendar the pastor exhorted his members to "work as hard for God's cause as people in all sorts of organizations work for carnivals."

18. Holyoke *Transcript,* May 16, 1947.

19. In 1947 the priests privately differed among themselves more over the

extent to which the church should use gambling as a financial source than perhaps any other issue. In the 1950's a new bishop considerably reduced the gambling activity among the city's Catholics.

20. *Catholic Mirror*, "Around the Diocese," May 1946, p. 36.

21. Holyoke *Transcript*, November 6, 1944, p. 10.

22. Holyoke *Transcript*, July 23, 1945.

23. The income to Protestant churches in Paper City from investments and trust funds is a very minor item in their assets. For example, the average annual income to the Second Congregational Church from such sources has over the past five years been $1,200; in the First Congregational Church, only $850 (studies of reports by church treasurers to the annual meetings).

24. In another upper-middle class church, First Congregational Church, 10 families (4 per cent of the congregation) in 1933 were contributing three-fourths of the income of the church. By 1943, the pattern of a small clique support had been broken somewhat, with 10 families contributing 40 per cent of the income. These conclusions were reached in a careful study of the recent financial history of the church by the pastor.

25. *The Log*, 1917-1947, a published and candid record kept by the pastor of parish problems and activities has been the source of this and considerable other information given here.

26. One of the major financial practices of the minister has been to secure money from wealthy Protestants for the decoration of particular rooms in the church in their memory. The young people complain that funds have been obtained for richly furnished display rooms but no money is available for a recreation room with ping pong table and informal lounging furniture. Alan Peabody, *Grace Church in Holyoke: a Case Study* (Religious Education and Field Work Project, Mss. Springfield College, 1946), p. 50.

27. Patrick J. Luccy, *History of St. Jerome's Parish* (Holyoke, 1931), p. 30; *Caravel*, Knights of Columbus publication, October, 1931, pp. 4, 6; Ducharme, *The Shadows of the Trees*, p. 151.

28. Interviews with scores of Protestant professional and business men established that a campaign was conducted and substantial gifts of as much as $500 made.

29. Records of the contributions of Catholic employees of the Lyman Mills kept by the company are obtainable from the Harvard School of Business Administration. Lucey, *op. cit.*, p. 39.

30. Conclusion reached after consultation with president of Water Power Company about specific grants and after study of church histories. *Caravel*, October 1931, p. 4, acknowledges grants of land to Catholic churches.

31. Ducharme, *Shadows of the Trees*, p. 151.

32. *Orphan Light*, May 1947, p. 1.

33. Holy Family League of Charity, "Are You Satisfied With Your Life?" (Holyoke, 1947). Deletions in testimonials are in the leaflet.

34. Holy Family League of Charity, "As An Orphanland Helper," (Holyoke, 1947).

35. For example, Sacred Heart parish published in offset print a "Census of Adult Members and Financial Report." This lists every adult member, street by street and indicates contributions in four categories: Sittings Received, Day's Pay, Heat, Church and School Funds. Children's contributions

are listed according to: Christmas, Easter, Offertory and Church Support. The report gives no accounting of how the funds are used, but a brief summary is made each year in an oral report by the pastor. Perpetual Help parish publishes a similar report. The Lutheran church is the only Protestant church which publishes each year a report on envelope contributions of each member. It has a system of clerical authority similar to the Catholic churches in one respect: the strong sense of official charisma in the ministry.

36. The pastor of Perpetual Help parish reports almost every Sunday on how much money was given the previous Sunday and appeals for greater giving. The comprehensive and continuous nature of Catholic financial appeals cannot be grasped until the nonparish appeals are added: various societies and orders make periodic door-to-door canvasses for funds. Most local bars and grocery stores have "Help an Orphan" coin containers. Children are recruited into the Holy Family Association to "donate a penny a month for the salvation of pagan children." (*Century of Catholicism*, p. 226.)

37. One study was attempted by the author comparing the giving in the Lutheran church and the Sacred Heart parish, since both publish fairly carefully prepared records of the contributions of each member, both use envelope systems as their primary source of support and both parishes refuse to raise funds by gambling activities or by solicitation of large gifts from well-to-do people. The parishes each have a combination middle-labor class membership. Income from children and adults was included in study of both parishes. Contributions to various religious benevolences were not counted—only the contributions to regular local church support—since comparable data was not available for the giving to benevolences and charities by members.

The Sacred Heart parish received in 1946 from its members for sittings, day's pay offering, heat offering, church and school fund contributions, and from children's offerings, $50,578. With a membership of 6,519, the average contribution of each member was approximately $7.70. The Lutheran church received for local parish expenses $12,649, from 1,021 members. The average contribution was approximately $12.30. The Lutheran giving was compared with other Protestant middle-labor class churches and found to be slightly higher than the average, considerably greater than that of Grace Church. Sacred Heart parish could not be compared with other Catholic churches because of inadequate data.

38. Evaluation of the assessor's estimates, some Protestants argue, should take into account the possibility that a Catholic-controlled city government may have purposely placed lower estimates on the property of the Catholic churches than on that of the Protestant churches to protect the Catholic church's financial interests in case tax exemption of certain property should end. The estimates given are close to the amounts given in parish histories as to the initial cost of the church buildings in both cases. But both Protestant and Catholic estimates are below what the pastors now give in yearbook reports and interviews as the value of the property. The estimates on Catholic school property are usually lower than Catholic histories indicate the initial cost to have been. Even if the amount given for the value of the Catholic schools were doubled, the Catholic property in Paper City would be only $117 per Catholic person.

39. *Century of Catholicism*, p. 148; Holyoke *Transcript*, May 19, 1947, p. 1; *Paroisse du Precieux-sang; 75e Anniversaire de sa Fondation* (Holyoke, October 22, 1944), p. 23.

40. *Century of Catholicism,* p. 8.

41. Constance M. Green, *Holyoke, Massachusetts,* p. 125. In the words of some leading Protestant government officials in 1869: "We believe that the truest and best interest of a church consists in making provision for its own poor, and if the Roman Church would give attention to this important element of living Christianity, by following the Christian rule adopted by every other religious denomination in town, in providing for its own poor . . . it would secure a more abiding and heartfelt respect for their religion." Holyoke *Town Records,* 1869, p. 9.

42. The identification of wealth and power with the "correct" religion for many Catholics is indicated by the comment of a Catholic mill worker to a sect minister, "If your religion is so good, why do you have to worship in a store?"

Chapter 10

Tolerance and Religious Liberty

1. The *Catholic Mirror* quotes Pope Pius XI's encyclical on *The Christian Education of Youth* to the effect that the church does not say "that morality belongs purely, in the sense of exclusively, to her. She has never maintained that outside her fold and apart from her teaching man cannot arrive at any moral truth." *Catholic Mirror,* "Catholics and Freedom," April 1947, p. 15. (When no author's name is indicated for articles which appear in the *Catholic Mirror,* the item is an editorial of the publication.)

2. This is illustrated in the answers written by the director of the parochial schools in Paper City to the following two questions:

"Q. What do you think is the most constructive way for teachers to approach the area of interreligious relations in their teaching?

"A. To strive to inculcate in the hearts of the children the necessity of forbearance and at the same time to be so well-grounded in the truths of their holy religion as to be able intelligently to explain it and above all to strive by good example to encourage those outside the faith to desire to practice it.

"Q. What does your school teach in civics, history, and doctrine courses about relations between the various religious groups in Paper City? That is, what is the nature of the tolerance taught the children for other religious groups and what information is given as to their religious beliefs in comparison with Roman Catholic beliefs?

"A. Training in good citizenship is one of the first objectives of our school and it must be thought and lived. The school strives ever to set up high ideals and the practice of these ideals in everyday life which necessitated tolerance, patience and charity, of which St. Paul speaks so beautifully, in his Epistle to the Corinthians. Christ established only one Church, namely the Holy Roman Catholic Church."

3. The controversies examined in Paper City Catholicism go on among Catholics in America and in Europe. A number of exchanges between Catholics have clarified to some extent the points of tension. Several Roman Catholic publications in America have tried to differentiate, for example, between what may be a valid position on religious diversity in Spain and what for them would be valid in the United States. See the comments of *America,* a Jesuit organ, April 5, 1952, upon a pastoral letter of Cardinal Segura of

Seville regarding Protestantism in Spain. (For example: "The Cardinal is certain that in the religious situation of Spain religious liberty would be contrary to divine law. That is a prudential judgment. One can argue that in the situation of the world at large religious liberty in Spain is an ethical imperative.") See also the *Pilot's* critical comment upon an address of Cardinal Ottaviani of the Sacred Congregation which condemned the "liberalizing thesis" on church-state relations (March 7, 1953).

In 1953, Pope Pius XII presented a "Discourse on Religious Toleration" to the National Convention of Italian Catholic Jurists which deals at length with the relation and meaning of the two fundamental principles debated at length among Catholics in Paper City. Religious News Service issued the entire text in English translation December 15, 1953. The statement appears to some Protestants to encourage American "liberal" theorists, such as John Courtney Murray, while not rebuking the traditionalists. See *Memorandum,* Committee on Religious Liberty, National Council of Churches of Christ in America (January 1954).

The general position of the Roman Catholic clergy in their majority role in Paper City is to be identified with the more conservative and traditional positions expressed in American Catholicism.

4. "A Legend Ends," *Catholic Mirror,* August 1946.

5. These themes probably in general contribute to religious tension in the community, but their influence cannot be evaluated apart from the larger context of religious relations. Robin Williams, *The Reduction of Intergroup Tensions* (Social Science Research Council, Bulletin 57, 1947), p. 64, holds as an hypothesis supported by much of present research on intergroup relations, "The likelihood of conflict is reduced by education and propaganda emphases common to various groups rather than upon intergroup differences. But there is danger that attitudes thus created may lead to expectation of greater similarity than later experience demonstrates, and this can lead to disillusionment and secondary reinforcement of hostility." Williams also believes that present research suggests the position that reduction of intergroup hostility is through minimizing or carefully appraising the threat to one's group commitments by changes in intergroup relations, rather than by encouraging defensive action. P. 63.

6. Samuel Knox Wilson, *American History* (Chicago, 1946), pp. 18-20. This textbook was one of those used at the time of this study, according to a list prepared by the director of the parochial schools and the Mother Superiors in charge of the various schools.

7. Hugh Dunn, "The Counter-Offensive of the Sixteenth Century," *Catholic Mirror,* July 1945, p. 15.

8. In *Catholic Comics,* a comic book published as a business enterprise by laymen in Holyoke, Luther is described as a "proud, heretical, jealous Augustinian monk. When he was not chosen to preach throughout Europe for the Pope, he began a Protestant religion." *Catholic Comics,* Vol. I (Holyoke), November, 1946, p. 7.

9. Rev. Myron Florey, *Supermen of Church History* (Scranton, Pa., 1947), Sunday-school pamphlet distributed to pupils in the city's Catholic churches. Pages unnumbered.

10. "United States Drifting Into War," *Caravel,* March 1940, p. 5.

11. "A Legend Ends," *Catholic Mirror,* August 1946, p. 19.

12. "Loss of Religion" in Editorial Ripples, *Catholic Mirror,* April 1946, p. 17.

13. Rev. Daniel A. Lord, *Let's See the Other Side* (St. Louis, 1938), p. 20.

14. *Ibid.,* pp. 34-35.

15. Conclusion of a careful population study by the Massachusetts Council of Churches, 1944. Even in communities in the diocese where Catholicism is not the major faith, great numbers of Catholics have risen to positions of status high in the social structure and Catholic ethnic assimilation has been extensive.

16. See for example the *Catholic Mirror,* March 1945, p. 23; June 1946, p. 20; "The Rising Tide of Bigotry," April 1945, p. 7; Wilson, *American History,* p. 579; *A Century of Catholicism in Western Massachusetts* (Springfield, 1931), p. 143.

17. See Solomon Anhill Fineberg, "Strategy of Error," *Contemporary Jewish Record,* February 1945, pp. 25-30, for a brief analysis of Roman Catholic communications strategy in answering charges.

18. Robin Williams, *op. cit.,* p. 58, concludes that one of the major hypotheses supported by intergroup research is the ability of outside threats to increase the internal unity of a social group which is a "going concern."

19. See "Bishop Oxnam—Bigot," *Catholic Mirror,* June 1946, p. 20, and "Rising Tide of Bigotry," *Catholic Mirror,* April 1945, p. 7.

20. The single mention of Protestant mission activity in the diocesan press in the years 1946-47 appeared in this context: "Europe would seem to have almost completely succumbed to Moscow's rule, while south of our border infiltration of red propaganda and unabashed protestant proselytism threaten the Catholic life of millions of people." From the mission page—"Go Teach All Nations," conducted by the diocesan director of missions, *Catholic Mirror,* September 1946, p. 29.

21. "Encouraging the Reds," reprint from *Our Sunday Visitor* by the *Catholic Mirror,* October 1946, p. 24.

22. *Ibid.,* and "The Rising Tide of Bigotry," *Catholic Mirror,* April 1945, p. 7; "Bishop Oxnam—Bigot," June 1946, p. 20.

23. "Troublemaker Bishop," *Catholic Mirror,* April 1947, p. 40. Another attack in the *Catholic Mirror* on Oxnam says: "He pays lip service to freedom, is silent on the rape of Poland and of the Baltic States and of the Balkans. He praises the Red terrorists who drenched Spain with the blood of Christ's priests and nuns . . ." Everett Conway, "Bishop Oxnam—Bigot," *Catholic Mirror,* June 1946, p. 20.

24. "Fearful News," *Catholic Mirror,* January 1945, p. 9.

25. "On Who Will Do the Driving," *Catholic Mirror,* August 1946, p. 34.

26. Interview, June 11, 1947. Over 100 Catholic laymen were interviewed for this study. The sample included Catholic parish and city-wide society leaders and rank-and-file members from the major ethnic and class categories given in Chapters 12 and 13.

27. "Doctrine is Essential," *Catholic Mirror,* February 1946, p. 7; editorial, *Caravel,* publication of the Paper City Chapter, Knights of Columbus, November 1931, p. 2.

28. *Catholic Mirror,* April 1947, p. 40.

29. At the time of the study, a new constitution was being written for Italy.

30. "Catholics and Freedom," *Catholic Mirror,* April 1947, p. 16.

31. "Committee for Constitutional Government," *Catholic Mirror,* November 1944, p. 9.

32. "Religious Liberty," *Catholic Mirror,* January 1946, p. 9.

33. The journal also rebukes the Federal Communications Commission for its ruling permitting atheists to present their views on the air, observing that "there are no unchangeable principles unless there is a God. The FCC ruling on atheism is a ruling in favor of anarchy." "Freedom of Speech," *Catholic Mirror,* February 1947, p. 22.

34. In the position developed by such American Catholic theologians as Father Murray, who is seeking to adapt to the modern democratic society the distinctions developed by John of Paris between the spiritual and temporal orders, freedom of religious association and free expression of religious opinion, while conceived to be liberties with a distinct importance of their own, are like freedom of speech, press and association at the heart of the modern democratic state. These freedoms are natural freedoms. Father Murray holds that it is not politically possible to exempt one of the freedoms—such as religious liberty—and to maintain the others. John Courtney Murray, "Contemporary Orientations of Catholic Thought on Church and State in the Light of History," *Theological Studies,* Vol. X (Woodstock, Maryland), June 1953.

35. The words quoted in this and the following paragraph are those of three Roman Catholic pastors, and represent the general position taken by all Catholic clergy in Paper City on the relation of civil and religious liberty.

36. See Chapter 18 for description of the Catholic interpretations of the boundaries of the natural and supernatural areas. What issues the Catholic considers religious and therefore the province of the church have a great deal of influence upon the degree of freedom and autonomy available to other religious groups in a community where the church has great influence.

37. The use of economic boycott was the concrete method on which leaders' attitudes were tested. The use of physical coercion was not at issue here.

38. The boycotting activity has been used chiefly against people in business or economic activity where consumer pressure is most directly felt, such as shoe repair shops, grocery stores, banks, and the like. The managers and owners of manufacturing establishments in Paper City believe that tension over religious issues can disturb labor morale and harmonious relations between management and employees during work, but the vulnerability of such businesses to Catholic economic action is slighter than in retail areas. Interviews were conducted with Protestant business men involved in boycotts and with managers of eleven manufacturing concerns in Paper City, August, 1947.

39. Interviews were held with the Protestant bank director who talked with the priest and with the two bank clerks who signed the petition. The clerk involved in the director's conversation with the priest was not informed that the proposal was to be made to the priest that the clerk talk with him.

40. Interviews were conducted with the mayor, members of staff and board of directors of the Family Welfare League, the pastor of Polish Evangelistic Assembly, the pastor of Mater Dolorosa Church, the editor and a member of the staff of the newspaper involved.

41. The unpublished data of the Yale Intergroup Research Project, a study of Protestant Sunday school literature under the sponsorship of the American

Jewish Committee, documents the tremendous attention now being given to Catholic-Protestant relations in such material.

42. The sermons of three pastors on religious relations delivered over the past three years were available in manuscript form. Two-thirds of the Protestant sermons preached by pastors over the past three years in the largest churches in the city dealt with Protestant New England bigotry from a critical viewpoint.

43. Interviews with fifteen converts to four Protestant churches in 1947 disclosed that only four had received religious instruction before being accepted as members. One convert reported that the chief help he received in understanding the nature of Protestantism was from a comic-book Bible given him by a friend.

44. The pastor conducts one class in comparison of his denomination's basic doctrine with Protestant and Catholic beliefs. All other Lutheran church school classes for people in the teen ages or beyond develop explicitly and systematically the doctrinal likenesses and differences of the major Christian positions and define norms for relations of Lutherans and non-Lutherans. The sects also deal regularly with Roman Catholic and Protestant differences in their educational programs.

45. The definition of religious liberty developed by the Federal Council of Churches of Christ in America could be said to be an adequate and concise statement of the consensus of the Paper City pastors: "Religious liberty shall be interpreted to include freedom to worship according to conscience and to bring up children in the faith of their parents; freedom for the individual to change his religion; freedom to preach, educate, publish, and carry on missionary activities; and freedom to organize with others, and to acquire and hold property, for these purposes." (Adopted by the Federal Council of Churches of Christ in America, March 21, 1944.)

Chapter 11

Interfaith Association

1. See, for example, two canon law studies: Thomas J. Clarke, *Parish Societies,* Canon Law Studies, No. 176 (Catholic University of America, Washington, D. C., 1943); and Rev. Stephen Joseph Kelleher, *Discussions with Non-Catholics,* Canon Law Studies, No. 180 (Catholic University of America, Washington, D. C., 1943).

2. Constance M. Green, *Holyoke, Massachusetts* (New Haven, 1939), p. 334; G. C. Osgood, *Story of the Holyoke Churches* (Holyoke, 1890) pp. 1-12.

3. Green, *op. cit.,* pp. 95-98.

4. The canon law under which the priests operate comprehends private as well as public discussion (Kelleher, *op. cit.,* p. 33). Church interpreters of the law believe that the dangers involved in private disputations "will ordinarily far outweigh the possible good results to be expected." (Kelleher, *op. cit.,* p. 42.) So the church deems it necessary to prohibit private disputations without permission from the Holy See, or in urgent cases from the local bishop. (Kelleher, *op. cit.,* p. 68.)

5. Some exploratory contacts have been made by the Roman Catholic church for union of the Greek Orthodox church pastor with the Roman church

through visits by seminary students to the Greek pastor to remind him that the Roman church is always ready to receive him and his people back, and permit him to remain a priest.

6. Kelleher, *op. cit.*, p. 48.

7. Kelleher, *op. cit.*, pp. 48, 68. The discussions which do not aim at cooperation are termed disputations in canon law and are viewed as "debates in which opposing parties, by force of argument and rhetoric, strive to convince their adversaries and the audience of the truth of their respective opinions." (Kelleher, *op. cit.*, p. ix.) The morality of disputations is determined ultimately by the circumstances in each particular case, the major factor in the situation being an anticipation of whether the Catholic participant will be able to effect a reaction favorable to the church. (Kelleher, *op. cit.*, p. 3.)

8. Green, *op. cit.*, pp. 331-332.

9. Interviews were conducted with the rabbi and Protestant pastor involved in the incident, but the incident was not checked with the senior priest or curate.

10. The pessimism of religious leaders about cooperation on social and moral issues is particularly significant for interfaith relations. The most effective use of interfaith contacts if the goal is reduction of hostility and increase of understanding appears from most research to be the type of intergroup participation focused upon a common interest or task, and providing opportunity for individuals to function as equals. Robin Williams, *The Reduction of Intergroup Tensions* (Social Science Research Council, Bulletin 57, 1947), pp. 69, 71.

11. Two of the ministers read at least one Catholic periodical "frequently" (average of once a month); both read the diocesan magazine; the remainder read Catholic periodicals without plan and only as they "happen onto them" —in trains or in other public places. *The Converted Catholic* and *The Protestant* magazines have over the past decades been read more frequently among the Protestant pastors than all Catholic magazines combined.

12. In general, the Catholic pastors felt that they "learned enough about Protestantism in [their] seminaries to know its errors," and therefore make no effort to read any of its official publications. None of the pastors reads a Protestant church periodical "frequently" (once a month); two, "occasionally" (average of three times a year). One of the pastors could not recall the name of the publication he read "occasionally"; the other named the *Christian Science Monitor*.

13. "Diocesan Notes," *Catholic Mirror*, January 1947, p. 38.

14. Interviews were held with the senior pastor, the nurse who had conversation with the priest, and the Baptist minister.

15. Interviews were conducted with all three of the participants.

16. Thomas J. Clarke, *op. cit.*, p. 49.

17. *Catholic Mirror*, February 1945, p. 31.

18. Surveys were made of all of the Protestant funeral directors and a sample survey taken of Catholic directors.

19. Letter of Michael Ryan, no title (private printing, Holyoke, 1933).

20. The upper class of Catholics provides the major source of leadership in the religion for community welfare programs which involve all faiths. A study of the economic class background of the officers in the six major city-wide Catholic societies, such as the Knights of Columbus, Catholic Library Association, Catholic Girls Association and Catholic High School Alumni As-

sociation, indicated that leadership of these is drawn almost entirely from middle and particularly upper-middle class ranks (96 per cent middle class, 4 per cent upper class).

21. Interviews were conducted with and questionnaires submitted to over fifty business and professional men in Paper City.

Chapter 12

Class and Parish

1. Class characteristics most directly associated with economic factors have been the major concern of Chapter 12. Objective criteria of occupation, income and material possession were given chief attention, with the assumption that occupation represents the most reliable composite index. However, three other criteria are also considered in development of the class structure of the churches and the city: (a) residence and type of dwelling, (b) participation in community and social affairs, and (c) reputation and personal prestige. These criteria in some cases give persons or families a different class status than occupation alone would indicate, but such deviations are too few to distort the total picture.

At the time of the first field study, all mill workers and service employees and most middle-class workers were within the $3,500 or less category of income distribution. A United States Bureau of Census sampling study of 1945 incomes estimated the median money income for spending units at $2,673. Families and individuals living on $2,500 a year or less composed 62.8 per cent of Paper City's population. Only 1 per cent of the people received $10,000 or over, and 36.2 per cent had between $2,500 and $10,000. Paper City citizens, asked to designate classes by income, generally agreed that these income groups represented, respectively, lower, upper and middle class.

2. The social rank given occupations can be correlated with income only in a general way. There are significant deviations. For example, the annual money income of clerks and other nonmanual white-collar workers employed in the city government (excluding technical and professional personnel), was $1,693 in 1946; that of manual workers in the street, highway and public works department, $2,084. But people in Paper City and elsewhere tend to rate the former group of workers higher in economic and social status than the latter. State Department of Labor and Industries, Division of Statistics, "Employment and Pay Roll Earnings in Manufacturing," 1947.

It should be noted also that some clergymen and teachers rank considerably higher in social status than many others with comparable income who do not belong to professions so highly regarded in the community.

3. An intensive study of English-speaking Protestant and Roman Catholic churches in each of the three class-type churches—upper-middle, middle-labor, and labor—reveals other important differences in the social composition of the two religions. The occupational composition of the churches indicates important differences between the churches within each class type and accentuates the fact that class lines are more closely drawn in the Catholic than in the Protestant churches. The Protestant upper class is drawn more largely from the mill owners, large proprietors, mill officials and managers than from the professions, while the Catholic upper class is drawn largely from the professions with a small representation from the construction industry, retail and

wholesale merchandising and mill managers. The Catholic middle class is represented more extensively in the mill officials below superintendent, in the semiprofessional, in the small proprietor and protective services (firemen, policemen) than the Protestant middle class. A larger proportion of Roman Catholic housewives work in the mills as operatives than do Protestant housewives. The Protestant churches in each class have a larger proportion of people of high school or college education than the Roman Catholic churches.

The class structure of churches is indicated not simply by the composition of the membership but also by the positions of influence and prestige in the church policy-making committees and parish societies held by representatives of the various occupational groups. In both Protestant and Roman Catholic churches, congregational or parish leaders are of higher social and occupational status than rank and file members, and church boards do not have proportional occupational or class representation. This is more clearly the situation in the Protestant churches.

4. If it could be assumed that the social stratification of the nonchurch-affiliated population corresponds generally with that of the church-affiliated, then the class percentages given for the religious population might be taken to represent the class divisions of the entire city. Data on the class or occupational composition of the people not formally affiliated with religious institutions is very meager, but available data on social participation indicates that the largest proportion of non-affiliated people is in the low income area. The membership of all churches—Protestant and Roman Catholic—is composed of 2 per cent upper class, 38 per cent middle class, and 60 per cent lower class. Roman Catholics and Protestants together comprise 78.3 per cent of the total population of Paper City.

5. Interviews, Yankee industrialist, June 30, 1947; major industrial historian of the city and president of the Water Power Company, June 19, 1947. Paper City's ecological lines are so stark that little schematization of data for presentation in maps has been necessary.

6. For decades the Yankee-controlled Water Power Company, which owned most of the land during the first half of the city's history, fought the building of a bridge across the river cutting off the community on two sides from the surrounding countryside. The bridge would have made home sites accessible to workers in a day of slow transportation and would have reduced the pressure on land within the city owned by the company. Constance M. Green, *Holyoke, Massachusetts* (New Haven, 1939), p. 117.

7. Jacques Ducharme, *The Delusson Family* (New York, 1939), p. 39. If a family reached the Highlands, it was through more than one generation and with a period of residence at some interim point up the slope from the Flats.

8. Since it was important to the development of interview questions and to the selection of people to be interviewed that the researcher's knowledge of the city during part of his field work include class and ecological aspects of the community, part of the study was done with the most recent census data available at the time. This included the 1940 census data and a 1938 study of *Substandard Housing in Holyoke* by the Holyoke Housing Authority. The 1950 census data does not alter the social-ecological picture of the city presented here, such as order of social rank of the wards.

9. The ethnic make-up of the wards cannot be indicated more exactly because of the difficulties in securing adequate data. The information given in

this study is the result of weighing and sifting data from a variety of sources: (1) the census data on percentage of foreign born and on the population of each ward; (2) the data from studies of Catholic parish ethnic composition, (3) the data on location of Protestant members through spot maps, (4) interviews with real-estate dealers; (5) interviews with recognized leaders of the various organizations composed on an ethnic basis; (6) data from sampling studies by the Public Housing Authority; (7) data from Protestant efforts at a religious census of a few areas of the city in 1946; (8) observations by historians, newspaper reporters of early colonizing of the ethnic groups and present location.

10. The percentage of foreign-born whites in the wards, in the order of the least to the largest, are as follows: Ward 7, 15.4; Ward 5, 21.9; Ward 3, 22.1; Ward 6, 22.5; Ward 1, 23.8; Ward 2, 24.8 and Ward 4, 26.6. Source: United States Census, 1940, Vol. II, Part 3, *Population,* and Housing Supplement, Holyoke Block Statistics.

11. This conclusion seems warranted by a limited canvassing of blocks in the worker wards in a Protestant Ministerial Association study attempted in 1946.

12. The manner in which Protestant and Roman Catholic churches respond to social ecological developments gives important evidence as to their approach to social diversity in the community. Yet the sociologists of religion have made little study of parish lines in relation to social differentiation.

13. The medieval concept of the parish comprehended the entire population of a territory, and coordination with and recognition by the state system. See M. Searle Bates, *Religious Liberty* (New York, 1945), p. 151.

An authoritative definition of a Roman Catholic parish interprets it as: ". . . a gathering of the faithful living within a territory marked off by well defined limits over whom a proper priest is placed to exercise the care of souls. The essential elements of a parish are a group of the faithful determined by a definite territory and directed by a specific priest. The concept of the parish has developed into that of an ecclesiastical entity. Its members are determined by strict territorial limits. Its pastor has the care of souls of all who live within these boundaries. This does not include non-baptized persons . . . The parish . . . should be the center of all spiritual or religious activity of the layman. There are exceptions, of course, but ordinarily works of piety and charity as well as any other public act of devotion should center around the parish. Societies should operate or function in conjunction with or as parish activities . . ." Thomas J. Clarke, *Parish Societies,* Canon Law Studies No. 176 (Catholic University of America, Washington, D. C., 1943), p. 33. Clarke gives as his sources in Canon Law for the summary statement: John Joseph Coady, *The Appointment of Pastors,* Canon Law Studies No. 52 (Catholic University of America, Washington, D. C., 1929), p. 62. Canon 216, S1 and Canon 451. Also Ludovicus Fanfani, *De Iure Parochorum,* altera edito (Taurini; Marietti, 1936), p. 2.

14. Joseph H. Fichter, *Dynamics of a City Church* (Chicago, 1951), pp. 1, 11; John J. Harbrecht, *The Lay Apostolate* (St. Louis, 1929), pp. 18, 19.

15. Patrick J. Lucey, *History of St. Jerome's Parish* (Holyoke, 1931), p. 39; Green, *op. cit.,* p. 332; Holyoke *Transcript,* August 1, 1863 and July 17, 1865.

16. Green, *op. cit.,* p. 334; Lucey, *op. cit.,* p. 41; G. C. Osgood, *Story of the Holyoke Churches* (Holyoke, 1890), pp. 75, 76.

17. The historian of Holy Cross parish records the income that day as $44.00.

"The outlook certainly was not very encouraging—a debt of $20,000 on the lot, accrued interest on same of $425, no parish home, no place within the parish confine to hold public service, in the depth of winter and the Rt. Rev. Bishop on his visit to Rome." *Holy Cross Dedication* (Holyoke, 1929), p. 4.

18. *A Century of Catholicism,* edited by the *Catholic Mirror* (Springfield, 1931), p. 151.

19. *Holy Cross Dedication,* p. 32.

20. Ward 1 and parish lines for Holy Rosary and Immaculate Conception are alike and encompass the first of the workers' residential areas. Ward 2 and Precious Blood parish lines are similar and compose the second of the workers' residential areas. Ward 4 and St. Jerome's parish lines are almost coincident, except that the parish lines conform more closely to a low income housing area than the ward lines. Ward 7, the parish lines for Holy Cross and the social area of the Highlands are very similar. The remaining wards, 3, 5 and 6, are not like the parish lines of Blessed Sacrament and Sacred Heart which conform more closely to the social areas in the three wards. For example, Blessed Sacrament parish lines follow fairly neatly the middle-class housing areas of Oakdale and Elmwood. The parish includes all of Ward 3 except a definitely laboring class area called Springdale. Study based on use of block statistics from the "Housing Supplement to the First Series, Holyoke," 1940 United States Census.

21. When the lines of Blessed Sacrament parish were established, a triangular area including part of Elmwood was left in another parish. A delegation of laymen, with the encouragement of the pastor of Blessed Sacrament, visited the bishop and urged him to put the area in the Blessed Sacrament parish, on the grounds that the parish lines would separate some families and friends, so much of a social unit was the Elmwood area. The recommendation of the laymen was accepted. No changes in the lines have been made since then.

22. See R. J. R. Kennedy, "Premarital Residential Propinquity and Ethnic Endogamy," *American Journal of Sociology,* March 1943, pp. 580-584.

23. Measured by membership residential location, the Second Congregational Church is more concentrated in the Highlands than any other Protestant church, but its worship and educational center is in the business district of the city. In 1915, 70 per cent of the Second Baptist church membership was located within a four-block radius of the church building. Now only one Baptist family known to the church lives in the area. In the four blocks immediately surrounding the First Baptist Church of Elmwood, no two Protestant families in a block attend the same church.

24. Spot maps were prepared for the major Protestant churches, locating church membership. In a few cases, the ministers had already made such studies.

25. For example, the First Congregational and the Second Congregational churches have no members below High Street and five in Ward 4. The Episcopal Church has seven members below the business district and twelve members in Ward 4.

26. Green, *op. cit.,* p. 326.

27. This is the observation of the historians of the individual Protestant churches, for example, Osgood, *op. cit.,* p. 9; Rev. J. L. R. Trask and others, *Fiftieth Anniversary, Second Congregational Church* (Holyoke, 1900), p. 131;

Holyoke *Transcript, Thirtieth Anniversary Issue, History of Holyoke, 1882-1912* (Holyoke, 1912), p. 6; Green, *op. cit.*, p. 330.

28. The four sects—Gospel Hall, Jehovah's Witnesses, Polish Evangelistic Assembly and the Polish Study Group—all meet in halls or rooms located within a block of each other and in a run-down business section of the city.

Chapter 13

The "Foreign" and the "Native"

1. Constance M. Green's study, *Holyoke, Massachusetts; A Case History of the Industrial Revolution in America* (New Haven, 1939), provides a careful description of immigrant groups, their growth in the population, the social conditions under which they lived and the Yankee ethos from 1850 to 1922. Unless otherwise indicated, information on these areas is from this valuable source.

2. Holyoke *Transcript, Thirtieth Anniversary Issue, History of Paper City, 1882-1912* (Holyoke, 1912), p. 13.

3. *Sixteenth Census of United States, 1940, Population,* Vol. II, Part 3, p. 639.

4. Green, *op. cit.*, pp. 2-6.

5. *Fiftieth Anniversary, Second Congregational Church* (Holyoke, 1900), p. 20.

6. Holyoke *Transcript, Thirtieth Anniversary Issue,* p. 18.

7. "Book Tour," *Catholic Mirror,* October 1948, pp. 29-30.

8. Holyoke *Transcript,* March 14, 1947, p. 1.

9. *Caravel,* April 1940, p. 6.

10. Jacques Ducharme, *Shadows of the Trees* (New York, 1943), p. 3.

11. *Ibid.*

12. Interviews, officers of French Canadian societies.

13. Patrick J. Lucey, *History of St. Jerome's Parish* (Holyoke, 1931), p. 23.

14. Both of the terms "isolation" and "segregation" are used in describing the separation of peoples in Paper City. Both processes operate. Members of ethnic groups may in part choose to live together, that is, to isolate themselves from other groups, particularly in the early years in a city. But this may also be a reaction to discrimination and pressure against them as they move out from their first residential areas.

15. Holyoke *Transcript, Thirtieth Anniversary,* p. 5.

16. *Paroisse du Precieux-Sang: 75e Anniversaire de sa Fondation* (Holyoke, 1944); pp. 24-25.

17. Green, *op. cit.*, p. 332, and Lucey, *op. cit.*, p. 39.

18. Interviews with Roman Catholic priests were the major source of insight into ethnic rivalry within the church.

19. The clergy were not asked directly to rate ethnic groups for the vigor and excellence of their Catholicism, but an ethnic "pecking order" became clear as the priests volunteered judgments about fellow Catholics in the course of discussion of various topics in formal interviews.

20. Patterns of ethnic cleavage and adjustment of the Catholic church have been observed by Caroline Ware, *Greenwich Village, 1920-1930* (Boston, 1935), p. 305, and Stanley H. Chapman, *New Haven Churches, Aspects of*

Their Structure and Function, Ph.D. Dissertation (Yale University, 1942) pp. 59 ff.

21. Green, *op. cit.*, pp. 362, 367 and 113; and *Paroisse du Precieux-Sang: 75e Anniversaire de sa Fondation* (Holyoke, October 22, 1944), p. 24.

22. J. J. McCoy, "Diocese of Springfield," *History of the Catholic Church in the New England States,* Vol. II (Boston, 1899), pp. 681-682. Facts about the Polish parish are from this source.

23. T. Lincoln Bouscaren, *The Canon Law Digest,* Vol. II (Milwaukee, 1943), pp. 79-80. Comment on Canon 216, "Foreign-Born Catholics and Their Children: Parish Affiliation."

24. Interviews were conducted with Catholic laymen who have experienced such sanctions and penalties.

25. Ducharme, *Shadows of the Trees,* p. 212.

26. A content analysis was made of *Caravel* from February 1932 to August 1947.

27. Holyoke *Transcript,* April 11, 1947, p. 17; *Catholic Mirror,* March 1946, p. 41; March 1947, p. 23; and December 1945, p. 45.

28. The pattern of bias in the diocesan press is based on a study of its content for three years, 1945-47. The number of article pages given to Irish history and tradition in comparison with that of other nationals and the frequency of pro-Irish editorials in comparison with those favoring other groups was noted. The ratios in each case were approximately as follows for Irish, Polish, French: 8:2:1.

29. *Brief History of the Evangelical Lutheran Church, Holyoke,* issued at the Seventy-Fifth Anniversary of the church (Holyoke, November 1, 1942), p. 5.

30. Article, "From Many—One," written by the pastor for *Home Missionary Society,* Grace Church Scrapbook, 1916. Quotations about Grace Church and the ethnic program are from this article.

31. *Paroisse du Precieux-Sang,* p. 18.

32. Green, *op. cit.*, p. 301.

Chapter 14

The Churches and Recreation

1. If parish societies are "erected" formally by the bishop, the society is considered an ecclesiastical society; if the bishop merely commends and does not give authoritative approval, the society remains lay. Thomas J. Clarke, *Parish Societies,* Canon Law Studies, No. 176 (Catholic University of America, Washington, D. C., 1943), p. 34-37.

2. Clarke, *op. cit.*, p. 56.

3. The religious aspect of the association by nature of the church's polity must be directed not by the laity but by the priest. The priest's power over members in a parish society does not exceed the power of the pastor, which is to enforce, not make, moral laws. Lay societies are under jurisdiction of the bishop not as societies but as composed of individual souls or members in care of the bishop. Thomas J. Clarke, *op. cit.*, p. 94.

4. Caroline Ware's *Greenwich Village,* 1920-1930 (Boston, 1935), p. 307, observes the same alarm of the Catholic clergy at the increased association of Catholics with non-Catholic groups.

5. The Catholic church has possibly been forced to adapt more slowly than the Protestant churches to the pluralism of Paper City culture, since it has historically been more generally associated with a people of lower income than Protestants, of more recent ethnic background and with less diversified associations.

6. Golden Anniversary Letter to Knights of Columbus by a Catholic Bishop, explaining the purpose for founding the Knights, *Caravel,* March 1932, p. 1.

7. *Caravel,* May 1947, p. 4.

8. Greater attention is given in the Protestant church than in the Catholic church to women's organizations. The Protestant churches have a city-wide women's organization, but no city-wide men's organization. The opposite is true of the Catholic church. The Protestant Council of Churches has a women's division but no men's division. Every Protestant church has an adult women's Sunday school; half have no men's religious education group.

9. Sources of information about the Catholic Girls' Leagues and Protestant Girls' Association were: By-laws and minutes of the organizations, interviews with leaders and members of the associations, and Holyoke *Transcript,* March 24, 1947, p. 11.

10. Paper City in 1947 had the following number and types of girl and boy scout troops:

	Girl Scouts	*Boy Scouts*
Mixed faith membership		
Protestant church sponsored	6	5
Civic sponsored	12	8
One faith membership		
Jewish sponsored	2	1
Protestant church sponsored	2	2
Catholic church sponsored	11	12
Total	33	28

The sources of this information and much data to follow on Paper City scouting were interviews with members and several troop leaders.

11. *Scouting for Catholics* (The Catholic Committee on Scouting, New York, 1939), p. vi.

12. "Scouting for Catholics," pp. 59-60.

13. *The Scout Program in Protestant Churches* (The Protestant Committee on Scouting, New York, no date), p. 4. The Committee also notes: "Now it is quite essential that these Scouts shall acquire knowledge of American traditions, an understanding of American institutions, and a thorough grounding in American principles of democracy and the Christian religion, if they are to pass on to succeeding generations, these fundamentals as our spiritual heritage. What an opportunity for the Christian churches to safeguard our finest political and religious traditions and to fortify our first line of defense for the free institutions which are so essential to the welfare and happiness of our American people." *Op. cit.*, p. 13.

14. *The Scout Program in Protestant Churches,* pp. 19-21.

15. The adaptability of the scout movement to the associational and educational policies of the Catholic church has been indicated by the Pontifical bless-

ing bestowed upon the scouting organization as early as 1929. The primacy of the Catholic scouts' loyalty to the church and of the church's awareness that the movement can appropriate many of the characteristics of Catholic Action, including the development of a "well-guarded" organization of the young, free from "danger," is made clear in the *Scouting for Catholics* manual. See *Girl Scouting and the Catholic Girl* (Girl Scouts National Organization, New York City, no date), p. 3, and *Scouting for Catholics*, p. iii.

16. "The Scout Program and Protestant Churches," pp. 6-7.

17. The Ministerial Association has on two occasions passed resolutions requesting "Scout leaders to urge all scouts to attend their respective churches." Minutes, Ministerial Association, April 26, 1944; January 25, 1945.

18. The national official scout pamphlet, *Girl Scouting and the Protestant Churches,* distributed to Protestant pastors in Paper City, has a pastor observe that "The Girl Scout troop is ideal for encouraging respect for all religions. . . . The Girl Scout troop offers an opportunity for real unity and cooperation between classes, creeds, races and nationalities," p. 6. A similar pamphlet, *Girl Scouting and the Catholic Girl,* has no comment on the development of tolerance or associations across creedal lines.

19. Clarke, *op. cit.*, p. 61.

20. *Ibid.*

21. Clarke, *op. cit.*, p. 82.

22. Clarke, *op. cit.*, p. 83.

23. Interviews were conducted with leaders of YWCA and YMCA, Catholic and Protestant members of the YWCA and YMCA boards of directors and executive sessions of the boards observed.

24. "YMCA," *Catholic Mirror,* January 1921, p. 5. The Catholic who joined the "Y" committed a sin of the same kind as joining a Protestant sect. *Catholic Mirror,* June 1921, p. 12. The bishop of Springfield was taking the same attitude as other members of the hierarchy during this period. See C. Howard Hopkins, *History of the YMCA in North America* (New York, 1951), pp. 530-531.

25. Hopkins, *op. cit.*, p. 49, 733.

26. Interviews were held with all the presidents or vice presidents of the service clubs and with several rank and file members. The position expressed here is general across the nation. See Claris E. Silcox and Galen Fisher, *Catholics, Jews and Protestants* (New York, 1934), p. 83.

27. "It is not expedient that Ordinaries give permission to their clerics to join Rotary Clubs or to be present at their meetings," reads a ruling of the Sacred Congregation of the Consistory, February 4, 1929. See Henry A. Ayrinhae, *Administrative Legislation in the New Code of Canon Law* (New York, 1930), p. 466.

28. The rank of service clubs by social status (if the rating of occupations in Chapter 12 is taken as the chief criterion) is Rotary, Kiwanis and Lions. The lower the club ranks in the social structure, the smaller is the percentage of Protestants and the larger is that of Catholics and Jews: Kiwanis (52 per cent Protestant, 45 per cent Catholic, 3 per cent Jews); Lions (38 per cent Protestant, 48 per cent Catholic, 4 per cent Jews). With approximately equal numbers of Catholics and Protestants, the last two clubs have developed a tacit understanding that the presidencies of the clubs will alternate between

Catholics and non-Catholics. The understanding is adhered to with a good deal of uniformity by the nominating committees.

29. Interview with an officer, August 7, 1947. Another source of information about Junior League membership is "Report of Placement Chairman, 1947," Archives of Junior League, Holyoke.

30. "Catholic Attitude on Masonry," *Catholic Mirror*, March 1946, p. 33.

31. "Fraternal Warning," *Catholic Mirror*, January 1947, p. 24.

Chapter 15

The Churches, Business and Industry

1. Data on early industrial history are from Constance McLaughlin Green, *Holyoke Massachusetts; A Case History of the Industrial Revolution in America* (New Haven, 1939) unless otherwise indicated.

2. Interviews with two businessmen, one a secretary of Chamber of Commerce, one an industrial banker—both of whom have done historical studies of Paper City's commercial history.

3. Jacques Ducharme, *Shadows of the Trees* (New York, 1943), p. 160.

4. For fifteen years, the Water Power Company permitted its canal fences to be so neglected "that from six to ten children were mathematically certain to fall to their death each year." The situation was remedied in 1900. Holyoke *Transcript Thirtieth Anniversary Issue, History of Holyoke 1882-1912* (Holyoke, 1912), p. 12.

5. Holyoke *Town Records*, 1857, p. 11.

6. In 1880, New York, with 16.37 persons per dwelling, and Hoboken, with 11.50 persons, were more crowded than Paper City with 10.52 persons per dwelling. In 1908, a survey of Paper City housing made by a doctor and a social worker indicated that only eleven of thirty-odd cities of over 100,000 inhabitants had proportionately more tenements than Paper City with a population of 55,000. Green, *op. cit.*, pp. 260, 282.

7. *Caravel*, June 1940, p. 2.

8. Quoted in Green, *op. cit.*, p. 254, from Holyoke *Transcript*, February 15, 1879.

9. An extensive study of the present religious alignments of Paper City industry and business was made through facilities and staff of one of the major business associations.

10. By the turn of the century, half of the stores in the two blocks composing the main retail shopping area were Catholic owned or managed. Today the ratio is one Protestant store to two Jewish stores to three Catholic stores. The one large department store in the city is Protestant owned.

11. Study made in co-operation with an officer of the local bar association. The parents of the leading Roman Catholic lawyer were mill workers who on arrival in Paper City lived in "Shanty Town" where many of the houses were constructed from packing cans given employees of the mills.

12. Study made in co-operation with a leader in the Paper City Medical Association.

13. This is a development which has been traced in numerous studies of business and industry recruitment patterns. See, for example, John W. Mc-

Connell, *The Evolution of the Social Classes* (Washington, D. C., 1942), p. 93; W. E. Moore, *Industrial Relations and the Social Order* (New York, 1949), pp. 132-152; W. Lloyd Warner and J. O. Low, *The Social System of the Modern Factory* (New Haven, 1947), p. 66.

14. Constance McLaughlin Green, in her careful study of industrial Holyoke reaches a similar conclusion, supported also by several unpublished manuscripts of other authors: a short paper by the secretary of the Chamber of Commerce on "Holyoke, Fiftieth Anniversary," and a thorough study of the social history of the community by a trustee of the Holyoke Library Association (Mss. Holyoke Public Library, 1942).

15. The primary purpose of the inquiries was to discover the extent of the alignment of religious and status lines in the various industries, and to analyze the factors within the industrial or factory system which appear to heighten or diminish the importance of religious differentiation in the struggle for status, wealth and influence. The key decision-making centers examined within the factory system were top management and foremen.

The eleven companies represent the major types of firms in the city in terms of such crucial variables as size of organization and pattern of ownership and control (that is, local or absentee; Catholic, Protestant or Jewish). The adequacy of the sample was checked by examination, with less depth, of ten additional firms. The first sample included two plants absentee-owned by nationally known corporations with several manufacturing centers and with carefully developed policies of management selection; a paper manufacturing plant now partially absentee-owned by a mixture of Jewish, Catholic and Protestant interests; three paper processing plants and a metal processing factory, all owned by old Protestant Yankee families; the Water Power Company, of Protestant ownership; a textile plant with controlling ownership by a Paper City resident of Jewish background; and two machine shops owned by Catholic families.

16. A great deal of work has been done by industrial sociologists on the "job context" of the factory status system which substantiates or illuminates further the general observations made here. See Moore, *op. cit.*, pp. 122-123, 269-352.

17. See Warner and Low, *op. cit.*, pp. 66-89.

18. C. Wright Mill's *White Collar* (New York, 1951), has a great deal to say about the increasing importance of "selling oneself" and of working for the sake of leisure time pursuits in modern industry.

19. For example, on both salary and wage earner levels, several candidates for a job or for an advancement usually possess the technical efficiency required. Therefore, other qualifications become important. For studies of the ethnic factor in the factory social system, see Orvin Colbine, "Ethnic Behavior in Industry: Sponsorship and Rejection in a New England Factory," *Journal of Sociology,* January 1946, pp. 293-98. In this factory in Somerset, ethnic identification was "the most important" factor in job expectations. See also Warner and Low, *op. cit.*, pp. 92-98.

20. In 1947, Masonic leaders had knowledge of 225 members in "Square clubs" concentrated in three firms and most active in supervisory, white-collar, salaried positions. The officials of the Knights of Columbus reported that they had no record of the membership in "K. of C." factory groups.

21. Prospective employees are usually interviewed by the foreman or super-

visor, and if he disapproves of the man the personnel or employment office is not likely to hire him. Personnel officers are not often able to see the type of work a man does each day and depend upon foremen for detailed evaluation to guide promotion.

22. This conclusion is based only on a sampling study of worker opinion (below foremen). In one plant a study was made of the religious affiliation of employees at the beginning of the service of a Catholic foreman who engaged in religious discrimination and after a twelve-year period of his activity. The percentage of Catholics in his department (a shipping department of a local mill) had increased from 62 per cent Catholic (1935) to 88 per cent Catholic (1947). The shift is probably related to differences in the supply of Protestant and Catholics available in the depression and prosperity, but it is also clearly influenced by the Catholic foreman's acknowledged policy of "fair play for Catholics," of having "as large a percentage of Catholics in the department as are in the city." The percentage of Catholics in Paper City for him was "between 85 and 88 per cent." Almost no efforts are made by Protestant foremen to develop dominantly Protestant departments. Crucial factors in this are the unavailability of Protestant workers and the fear of accusation of favoritism from the numerically superior Catholic workers.

23. Evidence as to the use of religion as a criterion in employment in Paper City was obtained from a study of various employment agencies in the community, including the local branch of the state employment office, in addition to data developed in the intensive study of eleven companies. The staffs of the agencies report that the majority of requests for workers—approximately 90 per cent—make no effort to indicate ethnic or religious preferences. However, requests stating religious preferences are received regularly. These requests are made in various ways and with various reasons stated. Usually religion is not referred to directly. Requests for parochial-school or nonparochial-school graduates indicate religious preference. The employee of an agency who is Protestant is singled out by Protestant employers "as one of our kind" and therefore able to help find them the worker they want; or Catholic employees are singled out for similar requests. Many employees give religious qualifications on the basis that they are trying to carry out a policy of avoiding tension, either by keeping a balance of ethnic-religious representation, or by keeping an entirely homogeneous work group. These requests to agencies with a "mixed" religious staff, such as the United States Employment Service, for aid in locating an employee of a particular religion come to staff members "after hours." The most frequent requests by employers designating their religious requisites are for personal secretaries. Employment offices of business colleges receive a higher percentage of requests for employees indicating religious qualifications than any other organizations engaged in job placement work in the city.

24. In most of the factories studied and particularly in the family firms, patterns of job expectancy have developed in which workers assume that foremen of a particular nationality and religion will be replaced by men of the same characteristics. In three firms in which patterns of foremen recruitment were studied carefully for the period from 1926 to 1946 when little change took place in the general proportion of Catholics to Protestants in the city (these firms were two Protestant family-owned companies and one absentee-owned corporation plant), shifts in foremen positions from representatives

of the majority religion to Protestant foremen were more rare than shifts in foremen from Protestant to Catholic.

From 1926 to 1946 there are records of 24 changes to foreman personnel; 75 per cent (or 18) involved no shift in the religious allegiance; 20 per cent (5) involved a shift from Protestant to Catholic foremen; 5 per cent (1) involved a shift from a Catholic to a Protestant foreman. The rise in satus, skill and numbers of the Irish, French and Polish workers has been accompanied by a decreasing proportion of Protestant foremen in the paper and textile mills and the increase of representatives of Catholic groups. Records available for one of the Protestant family firms in existence during this century had in 1906, when Catholics represented approximately 70 per cent of the population, but 45 per cent Catholics in its foremen ranks; in 1946, 75 per cent were Catholic. The foreman positions which have remained Protestant in the large family firms have chiefly been in the departments which still employ a great number of German, English and Scotch Protestants.

25. Such rumor barrages were in operation in two of the plants when the study was made. In one plant, several Catholic workers talked to informally in a testing department reported that a particular foreman was soon to be fired, that he was an "APAer" or anti-Catholic, and that the foreman was in danger of being captured by Masons, etc. According to the managers of the factory, the foreman was under no threat of dismissal, but the foreman was fearful of his relations with the workers, highly careful not to offend Catholic workers for he believed his job was "being shot for" by a group of Catholic workers. The department actually had four foremen, three of whom were Catholic.

Chapter 16

The Churches and the Labor Movement

1. Chief sources for the labor history of the city are Constance M. Green, *Holyoke, Massachusetts: A Case History of the Industrial Revolution in America* (New Haven, 1939), particulary pp. 216-229, and extensive interviews with all the major labor leaders in the city.

2. *Paper World*, trade paper published from 1880-1898. (Holyoke: 1880-1887, Springfield: 1887-1898).

3. *The Artisan* was a labor paper published in Holyoke from 1910-1914.

4. Green, *op. cit.*, p. 225 ff., reports on attitudes reflected in Holyoke *Transcript*.

5. Pope Leo XIII promulgated in 1891 the famous social encyclical *Rerum Novarum*, "On the Condition of the Workers." This encyclical set the background for Roman Catholic church concern for the organization of laboring men in the modern industrial era. Pope Leo declared that "associations of workers occupy the first place [in the modern economy], and they include within their circle nearly all the rest." The encyclical has strong criticism of the "individualism" of capitalism which is largely responsible for the condition of the workers, and of collective "socialism," the most widely proposed remedy. The church is called upon to bring men to acts of Christian justice and charity which will correct the evils of capitalism and prevent the evil of socialism.

Pope Pius XI, forty years later, commended the effects of the earlier encyclical and developed further the principles which were to guide Catholics in developing a more Christian social order. He sought to indicate in somewhat concrete terms, what a return to the conceptions of function, status, common good, harmony and justice, which underlay the medieval society and guild system, might mean for modern society. Yet the encyclical is quite clear that Catholics are not to try to apply the guiding moral principles of the social encyclicals in a hard-and-fast way, but rather in relation to the different historical situations they confront.

6. Green, *op. cit.*, p. 27.

7. E. P. Bagg, Jr., *History of Second Congregational Church* (manuscript, in church offices), p. 19; Green, *op. cit.*, p. 71.

8. Patrick J. Lucey, *History of St. Jerome's Parish* (Holyoke, 1931), p. 5.

9. No record of public support of the right of labor to organize by Catholic priests is indicated in *Tho Artisan*, labor paper published from 1910-1914.

10. Interviews with labor leaders who made the contacts with the priests, July, 1947.

11. Labor leaders claim that the pastor of Holy Rosary disapproved of the activity of the curate so greatly that he provided less furniture for his room than for the other curates. One president of a local union supplied a chair and a lamp for the curate's room. Source: interviews with labor leaders who kept in close contact with the curate during his stay in Paper City and after he left.

12. For example, an editorial, "Striking and Strikers," *Catholic Mirror*, July 1946, p. 11, explains current strikes as the result of "the inability of a majority to achieve a decent livelihood."

13. "On the Good of Labor and the Common Good," *Catholic Mirror*, January 1947, pp. 13-14. Several of the local clergy followed the bishop's lead and preached against provisions in the act, but this was the only position which most of the pastors took during the year on a specific labor issue.

14. The history of the labor education program in the Springfield and Boston dioceses was described by the Rev. Thomas E. Shortell in a speech delivered before a Seminar at the Harvard University Graduate School of Business Administration, July 5, 1956. Manuscript in possession of Father Shortell. Father Shortell was interviewed by the author, a co-director of the seminar, on July 5, 1956.

15. Father Shortell, for example, delivered a speech at the State House in favor of the closed shop in 1947, at a time when neither the bishop of the diocese nor any of the local pastors of Paper City were being so explicit as to what Father Shortell called "the security clauses" which protect "the fundamental reasons for the existence of a labor union." Holyoke *Transcript*, March 26, 1947, p. 6.

The hierarchy has recognized that attempts to relate Christianity to a highly specialized area of social life, such as the contemporary labor movement, may lead to many mistakes of strategy and doctrine, and the "labor priests" have been given considerable freedom of operation. See the discussion by Rev. John F. Cronin, *Catholic Social Action* (Milwaukee, 1948), of the Catholic labor program. Father Cronin is Assistant Director of the National Catholic Welfare Conference, Department of Social Action.

16. The organization of Catholic labor schools is widespread throughout the country. An appendix to Cronin's *Catholic Social Action* selectively lists 65. Cronin says there are permanent schools in 48 cities in 22 states. This book

summarizes the general purposes of the labor schools in America. The Detroit area alone has at least 41 schools, according to Rev. Joseph Oberle, *The Association of Catholic Trade Unionists* (Paulist Press, New York, 1951).

17. Green, *op. cit.*, p. 249; *Holyoke Labor College Classes for Workers*, a pamphlet (Holyoke, 1930); interview, local director of the college for seven years, August 6, 1947.

18. Evaluation of the Workers Education Bureau *News Letter*, American Federation of Labor, October, 1949. The school probably ranks in national prominence close to the Sheil School of Social Studies in Chicago, Illinois, and the Xavier School in New York City. Father Shortell no longer directs the school, having found the work too heavy a task for his later years. He is now a professor of moral philosophy at Boston College.

19. The only record of the speech is that of the secretary of the institute, a member of a Baptist church in Paper City and secretary of a machinists' union. He had professional training as a stenographer and his record of the session, although not verbatim, contained considerable direct quotation from the speakers.

20. Transcript of 1945 institute sessions by the secretary of the institute.

21. Analysis of mimeographed literature given representatives of Holy Cross Institute of Labor, 1945, and transcripts of the major course lectures and discussions.

22. Some unions also pay the expenses of officers or representatives of the union to Catholic religious retreats. Interview, president, Central Labor Council, July 4, 1947.

23. For example, "Conflicting Views on P.A.C." and other material for "Current Labor Problems Class," Holy Cross Institute of Industrial Relations, November 13, 1945.

24. Interviews were conducted with a number of Catholic editors and scholars in Massachusetts. The author also observed a presentation by Father Shortell of the approach and history of his labor school to a group of Catholic and Protestant scholars at the Harvard Graduate School of Business Administration, July 5, 1956. The presentation was discussed at length.

25. *The Artisan*, September 4, 1914, p. 4.

26. Grace Church Scrapbook, 1911, 1913, 1919.

27. *The Artisan*, September 4, 1914, p. 4. It is significant that this statement was written by the pastor of Grace Church in collaboration with the editor of *The Artisan*. Mutual institutional promotion appearing in *The Artisan* was approved by the pastor.

28. Grace Church Scrapbook, 1911; *The Artisan*, September 8, 1911, p. 1.

29. Holyoke *Transcript*, November 14, 1934.

30. A Protestant labor leader correctly observed two characteristics of opening sessions of state labor conventions: 1) a Catholic priest always opens the convention with prayer. A Protestant pastor opens the second day's session; 2) the priest stays after the prayer through the convention while the Protestant pastor leaves.

31. This estimate is based on a study with officers of the unions of rolls of six unions representing a wide sample. The unions were in these economic areas: electrical and radio work, paper, textiles, building trades and printing.

32. The study made in 1947 discovered an undercurrent of religious and ethnic interest in most union elections. These are combined with other elements

of concern, such as finding people who will accept the responsibility of leadership, who have particular skills such as speech-making or secretarial ability. Most nominating committees of unions with mixed religious membership purposely break the nominations up so that the major nationalities and religions will be represented. No occasions were found in recent years when district organizers or other superior officers of the unions have investigated local union elections or declared them invalid on the basis of racial or religious discrimination. Many of the unions—all the CIO in the city and machinist (AFL) and textile (AFL)—have constitutions permitting withdrawal of charters of locals for racial and religious discrimination in choice of officers.

Catholics running for office in unions against Protestants have at various times in the past five years introduced the religious issue in order to solidify Catholic support. An election recently in a local union, in which a French Catholic defeated a Protestant secretary seeking re-election, illustrated the way in which Catholic-Protestant tension can be developed. The district organizer wished to investigate the election but the Protestant requested that he not do so. The French Catholics in the union achieved control of every office. They campaigned at a meeting of the Franco-American club on the basis that Yankee-Masons were trying to run the union. A French curate visited a meeting of a women's sodality of the union and said a few words in behalf of the French candidates. The Protestant was defeated by only six votes. In the next election, he concentrated his campaigning among union workers who were World War II Catholic veterans, whom he found to be highly opposed to religious bloc voting. He believes this aided him in winning the election.

33. The study of officers including stewards was made of six representative unions. In four textile locals with only two Protestant top level officers out of eleven, almost half of the shop stewards are Protestants. These locals are composed chiefly of girls. The major reasons given by the workers for the concentration of Protestants in shop steward positions were highly ethnic and religious. Protestants were thought to be more often willing than Catholics to accept the additional responsibility of this position. But the principal reasons given was that worker groups composed of Polish, French-Canadians and Irish were more ready to entrust the representation of their problems to management to a Protestant than to a person of one of their own Catholic ethnic groups. The steward, it should be noted, is made responsible to fellow workers by election and has a different relationship to workers and different rewards than the foreman. Therefore, Catholic workers view Protestants in stewardship positions differently than in foreman positions.

34. Holyoke *Transcript,* May 13, 1906.

35. Holyoke *Transcript,* November 4, 1946.

36. This quotation is based on the president of the Council's recall of the content of the note. The note was not in the files of the Council.

37. *Quadragesimo Anno,* quoted in William L. Miller. "A Catholic Plan for a New Social Order," *Social Action,* February 15, 1951.

38. In general, Catholic corporatism accepts the principle of private productive property which has characterized capitalism, but tempers the principle with emphasis upon the social responsibilities of property holders. The Catholic leaders do not condemn socialization of property, as such, but rather recognize its opportuneness when it is not practiced to excess and when it prevents exploitation contrary to the public good. See, for example, an editorial making

this point in the *Catholic Mirror,* January 1947, p. 19. See Eugene O. Golob, *The "Isms"* (New York, 1954), pp. 541-598 for a history of Catholic Corporatist thought.

39. The principal groups in American Catholicism which produce literature on the industry council that is read at least by a few Paper City Catholic leaders include: (a) The social action department of the National Catholic Welfare Conference. This literature apparently is the most widely circulated. For example, Rev. Raymond A. McGowan, "Economic Security for the Family," *The Family Today: A Catholic Appraisal* (Washington, D. C., 1944). (b) The School of Social Science of the Catholic University in Washington, D. C. From this school comes such academic work as Joseph David Munier, *Some American Approximations to Pius XI's Industries and Professions* (Washington, D. C., 1943). (c) The Industry Council Plan Committee of the American Catholic Sociological Society. Little of the material produced by this society is distributed in Paper City.

40. An example of this approach is "Labor's Contribution to Democracy," mimeographed literature distributed to Holy Cross Labor Institute, March 19, 1946. See also the resolution of the tenth annual national convention of the CIO, endorsing the industry council plan.

41. *Catholic Mirror,* March 1933, p. 5; February 1946, p. 19.

42. Interviews, 1947, samples of twelve labor leaders and twelve businessmen, about their understanding of the nature of Catholic industry council proposals.

43. Some of the first industry council proposals which appeared in the Paper City diocesan journal following leadership of the National Catholic Welfare Conference, simply proposed boards of employees and employers "with legislative powers" for "each industry separately and for all industries jointly." The machinery for selection of representatives to these boards was not indicated, nor the proportions of representation.

44. Some industry council planners evidently think chiefly of the existing special interest organizations as the sources of representation. They refer in agriculture to joint councils based upon farm cooperatives and in industry upon councils based upon trades associations and labor unions. *Catholic Mirror,* March 1933, pp. 5, 6.

45. *Catholic Mirror,* February 1946, p. 19.

46. *Catholic Mirror,* September 1933, pp. 12-15; McGowan, *op. cit.,* p. 84; Munier, *op. cit.,* p. 8.

47. See Chapters 14 through 17 for detailed discussion of the relation of the Catholic church to political institutions for public policy formation.

48. Munier, *op. cit.,* p. 8.

49. Rev. P. Henry Sullivan, *Double Novena to the Holy Family* (Holy Family League of Charity, Worcester, 1946), pp. 24, 29.

Chapter 17

The Morality of Politics

1. See the following efforts of political scientists and economists to describe and to reconcile these various approaches: J. M. Clarke, *Alternative to Serfdom* (New York, 1948); John K. Galbraith, *American Capitalism, The*

Economics of Countervailing Power (New York, 1952); Arthur N. Holcombe, *Our More Perfect Union* (Cambridge, 1950); David Truman, *The Governmental Process* (New York, 1950); E. E. Schattschneider, *Party Government* (New York, 1942); and American Political Science Association, Committee on Political Parties, *Toward a More Responsible Two Party System* (New York, 1950).

2. See Gabriel Almond, *The American People and Foreign Policy* (New York, 1950); Paul Appleby, *Policy and Administration* (New York, 1949); Karl Mannheim, *Man and Society in an Age of Reconstruction* (New York, 1949); and Karl Mannheim, *Freedom, Power and Democratic Planning* (New York, 1950).

3. This observation has been made by a number of historians and social scientists. See, for example, Karl Polanyi, *The Great Transformation* (New York, 1944); E. H. Carr, *Conditions of Peace* (New York, 1942), particularly pp. 70-104; Joseph A. Schumpeter, *Capitalism, Socialism and Democracy* (New York, 1942).

As Polanyi observes, three other institutions were deeply related to and greatly dependent upon the market mechanism: the gold standard as an attempt to extend the domestic market system to the international level; the balance of power political system which worked chiefly through the laws governing the market economy; and the liberal "laissez faire" state predicated on the just operation of the self-regulating market.

4. Only four of the twenty-one officers of the government were Catholic —a superintendent of the streets, two assessors and a water commissioner. *Holyoke: Past and Present, 1745-1895* (Transcript Publishing Company, Holyoke, 1896), p. 69; Constance M. Green, *Holyoke, Massachusetts: A Case History of the Industrial Revolution in America* (New Haven, 1939), pp. 251-252.

5. Green, *op. cit.*, pp. 251-285 is the source of most of the historical data of this chapter unless otherwise indicated.

6. One of the city's earliest and most persuasive Irish politicians was a watchman of the municipal reservoir. His enjoyment of argument was so great that he sometimes visited town meetings of neighboring communities and championed whatever appeared to be the losing positions on local issues. (*Thirtieth Anniversary Holyoke Daily Transcript*. Holyoke, 1912, p. 3.) A relative of his, now an alderman and Democratic party leader, displays the same zest for the status and influence of political office. He said in an interview: "It costs me money to be an alderman, but I like it. I understand my grandfather was like I am—a big fellow who loved people and who always wanted to run every organization he was in. I like to lead and I know I can, and that gives me a big kick. I see Protestant lawyers and doctors and industrialists trying to be aldermen and I see they don't do as good a job as I do, that I have to teach them a lot of the ropes. So I know I'm doing O.K."

7. Municipal Register, 1895, pp. 67-84; Holyoke *Transcript*, August 28, 1897, p. 1.

8. Holyoke *Transcript*, January 3, 1898, p. 1. April 18, 1898, p. 1.

9. Holyoke *Transcript*, November 26, 1898.

10. Interviews were held with friends of Hall and with Catholics and Protestants who were active in the Hall political machine. Private memoirs, diaries and scrapbooks were of particular aid.

11. Interviews with Protestant corporation owners and managers, July-August 1947.

12. Holyoke *Artisan,* February 12, 1915, p. 1.

13. Holyoke *Transcript,* December 1, 9, 13, 14, 22, 1897; *Thirtieth Anniversary,* p. 8.

14. Interviews with present and former leaders of the "G and E" machine, 1947.

15. Interviews, businessmen who sought to organize Taxpayers Association in 1930. August 1947.

16. Taxpayers Association minutes, July 12, 1932.

17. A systematic study was made of the membership rolls in 1947. The largest number of Catholic members was French; the next largest group was Polish. Irish Catholics composed only 2 per cent of the entire membership. The concentration of the association upon city government expenditure and the Irish identification of the government as an Irish-controlled institution is believed by the officers of the organization to be an important factor in the Irish refusal to support the association. The second president of the association was a French Catholic (Holyoke *Transcript,* October 10, 1937, p. 3).

18. The average pay for labor in the city government was between 50 and 58 cents an hour, in comparison with 40 cents an hour in industry. Paper City *Transcript,* November 4, 1932, p. 1.

19. Holyoke *Transcript,* October 11, 1932, p. 1; minutes and accompanying documents of the Taxpayers Association, June 24, 1932.

20. Holyoke *Transcript,* November 4, 1932, p. 1.

21. Editorial, "A Time of Thinking," prepared by the Taxpayers Association as an expression of its position in 1932. Publicity scrapbook of Taxpayers Association.

22. Holyoke *Transcript,* December 7, 1932, p. 1.

23. Holyoke *Transcript,* July 19, 1945, p. 14.

24. Interview, executive secretary, Taxpayers Association, July 7, 1947.

25. Interviews, July-August 1947, were made with fifteen Republican politicians on various levels of activity. Press books of past campaigns were examined.

26. For example, the mayor supported the Republican governor's advocacy in 1947 of a state sales tax, a relatively "regressive" tax in that it takes a larger fraction of the poor man's income than of the rich man's; he attacked the Democratic state senator from Paper City and state Democratic party organization who opposed it. Holyoke *Transcript,* March 22, 1947, p. 1.

27. Data on the composition of the city government is the result of a study conducted with the aid of four municipal employees who knew the religious affiliations and church habits of the people in the government. The importance of religious affiliation is illuminated in the accuracy displayed by the individuals participating in the study. Cross-checking of varied sources for over five hundred names necessitated only three corrections.

28. Only Ward 7 chose a Protestant alderman in the last election. In the past three decades, the largest number of Protestant aldermen serving simultaneously was seven; this was in 1932 after the Taxpayers Association crusade to cut government costs.

29. The fire department, which employs 112 people, has 10 Protestants in it, 4 Polish Catholics, 15 French Catholics, 83 Irish Catholics. The police

department, with a staff of 109 regular policemen, has 13 Protestants, 2 Polish Catholics, 9 French Catholics, and 85 Irish Catholics.

City employees who are not elected to offices have been under state civil service since 1936. Workers in the water, fire, police, municipal gas and electric departments and in the board of public workers are now under civil service. The service provides security from political changes taking place in the top offices of the government, but does not completely prevent the selection of job holders for political purposes.

In Paper City the civil service office is managed largely by Irish Catholics. Only one Protestant, an expert trained in the English employment exchange service, is employed among 28 workers. Lobbying can place a person at the top of the list from which appointments to a position are made, and the special knowledge stated as required for the position is not necessary if the political influence of the applicant is great.

30. At a recent one he made a short speech on the theme that he "no longer fears the spread of any isms such as communism, when I look out upon our strong forces of watchfulness, the Knights of Columbus." Quotation from stenographic report of speech at Knights of Columbus communion breakfast, 1947.

The mayor, who is the chief contemporary political figure in this study, died a few months before this book was prepared for publication.

31. The Irish were rising to political power in the nation as well as in Paper City. By 1880, the Irish, who settled chiefly in the large urban areas of the nation, had become the Northern mainstay of the Democratic party. (Milton L. Barron, "Intermediacy: Conceptualization of Irish Status in America," *Social Forces,* March 1949, pp. 256-263.)

The Northern urban vote has become increasingly crucial in the national election. In 1862, 20 per cent of the population was urban; in 1940, 56.5 per cent was urban. In 1944, majorities in the following seven cities were enough to determine the result in presidential election for their respective states: New York, Chicago, Philadelphia, Detroit, Baltimore, St. Louis and Jersey City.

32. See Elin L. Anderson, *We Americans; A Study of Cleavage in an American City* (Cambridge, 1937), pp. 211-212; and Francis James Brown and Joseph Slabey Roucek (editors), *One America* (New York, 1952), p. 649 for discussion of similar developments in other urban centers.

33. Jacques Ducharme, *The Delusson Family* (New York, 1939), p. 44.

34. Samuel Lubell, *The Future of American Politics* (New York, 1952), pp. 61-67, observes that the drive of the "later ethnics" toward middle class status has been reflected in shifts in power, similar to those in Paper City, all over the United States.

35. Paul Lazarsfeld in *The People's Choice* (New York, 1944), p. 109, observed the same difference between Protestant and Catholic party loyalty in upper-income brackets in Erie County, Ohio, during the 1940 presidential election.

36. Jacques Ducharme, *The Shadows of the Trees* (New York, 1943), pp. 176-178.

37. Holyoke *Transcript,* November 7, 1956.

38. Lubell, *op. cit.,* p. 47, observes that this religious alignment of Catholics with Democrats and Protestants with Republicans has held throughout eastern

United States until 1952, when Roman Catholics broke away in considerable number from the Democratic party to vote for Eisenhower for president.

39. In 1944, 10,955 registered voters did not identify party affiliations; 17,331 voters did. In the off-year election of 1946 the number of unenrolled was the highest in Paper City history—14,442 voters, approaching the 17,218 party affiliations. Holyoke *Transcript,* March 24, 1947, p. 14.

40. This is indicated by a comparison of registration in Ward 4 and Ward 7. Ward 4 had a population in 1940 of 7,461, composed chiefly (see Chapter 12) of low-income, Polish Roman Catholics. Ward 7 has approximately the same size population, 7,320. The proportion of the population eligible for voting in Ward 7 is greater than in Ward 4, making approximately 200 more potential voters in Ward 7. Yet Ward 7 in 1940 registered 4583 voters (1919 Democrats, 1512 Republicans) while Ward 4 registered only 3571 voters (2164 Democrats, 408 Republicans).

41. French Catholics cannot be counted upon to cast a "bloc vote" for one of their own people. The French-dominated Wards 1 and 2 in 1936 voted about 3-to-1 for two Irish candidates over the French candidate for County Commissioner. Moreover, Ward 4, heavily Polish in population, in 1944 gave a Polish Catholic candidate for the state senate 823 votes and an Irish Catholic candidate 1,665 votes.

As to a "religious vote," it is clear from the political record that Catholics do not regularly cast a solid vote for members of their own religion. In 1944 a Protestant Republican candidate for the United States Senate running against a Catholic Democratic candidate received 3,216 more votes in Paper City than Thomas Dewey was able to poll in the presidential race against Roosevelt. And in 1940 a Republican Protestant candidate for Congress broke through a solidly Democratic party victory in the city to defeat an Irish Catholic Democrat 15,008 to 11,535.

For national studies see Johan J. Smertenko, "The Emerging Hyphen," *Harper's,* August, 1951, pp. 63-71. The author reports a national survey which also sees ethnic factors as decreasing in importance in voting. *U. S. News and World Report* published August 10, 1956, a study conducted by backers of Senator John F. Kennedy of Massachusetts for the Democratic party vice-presidential nomination. The study argued that there was a Catholic vote. An article, August 17, argued there is little "bloc voting on religious lines, more on ethnic lines."

42. This is true of some other areas of America. Lazarsfeld, *op. cit.,* p. 111, observes about the voters of Erie County, Ohio, that if only one group affiliation of a citizen could be learned, religion was the most helpful in the prediction of voting behavior. This was not because religion determined voting patterns, but because so many more important factors such as economic status, residence, etc., could be roughly correlated with religious affiliation.

43. Lubell, *op. cit.,* p. 50.

44. Thus in 1944, the traditionally Democratic Wards 1, 2, 5 and 6 supported the Protestant Democratic candidate for the House of Representatives against a Catholic Republican. The French Wards 1 and 2, which are also traditionally Democratic (the usual proportions are one and three-fourths Democratic vote to one Republican vote), supported the Irish Catholic Democratic candidate for the State House of Representatives against a French Catholic Republican candidate. Holyoke *Transcript,* November 8, 1944, p. 12.

45. Political advertisements in Paper City *Transcript,* October 23, 1945; November 1, 1946. People have used various devices—particularly whisper campaigns—to make clear the religious affiliation of a candidate with an ambiguous name, such as Burke.

46. This campaign marked off in the nation the social, economic and religious lines on which politics in America have been fought ever since, as Lubell observes in *The Future of American Politics,* p. 35.

47. Another test of a particular facet of Catholic religious-political support came in 1936, when Lemke, presidential candidate of Father Coughlin, polled 1697 votes in Paper City to Landon's 6,621 and Roosevelt's 17,118. In Ward 1 Lemke polled about as many votes as Landon, 166 to 191. Holyoke *Transcript,* November 4, 1936, p. 8.

48. Significantly, the manipulation of religious prejudice was introduced most boldly in a local campaign in this century when a Catholic was pitted against a Catholic. In the closely fought mayoralty contest in which a new Irish machine centered in the municipal Gas and Electric Company revolted against the old Hall machine, a whisper or rumor campaign was conducted in the closing days against the Hall candidate. This man was a nominal Catholic but was not active in Catholic church organizations. Opponents spread stories that the Hall candidate was an "APAer," a "KKK type of Protestant," a "convert to Protestantism." The Hall candidate was narrowly defeated. Interviews were conducted with several political leaders of both factions who participated in this campaign.

49. See Chapter 18.

50. In Paper City in 1942, 53.9 per cent of the voters opposed the referendum (10,755 votes); 28.8 per cent favored it (5,754 votes); about as many, 27.3 per cent, were undecided or did not vote on the referendum. In 1948, 59.7 per cent of the voters opposed the referendum, almost exactly the same percentage favored it as in 1942, 28.7 per cent; and a much smaller percentage, 11.4 this time, were undecided on the issue. Data from study by the Springfield Council of Churches, 1948 and by a Springfield Protestant laymen's study in 1950. (Copies of both studies in possession of author.)

51. The Democratic vote for governor in Paper City increased from 10,748 in 1942 (59.5 per cent) to 19,215 (65.1 per cent) in 1948. It should be noted that the percentage increase in opposition to the birth-control referendum in the presidential year was only half as much as the increase in the Democratic gubernatorial vote.

52. Study by Springfield Council of Churches, 1948. Data on file in offices of Springfield Council of Churches.

53. The pro-birth control referendum vote in 1942 was 5,754; in 1948, 8,529. The vote for the Republican candidate for governor in 1942 was 8,750; in 1948, 9,471. The vote for the Republican candidate for president in 1948 was 9,394.

Chapter 18

The Politics of the Churches

1. See Max Weber's essay on "The Morality of Politics and the Politics of Morality," in H. H. Gerth and C. Wright Mills (eds.), *From Max Weber: Essays in Sociology* (New York, 1946), pp. 228-35.

2. The statements of Catholic priests, lay leaders of parish societies and editors on the nature of the church in contradistinction to society cite the familiar points of modern encyclicals such as *Immortale Dei.* See, for example, *Catholic Mirror,* June 1947, p. 27. For *Immortale Dei,* see Joseph Husslein, *Social Wellsprings,* Vol. 2 (Milwaukee, 1942), pp. 61, 70-72.

3. "Whatever belongs to the salvation of souls or to the worship of God is subject to the power and judgment of the church. Whatever is by reason or by its nature to be classified as political is rightly subject to the civil authority." *Immortale Dei.*

4. Interview, editor of the *Catholic Mirror,* June 11, 1947.

5. Pope Pius X has said, for example, "We do not conceal the fact that we shall shock some people by saying that we must necessarily concern ourselves with politics. But anyone forming an equitable judgment clearly sees that the Supreme Pontiff can in no wise violently separate the category of politics from the supreme control of faith and morals entrusted to him." Quoted in Jacques Maritain, *The Things That Are Not Caesar's* (London, 1939), p. 191.

6. In *Ubi Arcano Dei,* Pius XI stressed the reign of Christ in *all* areas of life, civil society included. Christ's Kingdom, the Pope indicates in *Ubi Arcano Dei,* is indeed spiritual, and he rejected earthly power, but it is a grave error to exclude Christ from authority in civil affairs, for God has committed all things to his rule. See also editorials dealing with the implications of the social encyclicals for a wide range of critical stages in the nations' domestic political-economic situation: *Catholic Mirror,* March, 1933, pp. 5-6; September 1933, pp. 12-13; February 1946, pp. 19-20.

In *Quadragesimo Anno* Pius XI makes this clear and sweeping statement of the church's authority: "For the deposit of truth entrusted to us by God and our mighty office of declaring, interpreting, and urging in season and out of season the entire moral law, demand that both social and economic questions be brought within our supreme jurisdiction, in so far as they refer to moral issues." The Catholic church in its encyclicals and other official pronouncements seems to prefer the phrase "economic and social" to "political." A very narrow interpretation is usually given the term "politics," restricting it to the contest of personalities, factions and parties. Social and economic issues are viewed as super-political, but often involving political clashes.

Quotations of the encyclicals are from the translations appearing in Joseph Husslein, *Social Wellsprings,* Vol. 2 (Milwaukee, 1942).

7. "On the Social Order," *Catholic Mirror,* January 1947, p. 16.

8. "The Road We Travel," *Catholic Mirror,* October 1939, p. 12.

9. "The Catholic Claim," *Catholic Mirror,* June 1946, p. 27.

10. Editorial, "The Pope on the Relation of Church and State," *Catholic Mirror,* June 1947, p. 27. The statement is held to be the central theme of the Pope's 1946 lenten message.

11. Almost every issue of the diocesan magazine deals with Catholic doctrine in relation to some major political issue such as housing, wage negotiations, governmental welfare measures, the evils of communism, the general social structure of American society.

12. The activity of Catholic women's sodalities, studied in 1947, was, for example, confined almost entirely to support of Catholic church organizations —the financing of the local parish education, the reading of Catholic devotional

literature dealing with problems of personal life, the sending of gifts to orphanages and to other Catholic charities. Some activity involved support of overseas relief projects—Catholic and non-Catholic. The chief attempt to make contact with political issues was represented in speeches—average two a year—by priests on the threat of communism. These talks did not usually deal with the ways in which the political activity of the community was involved in specific policy decisions of state and national governments concerning communism. This data was secured by survey of sodality programs with the co-operation of officers of organizations in three sample parishes.

13. The curates are apparently interested in developing the implications of Catholic doctrine for a wider range of political issues than are the pastors. Analysis of political concerns focus on the Catholic pastor and the Protestant minister, not on curates or assistant ministers, since these men have the major responsibility for the activity of the churches and since, in this group, all the men could be questioned—not just a sample.

There are slight differences in the breadth of issue concern on ethnic lines among the pastors, the French and Polish pastors being somewhat narrower in their definition of moral areas than the Irish pastors. The differences in concern of the pastors seem to be more deeply related to theological perspectives than to the ethnic or class composition of their constituency. This is so also of the Protestant church clergy.

14. Roman Catholic clergy vary some on moral-political emphases. The "gambling" priests such as Father McMichael of Holy Rosary parish are deeply concerned with maintaining the co-operation of the municipal government in the conduct of lotteries and circuses for a labor parish. An antigambling priest such as the pastor of Sacred Heart parish talks privately to the mayor about keeping "gambling activities" out of his middle-class parish.

15. Each of these areas were suggested to the priests and described as to meaning when necessary. The basic question was as follows: "Have any moral issues been involved over the past five years in Holyoke in this area making it of concern or action to the pastor or to the Roman Catholic Church?"

16. Interviews were conducted with party leaders, various city officials such as the mayor, aldermen, and city clerks. March-August 1947.

17. Interviews with aldermen, a priest and a public housing official who attended the meeting. Interviews also with the director of the local housing authority office, chairman of the housing commission, four of the leaders for the projects and three of the major opponents of the housing projects.

18. The health department was studied by a series of interviews with the director, the chairman and members of the public health commission, the major social service workers in the city, and the director of a recent study of the public health situation in the community. Staff meeting of public health department was observed.

19. For Paper City, 73.4 per 1,000 for a five-year average; 59.4 in the state; 30.6 in a nearby industrial city of comparable size. *Report of Tuberculosis Survey in Holyoke,* Made by the Emergency Relief Administration in Cooperation with the Holyoke Tuberculosis Association, January 1935.

20. Most sect leaders will not even make distinctions between the moral and religious concerns of the Protestant and the Roman Catholic churches. All but the sect group itself are aligned "with the Kingdoms of this earth," all

"have lobbies in Washington," all are "nothing but political organizations." Interviews, June 5, 8, 1947, with leaders of Jehovah's Witnesses and Polish Bible Study sects.

21. See study of treatment of international relations issues in journals of denominations represented in Paper City by Gordon Shull, "Post War Issues in International Politics and the Church Press," (M.A. Thesis, unpublished, University of Illinois, 1953).

22. Almost the entire financial contributions of the Protestant churches to world affairs, and most of their adult educational programs on world events in the three years following the Japanese surrender, represented efforts to apply an ethic of charity and stewardship to the international scene, through the giving of money to private relief and rehabilitation agencies. Analysis was made of Annual Reports of the men and women's organizations of the Protestant churches, 1945-1947; budgets of all Protestant churches for 1945-1947 were studied and interviews held with professional religious educators, and laymen in charge of program arrangements.

23. Minutes, Ministerial Association, October 19, 1936.

24. No Protestant publication originates within the Paper City area to be contributed to by the local clergy as is the case in the Roman Catholic church. Comparison cannot be justly made between the *Catholic Mirror* and religious publications read by the Protestant clergy, for awareness of moral issues in politics.

25. "Report of the Women's League," (mimeographed), Annual Report, 1946.

26. The Ministerial Association commended for study by the Council of Churches, the "social relations program" of the Council of Churches of a neighboring city which focused on four areas: "elimination of slot machines, securing of vacation clubs for wholesome recreation, relating religion and nature study in the public schools, and defeat of horse racing." Report of the annual meeting, Council of Churches, May 25, 1943.

27. A survey by a college economics department concluded in 1931 that the depression hardships of the people of this church were probably as great as those of any parish in six New England communities surveyed. Of this church's wage earners 21.3 per cent were without work and 37 per cent only partially employed. "The Amherst Survey of Unemployment in Holyoke," *Amherst Quarterly*, May, 1931, pp. 151-158.

28. The liquor issue has been the only social problem in the history of the community on which Roman Catholic and Protestant churches have cooperated in influencing the politics of the city (Minutes, Ministerial Association, November 16, 1914; Grace Church Scrapbook, August 16, 1912). At present the churches carry on no united campaign, and most Protestant pastors, the Lutheran pastor excepted, look upon the Catholic church permission of service of liquor at social events associated with the church as a contribution to intemperance.

Chapter 19

The Churches and Political Reform

1. The Holyoke *Transcript* reports several details of the controversy, May 9, 12, 13, 15 and 19, 1947. Interviews were conducted with all the pastors and politicians directly involved and quoted.

2. Roman Catholic political leaders of the Democratic party generally believe that the mayor did nothing to eliminate gambling in the city during the controversy as much to retain the financial support he received for his campaigns from the liquor and gambling interests as to defend the interests of the Catholic church.

3. In 1934, the state legislature amended laws on gambling to exclude "the game called beano, or substantially the same game under another name . . . provided, that the proceeds . . . in such game are donated solely to charitable, civic, educational, fraternal or religious purposes." A license had to be authorized by the mayor or the selectmen and the game played under terms and conditions prescribed by them. Acts, 1934, Chapter 371, Approved June 29, 1934. Beano was further regulated by a limit of $10.00 in value on each prize, the requirement of a statement of the total proceeds and expenses, and of a member "in good standing in full control and management of the game at all times." Acts, 1936, Chapter 222, Approved April 14, 1936. In 1945, the sections of the 1934 and 1936 laws including beano as a legal game for religious organizations were stricken out and amended to include only "the game of cards commonly called whist or bridge, in connection with which prizes are offered to be won by chance." Acts, 1943, Chapter 267, Approved May 14, 1943. The 1943 amendment was approved upon referendum at the state election November 7, 1944. See Footnote: Annotated, Laws, Vol. IX. For decisions under the provisions of these laws and amendments see Commonwealth versus O'Connell, 293, Massachusetts 459, 200 N. E., 269, 103 ALR872.

4. The pastor of Holy Rosary parish included the mayor in the annual trip to Washington, D. C. sponsored by the parish. The pastor believed this aided the mayor politically, claiming that the parish gave in past elections "practically a 100 per cent vote to the mayor." The pastor felt that "the mayor had a tough time for two weeks while the probationary officer was acting up, but he stood by us well."

5. Some of the articles in Catholic journals with this as a dominant or important motif are: *Catholic Mirror,* April 1935, pp. 21-22; August 1949, p. 9; October 1949, p. 23; December 1949, p. 17; January 1949, p. 31.

In 1947, Msgr. Fulton Sheen told an audience of 750 persons in the high-school auditorium in a lecture sponsored by the Catholic Library Association, "American opinion has only in recent months awakened to the menace of Communism." Msgr. Sheen reviewed his early warnings which met with considerable unpopularity and remarked, "The church was right and the world was wrong." Holyoke *Transcript,* May 17, 1947, p. 8.

6. The opposition of the Catholic church to Russian communism was voiced early. For example, the *Catholic Mirror* observed editorially in 1933, that "recognition of Russia was a betrayal of Christianity. Russia has not changed. She still denies the common rights of humanity to her citizens. She still defies the public opinion of the world in her treatment of her citizens." *Catholic Mirror,* March 1933, p. 10.

7. In some writings in the *Catholic Mirror* and in some statements of the local pastors, the Catholic church appears almost as the single Christian movement which has alerted the world against communism. Thus, "The communist crusade has singled out the Roman Catholic church as a supreme obstacle to its plan of global dominion. Except for a brief and minor flurry involving a

Lutheran Bishop and a group of Lutheran and Baptist ministers in Bulgaria, no Protestant sect has yet been molested beyond the Iron Curtain. . . . Communism has no fear of the Greek and Lutheran sects, because they have in general shown little scruple against serving as departments of political government." *Catholic Mirror,* December 1949, p. 17. More recently the Protestants have been noted as resisting communism with the Catholics. An editorial in the *Catholic Mirror* on "Heroism of German Protestants and Catholics," discussed Protestant and Catholic pastors who in sermons denounced communism in the Russian Zone of Germany. "Communists have not found Catholics or Protestants cowardly. That public protest and defiance, unitedly proclaimed from Catholic and Protestant pulpits, was the act of brave men." *Catholic Mirror,* June 1950, p. 14.

8. *Catholic Mirror,* "Catholics Versus Communism," April, 1945, p. 21. This summary answer to the question, "What is Communism?" was made by the *Catholic Mirror:* "1. Communism is an atheistic, anti-God and godless totalitarian system. . . . 2. Communism is a system of godless government . . . run by a clique of men with no principle . . . no morals . . . no respect for the dignity of man. 3. Communism is slavery. . . . 4. Communism is built on trickery, deceit, terror. 5. Communism seeks the minds of youth. . . . 6. The Communist Party owes its loyalty only to Soviet Russia. . . . 7. The principal aim of the Communist Party is overthrow of government by any means possible. . . ." *Catholic Mirror,* February 1950, p. 20.

Content analysis was made of the local Catholic press, the *Catholic Mirror* and *Caravel,* in its approach to communism for three years beyond the time limit of 1947 set for other areas of research, in order to have a more adequate picture of the influence of international events upon the programs of the churches than the immediate postwar period would provide.

9. *Caravel,* May 1946, p. 3.

10. *Catholic Mirror,* March 1946, p. 27. "Today Congress is on the way to enacting labor laws such as the Taft-Hartley Act to cripple unions so they cannot enforce demands for a living wage. Let us pray that Congress will not so cripple labor. When families starve and cupboards are empty workers are much more likely to listen to communist agents. Mary, Mary, Mother of God, enlist God's aid in influencing Congress to see that while it has appropriated funds for Greeks and others to fight communism abroad it may find that by crippling labor legislation it has opened the door to communism in the United States." Observation, sermon preached in Holy Cross parish, May 25, 1947.

11. Aleck Richards's article, "Czecho-Slovakia at the Crossroads," *Catholic Mirror,* December 1946, p. 34, gives a clear statement of this recurring theme in the diocesan journal. "President Roosevelt, President Truman and Winston Churchill should have known from the history of Europe that the Polish people have been *the* defenders of the Western culture against Russian aggression. . . . How could they have failed to comprehend that history is repeating itself in the current history of Russia. . . ." *Catholic Mirror,* May 1946, p. 16.

12. As early as 1920 the *Catholic Mirror* was explaining politics in terms of the alleged moral stupidity and blindness of a few leaders. "One man [Woodrow Wilson] was responsible for making England into the humble beggar, the haughty murderer of 1920—the man who saved her from the hands of Germany." *Catholic Mirror,* November 1920.

13. *Catholic Mirror,* February 1950, p. 25. For an example of the publication's description of Roosevelt in his relations to the American people see November, 1945, p. 22.

14. Editorial, "Catholics Versus Communism," *Catholic Mirror,* April 1945, pp. 21-22.

15. The programs of all the adult discussion groups of the Protestant churches were studied for 1947. The liberal Protestant pacifist has been described in detail by Vernon H. Holloway, "A Review of American Religious Pacifism," *Religion in Life,* Summer 1950, pp. 156-176.

16. Minutes, Ministerial Association, October 28, 1941.

17. Agencies chiefly under attack were the Council for Social Action, Congregational Christian Churches, and the Federal Council of Churches of Christ in America—now the National Council of Churches of Christ in America.

18. As early as 1933, the *Catholic Mirror's* protest against recognition of Russia was accompanied by an attack against the domestic "New Deal." "Perhaps a government based on the twin hatreds of capitalism and religion is perfectly legitimate, but we fail to recognize any obligation to recognize a government built on murder and brutal persecution." (*Catholic Mirror,* March 1933, p. 10.) The *Catholic Mirror* has been much happier with the social ethics of the American Council of Churches than with the Federal Council of Churches of Christ in America. The former was held to be much more aware that socialistic economic measures adopted by the New Deal were leading America toward communism. *Catholic Mirror,* January 1950, p. 16.

19. The *Catholic Mirror* has manifested at various periods of American foreign-policy debates an isolation guided by Irish ethnic distrust of the English. It rejected the "League of Nations fiasco, which would deliver up to Great Britain the mastery of the civilized world. We have merely voted now to give England what our boys died to prevent Germany from obtaining." (*Catholic Mirror,* December 1920, p. 7.) When Mussolini entered Ethiopia, the *Catholic Mirror* characterized this action of Italian fascism as promising nothing worse for Ethiopia than English imperialism, noting that at least the fascist leader did not engage in "pious hypocrisy that it was done for Ethiopia's good." (*Catholic Mirror,* December 1945, p. 43.)

20. One of the clergymen called attention to the voting record of one Republican candidate for re-election to Congress, who was backed by several laymen in his congregation. The Legislative Committee, Council for Social Action, Congregational Christian Churches, had charted the man's voting record. He had voted against arming Greece, against giving the Army and Navy more aircraft in 1940, against sending guns and supplies to countries fighting Hitler in 1939 and 1940, and in 1945 and 1946 against extension of UNRRA. From a mimeographed statement, "Our District Needs Better Representation in Washington" by a group of "residents of South Hadley Center."

21. Observation of a meeting of Democratic party leaders in October, 1947.

22. For example, *Catholic Action: What is It?,* and "Catholics Are Not in Politics," *Catholic Mirror,* July 1945, p. 15.

23. Several of the encyclicals of the Popes have emphasized the indirect approach to the temporal order: *Immortale Dei* (cf. Joseph Husslein, *Social Wellsprings* (Milwaukee, 1942), Vol. 2, p. 74); *Ubi Arcano Dei* (cf. Husslein, *op. cit.,* Vol. 2, p. 22); *Non Abbiamo Bisogno* (Washington: National Catholic Welfare Conference pamphlet), p. 5. See these scholars for discussion of "in-

direct power" in politics: John F. Cronin, *Catholic Social Principles,* pp. 42ff.; Jacques Maritain, *Scholasticism and Politics* (New York, 1940), pp. 156ff.

24. These activities were freely reported by the priests. The instance of a priest seeking election occurred when the pastor was located in another community. He was defeated.

25. "Merciless Teacher," by Rt. Rev. P. A. Bojanowski, *Catholic Mirror,* January 1947, pp. 11-12, 25. See also articles in the *Catholic Mirror* on Truman administration in December 1949, p. 18; April 1950, p. 45; October 1950, p. 42.

26. "God or Atheism," *Catholic Mirror,* May 1946, p. 16.

27. *Catholic Action: What is It?* pp. 8, 9.

28. Holyoke *Transcript,* April 14, 1947; observation of speech.

29. Interviews were conducted with all Catholic pastors; with curates in all but three of the parishes, and with 22 political leaders in the city, who gave their own impressions of the attitudes of Catholic clerical leadership toward the church's responsibility for knowledge of political activity.

30. The May minutes of the Ministerial Association in 1937 report that the "Committee on Pending Federal Legislation and Certain Issues at Oxford [an Ecumenical Meeting in England] continued for the purpose of reporting at a later meeting." The minutes of the next meeting note that "the Committee on Federal Legislation and Certain Issues at Oxford reported that time for action is passed and therefore no report is needed. This committee was therefore discharged with appreciation for its efforts." Minutes, Ministerial Association, May 25, October 29, 1937.

31. The most influential woman in the politics of the city—an alderman for thirteen years, one-time president of the National Federation of Republican Women's Clubs, chairman of the Committee on Women's Activities of the Republican Party in the state—is a Congregationalist. She has never been asked by a pastor to participate in any activity of the church seeking to relate the Christian faith to her major field of interest, or to provide some opportunity for serious exchange of views on what is actually occurring in contemporary politics. This separation of the Protestant educational program from the roles of laymen as politicians is duplicated in the experience of the major Protestant political figures in the city.

32. The Ministerial Association held study sessions on the methods of political action during efforts to reduce the number of licenses for saloons. The association sent representatives to speak on its behalf at hearings on liquor bills in the state legislature and at trials of liquor dealers, and made public appeals to many politicians for action. The pastors co-ordinated assignments of specific responsibilities to various church members; they brought authorities on the social conditions of the community to the association to brief the pastors; they "stood up to the knees in mud" in alleys to observe the "evils in cellar bars."

Chapter 20

The Churches and Political Compromise

1. Mimeographed statement circulated by members of the two Baptist churches, December 9, 1941.

2. Springfield *News,* December 10, 1944. The author of the report was a Catholic layman on the newspaper staff.

3. In 1947 only one Catholic pastor believed the Protestant clergy were correct in seeking to submit the issue to the voters. The general position of the Catholic clergy was expressed succinctly by the pastor of Holy Rosary parish: "The justice of the Roman Catholics receiving this aid from the state for taxes they have paid is so clear that there is no need at all for submitting the issue to the voters."

4. Interviews were conducted with a grocery store owner, a bank clerk, a shoe repair shop owner who were boycotted.

5. The church assumes that it is able to describe a Christian civilization and Christian politics. The church is not in any way one among other political forces in a nation; it is a force that redeems and unites all other institutions. "What is the aim of Catholic Action?", a widely used pamphlet in Paper City Catholic churches asks. The answer: "Ultimately the aim and object must be to bring Christianity into legislation and to bring up a truly Christian civilization in every country. There should be a sound Christian civilization in France, Spain, Portugal, Austria, Hungary, Italy, Ireland, Belgium, Poland, Lithuania, Mexico, in all the countries of South America because they are predominantly Catholic." *Catholic Action: What is It?* p. 9.

6. Twenty-five politicians—elected officers, appointed administrators, aspirants to office—were interviewed, and the effects of Roman Catholic clerical pronouncements on political controversies were discussed in detail.

7. For example, the mayor was willing to use the resources of the government to aid the Roman Catholic church conduct fund-raising circuses in the city, but when one priest desired that he use the power of the government to prevent a circus of the Greek Orthodox church from locating in a central area of town, he refused on the basis that a "man in politics can't do one thing for one church and not do it for others if they want it done."

8. Only Catholic pastors were questioned on this issue. Opinions of curates and other priests were not sought, on the assumption that the pastors would on this subject constitute an adequate sample of the points of view of Catholic clergy.

9. An editorial in the diocesan press observed: "The Catholic church does not want union of church and state. Catholics read history, too, but with the distinctive difference that they like to read it in *complete* versions, which do not overlook the sinister union of church and state which prevails, for example, in England, and in Russia, and elsewhere, to which those who blatantly warn against the 'encroachments of Rome' seem strangely non-allergic." *Catholic Mirror,* December 1945, p. 18.

10. See Chapter 9, for detailed developments of the implications of this position for religious liberty. The encyclical of Pope Leo XIII, *Immortale Dei,* states the "ideal" relation of church and state reflected in the views of the minority of Paper City clergy. Principles enunciated in the encyclical include: 1) the state is "bound" to make a public profession of religion to "the only true religion"; 2) the state is condemned which "disregards all religious duties" or which "holds in equal favor different kinds of religion." An orthodox American interpretation of this "ideal" can be found in John A. Ryan and Moorhouse F. X. Millar, *The State and the Church* (New York, 1922), and John A.

Ryan and F. J. Boland, *Catholic Principles of Politics* (New York, 1928). On p. 314, Ryan and Boland conclude from Catholic encyclical doctrine that "no state is justified in supporting error or in according error the same recognition as truth."

The minority position among the Catholic clergy in Paper City is best represented in the general theory by John Courtney Murray. See for example his article, "St. Robert Bellarmine on the Indirect Power," *Theological Studies,* December, 1948, pp. 491ff.

11. The Everson case places bus transportation of parochial students in the category of "indirect" aid.

12. See Chapter 16 for detailed descriptions of the corporatist proposals of the Catholic church. See the *Catholic Mirror,* March 1953, pp. 5-6; September 1933, pp. 12-13; February 1946, pp. 19-20 for samples of discussions of the implications of the social encyclicals and industry council proposals at critical stages in the nation's domestic political situation. See also the Catholic works read by various lay leaders in Paper City: John Francis Cronin, *Catholic Social Principles* (Milwaukee, 1950), Chapter VII; William Ferres, *Introduction to Social Justice* (New York, 1948); *Catholic Action, What is It?* (Huntington, Indiana, 1944). The last booklet, which seeks to define Catholic Action, notes in regard to politics only that the citizenry are to be educated to the nature "of equitable laws for recognition of the sovereignty of God," to which legislators will then be certain to defer. The Catholic Action programs envision "no effort to change the form of government . . . , no alliance with any particular party." (P. 11.)

13. Study literature presented to students at the Holy Cross labor school and smaller schools in Paper City and neighboring cities were analyzed, for the years 1944-47. Also notes of students at the schools and secretarial minutes of meetings of schools were examined.

14. The PAC literature described the important activities of the parties and strongly urged work within them to secure broad economic goals of the labor movement. Members were asked not simply to vote or give money but to accept greater responsibility for discussing party positions on public policies, and recruitment of supporters. The PAC was out to sell the parties "labor's liberal program," and the problem of possible compromise of a union program in order to work within a major party was debated in union halls, the daily press, and business service clubs. For this aspect of the study literature distributed in Paper City by the CIO unions on the PAC program during the years 1944-1947 was examined. Joseph Gaer, *The First Round* (New York, 1944) contains much of the literature generally distributed.

15. The *Catholic Mirror* presented a "Symposium" on the "CIO-PAC Controversy." Its symposium dealt only with the "communist issue" and quoted only from the Catholic press and from priests who were generally sure that the PAC was communist-dominated and who held that "proceeding from the moral angle of such co-operation, we cannot approve of PAC from a civic and common sense point of view." "Symposium on Catholic Press CIO-PAC Controversy," *Catholic Mirror,* February 1945, pp. 17-19.

16. The literature of the Catholic labor schools went beyond the concerns of the local parish pastors in reconsideration of the political role of the labor movement. Labor leaders were asked in the Holy Cross Institute of Industrial Relations "whether it is 'un-American' for a pressure group to seek control of

a political organization [the Democratic party]"? See "Conflicting Views on PAC" (distributed in Current Labor Problems class, November 13, 1945). The basic questions posed for the labor leaders were cast in the categories of "industry council" thought: "Will PAC create an antagonism from other classes which will intensify the spirit of political action either with or without consent of the members?" "Should labor attempt to gain its aims chiefly through the state and the political instruments which control it, or should it continue to rely mainly upon direct economic activity?"

The Catholic "labor priests," who were more directly exposed to the debates going on in the unions than the parish priests, again reflected less of a single-issue approach to the PAC's program for labor politics than the local clergy. The Holy Cross Institute of Industrial Relations provided in its "Current Labor Problems" course of 1945, a carefully prepared digest of articles appearing in *America, Commonweal, Comment, Labor, Mineworkers' Journal, Saturday Evening Post,* and *Reader's Digest.* The issue of whether the CIO, and therefore PAC, was communist-controlled was but one of several considerations suggested in these articles for evaluating the program.

17. The pastor of the Second Congregational Church has participated in the attempts of the Council for Social Action of the Congregational Christian Churches to formulate a position on the relation of the Christian faith, ethics, and the policy sciences to the controversies now going on in American society over the nature of the political parties. See *Social Action,* November 1952.

18. This idea was developed at length in an unpublished paper by the First Congregational pastor. Entitled "Catholicism Past and Present," it was read to an informal discussion club of nominally Protestant laymen.

19. "Editor's Colorful Review of Holyoke Visit," *Caravel,* June 1946, p. 6.

Conclusion

1. H. Richard Niebuhr has stated many of these same convictions more adequately in the preface of *The Kingdom of God in America.*

Appendix

The Point of View

1. Joachim Wach, *Sociology of Religion* (Chicago, 1944), p. 11.

2. James M. Gustafson's unpublished paper on "A Study in the Problem of Authority in Congregational Church-Order" (Mimeographed, 1954, Social Ethics Library, Yale Divinity School) contributed to clarification of the basic assumptions of this study.

3. The first volume of a series of research studies in Roman Catholic sociology begins with the fundamental conviction: "The reintegration of modern Western society, particularly in the American scene, can take place only through the Catholic church." The only other force held capable of uniting the divergent interests of the West is Communism. Joseph H. Fichter, *Dynamics of a City Church,* Vol. 1 in a series titled "Southern Parish" (Chicago, 1951), pp. 1-3. The *Information Service,* bi-monthly publication of the National Council of Churches of Christ in America, has observed that the Protestant churches in contrast to the Roman Catholic churches, have fostered a cultural diversity which has more often achieved unified concern and action in the society on a volun-

tary basis than the Catholic approach to unity. "Secularism and Cultural Pluralism," *Information Service,* Central Department of Research and Survey, National Council of Churches of Christ in America (New York, February 9, 1952).

4. This can be observed, for example, in the works of Emile Durkheim, Ernst Troeltsch and Joachim Wach. Durkheim saw the chief function of religion as that of representing those collective beliefs and rites which provide the integration and solidarity of society. For Durkheim, religion symbolizes the dominant values in society. Social life without communal and devotional affirmations of universally accepted values is characterized by *anomie,* disorganization, normlessness, apathy—in short, the loss of society. Ernst Troeltsch in *The Social Teaching of the Christian Churches* posed as the "ultimate problem" in the study of religion and culture: Given a civilization in which there are decisive and powerful forces such as the state, economic organizations, and innumerable other formative powers, how do the religious institutions attempt to harmonize with these forces in such a way that together they will form a unity of civilization? Joachim Wach in his *Sociology of Religion* focuses the discussion of the sociological consequences of religion upon its "positive or cohesive integrating influence" and "negative, destructive, disintegrating influence." For Wach, the facts most relevant sociologically are those which indicate the degree and modes in which concepts, rites and forms integrate a religious group and separate it from the outside world. See Emile Durkheim, *Elementary Forms of the Religious Life* (trans. J. Swain, Glencoe, Illinois, 1934), pp. 10 and 206; Ernst Troeltsch, *The Social Teaching of the Christian Churches* (trans. V. Wyon, New York, 1931), Vol. I, p. 32; Wach, *op. cit.,* pp. 34-35.

5. Many general theories of religion in relation to society can be described in terms of two extreme approaches which were found to be inadequate for this study. The first extreme approach is in the tradition of Karl Marx and Feuerbach, in which religion is interpreted simply as incorporating certain patterns of structure, interaction and meaning found in the cultural matrix, and primarily conditioned by socio-economic factors. In a study of Roman Catholic and Protestant relations, sources of tension and harmony from this perspective would be located in the ethnic and economic groups composing the respective religious institutions. Theology and worship would be interpreted as involved in the interactions of the churches only in the sense that these behavior patterns were predictable from analysis of the *social* forces operating within the institutional forms.

The second extreme approach to religion in its relations to society would view religious interactions as the expressions which men give to their experience of the Holy Other, the Numinous, the objective reality or spirit which transcends culture. Joachim Wach in his *Sociology of Religion* tends toward this approach (see, for example, pp. 13-34). The social patterns of religious relations would reflect somewhat the cultural context in which they occur, but their formative source would always be the religious experience, interpreted as originating beyond history. In this view, Roman Catholic-Protestant interactions would be seen as the witness of members to different religious experiences.

This study's general approach to religion in its relations to society stands between these extreme positions, seeking to deal with its material from within the general methodological framework of Max Weber and Ernst Troeltsch. See, for example, Weber's *The Protestant Ethic and the Spirit of*

Capitalism (London, 1930), pp. 39-40, 55-56; Weber's "Social Psychology of World Religions," *From Max Weber* (New York, 1946), pp. 268-271; Troeltsch, *op. cit.*, Vol. II, p. 1002.

6. H. Richard Niebuhr, in his book, *The Kingdom of God in America* (Chicago, 1937), demonstrates the power of religious commitment to widen the areas of sociological and historical investigation (and of history to stimulate theological inquiry). Niebuhr explains that he wrote *The Social Sources of Denominationalism* (New York, 1929) to examine the influence of social forces on faith. But the knowledge of his own faith led him to write another book which would seek to understand Christianity in America as a movement, rather than as an institution, as "gospel rather than law," and as a force not to be explained only in terms of racial, class or sectional interests. See especially *The Kingdom of God in America*, pp. 11-12.

Index